AUDIT REPORTS

AUDIT REPORTS

A Practical Guide to Preparation Under SAS 600

David York

KOGAN PAGE

First published in 1994

Kogan Page Limited
120 Pentonville Road
London N1 9JN

British Library Cataloguing in Publication Data

A CIP record for this book is available from the British Library.

ISBN 0 7494 0829 4

Typeset from author's disk by Saxon Graphics Ltd, Derby.
Printed and bound in Great Britain by Biddles Ltd, Guildford and Kings Lynn.

PREFACE

Most auditors now use an audit manual (or 'system') that contains some guidance on auditors' reports. The topic is also dealt with in auditing text books. All these publications suffer from the same main problem: they deal with reports as just one of the topics within their covers. For example, the fifth edition of *The Coopers & Lybrand Manual of Auditing* contains more than a thousand pages devoted to other auditing matters.

This book is devoted entirely to auditors' reports. It was planned well before Statement of Auditing Standards 600 'Auditors' reports on financial statements' (SAS 600) saw the light of day as, even under the Auditing Standard that SAS 600 superseded, writing audit reports was always a difficult matter. While SAS 600 has made some matters easier, it has introduced a much longer standard report and allowed even that wording to be varied by auditors. To provide the necessary depth as well as breadth of analysis in this book it has been necessary to devote well over a hundred pages to the subject of the standard report alone.

Auditors faced with reporting under SAS 600, especially when their report is not a standard report, may expect to spend considerable time on drafting and agreeing the form of a report with others in their firm. This book gives auditors access to practical advice that has taken approximately £100,000 of professional time to research and write.

The author would like to express his thanks to the many individuals and organisations who have helped by providing information or other input to this book. Inevitably some names may have been omitted: A A Payne, Robert Dove, Hugh Morgan, Henry Blank, Ian Cherry, Brian Rich, Jonathan Chaytor, Isobel Sharp, Robert Charlesworth, Brian Shearer, Roger Housechild, Stephen Glover, J Tunk, Geoffrey Miller, Peter Allen, Robert Outram, John Constantine, Mary Arden, Martyn Jones, Stephanie Smith, Nina Nicholls, Eric Kerry, Nigel Macdonald, Tony Upson, Roy Burton, Maureen Dowling, David Masterson, Shelagh McAlpine, Matthew Patient, members of the Practical Auditing Discussion Group, Coopers & Lybrand, Kingston Smith, Macintyre Hudson, Moores Rowland, Pannell Kerr Forster, Price Waterhouse, Robson Rhodes and Touche Ross & Co.

The author is, of course, indebted to his long-suffering family: Susan, Joanna, Helen, Stuart and Nicholas and to the patient people at Kogan Page. This book is dedicated to Caroline York and the late Percy York, without whom it would not have been possible.

DAVID YORK
London
May 1994

CONTENTS

1 INTRODUCTION

1.1 Introduction

Statement of Auditing Standards 600 'Auditors' reports on financial statements' (SAS 600) was issued in May 1993. It was the first SAS issued by the UK Auditing Practices Board (APB) since it took over from the Auditing Practices Committee (APC) in 1991. For reports on accounts for periods ending on or after 30 September 1993, SAS 600 became mandatory and superseded the APC's Auditing Standard 'The audit report', which had itself last been updated in 1989.

Although the SAS encouraged auditors to adopt it before it became mandatory they had to bear in mind that the existing Auditing Standard had not been withdrawn. There was a danger that some forms of modification of the standard report might not comply with it. The APB had failed to introduce a satisfactory transitional measure.

Many Auditing Guidelines that included reporting matters were left high and dry by the new SAS and were also excluded from the APB's general revisions project to codify auditing standards in the United Kingdom. Although some Practice Notes are promised, auditors have had to look to the ICAEW for guidance through the issue of 'FRAGs', the modern term for 'technical releases'. Guidance has, therefore, been incomplete, and what there is has been piecemeal.

Auditors have been let down especially by the APB's failure to issue a SAS dealing with 'going concern'. SAS 130 'The going concern basis in financial statements' was the second exposure draft issued by the APB dealing with going concern. As it was issued in December 1993, any final SAS will be at least a year later than SAS 600. In the gap period, auditors are left to their own devices. At least one major firm decided not to adopt SAS 600 before it became mandatory because of the absence of a going concern SAS.

Against this background it came as no surprise that, when it was published, the booklet form of SAS 600 bore the title 'Auditors' report on financial statements', instead of bearing the correct title (with the plural 'reports').

This is not to say that SAS 600 is a bad Statement of Auditing Standards. It was produced by some very talented individuals who were well supported by the over-stretched and under-resourced secretariat of the APB. In the main it is a well thought out, well crafted and useful document that will do much to improve communication with the users of audited accounts.

This book aims to provide practical guidance for auditors on the application of SAS 600. The author knows that the book might have been welcomed more by auditors had it been published close on the heels of the SAS. Had that been possible the text would, however, have been less useful in practice. Even in the few months that major firms have had to report under SAS 600, practice has become established. The book is able, therefore, to include examples and present arguments that could not have been anticipated.

Practice has not, however, been uniform. Indeed, the 'Big Six' firms are split over such fundamental matters as whether to include a reference to cash flows in their reports.

The remainder of this chapter:

- explains how this book may be used and in doing so summarises its contents and explains the terminology used
- puts auditors' reports into context by examining the recent history of reporting by auditors
- highlights the difficulties that some auditors have had writing reports
- explains some aspects of the writing of this book.

1.2 How to use this book

The rest of this book is in chapters as follows:

- the standard report
- modified reports
- multiple modifications
- illustrative modifications.

The contents of these chapters are summarised below.

1.2.1 The standard report

Chapter 2 begins by setting out the relevant statutory and professional requirements together with a model report. A substantial section called 'Elements and options' then analyses these matters in detail. That analysis includes Audit Regulations, the explanatory material and example reports in SAS 600, and the options available to auditors drafting a standard report. The options in a SAS 600 standard report are many. The amount of detail in the section may be gauged from the fact that two and a half pages are devoted to a discussion of report titles alone.

The meaning of 'true and fair' is sufficiently important to merit a section devoted to it. Almost as significant in practice, and so accorded a similar treatment, is the topic of 'readability'. The overriding aim of SAS 600 has been to promote clear communication. A section of the chapter, therefore, explains measures of readability and offers a model report that is almost four times as readable as one based on SAS 600.

The chapter may be used by auditors to develop their own 'house style' for standard reports, or simply to understand more about the requirements, the options, and the way other auditors have approached the standard report. The flexibility for auditors is enormous; as are the risks of getting it wrong. A section on 'Developing a standard report' presents alternative designs for putting the building blocks of a report together. The section may be used by auditors who want to stay close to the examples in SAS 600, or use their firm's preferred approach, or even be avant-garde.

Although the chapter deals mainly with the standard report on a single company, it also covers other entities. The chapter deals with group accounts; with small, dormant and other non-standard companies; and with other entities in general, using pension schemes as an important example. The implications of the proposed abolition of the audit for very small companies are discussed, as is the adoption of SAS 600 for companies in Northern Ireland and the Republic of Ireland.

For many auditors, the signing and dating requirements of SAS 600 have seemingly introduced more practical problems that the whole of the rest of the SAS. Indeed, the auditing committee of the ICAEW entered into lengthy (but not prolonged) correspondence with the APB, unsuccessfully seeking to influence a relaxation of the SAS's onerous requirements. The chapter, therefore, concludes by looking at the signing and dating of reports, considering the consequences of issuing a deficient report, and discussing some phantom reporting problems.

1.2.2 Modified reports

Each main type of modification, such as for scope limitation, is discussed in its own section of chapter 3. The chapter also includes modifications that are outside the scope of SAS 600. The modifications that are required by law in appropriate circumstances are covered in detail in a series of subsections. Such modifications can be difficult on their own and are often present in multiple modifications involving, for example accounting records, information and explanations and a scope limitation.

The sections include skeleton reports, showing the shape of each modification, and generic word pictures. Word pictures show how each modification should be written to achieve clear communication. Specific examples are also provided to illustrate appropriate wording for common circumstances. In some cases, these illustrations make use of the examples in appendix 2 to SAS 600.

Guidance on modifications is also extended to groups and difficult circumstances, such as where auditors are prevented from reporting, or face adverse consequences of a modified report.

Two very important sections of the chapter examine:

- deciding whether to modify a report and the right form of modification
- writing and signing an effective modification.

A complex example is followed through a seven-stage analysis to demonstrate how problems may be converted into a tabulation of a proposed report. That analysis includes practical guidelines for assessing materiality. Decisions as to whether matters might give rise to the extreme forms of qualification (adverse or disclaimer) are discussed in the appropriate earlier sections of the chapter. The writing and signing of reports is then tackled, but only for single modifications. These principles may be applied to the more complex reports that are the subject of the next chapter.

1.2.3 Multiple modifications

Some modifications are frequently found together. Two that are inexorably linked are a SAS 600 limitation of audit scope and a modification because auditors have failed to receive all the information and explanations that they require. Such linked modifications are covered when discussing their associated primary modification. Chapter 4 mainly examines combining two or more 'stand alone' modifications. It proposes a general approach that may be used successfully for any number of modifications. That general approach shapes the chapter, which moves through the various combinations revealing their underlying structure with skeletons and word pictures.

The most complex reports may involve a disclaimer of, or adverse, opinion and so the later sections of the chapter set out a method for wording such multiple opinions to keep relevant information before the reader. Such matters have not been addressed in professional guidance.

1.2.4 Illustrative modifications

The last chapter of the book is a resource bank of modifications that auditors can use as a starting point for their own modified reports. The illustrative modifications are presented in sections dealing with areas of difficulty, such as going concern and the completeness of income in small companies. The sections provide background and discuss the practical problems as well as giving illustrative wordings. The last section of the chapter deals with the reading of reports by auditors at annual general meetings.

The illustrations in chapter 5, in common with most modified reports in this book, are in extract form. Only the parts of a report that differ from the standard report are shown. The illustrations are mainly single modifications for single companies. They may be adapted for other entities and groups of companies and tailored according to auditors' house styles as described in the earlier chapters. Because a disclaimer of, or adverse opinion differs from a lesser 'except for' opinion only in the wording of the opinion paragraph itself, illustrative modifications for the extreme qualifications may also be used for the related 'except for' opinion and vice versa.

1.2.5 Table of reports

Although this book may be read from front to back, it is likely that access for reference purposes will be in the other direction. The index may be used to find where topics are dealt with: it is designed to be helpful rather than being a comprehensive list of every occurrence of each entry. Illustrative reports, wherever they are in the book, are all listed in a comprehensive table following chapter 5.

1.2.6 Terminology

Auditors frequently use the words 'audit report' and 'audit opinion' interchangeably. Because of the need for detailed analysis the following terminology is used in this book.

Auditors' report: the entire material issued by the auditors.	The term includes the title and the signature as well as the material in between.
A **standard report**: one that contains no qualification or other modification and is not deficient.	Other terms, such as a 'clean' or 'unqualified' opinion, suffer from lack of precision and possible taints of value judgement. After all, why should a standard audit report be next to godliness?
A **modified report**: any non-standard audit report other than a deficient report. The modifications can be qualifications, paragraphs referring to fundamental uncertainty or even matters outside the scope of SAS 600.	The term 'qualified' is reserved for more specific use. Alternatives to 'modified' (according to a thesaurus) that were rejected are; 'changed', 'adjusted', 'converted', 'altered', 'reformed', 'shaped', and 'tempered'. 'Non-standard' was also considered but rejected as being too obvious and hence not English enough (in the American sense of English).
A **deficient report**: a report that fails to be a standard report or an appropriately modified report.	This term is necessary to allow a description of audit reports that are not standard, but for the wrong reason(s).
A **qualified report**: a report modified in respect of a matter affecting the truth and fairness (or equivalent term) of the accounts.	There is a temptation to make this term synonymous with 'qualified' as defined in company law. It is more practical, however, to use the term to refer to a report that has an 'except for', or adverse, or disclaimer of opinion.

1.3 Recent history of reporting

The Auditing Standard 'The audit report' was issued in the first tranche of material that the Auditing Practices Committee (APC) produced. It was revised in 1989 and almost immediately the APC began considering a further revision. This was well before the Auditing Practices Board (APB) took up the fight as the APC's successor. The fact that it took over 4 years to issue a new standard is a direct result of the slow process that the APB has continued, not any lack of importance of the subject matter.

Why then was the 1993 revision needed? There was a simple reason, in that the regulation of auditors had introduced a requirement that reports be signed as 'Registered Auditor(s)'. The following sections look at some more complex reasons:

- the expectation gap
- corporate governance
- globalisation.

1.3.1 The expectation gap

One of the reasons for the revision of reporting standards that was mentioned publicly was *'bridging the expectation gap'*. In other words, to help communicate to the users of accounts exactly what the auditors did and hence what their report meant. The APB includes many non-auditors. It is therefore more likely to consider the users of reports than was the APC, the members of which were almost entirely auditors. Some would say that this is not an ideal situation. If you were in hospital would you prefer to be operated on by a skilled team of surgeons or a team where half the surgeons were replaced by your fellow patients?

There have been several academic studies into the auditors' report as a communication device. As this book is a practical one, these will not be explored in detail.[1] The principal conclusion reached is that those who read the report form a more accurate perception of the audit if the report is expanded. Some professions seemed to have grasped this earlier than others. The following two reports appeared next to each other in the 1992 annual report of Brixton Estate PLC.

---

[1] The most recent relevant study to hand was *The Review Report: An Empirical Investigation* by Tom Brown, David Hatherly and John Innes. That report provides comprehensive references to earlier papers. It is published in the Winter 1993 issue of *Accounting and Business Research*, an essential source for auditors wishing to keep up with research issues. It is published quarterly by the ICAEW and is currently £75 per annum for corporate UK subscribers, £30 for individuals or £13 for students.

REPORT OF THE AUDITORS TO THE MEMBERS OF BRIXTON ESTATE PLC

We have audited the Accounts on pages 22 to 38 in accordance with Auditing Standards.

In our opinion the Accounts give a true and fair view of the state of affairs of the Company and of the Group at 31st December 1992 and of the profit and cash flows of the Group for the year then ended and have been properly prepared in accordance with the Companies Act 1985.

Ernst & Young
Chartered Accountants
Registered Auditor

REPORT OF THE VALUERS TO THE DIRECTORS OF BRIXTON ESTATE PLC.

As instructed, we have valued for the purposes of your Company's Annual Accounts the completed and let investment properties, including those in owner-occupation, owned by your Company and its subsidiaries in the United Kingdom, Continent of Europe, Australia and the United States of America; these are listed individually in our more detailed reports. The properties are all well known to us and re-inspections have been made of a substantial proportion in accordance with your requirement that each shall be seen at intervals of not more than three years. We have made relevant local enquiries and obtained such further information as we consider necessary for our purpose.

We confirm that this valuation has been carried out by us as External Valuers qualified for the purposes of the valuation and that it has been made in accordance with the Statements of Asset Valuation Practice and Guidance Notes published by the Royal Institution of Chartered Surveyors; it represents our opinion of the current open market value at 31st December 1992 of the relevant interest in each property. Properties in your Company's occupation have been valued for their existing use. No allowances have been made for any expenses of realisation, or for taxation or value added tax which might arise in the event of a disposal. In accordance with local custom, the values in Belgium have been expressed gross of costs of acquisition.

Having regard to the foregoing, we are of the opinion that the aggregate of the values of your company's interests in these properties is £600,808,000. The values of the overseas properties have been converted to sterling at the rates of exchange prevailing on 31st December 1992.

Finally, and in accordance with our standard practice, we must state that this valuation certificate is for the use only of the parties to whom it is addressed and no responsibility is accepted to any third party for the whole or any part of its contents.

Jones Lang Wootton
Chartered Surveyors

1.3.2 Corporate governance

SAS 600 was created at the time that the Cadbury committee was producing its report and corporate governance Code of Best Practice. The APB working party was chaired by a member of the Cadbury committee, which meant that the two documents kept in step. Corporate governance issues have affected reporting by auditors in areas outside their report on the financial statements:

- reporting on compliance with the Code of Best Practice itself (including on internal control and going concern — which have not been finalised)
- reporting on interim accounts
- reporting on preliminary announcements.

Some matters have, however, impinged on auditors' reports on financial statements because of the overlap between requirements and the fact that some companies wanted to bring in Cadbury matters before SAS 600 became mandatory. The draft Cadbury report encouraged the inclusion of a responsibility statement in the following terms: *'So that shareholders are clear where the boundaries between the duties of directors and auditors lie we recommend that a brief description of directors' responsibilities for the accounts should appear in the Directors' Report as a counterpart to a statement by the auditors about their reporting responsibilities . . . The appropriate position for the directors' statement is immediately before the auditors' report which in future will include a statement of auditors' responsibilities.'*

The final SAS 600 included only a brief mention of the auditors' responsibilities. Some companies that were quick off the mark with corporate governance disclosures might have preferred more detail. For example, the following was included in the 1993 annual report and accounts of Eastern Electricity PLC.

AUDITORS' RESPONSIBILITY IN RESPECT OF THE PREPARATION OF ACCOUNTS

> The auditors are responsible for forming an independent opinion on the accounts presented by the Directors, based on their audit, and to report their opinion to shareholders. They also have responsibility under the Companies Act 1985 to report to shareholders if particular requirements are not met. These requirements are:
>
> - that the Company has maintained proper accounting records;
> - that the accounts are in agreement with the accounting records;
> - that Directors' emoluments and other transactions with Directors are properly disclosed in the accounts and
> - that they have obtained all the information and explanations which, to the best of their knowledge and belief, are necessary for the purpose of their audit.
>
> The auditors' opinion does not encompass the Directors' Report on pages 22 to 25. However, the Companies Act 1985 requires the auditors to report to shareholders if the matters contained in the Directors' Report are inconsistent with the accounts.

The continuing problems of overlap between the corporate governance Code of Best Practice and SAS 600 are discussed in the following chapters where appropriate.

1.3.3 Globalisation

Although not given as much publicity as the expectation gap, the globalisation of auditing had a great influence on SAS 600. That influence is now affecting other pronouncements. At the time this book was finalised, Auditing Standards and Guidelines in the UK were well on their way to being revised to accord almost word for word with international auditing standards. The international influence is so strong that in the APB's exposure drafts, 'stocks' are now termed 'inventory' (for example in draft SASs 400 and 420).

Over the last two decades, most of the advances in auditing have emanated from the United States. It is probably not surprising that an economy which has more accountants than any other and which has spawned the global accountancy Big Six should have the resources to allow thinkers to develop auditing theory. The US reporting influence on the UK is undeniable when one compares the two standard reports. Apart from the effect of legislation, which accounts for the reference to the Companies Act 1985 and the use of the words 'true and fair' in the UK, the similarities between a SAS 600 report[2] and one in use in the US[3] are obvious.

Report 100
STD: Generic report in United States

INDEPENDENT AUDITOR'S REPORT ....

> We have audited the accompanying balance sheet of X Company as of December 31, 19XX, and the related statements of income, retained earnings, and cash flows for the year then ended. These financial statements are the responsibility of the Company's management. Our responsibility is to express an opinion on these financial statements based on our audit.
>
> We conducted our audit in accordance with generally accepted auditing standards. Those standards require that we plan and perform the audit to obtain reasonable assurance about whether the financial statements are free of material misstatement. An audit includes examining, on a test basis, evidence supporting the amounts and disclosures in the financial statements. An audit also includes assessing the accounting principles used and significant estimates made by management, as well as evaluating the overall financial statement presentation. We believe that our audit provides a reasonable basis for our opinion.
>
> In our opinion, the financial statements referred to above present fairly, in all material respects, the financial position of X Company as of [at] December 31, 19XX, and the results of its operations and its cash flows for the year then ended in conformity with generally accepted accounting principles.

---

[2] A model report based on SAS 600 is given in section 2.4 'A model report' of chapter 2 'The Standard Report'.

[3] The report is from section AU 508 of the American Institute of Certified Public Accountants' professional standards. It is on the financial statements for a single year.

1.4 Famous blunders

1.4.1 Introduction

This section of the introductory chapter presents reports, both real and illustrative, from the time before SAS 600. The errors made then will no doubt turn up again in the future wearing new clothes. As one contributor to this book commented, the public probably rates the unqualified reports issued just prior to a spectacular company failure to be the most famous blunders by auditors. The wording of such reports does not, however, provide any further useful information for the purposes of this book.

Of course, auditors' reports are not the only part of the annual report and accounts where errors can be found. 'Observer' of the *Financial Times* reported on 8 October 1993 a classic in the annual report of Thailand's Saha Union: a page at the front of the group's accounts was headed 'Massage to shareholders'.

1.4.2 The Joint Monitoring Unit

Jo Holden, the first head of the Joint Monitoring Unit, is reported as saying that he had come across examples of auditors sending in clients' accounts to Companies House that (almost) complied with the Companies Act 1948. He did not mention the wording of the attached auditors' reports. This section does not wholly relate blunders by auditors who have not noticed the passing of Companies Acts, hopefully the registration process will have persuaded them to quit while ahead.

In its official comments on the first full year of their operations, the JMU expressed concern that firms were making errors in auditors' reports.[4] It drew attention to:

- failure to refer to Auditing Standards
- referring to the *'historical cost convention'* (this reference has been reinstated by SAS 600)
- using *'comply with'* rather than *'properly prepared in accordance with'* the Companies Act 1985
- reference to the wrong Companies Act(s) or section numbers
- use of the superseded 'Example 6' report for small companies.

These matters are all simple and basic. Presumably the JMU found it harder to criticise reports on grounds of judgmental inaccuracy. Compliance of reports with SAS 600 is, however, one of the key questions that the JMU address on visits.

The JMU visits firms at random according to an overall scheme that ensures that auditors of listed companies are visited more frequently. In addition, some visits

[4] Printed on pages 116 to 118 of the September 1993 issue of *Accountancy* magazine.

are carried out in response to complaints about firms. For example, if the Financial Reporting Review Panel (FRRP) finds that an accounting treatment is unacceptable, but the auditors have not qualified their report, those auditors could receive attention from their institute's disciplinary arm or the JMU.

1.4.3 The golden age

Of course, some very weird reports by auditors turn up at Companies House. Sometimes it seems that whoever was doing the filing for the company concerned did not know that some of the financial statements, to use the term in its wider sense, did not need to go to the registrar. The following report would seem, however, to be a full report on statutory accounts. It seems to be not only pre SAS 600, but also a little out of the ordinary. Clear communication might have been assisted by some quantification, but the report perhaps should just be read for artistic impression rather than technical merit.

REPORT ON BESTDYNE LTD, ISSUED AUGUST 1990 (EXTRACT)

> I have examined the accounts on pages 2-6 in accordance with approved standards.
>
> In my opinion the balance sheet correctly states the assets and liabilities of the company subject to:
>
> (i) Accounts receivable contains sums due to over a year to which insufficient effort has been made to collect.
>
> (ii) The loan has been made on an internal basis and I have been unable to obtain satisfactory proof as to the underlying security.
>
> (iii) The company has not made a single payment to its suppliers for services rendered for over six months. This shows a lack of commitment by the directors.
>
> (iv) The company's tax status in the UK is unresolved.
>
> (v) The accounts have been prepared under the historical cost convention.
>
> The depreciation charge is low for the type of asset owned.
>
> The profit and source and application of funds for the company are correct and comply with the Companies Act 1985.

The above example was reported in a marvellous subscription magazine *Audit Report.*[5] In earlier years, *Audit Report* corrected the spelling and punctuation errors it found in reports used as examples. In recent issues it has not pulled its punches. Just as audit reports are subject to error, so too is that magazine. As a result, if errors have been made in reproducing reports they could have been

[5] A subscription magazine providing each month eight pages of extracts of published modified auditors' reports. It is available from Butterworths, Borough Green, Sevenoaks, Kent TN 15 9PH, 0732 884567.

imported into this book, as the reports quoted have not generally been checked back to Companies House. Neither have copies of reports sent in by those kind enough to respond to the author's pleas for help. If reports have been inadvertently misquoted it is hoped that those affected will accept appropriate apologies in advance. In most cases, with the exception of the larger firms, the name of the auditors has been withheld, so only very diligent research would reveal their identity.

The subsections that follow illustrate blunders that one would think are so obvious that they could never happen. Some blunders are seemingly unexplainable; others reveal their likely cause. As ever, if something can go wrong, it will. Perhaps the cautionary tales here, and the advice in the rest of this book (which mainly deals with the more technical things that can go wrong), will keep some reports out of the next edition.

Common to all these examples is a breach of the first golden rule of signing audit reports: read the report carefully before signing it.

1.4.4 Not quite the same as last year

Audits tend to happen annually. When they do not it is like a foot sticking out into the path of the unwary auditor. Even when the accounting reference date does not change and the reporting period is always a year, the very fact that 199Y is not still 199X can cause problems. It only needs the next Companies Act to arrive (you have been warned) to give an opportunity to that articled clerk who was renowned for including the date at the top of the column in its cast (easier in £ s d) to make a similar mistake as a partner.

1.4.4.1 One date is much like another

The following is a result of giving the task of updating the accounts from one year to the next (1990 to 1991) to an under-qualified or under-briefed trainee or word processing operator. Such initiative is often unrewarded.

> In our opinion the financial statements give a true and fair view of the state of affairs of the company at 31 December 1991 and of the profit and source and application of funds for the year then ended and have been properly prepared in accordance with the Companies Act 1986.

1.4.4.2 The impossible dream

A change of accounting reference date is clearly an unfair burden for the following auditor; he or she forgot the first line of the little rhyme. Perhaps this problem never happens in those firms that issue a diary to partners, staff and clients.

> In our opinion the financial statements give a true and fair view of the state of affairs of the company at[6] 31 September 1991 and of the profit and source and application of funds for the nine months then ended and have been properly prepared in accordance with the Companies Act 1985.

1.4.4.3 Too much knowledge

In the good old days (1947 was not good), Companies Acts came along with what seemed like increasing pace; 1948, 1967, 1976, 1980, 1981; then a widening of the gap until 1985. Now the only things that come along with increasing frequency are Statutory Instruments. The temptation for the newly qualified 'high flier' to modify the opinion for an SI is, one hopes, easier to resist, but the following opinion shows the history of the problem. No doubt there was a scathing comment on file somewhere about the error in the previous year's audit report.

> In our opinion the financial statements give a true and fair view of the state of affairs of the company at 31 December 1990 and of the profit and source and application of funds for the nine months then ended and have been properly prepared in accordance with the Companies Act 1989.

Some firms require all the audit reports they issue to refer to 'period' instead of 'year' to avoid problems when accounting reference dates are changed. This can be criticised for lack of precision; rather like the practice of referring to the profit or loss as a 'result'. People wait at a bus stop for a bus, not a 'form of transport'.

1.4.5 The qualified report that isn't

A now-you-see-it, now-you-don't blunder leaves a top and tail that shows a qualification was proposed, then removed without altering the final paragraph. At least that is what it looks like; it could always have been last year's qualification that was not repeated. This type of error is surprisingly common.

REPORT ON PEPSICO HOLDINGS LTD., JUNE 1989

> We have audited the financial statements on pages 4 to 12 in accordance with auditing standards.
>
> Subject to the adjustments, if any, which may prove necessary as a result of the above in our opinion the financial statements give a true and fair view of the state of the company's affairs at June 30, 1989 and of its loss and source and application of funds for the period then ended and have been properly prepared in accordance with the Companies Act 1985.

The above report was issued by Ernst & Young; proving that a Big Six firm is not immune to errors in reporting.

---

[6] In case some readers revisit this section having read later chapters it is worth pointing out that 'at' rather than 'as at' was favoured by the Auditing Standard that SAS 600 superseded.

1.4.6 Similar words and similar errors

Some words have the chameleon-like ability to seem correct in a particular context when they are not. The first extract is a classic error.

REPORT ON ALINVYNE INSTALLATIONS LTD., MAY 1989

> I have audited the financial statements on pages 3 to 7 which have been drawn up on a going concern basis, which assumes that adequate borrowing facilities will remain available. My audit has been carried out in accordance with Accountancy (sic) Standards except that the scope of my work was limited by . . .

In this context, lessons may be learnt from two reports by auditors of the London Society of Chartered Accountants. The first example, cherished for some years by a contributor to this book, comes from the accounts of a predecessor body for the year to 31 December 1958. Total income then was £2,030.

REPORT TO THE MEMBERS OF THE LONDON AND DISTRICT SOCIETY OF CHARTERED ACCOUNTANTS

> We have examined the above Balance Sheet and annexed Income and Expenditure Account. In our opinion they present a true and fair view respectively of the state of the Society's affairs as at 31st December, 1958, and of its income and expenditure for the year ended on that date.
>
> Sydenham, Snowdon, Nicholson & Co.,
> Chartered Accountants.
> Honourable Auditors.

There is no doubt that the auditors were honourable men, but they probably meant to say 'honorary auditors'.

The second extract is more modern. Total income has grown to approximately £490,000. The audit fee, if any, is not disclosed but only the treasurer is described as 'honorary'. The extract demonstrates how a *'directors' responsibilities'* section for a society may be drafted under SAS 600. That section and the extract from the beginning of the auditors' report that follows also demonstrate that, 35 years later than the first example, errors are just as common.

STATEMENT OF MEMBERS OF THE SOCIETY'S RESPONSIBILITIES

> The Society's Rules require financial statements to be prepared for each financial year which give a true and fair view of its state of affairs at 31 December 1993(Note 1) and of its income and expenditure for the year then ended. These statements are required to be audited by independent auditors and copies made available to members.

In preparing these statements the members of the Society will have due regard to:

— selecting suitable accounting policies and applying them consistently

— making judgements and estimates that are reasonable and prudent

— observing applicable Accounting Standards

— preparing the financial statements on a going concern basis

The members of the Society are responsible also for keeping proper accounting records which disclose with reasonable accuracy the financial position of the Society and for safeguarding its assets.

AUDITORS' REPORT TO THE MEMBERS OF THE LONDON SOCIETY OF CHARTERED ACCOUNTANTS

We have audited the financial statements on pages 14 to 17 which have been prepared under the historical cost convention and the accounting policies set out on page 16.

Respective responsibilities of Society and Auditors (Note 2)

As described above the Society is responsible for the preparation of financial statements. It is our responsibility to form an independant (Note 3) opinion, based on our audit, on those statements and to report our opinion to you.

The London Society's accounts make interesting reading as they apparently fail to comply with Statement of Standard Accounting Practice 12 'Accounting for depreciation' because fixed assets are not capitalised. One assumes that the effect is immaterial as they still get a 'true and fair view' opinion. There seems to be potential for confusion over whether the members, or the society, have responsibilities and are reported to by the auditors. Perhaps the average member should be alarmed that he or she has a responsibility to safeguard assets that are not even shown in the accounts.

Notes

1 Presumably, after a few years, members will get bored with receiving accounts always for the year to 31 December 1993 and will demand some for 1994, 1995 and so on.

2 Perhaps the word 'the' was omitted in order to make the heading resemble those in the examples in appendix 2 to SAS 600. Sociologists might spend years of research and still be unable to define the responsibilities of society. The root cause of this anomaly in the extract is, however, its overuse of capital letters.

3 Either the auditors (Kidsons Impey) or the printers can't spell 'independent' correctly.

1.4.7 Caught by the computer

Modern auditors use computers. Over-reliance on computers can, however, bring dire consequences. These are explored in more detail in chapter 3 'Modified Reports' as they are more likely to occur when the prose is non-standard.

Standard reports too may suffer from computer interference. Some popular accounts preparation software still does not incorporate a computer spelling check but if such a check is run on a report, errors may be introduced by inadvertently accepting a computer-suggested word as a substitute for one it thinks is misspelled. Imagine that you are a partner in one of the top firms in the UK (if you are such a person then you are allowed to not imagine). In a hurry, would you spot that your firm's name had been subtly (in some cases not so subtly) altered in this way? The following were all the product of the spelling checker of Microsoft Word for Windows 2.0c:

Chancery Hellcat
Clark Whitehall
dB Binder Hamlet
Earnest & Young
KCMG Peat Warwick
Kid sons Impel
More Stephen's
Mores Lowland
Panel Err Frostier
Price Warehouse
Robin Rhodes
Soy Haywire
TG Grant Thorn ton
Touch Ross & CO

One suspects that partners in 'Chancery Hellcat' might just notice the difference! As well as trying your own firm's name, the obvious way to avoid this problem is to make sure that the 'user' or 'custom' dictionary for such work includes its correct spelling.

Examples of similar changes are occasionally quoted in the press. For example, in the 26 September 1993 issue of the *Financial Times* 'Observer' reported that the spell check of Microsoft Word 5.0 had attempted to turn Michael Portillo MP into Mischief Bordello. Spell checking is a changing art; the current Windows version of the same software now does not object to 'Michael' and offers 'Portal' as the best alternative for his last name.

Any auditor who has run a computer grammar checker over an audit report will know that 'in our opinion' is wordy and the computer offers 'we believe' as a better alternative. So far, this particular blunder (if it is a blunder), has not been seen in published reports.

Auditors who have come to terms with computer induced errors will face new computer challenges in the mid 1990s: voice and handwriting recognition. Voice recognition is already a commercial reality in the US, with personal systems now coming below the $1,000 barrier and, despite its shaky start, handwriting recognition is featured in some personal organisers.

Voice recognition increases the possibility of words that sound alike being confused. This already happens with traditional dictation but computers will initially not have the ability of word processing staff to correct errors. Handwriting recognition has a much larger potential for error and the results are not always predictable. Computer magazines have delighted in reporting some of the more unfortunate mistakes (such as recognising 'Random House' as 'condom nose') but such incidents may be fabricated rather than real[7].

1.5 Writing this book

Those who have read the introduction so far will have gathered that this book is not aimed at the lay reader; the 'man on the Pentonville omnibus' (as he would have been known had John Ruskin not been misquoted). It is likely that the text will prove difficult for non-auditors because of the necessary use of jargon. On 22 December 1993 the *Financial Times* carried a letter from Prof. Ian Morrison pointing out (with tongue in cheek) that it was seasonally inappropriate to use the headline 'Accountants divided over goodwill' just five days before Christmas. Those who may think 'material' is cloth, or associate the letters 'ICAEW' more with a trade union are going to have a difficult read.

There are some facts concerning the writing of the book about which readers should be aware because it may affect their interpretation of, or use of, the text.

Many books that accountants and auditors use are a 'team effort', to quote the preface to the first edition of *UK GAAP, Generally Accepted Accounting Practice in the United Kingdom*. That book had three principal authors and editors, thirteen other contributing authors, eighteen named commentators and numerous credits for research, marketing and word processing.

Many books are also written in the course of the writers' employment for the benefit of their firm's marketing effort. The writers have access to inside information from professional committees and working parties of which they or members of their firm are members. Significant judgements may be confirmed by counsel's opinion.

The above does not apply to this book. It was written by one person, working on their own, in their spare time. Input was sought from others by means of:

- a letter published by *Accountancy Age*
- sending questionnaires to major firms
- involvement in discussion groups
- asking people directly for information or their views.

---

[7] From the back (less serious) page of *PC Week* 26 October 1993.

Having sought this input, the views expressed in the book remain those of the author alone. In some instances recommendations have been made that are justified by anticipated acceptability, not the author's own preferences. Auditors are free to accept or reject the practical advice offered.

The book was written on computer and delivered to the publisher in final form 'ready to print'. A significant advantage of this method of working is that the book is as up-to-date as possible throughout its whole text to the date that the final copy was sent to the printers (10 May 1994). A disadvantage of this method of writing is, however, that there are inevitably more 'rough edges' to the finished text.

SAS 600 is a young pronouncement. Developing practice will make a further edition of this book desirable. The author would be pleased to receive criticism of the current text and any further input towards that eventuality.

2 THE STANDARD REPORT

2.1 Introduction

This chapter deals with the 'clean', or 'unqualified', or, to use the term preferred in this book, the 'standard' audit report. Discussion of modified reports is postponed until chapter 3.

The text concentrates on auditors' reports on single companies. Reports on groups are included, but only in a separate section. Sections are also included that deal with non-standard companies (such as small companies) and other entities.

After this introduction, the next three sections (see the list of sections above) give the statutory and professional requirements and a model standard report.

Section 2.5 'Elements and options' is a major part of this chapter. It examines every part of the standard auditors' report in detail. Some significant aspects of the analysis (true and fair view and readability) are given sections to themselves. Section 2.8 explains how to develop a standard report. The section draws on the earlier analysis and on research into how major firms have implemented SAS 600.

The chapter ends with three sections that examine some practical aspects of the reporting process.

2.2 Statutory requirements

2.2.1 Introduction

This section deals with the statutory requirements for auditors reporting on companies and groups of companies generally. The main references are to the Companies Act 1985. There are similar requirements in Ireland.

Later in this chapter, section 2.10 'Non-standard companies' sets out the statutory requirements and other matters relevant to companies in Ireland. That section also covers the special circumstances of:

- small companies
- dormant companies
- single member companies
- very small companies.

The requirements for companies that are in specialised industries (such as banking and insurance) are not covered as such specific matters are outside the scope of this book. The general guidance on reporting on other entities (section 2.11 of this chapter) is, however, useful for such companies.

The main sections of the Companies Act 1985 that are relevant are:

- section 235 — sets out the duty to report, the form of the report and associated matters
- section 236 — governs the signature to the report
- section 237 — requires auditors to carry out certain investigations in preparing their report and to report on some matters by exception
- section 46 — deals with the meaning of 'unqualified report' for the purpose of determining the legality of distributions [s 43(3)].

These sections of the Act are discussed in the subsections that follow. Rather than quote the Act, the requirements are first presented in a form that could be used as a checklist.

2.2.2 Auditors' report

Section 235 contains the following requirements:

a report is made to the company's members[1]

b report is required on all annual accounts to be laid before the company in general meeting during auditors' tenure of office

---

[1] See section 2.10 of this chapter for a discussion of companies with only one member.

c report shall state if in auditors' opinion the annual accounts have been properly prepared in accordance with the Act

d report shall state if in auditors' opinion a true and fair view is given of:
- the state of affairs of the company as at the end of the financial year
- the profit or loss of the company for the financial year

and, in the case of group accounts, for the undertakings included in the consolidation as a whole, of:
- the state of affairs as at the end of the financial year, and
- the profit or loss for the financial year

so far as concerns members of the company

e auditors shall consider whether the information given in the directors' report is consistent with the accounts and, if of the opinion that it is not consistent, they shall state that fact in their report.

Notes

1 Those who like to anticipate obscure problems could query what happens if the members vote at the annual general meeting (AGM) not to re-elect the auditors earlier than the accounts are laid. There are two reasons why this is not actually a problem. The first is that auditors hold office from the end of one AGM to the end of the next (unless removed or resigning earlier). It does not, therefore, matter whether the members take the accounts or the reappointment of auditors first; the retiring auditors are still required to report. The second reason is that the members do not approve the accounts in the AGM, that is done earlier by the directors as required by section 233. AGMs nevertheless frequently minute the laying of the accounts as if the members were approving at least the receipt of them.

2 The Act refers only to the 'report'. The opinion is merely the way auditors make some of their required statements.

3 If, as is usually the case, the company's individual profit and loss account is omitted when group accounts are prepared, the auditors need not report on it.

2.2.3 The signature

The requirements of section 236 are that:

a the auditors' report shall state the names of the auditors and be signed by them

b every copy of the auditors' report shall state the names of the auditors if it is:
- laid before the company in general meeting, or
- otherwise circulated, published or issued

c the copy that is delivered to the registrar shall state the names of the auditors and be signed by them.

Notes

1 The section draws a distinction between the report (of which there is but one) and copies of it. Most copies need only state the name of the auditors but the copy sent to the registrar must also be signed. The auditors' name forms part of the report.

2 Section 236 makes it clear that where the office of auditor is held by a partnership (or a body corporate) an authorised person may sign in the name of the organisation. The reference to 'names' should not be taken to mean that auditors are expected to have at least one alias. The section allows for the relatively rare joint audit, where two or more firms report together.

3 The wording in (b) concerning circulation, publishing or issuing seems sufficiently wide to include, for practical purposes, any public use of the report made by the company.

4 The requirement to deliver in (c) to the registrar a signed copy of the report seems a little odd. The registrar certainly does not check the signature to ensure that it is genuine. The safeguard seems to be for the benefit of auditors who might otherwise never discover that their client has substituted a forged report. In such circumstances, however, the auditors would surely notice any changes in wording rather than rely on recognising a signature as bogus.

5 Section 236 contains teeth. If the statement of auditors' names is not made, or if the registrar's copy is not signed, every officer of the company is liable to a fine. The possible penalty is one-fifth of the statutory maximum (on summary judgement). In plain language, currently a fine of up to £1,000.

2.2.4 Reporting duties of auditors

The requirements of section 237 are that:

a the auditors shall carry out such investigations as will enable them to form an opinion as to whether:
- proper accounting records have been kept and proper returns adequate for their audit have been received from branches not visited by them
- the company's individual accounts are in agreement with the accounting records and returns

b if any of the matters in (a) above are not satisfactory, the auditors shall state that fact in their report

c if the auditors fail to obtain all the information and explanations which, to the best of their knowledge and belief, are necessary for the purposes of their audit, they shall state that fact in their report

d if the requirements of Schedule 6 of the Act (disclosure of information: emoluments and other benefits of directors and others) are not complied with in the annual accounts, the auditors shall include in their report, so far as they are reasonably able to do so, a statement giving the required particulars.

Notes

1 Section 237 requires auditors to carry out investigations towards specific objectives. Auditors perhaps assume that the work they do to make the report required by section 235 is sufficient to discharge their obligations under this section. The priority given to specific work to, for example form an opinion on returns from branches, is not high. As an illustration of this, the index to the fifth edition of *The Coopers & Lybrand Manual of Auditing* contains no entries where one might expect to find the words 'branch', or 'return'.

2 Lovers of trivia might like to dwell on the fact that the word 'branch' is not defined in the Companies Act 1985. Where a word is not defined it normally takes on its common meaning, such as 'a limb of a tree'.[2]

2.2.5 The meaning of 'qualified' opinion

The term 'qualified' in relation to auditors' reports has a particular meaning in company law. For example, the term is defined by section 262(1) for the purposes of part VII of the Companies Act 1985 (accounts and audit) as meaning:

> that the report does not state the auditors' unqualified opinion that the accounts have been properly prepared in accordance with this Act or, in the case of an undertaking not required to prepare accounts in accordance with this Act, under any corresponding legislation under which it is required to prepare accounts.

Issuing a qualified opinion is significant for other provisions of the Companies Act 1985 relating to distributions and the certainty of the net assets position:

- when the last annual accounts are the relevant accounts for determining the legality of a proposed distribution — section 271.

  If the opinion is qualified the company may not pay a dividend based on the accounts unless the auditors make a further report as to whether the qualification is material to assessing the legality of the distribution [s 271(3)].

- re-registration of a private company as a public company — section 43.

  If the opinion is qualified the company cannot change its status unless the auditors state in their report that the matter giving rise to the qualification is not material for the purpose. The purpose being to determine whether at the

[2] The definition of 'branch' is now a European matter, but still not without difficulty. The disclosure of the existence of branches outside the UK (for financial years commencing on or after 1 January 1993) required by SI 1992 No. 3179 The Oversea Companies and Credit and Financial Institutions (Branch Disclosure) Regulations 1992 is, however, outside of the scope of this book.

balance sheet date the amount of the company's net assets was not less than the aggregate of its called up share capital and undistributable reserves.

In this instance it is only the balance sheet that is relevant as 'unqualified' is defined by section 46 as *'stating without material qualification the auditors' opinion that the balance sheet has been properly prepared in accordance with this Act'.*

2.2.6 The elective regime

Under section 379A of the Companies Act 1985 a private company may elect to dispense with any of the following:

- holding annual general meetings [s 366A]
- laying of accounts and reports before a general meeting [s 252]
- annual appointment of auditors [s 386]
- the time limit on any directors' authority to allot shares [s 80A]
- the 95 per cent majority requirement for agreement to short notice (but a newly specified majority cannot be below 90 per cent) [s 369(4) or 378(3)].

The first three are interlinked and have much greater general application than the other items. Together they are frequently referred to as the 'elective regime'. The elective regime may be revoked by an ordinary resolution and it lapses if a private company becomes public.

The elective regime has no direct effect on auditors' reports. However, auditors need to be aware of its effect on the mechanics of their office as certain professional requirements are stated only in terms of the normal events, such as laying accounts before the members.

1 Reappointment as auditors

During the elective regime auditors are deemed to be reappointed on the expiry of the time for appointing auditors for each subsequent year (i.e. the expiry of a period of 28 days from the sending of accounts to members) unless (1) the company is dormant and resolves not to appoint auditors, or (2) a resolution is passed removing the auditors in accordance with section 393 (a written resolution cannot be used to remove auditors before their term of office expires) or (3) the auditors resign.

If the regime ends, auditors continue to hold office until the conclusion of the next general meeting at which accounts are laid.

2 Laying of accounts and reports

Accounts and reports must be sent to those entitled to receive them not less than 28 days before the end of the period allowed for laying and delivering them. This event (i.e. the sending of accounts) is a convenient substitute, for the purposes of professional standards, for laying of accounts.

3 Rights of auditors

Auditors who wish to exercise their right to be heard at the AGM are able to use a right given them by section 253. That section gives auditors 28 days, beginning with the day on which the accounts and reports are sent out, to require that a general meeting be held.

2.3 Professional requirements

This section sets out the professional requirements governing the wording of the standard report. The requirements derive from the individual Auditing Standards 600.2 to 600.5 set out in Statement of Auditing Standards 600 'Auditors' reports on financial statements'. In checklist form the requirements are:

a shape [SAS 600.2[3]]:
- title
- introductory paragraph
- appropriate headings for other sections
- sections dealing with:
  - — respective responsibilities of directors and auditors
  - — the basis of the auditors' opinion
  - — the auditors' opinion on the financial statements
- the manuscript or printed signature of the auditors
- the date of the auditors' report.

b in the respective responsibilities of directors and auditors section [SAS 600.3]:
- statement that the financial statements are the responsibility of the directors
- a reference to a description of those responsibilities when set out elsewhere in the financial statements or accompanying information
- if the directors' relevant responsibilities are not adequately described elsewhere, a description of those responsibilities
- a statement that the auditors' responsibility is to express an opinion on the financial statements.

c in the basis of opinion section [SAS 600.4]:
- a statement as to the auditors' compliance or otherwise with Auditing Standards, together with the reasons for any departure therefrom

---

[3] The abbreviation 'SAS 600.2' may strike some readers as odd. When referring to SAS 600, 'SAS' is short for 'statement of auditing standards'. Logically, an individual standard should be an 'auditing standard', that is 'AS 600.2'. The convention used in this book is, however, the one that the APB has adopted in its own SASs. Perhaps SAS can also stand for 'single auditing standard'.

- a statement that an audit includes:
  - — examining, on a test basis, evidence relevant to the amounts and disclosures in the financial statements
  - — assessing the significant estimates and judgements made by the directors in preparing the financial statements
  - — considering whether the accounting policies are appropriate to the reporting entity's circumstances, consistently applied and adequately disclosed
- a statement that the auditors planned and performed the audit so as to obtain reasonable assurance that the financial statements are free from material misstatement, whether caused by error or by fraud or other irregularity, and that they have evaluated the overall presentation of the financial statements.

d in the opinion section[SAS 600.5]:

- a clear expression of opinion on the financial statements and on any further matters required by statute or other requirements applicable to the particular engagement.

2.4 A model report

2.4.1 Introduction

This section presents a model standard audit report. Although it is based closely on the first example in appendix 2 to SAS 600 it takes a small amount of advantage of the flexibility of wording allowed by the SAS. The features of the report are discussed in detail in section 2.5 of this chapter 'Elements and options'.

The last part of this section explains how reports are shown in this book.

2.4.2 Model report

Report 200
STD: Model based closely on SAS 600

AUDITORS' REPORT TO THE SHAREHOLDERS OF ....

We have audited the financial statements on pages ..... to ..... which have been prepared under the historical cost convention [as modified by the revaluation of certain fixed assets] and the accounting policies set out on page ..... .

Respective responsibilities of directors and auditors

As described on page ..... the company's directors are responsible for the preparation of financial statements. It is our responsibility to form an independent opinion, based on our audit, on those statements and to report our opinion to you.

Basis of opinion

We conducted our audit in accordance with Auditing Standards issued by the Auditing Practices Board. An audit includes examination, on a test basis, of evidence relevant to the amounts and disclosures in the financial statements. It also includes an assessment of the significant estimates and judgements made by the directors in the preparation of the financial statements, and of whether the accounting policies are appropriate to the company's circumstances, consistently applied and adequately disclosed.

We planned and performed our audit so as to obtain all the information and explanations which we considered necessary in order to provide us with sufficient evidence to give reasonable assurance that the financial statements are free from material misstatement, whether caused by fraud or other irregularity or error. In forming our opinion we also evaluated the overall adequacy of the presentation of information in the financial statements.

Opinion

In our opinion the financial statements give a true and fair view of the state of the company's affairs as at .... and of its [profit / loss] for the year then ended and have been properly prepared in accordance with the Companies Act 1985.

Registered Auditors Date
Address

2.4.3 How reports are shown in this book

Reports in this book, whether full or extract, are numbered for ease of reference and have a heading that indicates their type and nature. The first digit of the number refers to the chapter, the other digits form a sequence within each chapter. The headings in this chapter mainly begin with the letters 'STD', which are an abbreviation for the word 'standard'. Other abbreviations are used, for example 'D' is a report modified because of disagreement. These abbreviations are explained in chapter 3 'Modified Reports'.

Full reports are not normally given. Only the relevant parts of a report are shown when illustrating a particular matter. The length of an example report shows whether it is a full report or just an extract. Some reports are given in skeleton or word picture form. The relevant text conventions for such reports are explained in chapter 3.

The following text conventions are used:

- a series of dots indicates that information should be filled in. Typical information is: the company's name, the pages referred to, and the balance sheet date
- plain text enclosed by square brackets [ ] should be included in appropriate circumstances. In the model report this is where there is a modification to the historical cost convention
- two or more words in plain text separated by a slash and enclosed by square brackets [..... / .....] are alternative wordings. The most common example is [profit / loss].

2.5 Elements and options

2.5.1 Introduction

This section explores the elements of the standard report. Because of its importance, one element, the discussion of 'true and fair view', has a section of this chapter to itself.

The objective of this section is to provide a basis for understanding and writing a standard report by:

- expanding on the requirements of SAS 600 dealt with in section 2.3 of this chapter by discussion of the related explanatory material and example reports in appendix 2 to SAS 600
- considering the interaction of the legal and professional requirements
- exploring the options available in wording auditors' standard reports.

Although readability is considered as part of the discussion of the elements it is easier to assess for the whole report. Readability is considered further, therefore, in a later section of this chapter.

2.5.2 Flexibility

The exposure draft of SAS 600 contained a proposed standard that would have required auditors to use the format and wording of the example reports contained in the SAS unless they considered that to do so would impair the clarity of their report, and thereby impair communication with the reader.

The proposed requirement was included to promote a degree of uniformity in the form and wording of auditors' reports to help the reader's understanding. Unfortunately, the proposed wording could have made the standard unworkable as pointed out in one letter of comment on it:

'*There has traditionally been a degree of divergence between firms. Alternative wording such as "state of affairs of the company" instead of "state of the company's affairs", and the continuing debate over "financial statements" or "accounts". Minor matters of divergence include whether to use punctuation and ordinals or plain numbers in dates. . . . Auditors are unlikely to be able to argue successfully that they must use their own house style or else the clarity of their report will be impaired. So is the APB really suggesting that the paragraph as it now stands will be enforced?*'

When issued, the SAS did not contain an absolute ban on divergence from the example reports in it. Instead the explanatory material to SAS 600.2 encourages the use of a standard format and common language in auditors' reports to assist the reader's understanding. The examples in appendix 2 to SAS 600 are referred to merely as examples '*to illustrate wording which meets the Auditing Standards contained in this SAS*'.

As discussed in the subsections below, auditors have considerable choice in wording. Some differences are of no real consequence, for example choosing to use '31st December' instead of '31 December'; others, such as whether or not to refer to cash flows, are more significant.

2.5.3 Position

There is no requirement in SAS 600 to position the auditors' report in any particular part of the package of information received by shareholders. The explanatory material to SAS 600.1 suggests that it will aid communication with the reader if the auditors' report is placed before the financial statements.

For smaller companies the auditors' report has usually been simply sandwiched between the directors' report and the accounts (in other words, complying with the SAS 600 suggestion). For larger companies, the auditors' report has also been found there, but a large minority of annual reports have relegated it to the end of the notes to the accounts.

The introduction of a statement of directors' responsibilities and other corporate governance disclosures has probably ended the practice of putting the report anywhere other than immediately before the accounts, because directors will normally want their statements to be reasonably prominent. The explanatory material to SAS 600.1 suggests that, where the directors set out their responsibilities themselves, an appropriate position for the description will be immediately before the auditors' report.

This coincides with the position favoured by the corporate governance Code of Best Practice which asks directors to explain their responsibility for preparing the accounts next to a statement by the auditors about their reporting responsibilities. The relevant note to the Code explains that the statement should be '*immediately before the auditors' report which in future will include a separate statement (currently being developed by the Auditing Practices Board) on the responsibility of the auditors for expressing an opinion on the accounts*'.

2.5.4 Layout

The layout of an auditors' report may be affected by such things as:

- the typeface or typefaces used
- whether elements are presented aligned to the left margin, or right margin, or centred
- whether elements are split between lines or are on a single line.

These matters are often out of the hands of the auditors and left to the judgement of the printer, or designer, or word processing operator who produces the accounts.

The requirements of SAS 600 are few. Apart from a title to identify the report, the only need is to ensure that the layout does not impede the required clear expression of opinion. A layout problem would have to be severe to cause a breach of SAS 600. For this reason such problems are not considered further in the subsections below.

Auditors do need to pay attention to layout, however, to avoid criticism of clarity, or just simply to avoid appearing unprofessional. Problems could be caused by:

- the date of the report being shown only in a page heading
- the printed signature of the auditors being misplaced from the foot of the report
- headings and layout that could confuse a reader into thinking that other matters were within the report, for example the description of the responsibilities of the directors
- unprofessional typefaces
- the report appearing superimposed over a distracting or inappropriate picture.

2.5.5 Title

2.5.5.1 The requirements

SAS 600.2 requires the auditors' report to include a title identifying the person or persons to whom the report is addressed. For a company, section 235 of the Companies Act 1985 requires the report to be made to the members.

2.5.5.2 Who reports

Auditors report, but the heading of the report varies between firms. There are different views about whether to use the singular or plural form of auditor, which makes placing an apostrophe important. The alternatives are:

- Auditors' report to . . . (plural)
- Auditor's report to . . . .

The examples in appendix 2 to SAS 600 use the plural form. The Auditing Standard that SAS 600 replaced used the plural form. Section 235 of the Companies Act 1985 uses the plural form.

The practical conclusion is that the use of the plural form is best practice. The singular form should only be used if the auditor is a sole practitioner.

Audit Regulations initially added to the confusion by forcing firms to use the singular description 'Registered Auditor'. This looked particularly odd when combined with the plural 'Chartered Accountants'. However, it is now possible to use either form of Registered Auditor(s) and so match the number in the title to the number after the signature.

Those who prefer the singular form point out that the Companies Act 1985 uses the plural form only because of the possibility of joint auditors. They may refer to section 384(1) of the Companies Act 1985, which states that '*Every company shall appoint an auditor or auditors in accordance with this Chapter.*'

They will then point to section 236(1) which is clearly aimed at joint auditors: '*The auditors' report shall state the names of the auditors and be signed by them*'. The important part of the above being the 's' at the end of 'names'.

To add trivia they may comment that in the unlikely event of the Secretary of State being called upon to fill a vacancy under section 387, the Secretary of State may only appoint a person (i.e. not joint auditors).

There is a very strong suspicion that the singular form is, in fact, the correct form (except for joint audits). However, it is unlikely that SAS 600 will be amended, or that major firms will alter their stance, so are there any further reasons to perhaps prefer the plural version?

Two spring to mind: the need to use a plural version to assist in avoiding sexist prose in SASs and, more importantly, the resulting problems with personal pronouns if the singular version is used. The normal standard report starts with 'We have audited . . .'. It would appear very odd if 'we' was changed to 'I', especially as the signature is likely to be that of a firm (and many sole practitioners also trade under a name that looks like more than one person).

Whatever the merits of the singular version, for practical purposes the plural should be used.

There is, of course, no reason other than conformity why 'Auditors' report to . . . ' should not instead read 'Report of the auditors to . . . '. Auditors might accept this start to a title if the annual report used a similar wording for the 'Report of the directors' or 'Responsibilities of the directors'.

2.5.5.3 Addressees

The normal mechanism for identifying the addressees has been to title the report 'Auditors' report to the members of . . . '. Many auditors will find the word 'shareholders', which is preferred by the SAS, unfamiliar.

Either term can be used, although the larger firms (with the occasional exception of Arthur Andersen[4]) seem to have a preference for 'members'.

Although familiar, and supported by the wording of section 235, the word 'members' is capable of misinterpretation. The person on the Clapham omnibus arguably finds 'shareholder' more understandable. 'Shareholder' means a holder of shares; 'member' could have several different meanings. For example, the report could be thought to be to members of the board of directors, or members of the workforce, instead of the shareholders.

This word 'member' is defined in section 22 of the Companies Act 1985. There are two ways to become a member. A subscriber of a company's memorandum becomes a member on its registration. The most common way is to agree to become a member of a company and to have ones name entered in the register of members. This normally coincides with becoming a holder of shares and for practical purposes the word shareholder is synonymous with 'member' except for companies not having a share capital as their members do not hold shares.

For a single member company there is an argument for auditors to address their report to the member by name. This can hardly be criticised and may be significant if there is litigation, such as after a change in ownership of the company.

Assuming that the client is not a single member company, the normal title identifies the addressees but does not limit those shareholders or members in any way (for example, by stating that only the shareholders as at the date of signing the report are being reported to). It would not be realistic to suppose that such a limitation could effectively reduce auditors' potential liability.

1 'Person or persons'

The wording of the requirement of SAS 600.2 results from the need to make it applicable to entities other than companies. The reference to 'person' in the singular, which was included in the exposure draft, was not, therefore, a clever anticipation of the introduction of the single member company[5].

Of interest to audit report trivia enthusiasts is the fact that section 235 has not been amended and continues to refer only to 'members'. This is not actually a problem as the statutory instrument that introduced the single member company contained a general relief such that any enactment or rule of law that applies in

---

[4] For example Senior Engineering Group PLC, 31 December 1993. The word 'shareholders' is also used by Pannell Kerr Forster in their report on the accounts of Booker PLC as at 1 January 1994.

[5] SI 1992 No. 1699 The Companies (Single Member Private Limited Companies) Regulations 1992 was brought into force on 15 July 1992. The Regulations permit private companies limited by shares or guarantee to be formed with, or have, only one member. Following the Regulations, groups having wholly owned subsidiaries may do away with nominee holdings.

relation to a private company limited by shares or guarantee applies with such modification as may be necessary to allow for the single member company.

2.5.6 Introductory paragraph

2.5.6.1 The requirements

SAS 600.2 requires auditors' reports to include an introductory paragraph identifying the financial statements audited.

2.5.6.2 Paragraph heading

The examples in appendix 2 to SAS 600 do not have a heading for the introductory paragraph. Auditors will normally not consider a heading for the introductory paragraph to be necessary. There is no reason, however, why auditors who want a heading should not use one. Possible headings could include:

- Introduction
- Financial statements audited
- Accounting policies
- Historical cost convention
- Modified historical cost convention
- Basis of preparation of accounts.

The last three examples above could be used to draw attention to a feature of the accounting convention or accounting policies. This could be done, for example, where the going concern basis was not used.

2.5.6.3 Methods of identifying the financial statements

The examples in appendix 2 to the SAS identify the financial statements by referring to page numbers. This will normally suffice, but there are dangers in brevity.

In reality, apart from other auditors, who always check that the page numbers are right (in case the directors' report is included in error), is it reasonable to expect users to pay attention to such small details? It is much more reasonable to suppose that users assume that the whole of an annual report is audited unless there is a 'health warning' about unaudited material.

The example reports could also be challenged as not complying with the requirement of SAS 600.2. If detached from the accounts (or used for typed and printed accounts) page numbers are insufficient identification. However, the alternative introductory paragraph suggested below is going against the call for brevity that went up from many of those who commented on the exposure draft. For example:

> We have audited the annual accounts of .... for the year to .... on pages ..... to ..... . The annual report and accounts, of which our report forms a part, includes the directors' report and other explanatory material that we have not audited.

While the above may seem to be a solution in search of a problem, some auditors have historically identified the financial statements by using words such as 'attached' or 'annexed'. This requires users to know the difference between financial statements and directors' reports and so is probably no longer acceptable.

2.5.6.4 Audited

Although the main thrust of the requirement is towards the identification of the financial statements, there is an implied need to make the reader aware that they have been audited. This is accomplished in the examples in appendix 2 to SAS 600 by the use of the opening words: *'We have audited . . . '*. This is a perfectly adequate way of doing things. The approach is familiar as it was also used in the Auditing Standard that SAS 600 replaced. Most auditors will use these words.

Some may want to use alternative words and, so long as the requirements are met, may do so. Possible wordings include:

- We audited the financial statements on pages . . .
- The audited financial statements are on pages . . .
- Our report refers to the financial statements on pages . . . .

The report under SAS 600 differs from its predecessor because the basis of opinion section makes it clear that an audit has been carried out. There is, therefore, no real need to state that fact in the introductory paragraph. If an introductory paragraph such as the last example above is used, the basis of opinion wording must also be changed from the examples in appendix 2 to SAS 600. It is no longer reasonable to commence that part of the report with the words '*We conducted our audit in accordance with Auditing Standards*' if it is not already obvious that an audit was carried out.

Some may wonder why the examples in appendix 2 to SAS 600 prefer the words 'we have audited' to 'we audited', as the latter form is shorter. The answer is that the first form of the verb is the present perfect or perfect tense, the second is merely the simple past tense. In the context of auditors' reports, the meanings are similar but the former is the stronger and more assertive construction. For example, in answer to the question 'have you audited?' the response 'we audited' sounds weak.

2.5.6.5 Accounting convention and accounting policies

The explanatory material below SAS 600.2 merely states that the introductory paragraph **may** include reference to the accounting convention and accounting policies. This is further emphasised by the examples in appendix 2 to SAS 600, which refer to the 'historical cost convention' and accounting policies.

The exposure draft gave examples of introductory paragraphs that were more in the nature of a 'health warning' that the accounts provide information only about past performance and financial position at a particular date. The change in emphasis was not one that could easily have been anticipated by commentators.

The current and proposed international standards (IAG 13 'The Auditor's Report on Financial Statements' and an exposure draft issued in February 1993) contain no reference to either the accounting convention or accounting policies. The APB seems, therefore, to be out on a limb in suggesting that the accounting convention and accounting policies be mentioned.

In the absence of a specific requirement, there is no need to mention the accounting convention or accounting policies. Larger firms seem to be divided about the merits of including such wording.[6]

1 Accounting convention

The Auditing Standard 'The audit report' was issued in 1980 and revised in 1989. The 1989 revision contained no mention of the historical cost convention. The reference first arose because of a Consultative Committee of Accountancy Bodies (CCAB) recommendation in 1976 (ICAEW U 20, ICAS 3.3, ICAI KJ 6 CICA S6). At that time, the reason for it was to differentiate between reports on historical cost accounts and reports on the new inflation adjusted accounts.

Why should auditors refer to the historical cost convention? Perhaps to draw attention to the fact that the accounts had not been adjusted for inflation and so provided less worthy figures than the 'smart' inflation adjusted ones. In other words, to reduce their possible liability. There do not seem to have been any claims against auditors that attacked the omission of such a reference. In recent years, the JMU has regarded reports referring to the historical cost convention as evidence that the auditors were not up-to-date.

To bring back a reference to the historical cost convention at the time when the Accounting Standards Board (ASB) has issued a discussion paper on the regular revaluation of assets can be seen as either a responsive or redundant move. There seems to be no prospect of a return to current cost accounting or any other method

---

[6] Arthur Andersen's house style (?) is particularly odd. A typical wording is '*. . . under the historical cost convention as modified by the revaluation of certain assets and the accounting policies on pages .....*'. This reads as if the accounting policies modify the historical cost convention!

of accounting for inflation (particularly when inflation in the UK is at a low level). So why are auditors being encouraged to mention in the audit report that the accounts have been drawn up on the normal basis?

One school of thought (the *'reporting by exception'* school) suggests that a reference is only necessary when the historical cost convention has been modified, for example by the revaluation of properties. This is a sort of *'emphasis of matter'*. The need to draw attention to this has diminished as Financial Reporting Standard 3 'Reporting Financial Performance' (FRS 3) includes a requirement for a note of historical cost profits and losses where there is a material difference between the result as disclosed in the profit and loss account and the result on an unmodified historical cost basis.[7] Is there really a need for auditors' reports to repeat information in the accounts?

If a reference is included, are readers expected to understand what is meant by the *'historical cost convention'*. This is professional jargon.[8] The Companies Act 1985 includes in Schedule 4 the term *'historical cost accounting rules'* and spends a dozen paragraphs setting out what that means. If auditors do want to attempt an explanation it is unrealistic to expect that they can do so in only a line or two.

The only real reason for including a reference to the historical cost convention in the report is to conform with the examples in appendix 2 to SAS 600 and so with what other auditors do.

2 Accounting policies

An automatic reference to the accounting policies also seems unnecessary. Why not make an automatic reference to the amount of share capital, or any other aspect of the accounts for that matter?

The *'reporting by exception'* school of thought says that a reference is unnecessary unless, for example there has been a departure from an accounting standard or a provision of the Companies Act 1985 in order to show a true and fair view. This approach uses a variation of the standard report in lieu of a modification and is self-defeating if not universally used. If the majority of auditors include or do not include a reference all the time, but a significant minority only do so as an exception, readers do not know whether a particular report is normal or trying to alert them to a significant matter.

The only readers who will know what a particular report is trying to achieve are those that are familiar with the mode of reporting by the audit firm concerned. There is a temptation for members of a firm (especially those writing the firm's

---

7 FRS 3 paragraph 26.

8 A close study of SSAPs shows that the prefaces to SSAPs 1, 17, 18, 19, 20, 21, and 23 refer to the historical cost convention (and the current cost convention) others do not. There is, of course, no reason for this.

audit manual) to assume that readers of audit reports understand as much about the firm's policies as they do. This trap should be avoided. The story about a client complaining a competitor received an auditors' report drawing attention to the fact that the company was a going concern (when the client knew the competitor was in financial trouble) is well known.

Again, the only real reason for including a reference to the accounting policies in the report is to conform with the examples in appendix 2 to SAS 600 and so with what other auditors do.

2.5.7 Respective responsibilities of directors and auditors

2.5.7.1 The requirements

Auditors should include in their report an appropriately headed section giving:

- a statement that the accounts are the responsibility of the directors
- a reference to a description of those responsibilities when set out elsewhere in the accounts or accompanying information
- a statement that the auditors' responsibility is to express an opinion on the accounts.

Where the financial statements or accompanying information (for example the directors' report) do not include an adequate description of the directors' relevant responsibilities, the auditors' report should include a description of those responsibilities.

2.5.7.2 Paragraph heading

The most popular heading seems likely to be *'Respective responsibilities of directors and auditors'* because that is used in the examples in appendix 2 to SAS 600.

The word 'respective' seems almost redundant. Alternative headings include:

- Responsibilities of directors and auditors
- Directors and auditors
- Responsibilities.

2.5.7.3 Reference to directors' description

When the directors describe their responsibilities outside the auditors' report the examples in appendix 2 to SAS 600 use wording that is commendably brief:

> As described on page ..... the company's directors are responsible for the preparation of financial statements.

The position of the description decides the type of cross-reference. Popular alternatives will be:

> As described in the directors' report the company's directors are responsible for the preparation of financial statements.

> As described above the company's directors are responsible for the preparation of financial statements.

A possible problem with using 'above' arises when the directors' description is not signed and dated on behalf of the board. A reader may understand the directors' description of responsibilities to be part of the auditors' report. Attention to layout may solve this potential problem if it is not possible to convince the directors that their description of responsibilities deserves a signature.

Further aspects of cross-referencing are dealt with below under the heading of 'Integrated presentation'.

1 Abbreviated accounts

Auditors may be influenced by the knowledge that their report on the full accounts will be reproduced in their report on abbreviated accounts. The form of cross-reference may be changed to avoid a 'thin air' reference, for example to an unfiled directors' report. The following wording would make it clear that the description is not available to readers of the abbreviated accounts:

> As described in the directors' report on the full accounts the company's directors are responsible for the preparation of financial statements.

2.5.7.4 Position of directors' description

The position of the directors' description of their responsibilities was mentioned briefly in the section above dealing with cross-references. The position can affect auditors' responsibilities towards the statement and that is considered in this section.

SAS 600 does not prescribe where the directors' description of their responsibilities should be if it is not in the auditors' report. Appendix 3 to the SAS gives example wording of a description of the directors' responsibilities for inclusion in a company's financial statements. 'Financial statements' are defined in SAS 600 as: '*the balance sheet, profit and loss account (or other form of income statement), statements of cash flows and total recognised gains and losses, notes and other statements and explanatory material, all of which are identified in the auditors' report as being the financial statements.*' So auditors and directors may be persuaded by the example to put the material in the accounts. However, the corporate governance Code of Best Practice may also be influential even for companies not obeying Stock Exchange rules. The Code requires the statement to be placed immediately before the auditors' report.

Appendix 3 to SAS 600 envisages that part of the directors' description of their responsibilities relating to the going concern basis of preparation of accounts may be the subject of a separate statement. This statement may be that required by the corporate governance Code of Best Practice or it may be a requirement for all companies to be set out in SAS 130 'The going concern basis in financial statements'. SAS 130 has been issued as an exposure draft for the second time but at the time of writing it had not progressed to a full SAS. There is no general requirement for a separate statement in the exposure draft, but surprises could always emerge. A Joint Working Group has prepared guidance for directors of listed companies but at the time of writing it has not been issued, other than as an exposure draft. That document prefers inclusion of a disclosure of the appropriateness of the going concern basis together with supporting assumptions as necessary as part of the Operating and Financial Review (OFR) proposed by the ASB. That position is preferred because the OFR will include a significant amount of discussion and analysis which will help put the statement on going concern into context. The draft offers as alternative locations, particularly if no OFR is included, the directors' report or a separate statement of the company's compliance with the corporate governance Code of Best Practice.

The status of the directors' description of their responsibilities is enhanced if it is properly signed and dated. This will happen if it is part of the accounts or directors' report and should happen even if it is elsewhere.

The following subsections consider the implications for auditors' reports of the directors' description of their responsibilities being:

- in the accounts
- in the directors' report
- a separate statement
- part of other disclosures, such as:
  - corporate governance disclosures
  - OFR.

In some instances the disclosures may be integrated with one or more aspects of the above disclosures. A further subsection examines the consequences of that form of presentation.

1 In the accounts

Putting the directors' description of their responsibilities in the accounts is unlikely to be a popular choice.

The statement should receive a reasonable degree of prominence and it is unlikely to sit well as one of the notes at the end of the accounts. This might be done if the auditors' report follows the accounts but that practice itself is not common.

A possible place for the directors' description of their responsibilities would be together with the accounting policies. The matters discussed relate in part to the policies, so that choice of position is logical.

Whatever the position in the accounts, the questions for auditors are:

- how to cross-refer to the directors' description of their responsibilities?
- should the page references for the financial statements include the directors' description of their responsibilities?
- if the directors' description of their responsibilities is included within the scope of the audit, what implications does this have?

Cross-referring

It is probably insufficient to refer readers to 'the accounts', or even 'the accounts on pages ..... to .....'. Either the note number, or the page reference, or both should be given.

Page references for the financial statements

The directors' description of their responsibilities should normally be included in the page references as it constitutes part of the accounts if presented in that way. Although this generally holds true, the wording of the statement and its layout need to be considered. For example, if the statement is reasonably distinct and positioned between the primary statements and the notes it might be intended to be separate from the accounts rather than part of them. The wording of the statement might also indicate its status. For example, if it refers to 'the attached accounts' it is unlikely to be part of them.

Within the scope of the audit

If included in the page references because it forms part of the accounts, the directors' description of their responsibilities must be considered in relation to the true and fair view as well as for its adequacy.

The description normally contains no financial information and would have to do so, or be wildly inaccurate, to affect the true and fair view. The likelihood of this is remote and, for practical purposes, auditors need only consider the adequacy of the description in the normal way.

2 In the directors' report

The directors' description of their responsibilities may be included in the directors' report. It could be a separate section at the end (to be close to the auditors' report) or dealt with earlier, perhaps immediately after the introduction where the directors identify the accounts that the report accompanies.

If the directors' description of their responsibilities is included in the directors' report, the questions for auditors are:

- how to cross-refer to the directors' description of their responsibilities?
- what are the implications of the directors' description of their responsibilities being included in the directors' report?

Cross-referring
As the directors' report is normally short it is probably acceptable to refer readers to 'the directors' report' without having to give page numbers. Obviously, a more precise reference may be given.

Within the scope of the statutory responsibility
Section 235(3) of the Companies Act 1985 requires auditors to consider whether the information given in the directors' report is consistent with the accounts. If the auditors believe that it is not consistent they should state that fact in their report.

Information
It is worth spending a few moments considering whether *'the information given in the directors' report'* includes all material comprising the report or whether some material (such as the description of directors' responsibilities) is not 'information'. If material is not 'information' auditors need not consider whether it is consistent with the accounts.

The Companies Act 1985 specifies the minimum content of the directors' report. Section 234 requires the report to contain:

- a fair review of the development of the business of the company and its subsidiary undertakings during the financial year and of their position at the end of it
- a statement of the amount (if any) which the directors recommend should be paid as dividend and the amount (if any) which they propose to carry to reserves
- the names of the persons who, at any time during the financial year, were directors of the company
- the principal activities of the company and its subsidiary undertakings in the course of the year and any significant change in those activities in the year.

The section also specifies that the report shall comply with Schedule 7 as regards the disclosure of the matters mentioned there.

In Schedule 7 the word 'information' is used to describe only two required disclosures:

- paragraph 2 (directors' interests) requires the information required by paragraphs 2A and 2B to be given in the directors' report, or by way of notes to the company's annual accounts, with respect to each person who at the end of the financial year was a director of the company
- regulations to be made under paragraph 10 (health, safety and welfare at work of company's employees) for certain classes of companies may require the disclosure of relevant information.

The matters to be included within the directors' report that are explicitly referred to as 'information' are, therefore, few. It is, therefore, probably untenable to divide the directors report into 'information' and other material. As a result, for the purposes of section 235(3), it is reasonable to regard the directors' description of their responsibilities as being the same as the remainder of their report.

Inconsistencies

Inconsistencies may arise in general between:

- actual figures or narrative appearing in both the accounts and the directors' report
- the bases of preparation of related items appearing in the accounts and the directors' report, where the figures themselves are not directly comparable and the different bases are not disclosed
- figures in the accounts and a narrative interpretation of the effect of those figures in the directors' report.

The directors' description of their responsibilities normally involves no figures and so inconsistencies are unlikely. It is theoretically possible for the directors' description of their responsibilities in the directors' report to be inconsistent with another description of their responsibilities in the accounts. There is no materiality test on the reporting requirement so, theoretically, it would have to be mentioned in the auditors' report. The report would also have to include a description of the directors' relevant responsibilities as required by SAS 600 because presumably at least one of the directors' descriptions of their responsibilities would be inadequate.

3 A separate statement

If the description of directors' responsibilities is presented as a separate statement outside the accounts and directors' report it is not within the scope of the audit. The description normally contains no financial information and would have to do so, or be wildly inaccurate, to affect the true and fair view. The likelihood of this is remote and, for practical purposes, auditors need only consider the adequacy of the description.

Cross-referring to the description may be achieved by the use of the word 'above' if that is where the statement is. This is the position favoured by the corporate governance Code of Best Practice. If the description is elsewhere, a page reference will normally be sufficient.

Although it does not have a direct effect, the status of the description is enhanced if it is signed and dated.

4 *Part of other disclosures*

The description of directors' responsibilities may be included as part of other disclosures, such as those required by the corporate governance Code of Best Practice. So long as the description is readily identifiable, such as by the use of an appropriate heading, there is no effect on the auditors' responsibilities. The cross-reference may be extended if necessary, in which case the guidance immediately below may be relevant.

5 *Integrated presentation*

If the directors' description of their responsibilities is part of the accounts or another statement it may be presented as an identified part, or its elements may be integrated into the other text. The former is anticipated by SAS 600 and so the SAS provides no guidance on integrated descriptions. It is even possible to envisage circumstances where part of the directors' description of their responsibilities is in the accounts and part is elsewhere (e.g. the directors' report).

The subsections above, dealing with the places where the directors' description of their responsibilities may be, remain relevant. This subsection examines only the possible problems arising from an integrated presentation.

Auditors have to consider:

- whether the presentation constitutes *'a description of those responsibilities'*
- the need for multiple cross-references.

Adequate presentation

Although an integrated presentation is not envisaged by SAS 600 it is difficult to criticise that approach if, after discussion with the auditors, the directors wish to adopt it. The following avoids any discussion of semantics and looks only at a practical reason for accepting an integrated presentation.

The only requirement for auditors is to consider whether the annual report includes *'an adequate description of the directors' relevant responsibilities'*. If auditors decide that an integrated presentation is not adequate they are required to include a description in their report. If this is done, assuming that auditors choose to use the same words that the directors' use, they would be repeating information in their report rather than providing it. Even if they use their own words (introducing a suspicion that there is a disagreement) the material adds nothing to a reader's knowledge. For this reason, auditors should accept an integrated presentation.

Multiple cross-references

Including multiple cross-references is a purely mechanical matter but a long cross-reference makes the normal sentence look odd. In addition, the cross-references set out in the subsections above, which were adequate when the statement was an identified part of another, are no longer sufficiently precise. These factors argue for a change in presentation. The following example shows what happens when a long cross-reference is put into the normal sentence:

> As described in the second part of the paragraph headed 'Annual Accounts' on page 1 of the directors' report and in sections (c) to (e) of note 1 to the accounts on page 8 the company's directors are responsible for the preparation of financial statements.

The above has a Flesch Reading Ease (FRE) of only 29.6.[9] To improve readability, the material is better presented in two sentences as follows:

> The company's directors are responsible for the preparation of financial statements. The directors' responsibilities are described in the second part of the paragraph headed 'Annual Accounts' on page 1 of the directors' report and in sections (c) to (e) of note 1 to the accounts on page 8.

Although the material is longer the readability has improved; the FRE is now 41.5. There is, however, a further possible improvement to consider. The normal paragraph dealing with the respective responsibilities of the directors and auditors is short and presents the responsibilities close together, allowing easy comparison. If the responsibility of the auditors is just added to the above two sentences the facility to compare easily is lost. A better alternative (with FRE 42.2) is to insert the sentence as follows:

> The company's directors are responsible for the preparation of financial statements. It is our responsibility to form an independent opinion, based on our audit, of those statements and to report our opinion to you. The directors' responsibilities are described in the second part of the paragraph headed 'Annual Accounts' on page 1 of the directors' report and in sections (c) to (e) of note 1 to the accounts on page 8.

---

[9] The Flesch Reading Ease is explained in section 2.7 of this chapter. 29.6 is 'very difficult' to read.

2.5.7.5 Description of responsibilities of directors

1 Introduction

There are, in effect, two types of standard auditors' reports: those including a description of responsibilities of directors, and those that refer to a description set out elsewhere in the accounts or accompanying information. This subsection examines the wording of such descriptions, wherever they are.

SAS 600 does not prescribe the exact wording of the description of responsibilities but it:

- sets out in the explanatory material to SAS 600.3 the contents of a statement that will normally be considered to be adequate
- presents (as appendix 3) an example wording for a description outside of the auditors' report.

Unfortunately, as explained below, the explanatory material and appendix 3 are not consistent with one another.

Those companies complying with the corporate governance Code of Best Practice are also influenced by its provisions. Again, there is a lack of consistency, this time between the Code and the SAS.

It is unusual for an auditing requirement to prescribe disclosures that ought to be the province of financial reporting standards. The auditing requirement lacks an effective mechanism for ensuring compliance so directors, especially those not concerned with corporate governance disclosures, may not feel compelled to provide the required description of their responsibilities.

Even if directors let auditors put words into their mouths it is important for auditors to explain what they are doing and obtain evidence that the directors accept the wording used is a reasonable statement. This can be done by the mechanism of a letter of representation or equivalent.

2 Example wording based on the SAS

The following two examples illustrate wording for a directors' description of their responsibilities and an auditors' report including such information. They are based on the example wording given in appendix 3 to SAS 600 as that is likely to be used most widely. After these examples the wording is examined in detail.

Report 201
RD: Outside of the auditors' report (SAS 600 appendix 3)

STATEMENT OF DIRECTORS' RESPONSIBILITIES

Company law requires the directors to prepare financial statements for each financial year which give a true and fair view of the state of affairs of the company and of the profit or loss of the company for that period. In preparing those financial statements, the directors are required to:

- select suitable accounting policies and then apply them consistently
- make judgements and estimates that are reasonable and prudent
- state whether applicable accounting standards have been followed, subject to any material departures disclosed and explained in the financial statements[10]
- prepare the financial statements on the going concern basis unless it is inappropriate to presume that the company will continue in business[11]

The directors are responsible for keeping proper accounting records which disclose with reasonable accuracy at any time the financial position of the company and to enable them to ensure that the financial statements comply with the Companies Act 1985. They are also responsible for safeguarding the assets of the company and hence for taking reasonable steps for the prevention and detection of fraud and other irregularities.

Report 202
RD: In auditors' report (SAS 600 appendix 3)

Respective responsibilities of directors and auditors

The directors are responsible for the preparation of financial statements. Company law requires the directors to prepare financial statements for each financial year which give a true and fair view of the state of affairs of the company and of the profit or loss of the company for that period. In preparing those financial statements, the directors are required to:

- select suitable accounting policies and then apply them consistently
- make judgements and estimates that are reasonable and prudent
- state whether applicable accounting standards have been followed, subject to any material departures disclosed and explained in the financial statements[12]
- prepare the financial statements on the going concern basis unless it is inappropriate to presume that the company will continue in business[13]

---

[10] Large companies only.
[11] If no separate statement on going concern is made by the directors.
[12] Large companies only.
[13] If no separate statement on going concern is made by the directors.

> The directors are responsible for keeping proper accounting records which disclose with reasonable accuracy at any time the financial position of the company and to enable them to ensure that the financial statements comply with the Companies Act 1985. They are also responsible for safeguarding the assets of the company and hence for taking reasonable steps for the prevention and detection of fraud and other irregularities.
>
> It is our responsibility to form an independent opinion, based on our audit, on the financial statements and to report our opinion to you.

It is reasonable to expect that descriptions within the auditors' report will normally be confined to smaller companies. However, the following description appeared in the auditors' report on a listed company with a turnover of over £40 million:

Report 203
RD: In auditors' report, Rexmore PLC, 3 April 1993, Coopers & Lybrand

Respective responsibilities of directors and auditors

> The directors are required to present for each accounting period financial statements which comply with the provisions of the Companies Act 1985 and give a true and fair view of the state of affairs of the Group and the company as at the end of the accounting period and of the profit and loss for that period. In preparing the financial statements, suitable accounting policies, framed by reference to reasonable and prudent judgements and estimates, have to be used and applied consistently. Applicable accounting standards have to be followed subject to any material departures being disclosed and explained in the notes to the financial statements. The directors are required to prepare the financial statements on a going concern basis unless it is inappropriate to presume that the company will continue in business. The directors are also responsible for maintaining adequate accounting records so as to enable them to ensure the safeguarding of assets of the Group and to prevent and detect fraud and other irregularities.
>
> It is our responsibility to form an independent opinion, based on our audit, on those statements and to report our opinion to you.

3 SAS 600

The statement in appendix 3 to SAS 600 differs from a similar statement included in the explanatory material to SAS 600.3 dealing with what is normally considered adequate. There seems to be no reason why appendix 3 should not be fully consistent. It would have been logical to extend the statement in the appendix to perhaps provide some increased detail (as is done for accounting records) but there are wording changes too. This is illustrated by the following statement which is based on the explanatory material. The changes necessary to transform it into the appendix 3 statement are highlighted. New material is shown IN SMALL CAPITALS; deleted material is shown ~~in strike through~~.

STATEMENT OF DIRECTORS' RESPONSIBILITIES

> Company law requires THE directors to prepare financial statements for each financial year which give a true and fair view of the ~~company's~~ state of affairs OF THE COMPANY ~~at the end of the year~~ and OF THE profit or loss OF THE COMPANY for ~~the year then ended~~ THAT PERIOD. In preparing those financial statements, the directors are required to:
>
> - select suitable accounting policies and then apply them ~~on a consistent basis~~ CONSISTENTLY ~~making judgements and estimates that are prudent and reasonable~~
> - MAKE JUDGEMENTS AND ESTIMATES THAT ARE REASONABLE AND PRUDENT
> - state whether applicable accounting standards have been followed, subject to any material departures disclosed and explained in the financial statements[14]
> - prepare the financial statements on the going concern basis unless it is ~~not appropriate~~ INAPPROPRIATE to presume that the company will continue in business[15]
>
> The directors are responsible for keeping proper accounting records WHICH DISCLOSE WITH REASONABLE ACCURACY AT ANY TIME THE FINANCIAL POSITION OF THE COMPANY AND TO ENABLE THEM TO ENSURE THAT THE FINANCIAL STATEMENTS COMPLY WITH THE COMPANIES ACT 1985. THEY ARE ALSO RESPONSIBLE for safeguarding the assets of the company and HENCE for taking reasonable steps for the prevention and detection of fraud and other irregularities.

The example in appendix 3 can be seen to comply with the criteria that allow it to be normally considered adequate, with the exception that the date of preparation of the balance sheet is not given (note the deleted words '~~at the end of the year~~'). Either this matter is not important and need not have been included in the explanatory material, or the example does not comply with the explanatory material.

This leads on to an analysis of the criteria for judging the adequacy of the directors' description of their responsibilities. The analysis is important because it allows statements for entities other than companies to be written and considered. Auditors will be influenced in their assessments of adequacy by the material in the SAS discussed above and also by the note 12 to the corporate governance Code of Best Practice. The notes do not form part of the Code itself but include further recommendations on good practice.

4 Code of Best Practice

Note 12 to the corporate governance Code of Best Practice suggests that the statement of directors' responsibilities should include:

- the legal requirement for directors to prepare financial statements for each financial year which give a true and fair view of the state of affairs of the

[14] Large companies only.

[15] If no separate statement on going concern is made by the directors.

company (or group) as at the end of the financial year and of the profit and loss for that period
- the responsibility of the directors for maintaining adequate accounting records, for safeguarding the assets of the company (or group), and for preventing and detecting fraud and other irregularities
- confirmation that suitable accounting policies, consistently applied and supported by reasonable and prudent judgements and estimates, have been used in the preparation of the financial statements
- confirmation that applicable accounting standards have been followed, subject to any material departures disclosed and explained in the notes to the accounts. (This does not obviate the need for a formal statement in the notes to the accounts disclosing whether the accounts have been prepared in accordance with applicable accounting standards.).

The Code and SAS 600 are intended to be consistent with each other. This was facilitated by the fact that the chairman of the working party of the APB that produced SAS 600 was also a member of the Cadbury Committee. The above points are reasonably consistent except in three areas:

- linking of judgements and estimates
- no mention of going concern
- confirmation.

The Code presents judgements and estimates as a supporting matter to the accounting policies. This is, in fact, also done in the explanatory material in the SAS, but not in the example in appendix 3 to the SAS.

The Code omits any reference to going concern in the directors' statement of responsibilities. This is because it is the subject of a separate requirement that the directors should report that the business is a going concern, with supporting assumptions or qualifications as necessary. Companies will not be able to comply with this until the necessary guidance has been developed. Before guidance on going concern is developed, directors following the wording suggested by the corporate governance Code of Best Practice will not, therefore, comply with the criteria in SAS 600 by which responsibility statements are normally considered adequate. This is a significant practical problem and one that was not picked up by, for example the Law Society working party considering directors' statements of responsibility.

The Code suggests that it is good practice for directors to confirm that suitable accounting policies have been used and that applicable accounting standards have been followed. The SAS merely suggests that such aspects are set out as being requirements. There is a clear conflict between the SAS and the Code as the example in appendix 3 to SAS 600 does not comply with the suggestions of the former.

Early indications from the published reports of directors and auditors of listed companies are that some directors follow the wording in the SAS while others give the confirmation preferred by the corporate governance Code of Best Practice (without mention of 'going concern'). Both descriptions have been judged adequate, in some cases by the same firm of auditors. For example, the following descriptions were both accepted by KPMG Peat Marwick:

Report 204
RD: Cable and Wireless PLC, 31 March 1993

DIRECTORS' RESPONSIBILITIES IN RESPECT OF THE PREPARATION OF FINANCIAL STATEMENTS

Company law requires the Directors to prepare financial statements for each financial year which give a true and fair view of the state of affairs of the Company and of the Group and of the profit or loss of the Group for that period. In preparing those financial statements, the Directors are required to:

- select suitable accounting policies and then apply them consistently;
- make judgements and estimates that are reasonable and prudent;
- state whether applicable accounting standards have been followed, subject to any material departures disclosed and explained in the financial statements; and
- prepare the financial statements on the going concern basis unless it is inappropriate to presume that the Company will continue in business.

The Directors are responsible for keeping proper accounting records which disclose with reasonable accuracy at any time the financial position of the Company and the Group and to enable them to ensure that the financial statements comply with the Companies Act 1985. They are also responsible for safeguarding the assets of the Company and the Group and hence for taking reasonable steps for the prevention and detection of fraud and other irregularities.

Report 205
RD: The Boots Company PLC, 31 March 1993

DIRECTORS' RESPONSIBILITIES STATEMENT

The directors are required by law to prepare accounts which give a true and fair view of the profit and loss for the financial year and of the state of affairs of the company and group at the end of that period. The directors confirm that suitable accounting policies have been used and applied consistently, applicable accounting standards have been followed, and reasonable and prudent judgements and estimates have been made. The directors are also of the opinion that the company and its subsidiaries have suitable internal controls for maintaining adequate accounting records, for safeguarding the assets of the group, and for preventing and detecting fraud and other irregularities.

There is, therefore every indication that auditors will be able to take a flexible view about the wording of directors' descriptions of responsibility when assessing their adequacy. As more experience builds up of compliance with the corporate governance Code of Best Practice it may be that the current apparent flexibility will diminish.

5 Law Society

The Law Society's committee on company law had its attention drawn to the way in which some companies had followed the corporate governance Code of Best Practice wording while others had followed that in SAS 600 (and earlier its exposure draft). The committee expressed its concern (in the Law Society Gazette of 3 November 1993) that responsibility statements were being published without legal advice being taken on the implications of so doing or upon the accuracy of the legal statements which appeared in them. The committee felt that companies ran the risk of extending the legal liability of directors unnecessarily.

While the committee endorsed the view that there was no one answer, and that companies should take legal advice on responsibility statements, it produced a draft form of responsibility statement. The statement was accompanied by explanatory notes and introduced as a draft that had been produced by a working party of the committee that included leading counsel. That being so, it would only be the larger listed companies that would ordinarily have access to legal advice from other leading counsel. The statement is likely to be authoritative, but as it is less well known than the form of words in the corporate governance Code of Best Practice or SAS 600 its use may not be widespread. It is primarily a corporate governance Code of Best Practice statement as prima facie it is inadequate for the purposes of SAS 600 as it does not include mention of the going concern basis of preparation of accounts.

Report 206
RD: Model, Law Society

STATEMENT OF DIRECTORS' RESPONSIBILITIES IN RELATION TO FINANCIAL STATEMENTS

The following statement, which should be read in conjunction with the auditors' statement of auditors' responsibilities set out below, is made with a view to distinguishing for shareholders the respective responsibilities of the directors and of the auditors in relation to the financial statements.

The directors are required by the Companies Act 1985 to prepare financial statements for each financial year which give a true and fair view of the state of affairs of the company and the group as at the end of the financial year and of the profit or loss for the financial year.

Following discussions with the auditors, the directors consider that in preparing the financial statements on pages ..... to ..... the company has used appropriate accounting policies, consistently applied and supported by reasonable and prudent judgments and estimates, and that all accounting standards which they consider to be applicable have been followed [subject to any explanations and any material departures disclosed in the notes to the financial statements].

> The directors have responsibility for ensuring that the company keeps accounting records which disclose with reasonable accuracy the financial position of the company and which enable them to ensure that the financial statements comply with the Companies Act 1985.
>
> The directors have general responsibility for taking such steps as are reasonably open to them to safeguard the assets of the group and to prevent and detect fraud and other irregularities.
>
> The directors, having prepared the financial statements, have requested the auditors to take whatever steps and undertake whatever inspections they consider to be appropriate for the purpose of enabling them to give their audit report.

The notes to the statement provided by the committee explain the purpose of some of its contents. The notes are not reproduced in this book but have been considered below when analysing the proposed statement.

The statement appears to be based primarily on the corporate governance Code of Best Practice. It presents judgements and estimates as a supporting matter to the accounting policies and includes confirmation that suitable accounting policies have been used and that applicable accounting standards have been followed. The prose is very difficult to read and this may discourage its adoption.

Its main features are:

- an introductory paragraph, cross-referring to the statement of auditors' responsibilities
- inclusion of group matters
- use of the word 'appropriate' rather than 'suitable' to describe the accounting policies
- the confirmation from the directors is expressed as an opinion
- the confirmation is introduced by a note that it is *'Following discussions with the auditors'*
- there is no reference to accounting records being either adequate or proper (the statement is confined to the requirements of section 221 Companies Act 1985)
- the reference to 'reasonable steps' is extended to include safeguarding assets instead of just in relation to fraud and other irregularities
- omission of reference to the going concern basis
- a concluding paragraph that implies that the audit has been at the directors' request, rather than under statute (and that the auditors could only begin their work after the accounts were prepared!).

Interestingly, the Law Society working party did not mention the signing and dating of the statement. The implication of this is that such matters are not considered to be significant and that auditors need not worry about accepting statements that are neither signed nor dated.

The draft statement is more defensive and so is more likely to protect the interests of directors than SAS 600 or corporate governance Code of Best Practice statements. For example, the introductory paragraph not only puts the statement in context, it also aims to limit the use to which the statement can be put.

Auditors may be concerned about the directors only being prepared to give an opinion on the use of appropriate accounting policies and the following of applicable accounting standards after *'discussions with the auditors'*. This appears to suggest that the directors have had confirmation from the auditors to that effect; which may not be the case at all.

For the purpose of their report on the financial statements, auditors have to consider only the adequacy of the directors' statement. Many of the matters suggested by the Law Society working party have no bearing on that assessment.

Some auditors objected to aspects of the Law Society model, in part because auditors had not been consulted before it was published. A later issue of the Law Society Gazette carried further information for interested directors. After discussions with the APB, the Law Society committee felt the need to remind companies that:

- the committee did not seek to suggest that there is a single formulation for such statements which is appropriate in all circumstances for all companies wishing to comply with the Cadbury Report
- the draft statement did not purport to provide an exhaustive explanation of the responsibilities of directors in relation to both group accounts and separate company accounts
- companies issuing responsibility statements, including those based on the draft, should take legal advice on them.

In particular, they drew attention to the references in the draft wording to the audit process, which included a reference to:

- accounting policies and accounting standards, which was prefaced by: *'Following discussions with the auditors'*
- actions taken by the auditors (only) after the directors had prepared their financial statements.

The Law Society committee commented that, whether or not the wording is to be included in the directors' responsibility statement referring to the process involved is a matter on which companies should seek legal advice. Wording of this kind should only be considered if it can accurately reflect what has occurred in practice.

The committee further commented that it is particularly important that any wording describing the process should not be capable of being interpreted as a comment on the legal responsibilities of those concerned. If the auditors consider that the wording is capable of this interpretation, they may wish to clarify the matter when referring to the directors' responsibilities in their report. Consequently, if any such wording is to be proposed its inclusion should be discussed with the auditors in question in conjunction with the wording describing the auditors' responsibilities and the basis of their opinion.

Indeed, the directors' responsibility statement, and the wording describing the auditors' responsibilities and the basis of their opinion should, in the committee's view, in all cases, be considered together so as to avoid inconsistency and yet correctly reflect the legal and factual position.

6 *Origins of the directors' responsibilities*

The important aspects of the directors' responsibilities as envisaged by SAS 600, and their sources are:

- requirement results from company law [Companies Act 1985]
- accounts have to be prepared for successive periods (termed 'financial years') [s224 and s226]
- accounts must give a true and fair view of the state of affairs at the end of the financial year and profit or loss for the year then ended [s226]
- suitable accounting policies must be selected [no specific reference but stems from need to give a true and fair view] and used consistently [Sch 4 p11 (within and from one year to the next)]
- judgements and estimates must be prudent [Sch 4 p12] and reasonable [no specific reference but stems from need to give a true and fair view]
- accounts must state whether applicable accounting standards have been followed, subject to any material departures disclosed and explained in the accounts[16] [Sch 4 p36A]
- accounts must be prepared on the going concern basis unless it is not appropriate to presume that the company will continue in business[17] [Sch 4 p10]
- the directors are also responsible for:
  - — keeping proper accounting records [s221 but using the term 'proper' from the auditing requirement of s237]
  - — safeguarding the assets of the company and hence for taking reasonable steps for the prevention and detection of fraud and other irregularities [no specific reference but stems from fiduciary duty of directors towards company and auditors' mentioning their own responsibilities towards fraud].

---

16 Large companies only.

17 If no separate statement on going concern is made by the directors.

Omissions from the above are as follows:

- there is no direct reference to the legislation. The words 'company law' are not specific
- there is no reference to the time limit within which the directors must prepare accounts
- there is no mention of laying accounts before the members or of delivery to the registrar
- the requirements of section 226 of the Companies Act 1985 that are not mentioned are:
  - accounts comprise a balance sheet as at the last day of the year and a profit and loss account
  - accounts must comply with Schedule 4
  - further information must be given if necessary for a true and fair view
  - provisions of Act must be departed from to the extent necessary to give a true and fair view
- group accounts are not considered
- there is no mention of the requirements to make the disclosures required by Schedules 5 and 6
- the directors' report or other statements are not mentioned
- for affected companies there is no mention of Stock Exchange requirements.

The following directors' description of their responsibilities is of interest because it includes some aspects listed above as omissions from SAS 600. The matters have been highlighted below by the use of bold type. It also includes a confirmation as suggested by the corporate governance Code of Best Practice. The description was accepted by Coopers & Lybrand.

Report 207
RD: Marks and Spencer PLC, 31 March 1993

DIRECTORS' RESPONSIBILITIES FOR PREPARING THE FINANCIAL STATEMENTS

The directors are obliged under company law to prepare financial statements for each financial year **and to present them annually to the Company's members in Annual General Meeting**.

The financial statements, **of which the form and content is prescribed by the Companies Act 1985**, must give a true and fair view of the state of affairs of the Company and the Group at the end of the financial year, and of the profit for that period, and they must comply with applicable accounting standards.

The directors are also responsible for the adoption of suitable accounting policies, their consistent use in the financial statements, supported where necessary by reasonable and prudent judgements.

The directors confirm that the above requirements have been complied with in the financial statements.

> In addition, the directors are responsible for maintaining adequate accounting records and sufficient internal controls to safeguard the assets of the Group and to prevent and detect fraud or any other irregularities.

7 A framework

Looking at what is, and what is not, required, the following scheme of necessary disclosure emerges. It may be applied to judge the adequacy of directors' description of their responsibilities for companies and should be applicable to other entities with appropriate amendment. Companies for which the corporate governance Code of Best Practice is relevant have further matters to consider as discussed above.

- basic legal framework
- periods of account (but not balance sheet date)
- requirement to give a true and fair view
- accounting policy selection (reasonable and consistent)
- prudent yet objective ('reasonable') assessments ('judgements and estimates')
- any specific disclosures of adherence to applicable accounting standards
- going concern presumption
- keeping accounting records (to satisfy requirements such as allowing preparation of financial statements that comply with the Companies Act 1985)
- taking reasonable steps to safeguard assets (and prevent fraud etc.).

If the framework is used to assess the adequacy of report 205 (Boots) it will be seen to comply except for the absence of any reference to the going concern basis. Report 207 (Marks and Spencer) also fails to include any mention of going concern. It could be argued that the use of the going concern basis is implicit in the accounts but it begins to look as if, before specific guidance on going concern disclosures is available, auditors are not modifying their reports for such an omission. The matter is retained in the framework however, because it will in future be required to comply with the suggestions of the corporate governance Code of Best Practice and ought arguably to be fundamental to the directors' description of their responsibilities.

The framework aims to help auditors assess whether a directors' description of their responsibilities is adequate. It takes a prudent approach, without going into too much detail and so includes going concern. Auditors who accept directors' descriptions of their responsibilities without a reference to going concern face a higher risk than those who do not. It remains to be seen if any auditors will modify their reports over such matters or if any professional criticism will arise if they do not. Past experience indicates that such events will simply not happen. Obviously, if auditors do modify their report they run an entirely different risk of losing the audit.

The application of this framework to other entities is considered in section 2.11 of this chapter.

8 *Readability and prose*

The example given in appendix 3 to SAS 600 is written as a third-party statement. The directors do not use the word 'we', they write about themselves as 'the directors'. This approach loses immediacy and encourages verbosity. Perhaps as a result the example manages a Flesch Reading Ease of only 26[18].

It is not just the impersonal approach that makes the statement difficult to assimilate. The example statement contains the following sentence. Even if 'the directors' is replaced by the word 'we', it seems designed to cause the reader maximum discomfort.

> The directors are responsible for keeping proper accounting records which disclose with reasonable accuracy at any time the financial position of the company and to enable them to ensure that the financial statements comply with the Companies Act 1985.

It may be grammatically correct but is it art? A Flesch Reading Ease that hits an almost all-time low of 11 on a scale of 1 to 100 is ridiculous for an attempt at clear communication. In any case, many would prefer 'that' to 'which' in the sentence, so perhaps it is not even grammatically correct. It remains to be seen how many directors are willing to let the APB put such words in their mouths.

The readability of the three examples given above is shown below:

Report	Flesch Reading Ease
204 Cable and Wireless	34.5
205 Boots	24.6
207 Marks and Spencer	29.1

The Law Society model (report 206) has a FRE of only 10.8; perhaps confirming what accountants always suspected about lawyers.

9 *The wording surrounding the section in the auditors' report*

The description of the directors' responsibilities, when included in the auditors' report, raises questions about the surrounding prose:

- does it constitute '*a statement that the financial statements are the responsibility of the directors*', so that the statement need not be made separately?
- should its wording agree to that used in the opinion paragraph?

[18] The Flesch Reading Ease is explained in section 2.7 of this chapter. 26 is 'very difficult' to read.

- how should auditors respond to pressure for changes to the wording of the their responsibilities:
  - — as a consequence of the insertion?
  - — when asked to extend a description of their responsibilities to balance the length of the directors' description?

A responsibility statement?

SAS 600.3 requires auditors to include in their report a statement that the financial statements are the responsibility of the reporting entity's directors. The wording of the example in appendix 3 to SAS 600 does not include an explicit statement of that fact. The nearest the example comes to such an assertion is *'Company law requires the directors to prepare financial statements'*, which is not entirely the same thing. After all, the directors could go on to say that *'the preparation of the financial statements has been carried out by the auditors who are responsible for them'*. Auditors should ensure that, if their report includes a description of the responsibilities of the directors (in the form suggested by appendix 3 to SAS 600), they still state that the accounts are the responsibility of the directors.

Report 202 above shows, therefore, the responsibility statement (*'The directors are responsible for the preparation of financial statements.'*) before the description provided by the directors.

Agreement to the opinion paragraph

The directors' statement refers to the fact that *'Company law requires the directors to prepare financial statements for each financial year which give a true and fair view of the state of affairs of the company and of the profit or loss of the company for that period.'*

This wording is similar to that of the standard opinion paragraph of example 1 in appendix 2 to SAS 600 which is: *'In our opinion the financial statements give a true and fair view of the state of the company's affairs as at 31 December 19.. and of its profit [loss] for the year then ended and have been properly prepared in accordance with the Companies Act 1985.'*

The problem is that the wording is not consistent. Even if it is only cosmetically different, *'state of affairs of the company'* is not the same as *'state of the company's affairs'*. The wording in a report should be internally consistent unless there is an overpowering reason why it should not be. Auditors may, therefore, feel that they have a further valid reason for not following the wording suggested by SAS 600.

Changes to the auditors' report as a consequence of the insertion

It is reasonable to expect that readers will be affected by the inclusion of a description of the directors' responsibilities. If the words in the example in appendix 3 to SAS 600 are compare to the words in the example of a GB standard auditors' report in appendix 2 to SAS 600, the new material is 176 words compared to 273. Of a combined word count of 449 the description of directors' responsibilities amounts to nearly 40%, which is highly material.

Auditors may consider:

- changing the headings in their report
- increasing the coverage of their own responsibilities.

Heading

The normal heading for the section looks out of place when almost all of the section is devoted to the responsibilities of the directors. It may be preferable to alter it to give more space to the directors' aspects or to deal with the directors' and auditors responsibilities under subheadings.

Balancing the length of the directors' description of their responsibilities

The directors may look at the auditors' disclosure of their own responsibilities and wonder if justice is being done. The APB has aimed at brevity through restricting the auditors' disclosure of responsibilities but it would cost little for the auditors to mention some of their 'silent' responsibilities as set out in section 237 of the Companies Act 1985.

10 Groups

For a group, the directors' description of their responsibilities must be considered carefully as some legal requirements are not directly relevant to the group as a whole. Reporting on group accounts is dealt with in detail in section 2.9 of this chapter.

11 Inadequate directors' description of their responsibilities

The framework given earlier may be used to assess whether a directors' description of their responsibilities is adequate. Auditors would normally hope to avoid reporting on directors' deficient statements by resolving such problems through negotiation. Some directors will, however, give an incomplete or inaccurate (in the auditors' view) description of their responsibilities and present auditors with problems of how to deal with the matter in their report. There are two possible approaches:

- ignore the directors' description and give the 'correct' version in the auditors' report
- overtly correct the directors' description in the auditors' report.

The first approach leads to potential confusion for readers. If the directors say one thing and the auditors another, who should the readers believe, especially if the auditors do not acknowledge the directors' views? The second approach is more informative for readers but it seems close to a modification.

Reports where the auditors do not consider the directors' description of their relevant responsibilities to be adequate are dealt with in chapter 3 'Modified Reports'.

2.5.8 Basis of auditors' opinion

2.5.8.1 The requirements

Auditors should include in their report an appropriately headed section explaining the basis of their opinion [SAS 600.4]. This is required to include three statements:

- the auditors compliance or otherwise with Auditing Standards, together with the reasons for any departure therefrom
- what the audit process includes
- that the auditors planned and performed the audit so as to obtain reasonable assurance that the financial statements are free from material misstatement, whether caused by fraud or other irregularity or error, and that they have evaluated the overall presentation of the financial statements.

The required statement of what the audit process includes has three parts:

- examining, on a test basis, evidence relevant to the amounts and disclosures in the financial statements
- assessing the significant estimates and judgements made by the reporting entity's directors in preparing the financial statements
- considering whether the accounting policies are appropriate to the reporting entity's circumstances, consistently applied and adequately disclosed.

2.5.8.2 Paragraph heading

The examples in appendix 2 to SAS 600 use the heading 'basis of opinion'. This is commendably short and to the point. Alternative headings are likely to be used only infrequently. Possibilities include:

- The basis of our opinion
- How we formed our opinion
- Forming our opinion.

The problem underlying the choice of title is that the section of the report deals with different aspects of the audit. This is even more obvious when disclosures of fundamental uncertainty are included.

2.5.8.3 *Description prescription?*

The basis of opinion section as required by SAS 600.4 has three main drawbacks:

- it covers a very wide range of material
- it almost prescribes the use of unwieldy prose
- it lapses into jargon.

These aspects are examined below in subsections dealing with the individual required statements. A concluding subsection 'Readability and usability' examines how far auditors can go to improve the clarity of this section of their reports. For example, does the order of the statements have to be maintained?

The chapter of this book dealing with modified reports continues the examination of this section of the report where it has to accommodate more wording, for example to report a scope limitation. If auditors want to be consistent in their approach to the basis of opinion between the standard report and the modified report they may have to deviate from the unmodified examples in appendix 2 to SAS 600.

2.5.8.4 *Compliance with Auditing Standards*

1 The requirements

The first requirement of SAS 600.4 is to state compliance or otherwise with Auditing Standards. The wording of the examples in appendix 2 to SAS 600 is consistent:

Basis of opinion

> We conducted our audit in accordance with Auditing Standards issued by the Auditing Practices Board.

If auditors have followed other auditing standards, such as The Code of Audit Practice for Local Authorities and the National Health Service in England and Wales, those words should be used instead.

This statement has been criticised in the following ways:

- the word 'conducted' is unprofessional
- the sentence is needlessly long
- the mention of the Auditing Practices Board (APB) is not a requirement
- it is illogical to begin the basis of opinion section with this statement before readers have been told what an audit is (i.e. what the audit process includes).

2 Conducted

Some words attract antagonism. 'Conducted' has been criticised because it is more suited to the issue of tickets on the Clapham omnibus or to the concert hall platform than its use in connection with an audit. The Auditing Standard that

SAS 600 replaced used the words *'we have audited . . . in accordance with Auditing Standards'.*

3 Length

In addition to the odd use of the word 'conducted', the sentence uses the wordy expression 'in accordance with' instead of the shorter 'according to'.

4 Auditing Practices Board

There is no requirement to mention the APB but the examples in appendix 2 to SAS 600 include reference to the APB as the issuing body. Such wording is an improvement over the earlier reporting standard which only required a statement that *'we have audited . . . in accordance with Auditing Standards'*, leaving unanswered the question 'which Auditing Standards?' Perhaps, therefore, it is the requirements that are at fault, as it is surely more sensible to tell readers which auditing standards have been used.

There are already signs that some auditors (for example Pannell Kerr Forster) are not using the words *'issued by the Auditing Practices Board'*. This may be because brevity is considered more important.

5 Order

In the examples in appendix 2 to SAS 600 readers are not informed what an audit is until after they have been told under what standards it has been carried out. The order used follows that in SAS 600.4.

The lack of logic in the order is best demonstrated by considering something that (some) auditors are less familiar with:

Basis

> We conducted our boasting in accordance with rules issued by the British association.
>
> Boasting is a basic part of the game of squash. It is playing the ball against a side wall to rebound onto the front wall of the court.

Although the order could be varied there is no evidence of auditors doing so. Few auditors are likely to deviate from the prose used in the examples in appendix 2 to SAS 600.

2.5.8.5 What the audit process includes

The remainder of the basis of opinion section is prescribed by SAS 600.4. The wording is set out clearly and indications so far are that auditors are following the wording in the examples in appendix 2 to SAS 600 word for word.

Some of the words used will, nevertheless, be unwelcome:

- on a test basis
- which
- misstatement
- fraud
- reasonable assurance.

1 *On a test basis*

Some audits (for example of dormant companies) do not involve any 'test basis'. The accounts are audited in full. SAS 600.4 is, however, prescriptive as to the use of the word 'test'.

2 *Which*

In the following context, the word 'which' is grammatically wrong (as far as anything can be wrong in grammar): *'We planned and performed our audit so as to obtain all the information and explanations* ***which*** *we considered necessary'.* The only real argument for using 'which' is that it is used in section 237 of the Companies Act 1985 on which the requirement is based. In that section, however, the context is different: *'If the auditors fail to obtain all the information and explanations which, to the best of their knowledge and belief, are necessary for the purposes of their audit, they shall state that fact in their report.'*

The grammatically correct word in the report's context is 'that'. The construction is known grammatically as a defining clause. The information and explanations in question being defined as those the auditors considered necessary. The use of the alternative word 'which' is supported by sufficient writers, however, to make it acceptable and in all probability the more common word. It is to be regretted that the APB did not take the advice of Sir Ernest Gowers who wrote in his revision of Fowler's Modern English Usage: *'if writers would agree to regard* ***that*** *as the defining relative pronoun and* ***which*** *as the non-defining, there would be much gain both in lucidity and in ease.'*

3 *Misstatement*

One of those who provided material for this book (and who wished not to be named) explained that he avoided the words 'material misstatements' because he had not yet found an English dictionary that included 'misstatement'. It is, indeed, a horrible word. 'Misstatement' appears in the corresponding international statement and US dictionaries. Auditors in GB now appear to be doomed to use it too.[19]

---

[19] As an exception to the rule for published reports, Pannell Kerr Forster used 'mis-statement' in their report on the accounts of Booker PLC as at 1 January 1994. In that report the words 'fifty-three' were also hyphenated.

4 Fraud

There is no objection to the word 'fraud' except that it could startle readers. Some auditors are wary of using language that could alert people to the possibility of suing them if something goes wrong. The only consolation is that the wording of the SAS 600 report has no bearing on any actual potential liability and that almost all auditors' reports will include the word.

5 Reasonable assurance

Auditors familiar with the APC Auditing Guideline 'Audit evidence' are used to the notion that they should obtain sufficient relevant and reliable audit evidence. The term 'reasonable assurance' is not so specific. The proposed revision of auditing standards and guidelines includes a new Auditing Standard on audit evidence. The proposed SAS 400.1 is *'The auditors should obtain sufficient appropriate audit evidence to be able to draw reasonable conclusions on which to base the audit opinion.'*

The words used in SAS 600.4, therefore, have no obvious support. Their origin is the exposure draft of a proposed international standard on auditing 'The Auditors' Report on Financial Statements', with which SAS 600 is, in the most part, remarkably consistent and to which few GB auditors raised any objection.

2.5.9 The opinion

2.5.9.1 The requirements

The auditors' report should contain a clear expression of opinion on the financial statements and on any further matters required by statute or other requirements applicable to the particular engagement [SAS 600.5].

The statutory requirements are set out in detail in section 2.2 of this chapter.

2.5.9.2 Title

The examples in appendix 2 to SAS 600 use the title 'Opinion', except where the opinion is qualified. This title will undoubtedly be the most popular. A possible alternative is 'Unqualified opinion'. Such a title might help readers where a fundamental uncertainty is discussed in the basis of opinion section.

The standard opinion in the model report in section 2.4 of this chapter is:

Opinion

> In our opinion the financial statements give a true and fair view of the state of the company's affairs as at .... and of its [profit / loss] for the year then ended and have been properly prepared in accordance with the Companies Act 1985.

Apart from some avant-garde variations the wording of the standard opinion can be affected by only two influences:

- house style
- reporting on other primary statements (e.g. cash flows).

2.5.9.3 House style

The opinion section is much less prescribed by SAS 600 than the basis of opinion section. Auditors may choose their own words so long as the opinion is clear and complies with the statutory requirements.

Words in the model opinion paragraph above that can be varied include:

- financial statements — accounts, accounts and notes, annual accounts
- state of the company's affairs — state of affairs of the company
- the date — 31 December 19xx, 31st December 19xx
- profit — results
- year — period, nine months, 9 months, 52 weeks.

House style is generally of no consequence and is not discussed further.

2.5.9.4 Other primary statements

The explanatory material to SAS 600.5 contains three paragraphs (44 to 46) headed 'Primary statements'. The topic is discussed firstly in relation to accounting standards and the SAS confirms the view that the further 'primary statements' (in addition to the balance sheet and profit and loss account) required by FRS 1 'Cash Flow Statements' and FRS 3 'Reporting Financial Performance' are normally necessary in order that the annual accounts give a true and fair view.

The SAS then makes the point that reference to such statements in the opinion is unnecessary. Indeed, such a reference may be misleading because it could appear to detract from the role of the additional primary statements in supporting the information reported on as required by law.

Paragraph 46 of the SAS then makes a very controversial point that is relevant to auditors requested to report separately on one or more further primary statements. Auditors need to ensure that no impression is given that the primary statement is other than integral to the financial statements as a whole. They should also ensure that it is clear to a reader that the primary statement is necessary to give a true and fair view of the state of affairs and profit or loss for statutory purposes.

There is no indication in their reports that those auditors who now give an opinion on other primary statements have made any effort to follow paragraph 46.

The following is an example of a report including an opinion on cash flows:

Report 208
STD: Generic opinion including cash flows

Opinion

In our opinion the financial statements give a true and fair view of the state of the company's affairs as at .... and of its [profit / loss] and cash flows for the year then ended and have been properly prepared in accordance with the Companies Act 1985.

The Big Six are divided on the issue of including an opinion on other primary statements.

Not included	Included
Ernst & Young	Arthur Andersen
KPMG Peat Marwick	Coopers & Lybrand
Touche Ross & Co.	Price Waterhouse

Despite the inclusion of references to further primary statements by half of the Big Six it is likely that the majority of auditors by number will not include such material. This is for two main reasons. Firstly, the influential examples in appendix 2 to SAS 600 do not include such references. Secondly, the complications of such references increase the chance of error and it is not worth taking the commercial risk. As a simple example, if a firm decides that it will normally report on cash flows it increases the chance that it will issue an inappropriate opinion on a small company that does not present a cash flow statement.

Coopers & Lybrand goes further than most. They seem to have used the implementation of SAS 600 to change their standard opinion from one that refers to cash flows to an opinion that also includes reference to another primary statement: the statement of total recognised gains and losses. The following two reports are examples of their opinions:

Report 209
STD: Opinion including total recognised gains and losses, BET PLC, 27 March 1993, Coopers & Lybrand

Opinion

In our opinion the financial statements give a true and fair view of the state of the affairs of the company and the group at 27th March 1993 and of the loss, total recognised gains and losses and cash flows of the group for the year then ended and have been properly prepared in accordance with the Companies Act 1985.

Report 210
STD: Opinion including total recognised gains, Pilkington PLC, 31 March 1993, Coopers & Lybrand

Opinion

> In our opinion the financial statements give a true and fair view of the state of affairs of the company and the Group at 31st March 1993 and of the loss, total recognised gains and cash flows of the Group for the year then ended and have been properly prepared in accordance with the Companies Act 1985.

Coopers & Lybrand seem to be flexible in the wording of their opinions as the second report refers to *'total recognised gains'* while the first refers to *'total recognised gains and losses'*.

For those auditors who choose to refer to further primary statements, the questions to address are:

- which primary statements?
- how to word the opinion on each statement?
- what is the best order for the opinions?
- whether and how to implement the paragraph 46 suggestions for improved clarity?
- whether to include material in the report other than in the opinion?

2 Primary statements

The ASB's draft 'Statement of Principles — Presentation of Financial Information' explains that *'accounting information is presented in the form of a structured set of financial statements comprising primary statements and supporting notes'*.

It lists as primary statements:

- the profit and loss account
- the statement of total recognised gains and losses
- the balance sheet
- the cash flow statement.

The essential quality of a primary statement is that it should be presented with the same prominence as the other primary statements. In plain words; at the front and with a big heading. Primary statements 'articulate' or interrelate because they show different aspects of the same transactions or events affecting an enterprise. They contribute, both individually and collectively, to meeting the objective of financial reporting.

3 Which primary statements

The issue of FRS 1 'Cash Flow Statements' was accompanied by a press release stating that a cash flow statement was necessary in order for the accounts within its scope to give a true and fair view. This odd method of promulgating GAAP was presumably decided upon to make it clear that the new statement could not be regarded in the same way as the statement of source and application of funds required by SSAP 10.

Eventually, in response the APB issued Bulletin No. 1 'Implications for auditors' reports of FRS 1'. The bulletin provided interim guidance for accounting periods before the date on which FRS 1 'Cash Flow Statements' became mandatory but as no further guidance was produced before SAS 600, its influence continued. In what some considered flawed guidance, the bulletin proposed including reference to cash flows in the opinion.

The exposure draft of SAS 600 continued that approach but also suggested inclusion of a reference to *'total recognised gains (losses)'* as it anticipated the issue of the accounting standard based on FRED 1. When that document emerged as FRS 3 'Reporting Financial Performance' it introduced three new statements:

- a note of historical cost profits and losses
- a statement of total recognised gains and losses
- a reconciliation of movements in shareholders' funds.

Where there is a material difference between the result as disclosed in the profit and loss account and the result on an unmodified historical cost basis, the note of historical cost profits and losses is presented always as a note, not a primary statement. It should however be presented immediately following the profit and loss account or the statement of total recognised gains and losses. So it is nearly a primary statement.

The statement of total recognised gains and losses is always a primary statement.

Paragraph 59 of the explanatory material to FRS 3 gives the reconciliation of movements in shareholders' funds a choice of whether to be a primary statement or a note and defines its position if the former: *'If included as a primary statement, the reconciliation should be shown separately from the statement of total recognised gains and losses.'* It is, therefore, an optional primary statement.

Auditors who decide to report on further primary statements have to decide whether to report on the following (there are other possible permutations but the discussion keeps to the practical alternatives):

- just cash flows (or just the statement of total recognised gains and losses)
- all further primary statements listed in the ASB's draft 'Statement of Principles — Presentation of Financial Information', i.e. cash flows and total recognised gains and losses
- all primary statements in the financial statements that are reported on.

4 Cash flows

Those who choose to report on just one further primary statement do so either because that was the way the APB suggested in Bulletin No. 1 or because they are aiming for international conformity. US auditors reporting under their SAS 58 refer to cash flows. The proposed international auditing standard issued in February 1993 included references to cash flows but no other further primary statements.

5 Cash flows and statements of total recognised gains and losses

Those who choose to report on all the further primary statements listed in the ASB's draft 'Statement of Principles — Presentation of Financial Information' presumably do so because of that document (or the logic underlying it). The fact that this approach was taken by the exposure draft of SAS 600 also contributes to the likelihood that such a form of opinion will be used.

The wording of the example reports in the exposure draft of SAS 600 did not agree to the eventual treatment of total recognised gains and losses in FRS 3. The ED referred to *'total recognised gains (losses)'* as if the matter being reported on was the sum at the bottom of the column; equivalent to reporting on the profit rather than the income and expenditure. FRS 3 made it clear that the statement of total recognised gains and losses enables users to consider all recognised gains and losses of a reporting entity in assessing its overall performance. It, therefore, includes the profit or loss for the period together with all other movements on reserves reflecting recognised gains and losses attributable to shareholders.

The sum at the bottom of the column does not have any special significance and the correct form of reference in auditors' reports is to the *'total recognised gains and losses'*. This holds true whether or not all of the figures reported on are, for example gains. Unless report 210 above (Pilkington) by Coopers & Lybrand contains an error it shows, however, that different interpretations can be acceptable. Auditors reporting on total recognised gains and losses do seem to have some flexibility in the words they use, although the words in this paragraph shown above in italics are likely to be used more often.

6 All primary statements

Although to do so would be logically consistent there has been no evidence of auditors referring to all primary statements in their reports. The following report is, therefore, hypothetical. The order of references to primary statements is arbitrary:

Report 211
STD: Generic opinion referring to all primary statements

Opinion

In our opinion the financial statements give a true and fair view of the state of the affairs of the company at .... and of its [profit / loss], total recognised gains

> and losses, cash flows and movements in shareholders' funds for the year then ended and have been properly prepared in accordance with the Companies Act 1985.

7 Order of opinions

The order of opinions on the primary statements is not prescribed. It makes sense to report on the balance sheet separately because the other primary statements cover a period of time and can share appropriate wording. This means that the opinions on the profit, total recognised gains and losses, movements in shareholders' funds and cash flows should be dealt with together.

The order of these opinions could be determined by factors such as:

- administrative convenience
- readability
- relative importance.

Administrative convenience

Because of the availability of exemptions, not all financial statements will include a cash flow statement. The reconciliation of movements in shareholders' funds (if normally reported on) may be presented as a note rather than a primary statement. These factors argue for an order of opinions that allows these items to be deleted easily. In other words:

1 state of affairs
2 profit (or loss)
3 total recognised gains and losses
4 cash flows
5 (if normally reported on) movements in shareholders' funds.

Items 4 and 5 may be reversed in normal order if auditors consider that the frequency of reporting on cash flows will be less than on statements of movements in shareholders' funds presented as primary statements.

Readability

There is a possible complication in the wording that is more obvious if the entity makes a loss. The opinion can then refer to:

> . . . its loss, total recognised gains and losses, cash flows and movements in shareholders' funds . . .

Because of the close proximity of the words 'loss' and 'losses' this looks odd. It would, however, look horrible if the order of opinions was changed:

> . . . its total recognised gains and losses, loss, cash flows and movements in shareholders' funds . . .

It is perfectly feasible to avoid this juxtaposition by reordering the opinions to separate the words 'loss' and 'losses' as much as possible:

> . . . its loss, cash flows, movements in shareholders' funds, and total recognised gains and losses. . .

Relative importance

Auditors who choose to report on further primary statements could order their opinions according to their view of the relative importance of the primary statements. This approach cannot be recommended as there is no right answer. Indeed, Ernst & Young launched an attack on the ASB in September 1993 for seemingly preferring the balance sheet to the profit and loss account. Whatever the theoretical reasons for preferring one primary statement to another, the order of preference would presumably alter depending on the particular financial statements. For example, the balance sheet of a property investment company is normally more significant to users than its profit and loss account.

2.5.9.5 Improved clarity

Paragraph 46 of the SAS asks auditors who report on a further primary statement to ensure that no impression is given that the primary statement is other than integral to the financial statements as a whole. They should also ensure that it is clear to a reader that the primary statement is necessary to give a true and fair view of the state of affairs and profit or loss for statutory purposes.

There is no indication in their reports that those auditors who now give an opinion on other primary statements have made any effort to follow paragraph 46. There has been no indication that those auditors have been disciplined in any way, so there may be no need to follow paragraph 46 at all. Assuming that auditors may wish to attempt to comply with the explanatory material to the SAS, how should they amend their reports?

Auditors could expand the opinion section or another part of the report. Changes to the responsibilities section are only appropriate if the auditors have been requested to extend their audit opinion to cover a further primary statement. In practice, it is more likely that clients will not have a view and a firm will report on, for example cash flows almost as a matter of house style. If this is the case, the auditors' responsibilities are unchanged.

It seems reasonable for the basis of opinion section to be amended to refer to the further primary statements rather than increasing the length of the opinion and perhaps reducing its clarity. The following two examples show extra wording (IDENTIFIED BY SMALL CAPITALS) in the basis of opinion and the opinion sections of the report. Either report complies with the preferences expressed by paragraph 46 of SAS 600.

Report 212
STD: Explaining opinion on further primary statements in basis of opinion

Basis of opinion

We conducted our audit in accordance with Auditing Standards issued by the Auditing Practices Board. An audit includes examination, on a test basis, of evidence relevant to the amounts and disclosures in the financial statements. It also includes an assessment of the significant estimates and judgements made by the directors in the preparation of the financial statements, and of whether the accounting policies are appropriate to the company's circumstances, consistently applied and adequately disclosed.

We planned and performed our audit so as to obtain all the information and explanations which we considered necessary in order to provide us with sufficient evidence to give reasonable assurance that the financial statements are free from material misstatement, whether caused by fraud or other irregularity or error. In forming our opinion we also evaluated the overall adequacy of the presentation of information in the financial statements.

OUR OPINION EXTENDS TO THE CASH FLOWS REPORTED IN THE STATEMENT ON PAGE ..... . THAT STATEMENT IS NECESSARY TO GIVE A TRUE AND FAIR VIEW OF THE STATE OF AFFAIRS AND PROFIT OR LOSS FOR STATUTORY PURPOSES AND IS INTEGRAL TO THE FINANCIAL STATEMENTS AS A WHOLE.

Report 213
STD: Explaining opinion on further primary statements in opinion

Opinion

In our opinion the financial statements give a true and fair view of the state of the company's affairs as at .... and of its [profit / loss] AND CASH FLOWS for the year then ended and have been properly prepared in accordance with the Companies Act 1985. THE STATEMENT OF CASH FLOWS IS NECESSARY TO GIVE A TRUE AND FAIR VIEW OF THE STATE OF AFFAIRS AND PROFIT OR LOSS FOR STATUTORY PURPOSES AND IS INTEGRAL TO THE FINANCIAL STATEMENTS AS A WHOLE.

2 Effect on remainder of report

Auditors may wish to change their standard report when including an opinion on further primary statements. This may be because of paragraph 46 as discussed above or simply because the examples in the SAS were drafted on the assumption that further primary statements would not be reported on. Where an opinion extends to further primary statements, therefore, auditors may consider that the responsibilities or basis of opinion sections of the report ought to be more informative.

The following report expands the responsibilities section to refer to the further primary statements.

Report 214
STD: Explaining opinion on further primary statements in responsibilities section

Respective responsibilities of directors and auditors

As described on page ..... the company's directors are responsible for the preparation of financial statements. It is our responsibility to form an independent opinion, based on our audit, of those statements and to report our opinion to you.

WE ARE REQUIRED BY LAW TO REPORT ON THE COMPANY'S STATE OF AFFAIRS AND [PROFIT / LOSS]. FINANCIAL REPORTING HAS DEVELOPED SINCE THAT LEGAL REQUIREMENT WAS ESTABLISHED. IN PARTICULAR THE ACCOUNTING STANDARDS BOARD HAS ISSUED FINANCIAL REPORTING STANDARDS 1 AND 3 REQUIRING THE INCLUSION IN THE FINANCIAL STATEMENTS OF FURTHER PRIMARY STATEMENTS WITH PROMINENCE EQUAL TO THAT OF THE BALANCE SHEET AND PROFIT AND LOSS ACCOUNT. ACCORDINGLY, OUR OPINION EXTENDS TO THE REPORTED CASH FLOWS [TOTAL RECOGNISED GAINS AND LOSSES, AND MOVEMENTS IN SHAREHOLDERS' FUNDS]. THESE FURTHER PRIMARY STATEMENTS ARE NECESSARY TO GIVE A TRUE AND FAIR VIEW OF THE STATE OF AFFAIRS AND PROFIT OR LOSS FOR STATUTORY PURPOSES AND ARE INTEGRAL TO THE FINANCIAL STATEMENTS AS A WHOLE.

3 Modified reports

Modified reports including reference to further primary statements are a difficult area. For example, by definition a problem with the cash flow statement can affect the true and fair view of the profit and state of affairs, but the converse is not necessarily true. These matters are discussed in chapter 3 'Modified Reports'.

2.5.10 Other prescribed contents

2.5.10.1 The requirements

SAS 600.5 requires that the auditors' report should contain, in addition to the opinion on the financial statements, a clear expression of opinion on any matters required by statute or other requirements applicable to the particular engagement.

2.5.10.2 How the requirements are implemented

The implementation of the requirements is illustrated in subsection 2.10.5.2 of this chapter as reports on companies incorporated in the Republic of Ireland are required to include opinions on matters (such as agreement of the financial statements to the books of account) that are dealt with by only exception in Great Britain.

Example 2 in appendix 2 to SAS 600 simply extends the opinion section of the report to include such matters. This is illustrated by the generic report below:

Report 215
STD: Generic other required matter

Opinion

In our opinion the financial statements give a true and fair view of the state of the company's affairs as at .... and of its [profit / loss] for the year then ended and have been properly prepared in accordance with the Companies Act 1985. In our opinion REQUIRED OPINION. REQUIRED STATEMENT.

2.5.10.3 Analysis

The obvious omission in reporting on other required matters is any change to the responsibilities or basis of opinion sections of the report. Those sections for a company incorporated in the Republic of Ireland are exactly the same as for a GB company, despite the fact that auditors of the former are required to report explicitly on:

- information and explanations
- proper books of account
- agreement of accounts to books of account
- consistency of directors' report with accounts
- net asset position.

The requirements in SAS 600.4 to disclose the basis of opinion all relate to the auditors' opinion on the financial statements. It would be possible to extend the section to deal with the basis of other opinions but that has not been done in example 2 in appendix 2 to SAS 600. To extend the section would, in any case, make the report seem repetitious; first stating perhaps that a matter was considered and then giving an opinion on it. If this approach was adopted, logically the report ought also to be expanded in the area of stating the respective responsibilities of directors and auditors. Such a report would be tedious in the extreme to read, even if it was logically defensible.

A further approach would be to title the basis of opinion section 'Basis of opinion on the financial statements'. This is, in fact, what it really is.

Auditors faced with reporting on other required matters may adopt any of the above approaches and still comply with SAS 600. The more informative approach is to follow example 2 in appendix 2 to SAS 600, but:

- adapt the heading of the basis of opinion section
- refer in the responsibilities section to the auditors' responsibility to form an opinion on the further matters dealt with in the opinion paragraph.

The resulting form of report can be considered to be an alternative standard report rather than a modified report.

2.5.11 The signature

The dating aspects of SAS 600 have caused widespread concern. They are dealt with in section 2.11 'Signing and dating' of this chapter. This subsection examines only the words used at the end of the auditors' report.

2.5.11.1 The requirements

SAS 600.2 requires that auditors' reports should include their manuscript or printed signature.

The explanatory material to SAS 600.9 (mostly concerned with dating) includes a note that the report may be signed in the name of a firm (the normal approach), the personal name of the auditor, or both, as appropriate.

The explanatory material also notes that the report normally states the auditors' address and their status as Registered Auditors.

The statutory requirements of section 236 of the Companies Act 1985 are dealt with in section 2.2 'Statutory requirements' of this chapter.

2.5.11.2 Analysis

The normal signature and identification involves the following elements:

- a signature (where present — legible or not)
- the name of the firm
- the address of the firm or office of the firm
- the description of the firm, for example as 'Chartered Accountants'
- the status of the firm as a Registered Auditor.

1 Address

Although an address is not required, auditors normally indicate where the report was signed. The address can be given in full or just the city or town can be indicated. Listed company auditors may choose to disclose just, for example 'Glasgow' in the knowledge that the report and accounts disclose the names and full addresses of the company's auditors and other professional advisors. It is permissible for auditors of other companies to issue their report on their own headed paper and so achieve an equivalent level of publicity for their address.

The use of a full address when reporting on smaller companies may be thought to give potential clients a ready point of contact but there is little evidence of auditors including their telephone and fax numbers for this purpose.

2 Audit Regulations

Since 1 October 1991 only an individual or a firm that is registered with a recognised supervisory body has been eligible for appointment as a company auditor. Reports by auditors have been affected by this regime.

The correct term to use

The examples in appendix 2 to SAS 600 are attributed to 'Registered auditors'. At one discussion group, this choice by the APB drew an equivalent amount of scorn to its choice of 'shareholders', rather than 'members' as addressees.

The term that registered auditors are permitted to use has changed over the life of Audit Regulations. *Audit News,*[20] Issue No. 3, August 1991 set out the initial position as follows:

> A registered auditor will be required to sign an audit report relating to an appointment or reappointment accepted after s25 of the Act comes into force (1 October 1991) in the name of the firm and using the title registered auditor.

Those firms that were entitled to sign as Chartered Accountants were encouraged to do so and *Audit News* gave as alternatives:

R. Auditor & Co Registered Auditor Chartered Accountants
R. Auditor & Co Chartered Accountants and Registered Auditor
R. Auditor & Co Registered Auditor and Chartered Accountants

Presumably also acceptable would have been:

R. Auditor & Co Chartered Accountants Registered Auditor

As it is the firm that is registered it is strictly correct that the singular form of registered auditor should be used. However, in response to pressure from firms, a minor change to Audit Regulations was made *'to provide consistency between what firms can put on their letter-headings and their signatures on audit reports.'* *Audit News*, Issue No. 5, September 1992 recorded the change to regulation 3.06, which was thereafter to read *'. . . the words, "Registered Auditor" or "Registered Auditors" shall appear after such signature'.*

The initial capital letters used for the description are apparently not important.

Signing an audit report as registered auditor confirms that the particular audit has been carried out in compliance with Audit Regulations.

Signing as an individual

Some firms have allowed partners to sign audit reports in their own name. For that to happen under Audit Regulations that individual normally has to have separate registration as their name needs to appear on the public register. Alternatively the individual's name could be declared a 'trading name' of the firm, in which case any partner of the firm could also sign in that name

What reports must be signed as 'registered auditor(s)'

The Audit Regulation Policy Co-ordinating Committee decided that for reports required by various sections of the Companies Act 1985, use of the title 'registered auditor' was necessary if the person giving the report was required to be the

[20] A publication sent to all registered auditors.

company's auditor. A firm may choose to sign other reports as 'registered auditor' but is not required to do so.

Other reports

Some engagements may only be performed by those eligible for appointment as a company auditor under section 25 of the Companies Act 1989; in other words, registered auditors. Such engagements are governed by statutes as diverse as the Horticulture Act 1960 and the Building Societies Act 1986. The original legislation naturally makes no reference to the Companies Act 1989. The necessary changes in legislation were made by Statutory Instrument. In the good old days, in 1985, it required an Act to bring about similar changes. Schedule 2 to the Companies Consolidation (Consequential Provisions) Act 1985 contained amendments to many Acts that referred to aspects of company law. A typical change was altering a reference to section 161(1)(a) of the Companies Act 1948 into one to section 389(1)(a) of the Companies Act 1985.

SI 1991 No. 1997 The Companies Act 1989 (Eligibility for Appointment as Company Auditor) (Consequential Amendments) Regulations 1991 came into force on 1 October 1991, essentially at the same time as Audit Regulations. Under section 50 of the Companies Act 1989, the Secretary of State altered enactments mentioned in the Schedule to the Regulations, mainly to replace wording typically referring to *'members of the Accountancy Bodies'*, by a reference to those eligible for appointment as a company auditor under section 25 of the Companies Act 1989. In this process, some amendments to legislation (e.g. the Horticulture Act 1960) that had been effected by the 1985 Consequential Provisions were superseded by the Regulations.

As engagements under the various enactments may only be carried out by registered auditors, those firms often choose to advertise their status by signing reports in the same way that they sign company audit reports.

2.6 What is 'true and fair'?

2.6.1 Introduction

Because of its importance, the meaning of 'true and fair view' is dealt with in this section rather than as a subsection of the analysis of elements and options for reporting considered above.

Sometimes described as the holy grail of accountancy, the search for the meaning of true and fair view (the term is often contracted to 'true and fair') is doomed to failure as it can only be determined by a court when considering a specific case. Nevertheless, in order to avoid being a party to such a case, accountants have to attempt a definition every time they issue or audit a set of accounts.

Because this book deals with reports by auditors, the meaning of *'properly prepared in accordance with the Companies Act 1985'* is also investigated, as the two terms are closely related.

2.6.2 Statutory background

Section 226(2) of the Companies Act 1985 uses the words 'true and fair view' to describe what the balance sheet and profit and loss account shall give:

'The balance sheet shall give a true and fair view of the state of affairs of the company as at the end of the financial year; and the profit and loss account shall give a true and fair view of the profit or loss of the company for the financial year.'

Unfortunately, the Act does not define the term. A trawl through the text of the Act for a definition only reveals a circular route. Section 262 (minor definitions) states that, for the purposes of Part VII of the Act, true and fair view refers:

- in the case of individual accounts, to the requirement of section 226(2), and
- in the case of group accounts, to the requirement of section 227(3).

Section 226, which sets out the duty to prepare individual company accounts, does not include the words 'properly prepared'. It would have simplified matters greatly if it had.

Auditors are required by section 235 to state whether in their opinion the annual accounts have been properly prepared in accordance with the Act. The Act contains many requirements concerning disclosures in the accounts. The question for auditors to answer is whether proper presentation is the same as giving a true and fair view and, if not, what it does mean. This is examined in detail in subsection 2.6.4 below.

2.6.3 Legal opinions

In the absence of a definition of true and fair view in legislation it is necessary to look for legal precedent. The accounting standard setting bodies, the Accounting Standards Committee (ASC) and the ASB, sought and published legal opinions from counsel, so the results of such a search are available. The courts have only rarely touched on the matter, so much of the legal opinion relies on the views of the counsel asked to consider the question.

The legal views that are relevant are:

- opinion of Leonard Hoffman QC and Mary H Arden
- 'Littlejohn' case
- opinion of Mary Arden QC.

The ASC obtained a joint counsels' opinion in 1983 that clarified the meaning of true and fair view. The Companies Act 1981 had implemented the EEC Fourth Directive and imposed a rigid format on the profit and loss account and the balance sheet. This had introduced the possibility of conflict between accounting standards and the law and clarification was needed. The opinion was also sought at a time when inflation accounting was under review and the ASC had put forward for discussion the proposition that pure historical cost accounts no longer gave a true and fair view where a company was materially affected by changing prices.

The joint opinion should really be read in full, but its main conclusions were that:

- a court would view compliance with generally accepted accounting practice (i.e. the standards issued by the ASC) as persuasive, but not conclusive, evidence that a true and fair view is given
- accounts that give a true and fair view should contain the quality and quantity of information to satisfy readers' reasonable expectations
- the concept is capable of change over time
- radical changes in accounting practice, such as deciding that historical cost accounts no longer give a true and fair view, are not in conflict with the law despite the presumption in legislation that historical cost accounts will be the main accounts.

The validity of this opinion was confirmed with regard to the status of accounting standards by Woolf in his judgement in the case of Lloyd Cheyham v. Littlejohn [1987] BCLC 303 at 313. He held that standards issued by the ASC were *'very strong evidence as to what is the proper standard which should be adopted'*.

By the time of the 1993 opinion the law had been changed by the Companies Act 1989. That Act had:

- given accounting standards recognition in law [s 256 CA 85] and through that given statutory backing to the work of the ASB (which took over the development of accounting standards from the ASC in August 1990)
- required disclosure of:
  - — whether accounts comply with applicable accounting standards
  - — particulars of any material departure from those standards and the reasons for it
- provided a mechanism for revising accounts that were defective
- enabled the Financial Reporting Review Panel of the Financial Reporting Council Limited to decide whether accounts should be referred to a court to decide whether or not they were defective.

Counsel's view was that such changes had increased the likelihood that a court would hold that, in general, compliance with accounting standards is necessary for accounts to give a true and fair view. The changes in the standard-setting process, which had occurred after due consultation (the Dearing Committee), would also tend to enhance the status of accounting standards in legal proceedings.

1 Omissions

Counsel was not asked to give views on:

- the interaction between 'true and fair view' and 'properly prepared' and 'do not comply with the requirements of the Act' (defective accounts)
- the meaning of paragraph 15 in the foreword to accounting standards (issued by the ASB in June 1993) which states that *'Where accounting standards prescribe information to be contained in financial statements, such requirements do not override exemptions from disclosure given by law to, and utilised by, certain types of entity.'*
- the application of the true and fair requirement to the accounts of small companies taking advantage of exemptions available under Schedule 8 to the Companies Act 1985
- the arbitrary limits in law and accounting standards whereby in some instances a difference of £1 or 1 share could mean that accounts did not (or did) show a true and fair view (for example, a wholly owned subsidiary need not prepare a cash flow statement; a 99.9% subsidiary has to).

These problems are dealt with in appropriate parts of this book. The first matter above is considered immediately below.

2.6.4 Properly presented

The standard auditors' opinion includes the words:

- *'true and fair view'*, and
- *'properly prepared in accordance with the Companies Act 1985'*.

A failure of accounts to achieve the above conditions would result in them being defective, that is accounts that *'do not comply with the requirements of the Act'* (to quote section 245B of the Companies Act 1985).

In order to draft appropriately modified opinions under SAS 600, auditors have to understand the interaction between 'true and fair view' and 'properly prepared' in the Companies Act 1985. The understanding resolves into the answers to two questions:

- does a qualified report (i.e. not a true and fair view) always indicate that the accounts were not properly prepared?
- can a modification stating only that the accounts were not properly prepared exist in isolation?

The answers are considered in the two sections below. The answer to the second question is by no means easy and auditors are faced with a difficult choice.

2.6.4.1 Not true and fair ⇨ not properly prepared?

It is clear from section 235 of the Companies Act 1985 that the auditors' report is primarily concerned with whether the annual accounts have been properly prepared in accordance with the Act. Reporting on the true and fair view is a secondary matter introduced by the words *'and in particular whether a true and fair view is given . . . '*

It would seem much more logical for the standard opinion paragraph to read as follows:

Report 216
STD: Upside down opinion

Opinion

> In our opinion the financial statements have been properly prepared in accordance with the Companies Act 1985 and in particular a true and fair view is given, by the balance sheet, of the state of the company's affairs as at .... and, by the profit and loss account, of its [profit / loss] for the year then ended.

This upside down opinion is an interesting possibility for a standard opinion. It makes a report on group accounts easier to write in accordance with the requirements of section 235(2)(c) and could improve the clarity of some modifications. Although it complies with SAS 600 it is not dealt with further in this book as there is no real need to depart from tradition and the wording of the examples in appendix 2 to the SAS.

The first of the questions above is, therefore, reasonably easy to answer. If a true and fair view is not given it follows that the accounts are not properly prepared.

2.6.4.2 Not properly prepared ⇨ not true and fair?

The answer to the second question above (i.e. if accounts are not properly prepared can they still give a true and fair view?) depends on whether the definition of 'properly prepared' includes matters other than the true and fair view. This eventually comes down to legal semantics. It is always wise to consider the legislation before leaping to the 'obvious' conclusion. The obvious conclusion in this case being that some failures of proper presentation do not affect the true and fair view. For example, a disclosure required by Schedule 6 may be omitted so that the accounts do not comply with the legal requirements but that fact may not be material to the true and fair view.

The less obvious conclusion is that 'properly prepared' is the legal term meaning that the accounts give a true and fair view. Taking this view, minor matters, such as an immaterial Schedule 6 omission, have no bearing on proper preparation, just as they have no bearing on the true and fair view.

Those who wish to argue for this less obvious conclusion can draw some comfort for their view from the Companies Act 1985:

- section 46 which defines 'unqualified report' for the purpose of section 43(3), (re-registration of private company as public)
- section 262 which gives minor definitions for Part VII of the Act
- section 272(3) which includes a definition of 'properly prepared' in respect of interim accounts

1 Section 46

The section explains the reference in section 43(3)(c) to an unqualified auditors' report on the relevant balance sheet. Unqualified means stating without material qualification that the balance sheet has been properly prepared in accordance with the Act.

2 Section 262

The section defines for Part VII (sections 221 to 262A) 'qualified' for an auditors' report. Qualified means that the report does not state an unqualified opinion that the accounts have been properly prepared in accordance with the Act.

3 Section 272(3)

Defines 'properly prepared' as compliance with section 226, modified as necessary because the accounts are not for a year and, without prejudice to the foregoing:

- the balance sheet must give a true and fair view of the state of the company's affairs as at the balance sheet date, and
- the profit and loss account must give a true and fair view of the company's profit or loss for the period in respect of which the accounts were prepared.

The last two criteria are familiar to readers of section 226 which includes the requirements:

- the balance sheet shall give a true and fair view of the state of affairs of the company as at the end of the financial year, and
- the profit and loss account shall give a true and fair view of the profit or loss of the company for the financial year.

Section 226 requires the accounts to comply with the provisions of Schedule 4 and contains general true and fair provisions including the true and fair 'override'.

Other sections of the Act require disclosures. To pick just two:

- section 231 requires the information specified in Schedule 5 to be given in notes to a company's annual accounts
- section 232 requires the information specified in Schedule 6 to be given in notes to a company's annual accounts as to their form and content and the additional information to be provided by way of notes.

Those supporting the less obvious conclusion that 'properly prepared' is synonymous with the accounts giving a true and fair view will point to the special position of Schedule 4 to support their view. They argue that section 226 only refers to Schedule 4, all of the disclosures in which are subject to a materiality test [paragraph 86], so that a deficiency in such a disclosure would also be material to the true and fair view. This argument is not, however, sustainable because companies may choose to give voluntary disclosures that are not material. In addition , although a disclosure may be material, a deficiency in it need not also be material (e.g. the deficiency may affect only a small amount of the disclosure).

A further counter to this argument is provided by section 226 itself. The link between disclosures required by other provisions of the Act and 'properly presents' is via the general true and fair requirements in section 226. Section 226(4) notes that *'Where compliance with the provisions of that Schedule (i.e. Schedule 4),* ***and the other provisions of this Act*** *as to the matters to be included in a company's individual accounts or in notes to those accounts, would not be sufficient to give a true and fair view, the necessary additional information shall be given in the accounts or in a note to them.'*

The words in bold above include all relevant provisions of the Act within the ambit of 'properly present', not just those of Schedule 4. The way that the provisions are included is not, however, completely straightforward and the method of inclusion could lend support to the argument that 'properly presents' is equivalent to 'true and fair view'. Where compliance with the provisions is not sufficient to give a true and fair view, additional information is required. This is not the same as saying that compliance with the disclosure requirements is necessary in order that the accounts give a true and fair view.

All of Schedule 4 is subject to a materiality test. Paragraph 86 states that amounts which in the particular context of any provision of the Schedule are not material may be disregarded. Paragraph 5 of Schedule 4A contains a similar provision. Some paragraphs of Schedule 5 include a materiality test but some do not. There are no general materiality tests in Schedule 6, just certain de minimis provisions.

Where there is a materiality test, a matter need not be included unless it affects the true and fair view. A significant error in such a matter (i.e. not properly prepared) therefore affects the true and fair view and vice versa. Where there is no materiality test the position varies depending on the item. A Schedule 6 disclosure is a special case because auditors must give the required particulars in their report if they are reasonably able to do so. Other matters must be considered individually. For example, Schedule 5 paragraph 6, dealing with shares and debentures of a company held by subsidiary undertakings, requires disclosure of the number, description and amount of the shares in and debentures of the company held by or on behalf of its subsidiary undertakings. The information must be given, if relevant, regardless of materiality. Either this type of information is simply a 'required disclosure' that is not relevant to the true and fair view or there is no materiality test because it is always (in the Act's view) material.

What, in any case, are the provisions that are not subject to materiality or similar considerations? The following two examples from Schedule 5 are chosen to illustrate the information that should be provided where relevant for a company required to prepare group accounts:

- paragraph 19(a) requires disclosure of the reasons why a subsidiary undertaking's financial year does not end with that of the company
- paragraph 31 requires disclosure of the name of the ultimate parent company.

It would be intellectually satisfying if it were possible to assume that the omission of any such disclosure affected the true and fair view. In other words, 'do not comply' equates to 'not properly prepared' and 'not true and fair view'.

This might be reasonable for the name of the ultimate parent company but it is not a sustainable argument for a few bland words about one small subsidiary undertaking that has a different year end.

The discussion above has focused on the accounting definition of 'properly prepared', which draws on section 226. The words when used in section 235 in connection with auditors' reports are the same, but there is no internal logic to the Companies Act 1985 that says that a definition for interim accounts has to apply to annual accounts, nor that an accounting definition has to coincide with an auditing definition. The words in section 235 need not mean the same as in section 272, although a court may be influenced by the above reasoning.

The following practical solution is proposed to the question *'if accounts are not properly prepared can they still give a true and fair view?'* The solution requires the use of some new terminology in order to avoid using 'proper presentation' as a term covering every departure from the disclosure requirements of the Act:

- if a disclosure provision of the Act is breached — the accounts *'do not comply with the requirements of the Act'* (and the defective accounts provisions of section 245B could be invoked)

- if the breach is material to the true and fair view (e.g. a significant error in a Schedule 4 disclosure) — the auditors' report states that the accounts do not give a true and fair view and have not been properly prepared in accordance with the Act (this may theoretically include a material Schedule 6 matter)
- if the breach is not material to the true and fair view — the auditors' report states that the accounts give a true and fair view:
  - if the disclosure is required by Schedule 6 — the auditors' report gives the required particulars but does not say the accounts have not been properly presented
  - for other disclosures — the auditors' report is silent on proper presentation.

The proposed practical solution may strike some as risky. After all, auditors are being encouraged to remain silent about breaches of the disclosure provisions of the Act. Such breaches could result in the need to issue revised accounts.

It is important to remember that silence is only appropriate if the matter is not material to the true and fair view, so it is difficult to envisage a party suffering loss as a result. The second point is that the Act contains specific reporting requirements for Schedule 6 disclosures. If it was intended that auditors should report on other immaterial aspects of non-compliance with the disclosure provisions of the Act, surely Parliament would have introduced equivalent requirements to do so?

Auditors may, however, feel that every time a disclosure provision of the Act is breached they wish to report that the accounts have not been properly prepared. This would include Schedule 6 matters. Such a course of action would involve less risk of criticism that the auditors had failed to alert readers to a problem. Obviously, auditors face a different risk; that of damaging relations with their client. This is often a barrier to taking a cautious view in a grey area.

2.6.5 Equivalent terms

SAS 600 applies only to reports that express an opinion in terms of whether a true and fair view is given. Other terms such as *'presents fairly'* and *'properly prepared in accordance with'* also bring a report within the scope of the Standard, but only if such terms are prescribed by statutory or other specific requirements.

The practical implications of this guidance are that:

- a true and fair view opinion is to be used in preference to other terms where a choice is permitted by the terms of the engagement
- other terms are to be used only when prescribed by statutory or other specific requirements
- opinions resulting from an audit engagement should not be expressed in a way that limits them.

The last item above means that an opinion such as *'the accounts have been properly presented in accordance with the accounting policies'* is not acceptable. This is because, in order to be able to give an opinion on the true and fair view, auditors consider:

- whether the accounting policies are appropriate to the circumstances of the enterprise
- whether those policies have been consistently applied and adequately disclosed
- whether all information relevant to a proper understanding of the results and financial position is present.

In the US the equivalent to 'true and fair view' is *'present fairly, in all material respects . . . in conformity with generally accepted accounting principles'.* This is an acceptable form of report under SAS 600 if it is specifically required by the terms of the engagement. Auditors issuing such a report are likely, however, to be complying with US GAAS rather than Auditing Standards issued by the APB.

If auditors are asked to give an opinion in terms other than true and fair view or equivalent they should not issue a report that could be mistaken for a SAS 600 report. To do so may mislead users of the accounts as to the degree of reliance that may be placed on the auditors' work.

2.7 Readability

2.7.1 Introduction

The aim of clear communication was stressed from the start of SAS 600's consultation process. The standard report given as example 1 in appendix 2 to the SAS seems to emphasise precision of language, not readability, as the means of achieving clarity. Some auditors may believe that this is the wrong emphasis.

This section analyses the readability of the standard report as presented by the SAS and examines an alternative approach. Readability is even more important in modified reports and this section also acts, therefore, as an introduction to relevant sections of chapter 3 'Modified Reports'.

2.7.2 Measuring readability

There are many ways to judge readability. The most practical methods use a mathematical formula to measure the readability. Such formulae are distilled from reading and comprehension experiments on many different types of prose. In general long words and long sentences give rise to difficult prose.

The readability of the model report given in section 2.4 of this chapter is indicated by the following:

Words	281
Words per sentence	31.2
Characters per word	5.3
Flesch Reading Ease	26.7

The last indicator is an index calculated by the word processing program with which this book was written. It is explained briefly below.

1 Flesch Reading Ease

The Flesch Reading Ease (FRE) is derived from the average number of words per sentence and the average number of syllables per 100 words. Standard writing averages 17 words per sentence and 147 syllables per 100 words. The actual formula is:

Flesch Reading Ease = 206.835 - ((1.015 x average sentence length) + (0.846 x number of syllables per 100 words))

Readability	**Flesch Reading Ease**
Very easy	90 to 100
Easy	80 to 90
Fairly easy	70 to 80
Standard	60 to 70
Fairly difficult	50 to 60
Difficult	30 to 50
Very difficult	0 to 30

2 Number of words

The readability index only measures the prose that is present. Obviously, if two passages score the same but one is twice the length of the other the shorter passage is much more effective (so long as the same information is conveyed). It is difficult to measure this property of prose. A simple indicator is to assume that the shorter of two passages that are equally readable is the more effective by the ratio of their length. So, a passage that is half as long is twice as effective. This is shown below as a further measure for the better of two passages. It is called 'comparative readability' and is a number that expresses how many times the better passage is at communicating.

Expressed as a formula the comparative readability is FRE(1)/FRE(2) x W(2)/W(1), where FRE(1) refers to the better Flesch Reading Ease (designated as passage 1) and W is the number of words in passage (1) or (2).

2.7.3 The readability of the SAS 600 model report

In case any reader has been busy counting the words in the report given in section 2.4 'A model report' of this chapter, it ought to be stressed that any difference between total counted and reported words is entirely due to the way the computer counts 'words'. A separate computer count, not related to the measurement of readability, arrives at a total of 276 words, not 281.

The second paragraph under basis of opinion contains a mammoth 49 word sentence, so its readability score below comes as no surprise. The scores for the individual paragraphs, excluding headings, are:

Paragraph	Flesch Reading Ease
Introductory	26.3
Responsibilities	38.4
Basis of opinion (1)	18.3
Basis of opinion (2)	9.3
Opinion	44.9
Whole report	26.7

Some of the readability problems of the example report can be ascribed to poor choice of words. Some of these are effectively imposed on auditors by the Companies Act 1985. Section 235 requires the auditors' to state in their report whether in their opinion the annual accounts have been properly prepared in accordance with the Act. Unfortunately, *'have been properly prepared'* is passive rather than the more readable active voice and *'in accordance with'* is wordy (prefer 'according to'). Even the words *'in our opinion'* are open to criticism, *'we believe'* is more direct.

2.7.4 A more readable standard report

The following report complies with SAS 600 and improves on the readability of example 1 in its appendix 2.

Report 217
STD: Model, high readability

AUDITORS' REPORT TO THE MEMBERS OF ....

We have audited the accounts on pages ..... to ....

Responsibilities of directors and auditors

The directors are responsible for the accounts. They describe their responsibilities on page ..... . We express our opinion on the accounts.

Basis of opinion

We comply with Auditing Standards. An audit includes:

- examining, on a test basis, evidence about the amounts and disclosures in the accounts
- assessing the significant estimates and judgements made by the directors
- considering whether the accounting policies are appropriate, consistently applied and adequately disclosed

We planned and performed our audit so as to obtain reasonable assurance that the accounts are free from material misstatement, whether caused by fraud or other irregularity or error. We evaluated the overall presentation of the accounts.

Opinion
We believe that the accounts:

- have been properly prepared in accordance with the Companies Act 1985
- give a true and fair view of:
  - — the state of affairs of the company at .... , and
  - — the profit for the year then ended.

Registered Auditors *Address*
Date

The 'score' of this unfamiliar report is:

Aspect	New report	SAS example 1
Words	157	281
Words per sentence	14.3	31.2
Characters per word	5.3	5.3
Flesch Reading Ease	56.7	26.7
Comparative readability	3.8 times	not applicable

The comparative readability is calculated as (56.7/26.7) x (281/157).

You may reach your own conclusion as to which report communicates more clearly.

The drive for readability has made the report unbalanced. The basis of opinion is required to include much material that is wordy (its Flesch Reading Ease is only 39.4). It would be better if the basis of opinion could be less constrained. It is not wise, however, to breach Auditing Standard 600.4 on the grounds that complying with it impairs the clarity of the report!

2.8 Developing a standard report

2.8.1 Introduction

This section examines the process of writing a standard report on a company. It is aimed at those issuing standard reports and also at those writing audit manuals and similar guidance material.

There are so many building blocks available that the standard report is almost built rather than written. It is simply a matter of deciding what building blocks to use and how to put them together.

The design of the standard report determines how the building will eventually turn out. That design is driven by the objectives that auditors have for their reports. Obviously, any report must comply with SAS 600, beyond that auditors can have different objectives. If auditors wish to aim for high readability, the discussion in section 2.7 'Readability' of this chapter is relevant. Other objectives could include:

- I want to stay close to the examples in appendix 2 to SAS 600
- I have to use my firm's preferred approach
- I want to give more information to users
- I want to write as little as possible
- I want to be avant-garde.

This section uses the analysis in the earlier sections of this chapter, in particular section 2.5 'Elements and options'. That section provides further information on all the significant building blocks.

2.8.2 House style

Some differences between building blocks have no effect on the validity of a report. They merely reflect the house style of the auditors. For example, so long as auditors are described as 'Registered Auditor' or 'Registered Auditors', the appropriate professional requirement is satisfied.

If, however, house style is too wayward the professional requirements may not be met. This should be guarded against. For example, a description that read as follows would cause problems:

Example & Co.
Chartered Accountants
Registered for Auditing.

The specific wording required by Audit Regulations is not used and so the auditors have breached the Regulations.

2.8.3 Client style

Auditors' reports are not issued in isolation. The annual report and accounts may have its own house style with which the auditors' report is expected to conform. As well as the typeface and layout, typical matters that may be affected include:

- referring to financial statements or accounts
- format of dates
- capitalisation of words such as Directors and Group.

Most auditors are prepared to be flexible when asked to conform to the client's house style. This is a reasonable stance as the matters are not normally relevant to the validity of the auditors' report.

2.8.4 A basic report and flexibility

The discussion of house and client style above leads to a conclusion that auditors cannot expect simply to decide upon one standard report and issue it (changing the name and dates) at the end of every audit. However, the closer to this ideal a firm can approach the less likelihood there is of a simple error in a report.

The most practical way of deciding on a standard report is to:

- decide on an ideal report that follows every preference the firm has
- identify those aspects of it that:
  - are not changed on any audit (e.g. name of the firm and description)
  - must change for every audit (e.g. client name, year end, profit / loss, page references to accounts)
  - may change to suit client style (e.g. typeface, capitalisation of 'Directors').

Firms may choose to have a standard report for a single company and one for a group or treat the latter as a variation on the standard report.

Where a matter may change to suit client style it is important for a firm to establish a preference that is used when the client has no view and which is suggested when the client asks for the auditors' views.

The above categories are not fixed. Some firms may decide that a particular matter is to be mandatory while other firms may consider the same matter to be one that can change according to client style. For example, one firm may be adamant about the position of its report, another may be flexible.

If a firm anticipates flexibility in an aspect of the report it may nevertheless put boundaries on the flexibility. For example 'accounts' or 'financial statements' may be considered acceptable alternative terms, but 'accounts and notes' may not.

It is also important to decide what boundaries, if any, exist on the use of the report. For example is it to be used on dormant companies, or small companies?

The above scheme works well except where it is put under pressure by client demands. For example, a firm may have decided that its standard report will never include a separate opinion on cash flows. If a client demands such an opinion a mechanism of consultation must be in place to consider the circumstances and decide the issue.

2.8.5 Staying close to the examples in appendix 2 to SAS 600

If the objective of the auditors is to stay close to the example reports in appendix 2 to SAS 600 some decisions of house style have already been made, including:

- section headings and basic order of the report
- addressed to the shareholders
- introduction refers to the historical cost convention and accounting policies
- terms such as 'financial statements' are decided
- opinion does not extend to further primary statements.

The remaining decisions to be made are confined to deciding aspects of house style not addressed by SAS 600 and the degree of flexibility allowed to accommodate client style. For example, the SAS does not prescribe:

- the position of the report
- how to identify the firm.

The reporting partner must also consider whether the use of the report is sensible. For example, is the report on a dormant company?

2.8.6 Using my firm's preferred approach

If the reporting partner has a firm's preferred standard report available the decisions about general philosophy and house style have already been taken. Unless the firm's preferred standard is entirely mandatory (an unusual circumstance) there is still scope for accommodating client preferences. These can include:

- capitalisation of words such as Directors
- format of dates (e.g. 31 December 19xx, 31st December, 19xx, etc.)
- words used to refer to financial statements (e.g. accounts).

If the client wishes to alter aspects of the standard report that the firm considers fixed, appropriate consultation procedures should be used to resolve any conflicts.

2.8.7 Giving more information to users

The main opportunities to give more information occur when the report is modified. When a standard report is issued the areas where more information may be given are restricted to expanding:

- the responsibilities of the auditors (this expansion looks more in keeping if the directors' responsibilities are described in the auditors' report)
- the basis of opinion.

There is no limit to the information that auditors may provide so long as the extra material does not impair the *'clear expression of opinion'*. Candidates for further explanation include:

- an introduction to the new reporting regime in the first year of its use
- the historical cost convention
- how an objective opinion stems from independence
- what the APB is
- what misstatement is and what is meant by 'material' in this context
- the statutory basis for the audit
- the statutory requirements to consider such matters as adequacy of branch returns.

The following example report was provided by the senior partner of a firm that wished to remain discreetly unnamed. It excels in explaining the auditors' report (before SAS 600) on a small company to readers that are not familiar with the Companies Acts. The firm used it for all clients except those who prepared draft accounts (from their own records) ready for audit. Although it was occasionally greeted by raised eyebrows, it was accepted in use by banks, the Revenue and, of course, clients.

REPORT OF THE AUDITORS TO THE MEMBERS OF ....

1. Our report is based on the requirements of Section 235 Companies Act 1985 as enacted in Section 9 Companies Act 1989. In the following paragraphs 2 to 6 we have quoted extracts from the Companies Acts 1985 to 1989 to provide the background to our report. Paragraphs 7 to 10 set out our comments on the accounting records in relation to the audit requirements leading through to our concluding opinion in paragraph 11. The financial statements and the prevention and detection of irregularities and fraud are the responsibility of the Management of the company. Our responsibility is to express an opinion on these financial statements based on our audit. We have carried out our audit in accordance with Auditing Standards which require that we plan and perform the audit to obtain reasonable assurance that the financial statements give a true and fair view. Our audit included an examination, on a test basis, of evidence supporting the monetary amounts and disclosures in the financial statements, an assessment of the accounting principles used and significant estimates made by Management and an evaluation of the overall presentation of the financial statements. Management has provided assurances that all the company's transactions have been recorded in the

accounting records and we believe that these assurances together with our auditing procedures referred to in this paragraph provide a reasonable basis for our concluding opinion in Paragraph 11.

2. Under Section 237(1) Companies Act 1985, as enacted in Section 9 Companies Act 1989, it is our duty, as the company's auditors, in preparing our report, to carry out such investigations as will enable us to form an opinion as to:

(a) whether proper accounting records have been kept by the company, and

(b) whether the company's balance sheet and profit and loss account are in agreement with the accounting records.

3. Under Section 237(2) if we are of opinion that proper accounting records have not been kept, or if the balance sheet and profit and loss account are not in agreement with the accounting records, we must state that fact in our report.

4. Under Section 237(3) if we fail to obtain all the information and explanations which, to the best of our knowledge and belief, are necessary for the purposes of our audit, we must state that fact in our report.

5. Under Section 389A(1) Companies Act 1985, as enacted in Section 120 Companies Act 1989 we have a right of access at all times to the company's books, accounts and vouchers and we are entitled to require from the company's officers such information and explanations as we think necessary for the performance of our duties as auditors.

6. Before we can complete our report under Sections 235 and 237 it is necessary to state the requirements of Section 221 Companies Act 1985 as enacted in Section 2 Companies Act 1989.

[The requirements of section 221 are reproduced.]

7. In relation to Sections 221(3)(a), 221(3)(b) and 221(1)(a), although the company has prepared a statement of stock as at the balance sheet date detailed statements of stocktakings have not been prepared and continuous stock records are not maintained.

8. In relation to Section 237(1)(a), although the company does not maintain its accounting records on double-entry book-keeping principles on a day-to-day basis, in our opinion proper accounting records (as described in Section 221(1) and (2)) have been kept by the company so far as appears from our examination of those accounting records.

9. In relation to Section 237(1)(b), although the balance sheet and profit and loss account have been prepared after the company's accounting records have been analysed and extended by us on double-entry book-keeping principles, in our opinion the company's balance sheet and its profit and loss account are in agreement with the accounting records.

10. In relation to Section 237(3), although financial transactions can only be fully substantiated and become susceptible to control and verification when the appropriate documentation is created and the relevant entries are made in the accounting records, we have obtained all the information and explanations which to the best of our knowledge and belief, and taking into consideration cost-effectiveness, were necessary for the purposes of our audit.

11. In our opinion the balance sheet and profit and loss account have been properly prepared in accordance with the Acts, subject to minor modifications to the formats set out in Schedule 4, Companies Act 1985, as amended by Schedule 1, Companies Act 1989. These modifications do not restrict the information disclosed. In our opinion a true and fair view is given:

    (i) in the balance sheet, of the state of affairs of the company at the ...., and
    (ii) in the statement of source and application of funds, of the source and application of funds of the company for the [year / period] ended on that date, and
    (iii) in the profit and loss account, of the [profit /loss] of the company for the [year / period] ended on that date.

Firm
Chartered Accountants and Registered Auditors
Auditors of ....
Address, and at
Address of second office of firm

The firm issued guidance notes at the time the above report was issued (May 1989) explaining its features to staff. The main matters discussed were:

- paragraphs 7 to 10 highlighting factors taken into account in forming the opinion, someone else might form a different opinion. The purpose of this method is to try to restrict any potential liability to third parties relying on the accounts
- the audit report widely used in the profession in connection with small companies has recently been withdrawn with no adequate substitute. Accordingly, auditors are in an awkward position and now have to review their own reporting methods
- professional accountants have been concerned about their position in relation to:
  — Inland Revenue and Customs & Excise investigations of client's accounts
  — the increasing number of professional indemnity claims against auditors
  — the Insolvency Act 1985 under which it is possible for auditors to be implicated in the causes of failure.

  Accordingly it has become necessary for auditors' reports to become more detailed
- without the words in paragraph 8 a third party (e.g. the Inspector of Taxes) examining the accounts in detail might be misled into believing that the accounting system was perfect. In the firm's opinion it is virtually impossible to create perfect book-keeping systems and perfect internal control systems. The wording is therefore almost a protest against the wording of section 221 Companies Act, 1985 but also gives the client and auditor some protection against any difference of opinion arising from the examination of the accounts by third-parties. The firm is merely indicating that the records kept are not absolutely in accordance with a perfect system

- the report makes no reference in paragraph 8 to the whole of section 221, as 221(4) is not fully complied with in terms of detailed stocktakings. Also sales/purchase ledgers and control accounts are not maintained
- the report does not refer to the historical cost convention, because in the Companies Act 1985, Schedule 4 Part II Sections A and B covers the normal accounting principles and historical cost accounting rules, so compliance can be assumed in accordance with the wording of the report at paragraph 11
- quoting sections from the Companies Act helps both clients and staff to be aware of the requirements, and facilitates the understanding of the firm's comments in paragraphs 7 to 10.

There are no doubt more ways that auditors can give more information to users following SAS 600.

2.8.8 Writing as little as possible

If the objective of the auditors is to have as brief a report as possible a choice has to be made between starting from scratch or cutting down an existing report, such as example 1 in appendix 2 to SAS 600.

The first approach entails a careful study of the detailed requirements of the SAS with a view to writing only what is required. To a large extent that approach was taken when drafting Report 217 STD: Model, high readability, in section 2.7 of this chapter.

Cutting down example 1 in appendix 2 to SAS 600 can produce a much shorter report than the original without resorting to the devices used in the high readability report. It is possible to delete or amend the following matters:

- changing *'shareholders'* to *'members'*
- changing *'financial statements'* to *'accounts'*
- deleting references to the historical cost convention and accounting policies
- shortening the title to the respective responsibilities of directors and auditors section
- deleting the word *'company's'* from *'company's directors'*
- changing *'preparing accounts'* to *'the accounts'*
- replacing the responsibilities of the auditors material by wording that complies only with SAS 600.3, deleting words such as:
  — *'independent'*
  — *'based on our audit'*
  — *'form an . . . opinion of those accounts and to report our opinion to you'*
- in the basis of opinion section:
  — removing reference to *'issued by the Auditing Practices Board'*
  — changing *'examination . . . of'* to *'examining'* and *'an assessment of'* to *'assessing'*

— removing the words *'all the information and explanations which we considered necessary in order to provide us with sufficient evidence to give'*
— removing the words *'In forming our opinion'*
— removing the words *'adequacy of'*
— removing the words *'information in'*.

The following model report shows the end result:

Report 218
STD: Model, condensing the example in SAS 600

AUDITORS' REPORT TO THE MEMBERS OF ....

We have audited the accounts on pages ..... to ..... .

Responsibilities

As described on page ..... the directors are responsible for the accounts. It is our responsibility to express our opinion on the accounts.

Basis of opinion

We conducted our audit in accordance with Auditing Standards. An audit includes examining, on a test basis, evidence relevant to the amounts and disclosures in the accounts. It also includes assessing the significant estimates and judgements made by the directors in the preparation of the accounts, and on whether the accounting policies are appropriate to the company's circumstances, consistently applied and adequately disclosed.

We planned and performed our audit so as to obtain reasonable assurance that the financial statements are free from material misstatement, whether caused by fraud or other irregularity or error. We also evaluated the overall adequacy of the accounts.

Opinion

In our opinion the accounts give a true and fair view of the state of the company's affairs as at .... and of its [profit / loss] for the year then ended and have been properly prepared in accordance with the Companies Act 1985.

Registered Auditors Address
Date

There are some 190 words in the title and body of this report (down to the signature). This compares to 280 in the model report based on SAS 600 and approximately 160 in Report 217: STD: Model high readability.

2.8.9 Avant-garde reports

It is possible to construct some very odd looking auditors' reports and still comply with SAS 600. Such reports would not be used in practice. This subsection points to some possible areas for change to example 1 in appendix 2 to SAS 600 that might interest avant-garde auditors.

2.8.9.1 Title

The Proposed International Standard on Auditing 'The Auditor's Report on Financial Statements' issued on 1 February 1993 proposed that *'The auditor's report should have a title that includes the word "Independent".'* The examples in SAS 600 include the word 'independent' only in the body of the text.

There is obviously a further degree of emphasis to be achieved by putting the word in the title.

2.8.9.2 Giving an opinion on the audit

The Proposed International Standard on Auditing 'The Auditor's Report on Financial Statements' issued on 1 February 1993 proposed that *'The report should include a statement by the auditor that the audit provides a reasonable basis for the opinion.'* An explicit statement that there was no restriction on the scope of the audit (which is what the international wording is) could be of use to readers of the report.

A basis of opinion section including such wording could be as follows (new material shown in SMALL CAPITALS):

Report 219

STD: Explicit statement of adequacy of audit in basis of opinion

Basis of opinion

We conducted our audit in accordance with Auditing Standards issued by the Auditing Practices Board. An audit includes examination, on a test basis, of evidence relevant to the amounts and disclosures in the financial statements. It also includes an assessment of the significant estimates and judgements made by the directors in the preparation of the financial statements, and of whether the accounting policies are appropriate to the company's circumstances, consistently applied and adequately disclosed.

We planned and performed our audit so as to obtain all the information and explanations which we considered necessary in order to provide us with sufficient evidence to give reasonable assurance that the financial statements are free from material misstatement, whether caused by fraud or other irregularity or error. In forming our opinion we also evaluated the overall adequacy of the presentation of information in the financial statements. WE BELIEVE THAT OUR AUDIT PROVIDES A REASONABLE BASIS FOR OUR OPINION.

2.8.9.3 Further information

Subsection 2.8.7 'Giving more information to users' deals with one aspect of reporting that could be considered to be avant-garde. The inclusion of some further information, such as an explanatory paragraph introducing the new report in its first year, may seem sensible but there is little indication that the majority of auditors will do this.

Many of the matters discussed in the elements and options section of this chapter include suggestions for further or alternative wording. These could also interest the avant-garde auditor.

2.9 Groups

2.9.1 Introduction

This section examines the changes to a standard report on a company necessary to make it applicable to a group. The approach taken is to repeat the format of the early part of this chapter. The requirements are followed by a model report and then its elements and options are explored.

2.9.2 Requirements

In general the requirements for auditors' reports on group accounts are the same as for reports on companies. This is hardly surprising as section 227 of the Companies Act 1985 specifies that group accounts should comply with Schedule 4A, the first section of which requires group accounts to comply so far as practicable with the provisions of Schedule 4 as if the undertakings included in the consolidation were a single company.

For group accounts, section 235 requires the auditors to give an opinion as to whether, so far as concerns members of the company, a true and fair view is given for the undertakings included in the consolidation as a whole, of:

- the state of affairs as at the end of the financial year, and
- the profit or loss for the financial year.

The examples in appendix 2 to SAS 600 do not include a standard report on group accounts. Example 4 is a modification describing a fundamental uncertainty in the context of group accounts. Stripped of the modification, the underlying report is shown below as a model.

2.9.3 Model report on group accounts

Report 220
STD: Model, group accounts based closely on SAS 600

AUDITORS' REPORT TO THE SHAREHOLDERS OF ....

We have audited the financial statements on pages ..... to ..... which have been prepared under the historical cost convention [as modified by the revaluation of certain fixed assets] and the accounting policies set out on page ..... .

Respective responsibilities of directors and auditors

As described on page ..... the company's directors are responsible for the preparation of financial statements. It is our responsibility to form an independent opinion, based on our audit, of those statements and to report our opinion to you.

Basis of opinion

We conducted our audit in accordance with Auditing Standards issued by the Auditing Practices Board. An audit includes examination, on a test basis, of evidence relevant to the amounts and disclosures in the financial statements. It also includes an assessment of the significant estimates and judgements made by the directors in the preparation of the financial statements, and of whether the accounting policies are appropriate to the company's (sic) circumstances, consistently applied and adequately disclosed.

We planned and performed our audit so as to obtain all the information and explanations which we considered necessary in order to provide us with sufficient evidence to give reasonable assurance that the financial statements are free from material misstatement, whether caused by fraud or other irregularity or error. In forming our opinion we also evaluated the overall adequacy of the presentation of information in the financial statements.

Opinion

In our opinion the financial statements give a true and fair view of the state of affairs of the company and of the group as at .... and of the group's [profit / loss] for the year then ended and have been properly prepared in accordance with the Companies Act 1985.

Registered Auditors Address
Date

2.9.4 Elements and options

2.9.4.1 Introduction

The above model report would be expected to differ from that on a company in the following ways:

- the description of responsibilities of directors (not shown) refers to 'group'
- the accounting policies are assessed and reported in relation to the group's circumstances (though the example actually continues to use the word 'company')
- the opinion refers to the state of affairs of the group (as well as the company) and its profit.

The responsibilities of the directors and the opinion are discussed further below. This subsection concludes with an examination of the further wording that some auditors might wish to include in their reports on groups to provide readers with more information.

2.9.4.2 Responsibilities of directors

The directors and auditors of a parent undertaking are not in exactly the same position that they would be in for a single company. Group accounts are intended to report the activities and state of affairs as if there were a single company, but that is not always enough. A reasonably complex group can have many subsidiaries, some owned for only part of the year. The group accounts may include the results of associated undertakings that would be excluded from the accounts of a company. The reserves position of a group is not directly relevant to the distributability of profits. The consolidated accounts may include goodwill and reserves arising purely from the consolidation process (such as the merger reserve). The group accounts are accompanied by a balance sheet and associated notes for the holding company. The directors' report on a group differs from that on a single company.

Looking specifically at responsibilities the directors are required to:

- determine which entities shall be consolidated
- arrange coterminous accounting periods
- ensure the accounting policies are consistent across the group
- arrange access for the auditors to assistance from the directors and auditors of subsidiary undertakings
- take reasonable steps to secure that subsidiary undertakings keep such accounting records as to enable the directors of the parent company to ensure that any balance sheet and profit and loss account is prepared in accordance with the Act.

The following shows how the wording favoured by the example in appendix 3 to SAS 600 could be amended for a group. New words are shown IN SMALL CAPITALS and deletions ~~in strike through~~.

Report 221
RD: Outside auditors' report, group drawing on SAS 600 appendix 3

STATEMENT OF DIRECTORS' RESPONSIBILITIES

Company law requires the directors to prepare financial statements for each financial year which give a true and fair view of the state of affairs of the company AND THE GROUP and of the profit or loss of the ~~company~~GROUP for that period. In preparing those financial statements, the directors are required to:

- select suitable accounting policies and then apply them consistently
- make judgements and estimates that are reasonable and prudent
- state whether applicable accounting standards have been followed, subject to any material departures disclosed and explained in the financial statements
- prepare the financial statements on the going concern basis unless it is inappropriate to presume that the company AND THE GROUP will continue in business

> The directors are responsible for keeping proper accounting records which disclose with reasonable accuracy at any time the financial position of the company and to enable them to ensure that the financial statements comply with the Companies Act 1985. They are also responsible for safeguarding the assets of the ~~company~~GROUP and hence for taking reasonable steps for the prevention and detection of fraud and other irregularities.

Even the first part of the statement is controversial. The wording shown is being adopted more often than not by the directors of groups but there are significant variations. Other aspects are even less certain and variations are being accepted by different firms of auditors and, in some cases across the clients of a single firm. The variations are all concerned with whether references:

- remain to *'the company'* alone
- are changed to *'the group'*
- are to *'the company and the group'* (the variation *'group and company'* is only a matter of house style and is not treated as a separate variation).

Some annual reports of listed companies show wording with no reference at all. This may be a way of dealing with groups or it may represent a house style adopted for single companies as well.

The statement of directors' responsibilities for a group is not dealt with in SAS 600, but for companies complying with the corporate governance Code of Best Practice a group statement will be the norm. The following table shows which of the aspects of the framework set out earlier in this chapter for deciding whether a description is 'normally adequate' might be modified for a group:

- requirement to give a true and fair view
- going concern presumption
- keeping accounting records (to satisfy requirements such as allowing preparation of financial statements that comply with the Companies Act 1985)
- taking reasonable steps to safeguard assets (and prevent fraud etc.).

2 True and fair view

A survey of 24 annual reports of listed companies (on a first come first chosen basis) showed the following variations in describing the requirement to give a true and fair view.

The following fourteen companies gave a description referring to the group and company balance sheets and the group profit and loss account:

API Group PLC 2/10/93 Ernst & Young
Bradstock Group PLC 30/9/93 Touche Ross & Co.
Carr's Milling Industries PLC 28/8/93 Coopers & Lybrand
Cosalt PLC 29/8/93 Kidsons Impey
Dobson Park Industries PLC 2/10/93 Price Waterhouse

MEPC PLC 30/9/93 KPMG Peat Marwick
Polar PLC 1/10/93 Coopers & Lybrand
Richards PLC 30/9/93 Ernst & Young
Sturge Holdings PLC 30/9/93 Price Waterhouse
The BOC Group PLC 30/9/93 Coopers & Lybrand
The Intercare Group PLC 31/10/93 Price Waterhouse
Trace Computers PLC 31/5/93 Touche Ross & Co.
Trafalgar House PLC 30/9/93 KPMG Peat Marwick, Touche Ross & Co. (joint)
Watson & Philip PLC 29/10/93 Ernst & Young

A typical statement is:

> Company law requires the directors to prepare financial statements for each financial year which give a true and fair view of the state of affairs of the company and group and of the profit or loss of the group for that year.

Three companies referred to the group but not the company:

Burndene Investments PLC 2/10/93 Stoy Hayward
James Dickie PLC 31/8/93 KPMG Peat Marwick
Neotronics Technology PLC 30/9/93 Robson Rhodes

A typical statement referring only to the group is:

> Company law requires the directors to prepare financial statements for each financial year which give a true and fair view of the state of affairs of the group and of the profit or loss of the group for that period.

Two companies referred only to the company:

Greencore Group PLC 24/9/93 Coopers & Lybrand
Wescol Group PLC 31/7/93 Touche Ross & Co.

A typical statement referring only to the company is:

> Company law requires the directors to prepare financial statements for each financial year which give a true and fair view of the state of affairs of the company as at the end of the financial year and of the profit or loss of the company for that period.

Four companies did not specify whether the profit was for the group or the company:

Albert Fisher Group PLC 31/8/93 Ernst & Young
BASS PLC 30/9/93 Ernst & Young
Marks and Spencer PLC 31/3/93 Coopers & Lybrand
The Greenalls Group PLC 24/9/93 Ernst & Young

A typical statement that does not specify the profit may be derived from the Law Society model, which is:

> The directors are required by the Companies Act 1985 to prepare financial statements for each financial year which give a true and fair view of the state of affairs of the company and the group as at the end of the financial year and of the profit or loss for the financial year.

The survey also revealed an unusual approach (Denmans Electrical PLC 30/9/93 Coopers & Lybrand) in which the statement also referred to the profit and loss of the holding company (as normal, the profit and loss account of the holding company was not disclosed in the report and accounts, under the exemption allowed by section 230):

> Company law requires the Directors to prepare financial statements for each financial year which give a true and fair view of the state of affairs of the Company and of the Group and of the profit and loss of the Company and of the Group for that period.

Current practice, albeit only emerging practice, indicates that the preferred approach is to refer to a true and fair view of:

- the state of affairs of the company and group
- the profit or loss of the group for the year.

The order of the words 'company' and 'group' is almost invariably alphabetical, though that is unlikely to be the underlying reason for the order. The only exception to this in the survey is Sturge Holdings PLC 30/9/93 Price Waterhouse.

It has been accepted by auditors that, nevertheless, descriptions can refer only to the company, or only to the group, or be non-specific.

3 Going concern

When mentioning going concern directors in nine of the companies in the survey specified that it was in relation to the company. A further nine reports contained wording that did not identify whether going concern was related to the group or the company. Only five reports mentioned group to the exclusion of company. One description referred to both company and group: that was Trafalgar House where the joint auditors were KPMG Peat Marwick and Touche Ross & Co.

The survey shows that auditors are not too concerned about whether going concern is related to the company or the group. One argument is that both company and group ought to be referred to because balance sheets are presented for both. Those using just company or just group have to be able to justify a link such that a going concern problem for the company affects the group or vice versa. The arguments to justify those links are simple but not absolute. Those using just 'company' argue that the group accounts are prepared under section 227 for the members of the company and if the company is not a going concern, the group accounts can not be on a going concern basis. Those using just 'group' argue that the group includes the company. This is undoubtedly true but there could be significant going concern problems in subsidiaries that a parent undertaking could, nevertheless, chose to have liquidated rather than support.

Best practice would seem to be, therefore, to mention the company or the company and the group, but not the group alone. There are currently, however, sufficient supporters of the minority view (the five examples were each endorsed by a different Big Six firm!) to make that a viable alternative approach.

4 Accounting records

Despite the fact that the statutory requirements for keeping adequate accounting records are for the company and have no relevance for the group, a quarter of the descriptions in the survey referred to 'group'. So, while 'company' is preferred, 'group' is also acceptable based on current practice.

Auditors may be referring to the requirements of subsection (4) of section 221 of the Companies Act 1985 which obliges a parent company which has a subsidiary undertaking (to which the requirements of subsections (1), (2) and (3) do not apply) to take reasonable steps to secure that the undertaking keeps such accounting records as to enable the directors of the parent company to ensure that any balance sheet and profit and loss account prepared under Part VII of the Act complies with the requirements of the Act.

5 Safeguarding assets

The survey revealed five instances of safeguarding assets disclosed only in relation to the company, two disclosures relating to both the company and the group and the remainder dealing with the group. Obviously the investments in its subsidiary undertakings are some of the assets that the parent undertaking's directors are concerned to safeguard. So again there is no wrong answer. The preferred disclosure, however, must be for the group.

2.9.4.3 The opinion

There are two aspect of the opinion on group accounts that are different to that on a company: its scope and its wording. Obviously the opinion has to refer to the relevant financial statements, in this case the group balance sheet and profit and loss account and the company balance sheet. The words chosen can vary due to house style.

According to the Companies Act 1985, the opinion of the auditors is required to be on the view *'so far as concerns members of the holding company'*. The reason for the wording is lost in the mists of time. Some volumes on group accounting suggest that it is to focus the requirements to the needs of the members of the holding company and to absolve the consolidated accounts from having to present information that is directed towards minority shareholders of subsidiary undertakings.

Historically, this form of opinion has been used only infrequently. This is so much so that one of those providing material for this book sent a copy of an opinion issued by Spicer and Peglar that contained the phrase on the basis that he thought that it was very unusual, despite any tendency to comply with the wording of the Act. Auditors can be expected to continue to prefer to comply with SASs.

2.9.4.4 Further information

The responsibilities of holding company auditors towards the financial statements are affected by the arrangements for the audit of subsidiary undertakings. The holding company auditors normally form their view by a combination of their own tests on, for example the holding company, and reliance on the work of auditors of subsidiary undertakings. The existence of auditors of subsidiary undertakings is not mentioned in the report (see section 2.14 of this chapter 'Keeping quiet'). The main reason for that approach being a view that to mention them may suggest that the primary auditors are seeking to place some of their responsibility onto the secondary auditors. This has been the position when the report of the auditors has previously not dealt with their responsibilities or the basis of their opinion. Following SAS 600, is there a need to continue to hide information from readers? The description of an audit in the basis of opinion section is a compromise between the level of information given and the need for brevity.

It would make sense to provide some information about the audit of a group where it differs from that of a company.

> Where subsidiary undertakings are audited by other auditors we carry out sufficient work to satisfy ourselves that we may rely on their work for the purposes of our audit.

The responsibilities of the auditors as set out in the section dealing with the respective responsibilities of the directors and auditors are normally stated very briefly:

> it is our responsibility to form an independent opinion . . .

It would look out of place to expand the description only to include group matters. If, however, the description of responsibilities has been expanded for other reasons, such as to match the length of a directors' statement, it would be possible to add a few words about the responsibility of the auditors that are different in a group accounts context.

2.10 Non-standard companies

This section examines the effect of some legal provisions that can affect companies if they satisfy certain size or other criteria.

2.10.1 Small companies

Small companies (as defined by section 247 of the Companies Act 1985) may make use of exemptions in Schedule 8 to the Companies Act 1985 when preparing their annual accounts and directors' report.[21] The directors may choose which exemptions to take. The exemptions are not trivial. They include combining headings in the balance sheet. For example, 'stocks' (format item C1) need only have 'payments on account' and 'stocks' as subitems. The latter subitem being the total of (1) raw materials and consumables, (2) work in progress, and (3) finished goods and goods for resale.

The exemptions do not affect the basic requirement of section 226 that the directors must prepare accounts that give a true and fair view. However, paragraph 14 of Schedule 8 stipulates that the annual accounts of a company taking advantage of any exemptions are nevertheless deemed to give a true and fair view.

Paragraph 14 goes on to state that when auditors report on a company that has taken advantage of any exemptions, section 235(2) only requires them to state whether in their opinion the annual accounts have been properly prepared in accordance with the provisions of the Companies Act 1985 applicable to small companies.

Everything would have been simple had the DTI not changed the reporting requirements for auditors. It was done in response to pressure from those who were reluctant to report in 'true and fair' terms. The history of this reluctance includes auditors' reports on banks and insurance companies where earlier provisions allowed reports to state only whether the accounts had been properly prepared in accordance with the Companies Act 1985. The relevant industry Auditing Guidelines have included example audit reports with extra explanatory wording, such as *'properly prepared in accordance with the provisions of the Companies Act 1985 applicable to insurance companies'*.

This is changing as banks have to comply with a new Schedule 9 (introduced by SI 1991 No. 2705) that provides an alternative to Schedule 4, not just exemptions from it. Exemptions for insurance companies remain in a new Schedule 9A but they will go when an EC directive on insurance company accounts is put into UK legislation. The prospect is, therefore, that small companies will be the only class of company to receive special treatment in this way.

By allowing reports on small companies taking advantage of exemptions to omit reference to 'true and fair', the APB missed an opportunity to narrow choices.

---

[21] The exemptions were introduced by SI 1992 No. 2452 The Companies Act 1985 (Accounts of Small and Medium-sized Enterprises and Publication of Accounts in ECUs) Regulations 1992 (issued October 1992, effective for accounts for periods ending on or after 16 November 1992).

Appendix 2 to SAS 600 gives an example report for a small company that includes an opinion on truth and fairness. The form of report omitting reference to 'true and fair' is dealt with in a footnote. Auditors are also cautioned that reference to 'true and fair' may be necessary to comply with the requirement of SAS 600.1 for clarity in reporting.

The opinion paragraph preferred by the SAS is:

Report 222
STD: Small company

Opinion

> In our opinion the financial statements give a true and fair view of the state of the company's affairs as at .... and of its [profit / loss] for the year then ended and have been properly prepared in accordance with the provisions of the Companies Act 1985 applicable to small companies.

Because the above opinion is used in the SAS it is likely to gain widespread acceptance. This is the main reason for proposing it, in this book, as the standard report on a small company.

The alternative opinion allowed by SAS 600 is:

Report 223
STD: Small company omitting true and fair view

Opinion

> In our opinion the financial statements have been properly prepared in accordance with the provisions of the Companies Act 1985 applicable to small companies.

This report is not offered as a simple substitute for the preferred one; its adoption is not a matter of belief as to the 'real' meaning of Schedule 8. Instead, SAS 600 suggests that auditors may consider the report to be appropriate where a true and fair view is given only because that is deemed to be so. That is, the accounts have taken advantage of exemptions and by doing so would not give a true and fair view except paragraph 14(1) of Schedule 8 deems that they do.

The report is essentially a modified report, saying that the accounts are not true and fair and the reason for the failure to give a true and fair view is the taking of exemptions allowed by law. By taking this line, the SAS ruins the approach of auditors who want to use the above report on all accounts of small companies taking advantage of exemptions.

However, auditors may well be tempted to use the shorter report in the belief that they reduce their potential liability by not referring to 'true and fair'. The shortened report may be bad for the client, the users of the accounts, and the reputation of the profession:

- it is important to remember that the accounts of a small company making use of the available exemptions are still required to show a true and fair view, whether the audit report refers to that or not. The small company frequently relies on its auditors to prepare the accounts. The directors are entitled to expect the auditors to report that the accounts give a true and fair view
- the first time that users (including the directors) see a SAS 600 report the length of it will come as a shock. One of the dangers of the new report is that it looks different from the previous year and, because it is longer, it could be mistaken for a qualification. For a small company, if the auditors do not use the words 'true and fair view' it will look so much like a qualified report that there is a significant risk that it will be mistaken as one. This could damage the company's standing with suppliers, customers and providers of finance
- for the auditing profession as a whole, when trying to bridge the 'expectation gap' with more informative auditors' reports, it cannot make sense to give less information about truth and fairness or for different firms to adopt different forms of report.

There is a further possible approach. The opinion could simply be a normal one making no special reference to *'the provisions of the Companies Act 1985 applicable to small companies'*. The opinion in the SAS is to be preferred only because it gives more information compared to the non-small company standard opinion. Those who believe that the right place for such extra information is the accounts may point out that those accounts already include (as required by Schedule 8) a statement on the balance sheet that advantage has been taken of special exemptions applicable to small companies.

2.10.2 Dormant companies

So long as it passes a number of tests, a company is allowed by section 250 of the Companies Act 1985 to pass a special resolution exempting itself from the legal requirements relating to the audit of accounts.

Companies that were once active and still have auditors may pass such a resolution only at the AGM at which accounts are laid. To do so the company must have been dormant since the last balance sheet date.

The most obvious difference between the accounts of a dormant company and an active company is that the former need not present a profit and loss account. There are other possible complications, so this subsection examines the following circumstances:

- profit and loss account not presented
- likely use of Schedule 8 small company exemptions
- standard wording that may be inappropriate to a dormant company
- scope limitations and dormant status.

2.10.2.1 Profit and loss account not presented
If a profit and loss account is not presented, the auditors' report need only give an opinion as follows:

Report 224
STD: Dormant company

Opinion

In our opinion the financial statements give a true and fair view of the state of the company's affairs as at .... and have been properly prepared in accordance with the Companies Act 1985.

In the first year that a company is dormant there may be a profit and loss account presented only as a vehicle for the disclosure of comparative figures. Alternatively, it would seem that such figures can be given in a note to the accounts. It is probably acceptable to continue to use the above wording when a nil profit or loss account is presented. One argument for this is that:

- there are no transactions and no profit
- the accounts do not give, therefore, any view of the profit (normally a true and fair view)
- so there is no need for auditors to report on a view that is not given.

It is normal for the accounts to include a note explaining why no profit and loss account has been prepared. The omission of such a note need not cause auditors to modify their report further as the standard dormant company opinion already informs readers of the position.

2.10.2.2 Schedule 8 small company exemptions
Where the dormant company also makes use of the exemptions in Schedule 8 available to a small company the standard opinion would be:

Report 225
STD: Dormant company using small company exemptions

Opinion

In our opinion the financial statements give a true and fair view of the state of the company's affairs as at .... and have been properly prepared in accordance with the provisions of the Companies Act 1985 applicable to small companies.

2.10.2.3 Standard wording not relevant to a dormant company
The wording of a standard auditors' report on an active company may not apply fully to a dormant company because it does not have transactions that require recording in the accounting records. Similar considerations apply to the statement of directors' responsibilities. Auditors may, however, decide to use full reports and it is difficult to criticise that approach on grounds other than taste (or perhaps clarity). Unfortunately, SAS 600.4 is very specific on the content of the basis of

opinion and auditors are forced to retain wording about estimates and judgements and significant accounting policies, even if there are none. Auditors could decide to breach this Auditing Standard, but are then required to include in their report an explanation for their action!

A possible justification for using a briefer report is that to do so gives a better 'clear expression of opinion' as required by SAS 600.1. Auditing Standards do not, however, admit that one standard can be in opposition to another, or one be preferred to another.

Amendments to the wording of a standard report are probably restricted, therefore, to omitting reference to the historical cost convention and the accounting policies.

Auditors are required by SAS 600.3 to assess whether the description of directors' responsibilities is 'adequate'. For a dormant company, auditors are likely to consider quite brief statements to be adequate. Such statements ought to include, as a minimum, the material suggested by the SAS that parallels the wording required from auditors about the basis of their opinion. The following possible wording of a statement of directors' responsibilities for a dormant company is constructed from the example given in appendix 3 to SAS 600 by inserting the clarifying words 'at the end of the year' and deleting as much as possible elsewhere. Some auditors may feel that this goes too far and prefer to reinstate wording about proper accounting records, safeguarding the assets of the company and preventing fraud. Other auditors may consider even this to be too much for a dormant company.

Report 226
RD: Dormant company

STATEMENT OF DIRECTORS' RESPONSIBILITIES

> Company law requires the directors to prepare financial statements for each financial year which give a true and fair view of the state of affairs of the company at the end of the year. In preparing those financial statements, the directors are required to:
>
> - select suitable accounting policies and then apply them consistently
> - make judgements and estimates that are reasonable and prudent.

2.10.2.4 Scope limitations and dormant status

The scope of the auditors' work on a dormant company may be limited. This is likely to be a rare event but, in such circumstances, there could be extra reporting complications.

This possible problem is dealt with here for convenience although strictly it ought to be in the chapter dealing with modified reports. Imagine that the company acts as an agent for another company (T Ltd.) that effectively trades using the dormant company's name. The accounting entries of the trade will be in T Ltd.'s books. If the arrangement is properly constituted, auditors should be able to examine formal written agreements and minutes of the board and perhaps see evidence of an indemnity agreement. The accounts and directors' report of the dormant company would normally include a note about the arrangement, perhaps combined with an explanation for the absence of a profit and loss account.

If a scope limitation affects such matters directly or affects the accounting records of the trading company, the auditors may not be able to obtain sufficient evidence to issue a standard opinion. A report such as the following may be required:

Report 227
SL — d: AR: IE: Dormant company unrecorded transactions

Basis of opinion

We conducted our audit in accordance with Auditing Standards issued by the Auditing Practices Board, except that the scope of our work was limited as explained below.

An audit includes examination, on a test basis, of evidence relevant to the amounts and disclosures in the financial statements. It also includes an assessment of the significant estimates and judgements made by the directors in the preparation of the financial statements, and of whether the accounting policies are appropriate to the company's circumstances, consistently applied and adequately disclosed.

We planned and performed our audit so as to obtain all the information and explanations which we considered necessary in order to provide us with sufficient evidence to give reasonable assurance that the financial statements are free from material misstatement, whether caused by fraud or other irregularity or error. However, the evidence available to us was limited because we were unable to examine an agency agreement between the company and .... , a company trading under this company's name, as this previously fellow subsidiary company was sold by the ultimate parent company during the year. There were no other satisfactory audit procedures that we could adopt to confirm the absence of accounting transactions that might be required to be entered in the accounting records during the year.

In forming our opinion we also evaluated the overall adequacy of the presentation of information in the financial statements.

Opinion: disclaimer on view given by financial statements

Because of the possible effect of the limitation in evidence available to us, we are unable to form an opinion as to whether the financial statements give a true and fair view of the state of the company's affairs as at .... or of its profit or loss for the year then ended or whether the financial statements have been properly prepared in accordance with the Companies Act 1985.

In respect alone of the limitation on our work relating to the agency agreement:

- we have not obtained all the information and explanations which we considered necessary for the purpose of our audit; and
- we were unable to determine whether proper accounting records had been maintained.

2.10.3 Single member companies

Many statutory requirements refer to 'members', but it is possible for a private company limited by shares or guarantee to have only one member. The statutory instrument that commenced this on 15 July 1992[22] contained some specific amendments to the Companies Act 1985 and the Insolvency Act 1986 to put the regime in place.

These provisions deal with such matters as:

- the mode of forming an incorporated company
- the minimum membership for carrying on business
- contracts with sole members who are directors
- publicity for the sole member status
- quorum at meetings of the sole member.

In addition, regulation 2 of the statutory instrument contained a general relief such that any enactment or rule of law that applies for a private company limited by shares or guarantee applies with such modification as may be necessary to allow for the single member company. The application of this is generally common sense. For example, where section 235 requires the auditors to report 'to the company's members', that is taken as meaning 'to the company's member'.

It is possible, assuming that the identity of the single member is known, to address the auditors' report to the member by name. This may prove to have some relevance to restricting the liability of auditors to other users of the accounts, such as a subsequent member or members.

2.10.4 Very small companies

2.10.4.1 Introduction

The DTI has proposed to remove the audit requirement from very small companies. Such companies are likely to be those having a turnover below £90,000 and, as such, are likely to be restricted to labour only contractors. Slightly larger companies, with a turnover up to £350,000 are to have some sort of compilation report. Auditors should be interested in the transitional provisions by which their office ceases or commences if a company grows above the criteria. In the first year that a company grows and so has to have an audit, auditors will have a practical problem of reporting on the comparative figures. This contrasts with an analogous change in status from dormant to non-dormant company because auditing the comparatives in a recently dormant company is likely to be a trivial matter.

---

[22] SI 1992 No. 1699 The Companies (Single Member Private Limited Companies) Regulations 1992.

The abolition of the audit for wholly owned subsidiary undertakings has also been proposed by the ICAEW. Similar reporting problems may be anticipated if this ever comes to pass.

2.10.4.2 The proposals as at April 1994

The Department of Trade and Industry (DTI) issued a press notice dated 7 April 1994 announcing some details of the relaxation of the audit requirement for small companies:

- the Government intends to bring the measures into force in the summer of 1994 by regulations under the Companies Act 1985
- the intention, announced by the Chancellor of the Exchequer in the November 1993 Budget speech, to abolish completely the statutory audit requirement for companies with a turnover below £90,000 is confirmed as is the intention, for companies with a turnover between £90,000 and £350,000 a year that the audit requirement be replaced by a compilation report
- the regulations will provide that companies that satisfy the turnover thresholds would be automatically exempted from the statutory audit requirement provided also that:
  - — their balance sheet total (as defined by section 247, i.e. gross assets) does not exceed £1.4 million;
  - — they are not public limited companies, part of a group structure or subject to a statute-based regulatory regime, such as the Financial Services Act 1986
  - — the exemption has not been vetoed by shareholders holding 10 per cent or more of share capital
- companies whose turnover falls between £90,000 and £350,000 a year would have to provide a compilation report to be filed with their annual accounts at Companies House. This must be produced by a suitably qualified independent accountant ('the reporting accountant') and confirm that the annual accounts have been prepared from the company's accounting records in accordance with the relevant format and disclosure requirements of the Companies Act 1985
- members holding a current practising certificate from any of the following accountancy bodies, or anyone who is registered as an auditor with those bodies, would be eligible to act as reporting accountants: The Institute of Chartered Accountants in England and Wales, The Institute of Chartered Accountants of Scotland, The Institute of Chartered Accountants in Ireland, The Chartered Association of Certified Accountants, The Association of Authorised Public Accountants.
- the Government intends to bring these measures into force this summer by regulations amending Part VII of the Companies Act 1985. The Government will give precise details of the date of implementation once the regulations are laid before Parliament. Companies which satisfy the relevant exemption criteria and whose accounts are approved after the implementing regulations have come into force will be exempt from the audit requirements

- 'Balance sheet total' is defined in Section 247 of the Companies Act 1985, i.e. gross assets.
- companies taking advantage of audit exemption must still keep and maintain adequate accounting records in accordance with the Companies Act 1985 and must file accounts with the Registrar of Companies. Advantage may still be taken of the limited exemptions from accounting disclosure available to small and medium-sized companies under Section 246 of the Act.
- the directors of companies taking advantage of audit exemption will need to state in the accounts which are filed at Companies House that:
  - — the company is eligible to take advantage of audit exemption, and
  - — they are aware of their obligation to keep proper records and to prepare accounts which give a true and fair view of the company's position.
- an individual shareholder (or shareholders) who holds 10 per cent or more of the issued share capital can reverse the automatic opt-out from audit for the current financial year by depositing a notice in writing at the registered office of the company not later than one month before the end of that financial year.
- the Department will be undertaking a limited consultation on the detailed wording of the draft implementing regulations
- he detailed format of the compilation report and professional guidance for practitioners who are eligible to act as reporting accountants will be developed by the Auditing Practices Board.

The criteria for qualifying for exemptions look odd. However, they are really a result of trying to set out a two-stage process:

1 companies will have to qualify as small
2 small companies then have to pass a turnover threshold test.

The DTI seems to be committed to introducing the changes with early effect and it will be necessary for the Regulations to contain effective transitional provisions to avoid minorities loosing their right to demand an audit in the first year.

2.10.4.3 Reporting

Auditors may wish to draw attention to the fact that the company is being audited for the first time (or has not been audited for some years). If there is no uncertainty in their opinion, they may do so by adding explanatory material that is outside the Scope of SAS 600 (see chapter 3).

Although modified reports are dealt with mainly in chapter 3, the following report is presented here to keep all the material for very small companies in one place. If possible, auditors should narrow down the area of uncertainty (perhaps only to stock). The report assumes that adequate assurance will be available on the closing balance sheet.

Report 228
SL — d: Opening position for company that was very small

Basis of opinion

We conducted our audit in accordance with Auditing Standards issued by the Auditing Practices Board except that the scope of our work was limited as explained below.

An audit includes examination, on a test basis, of evidence relevant to the amounts and disclosures in the financial statements. It also includes an assessment of the significant estimates and judgements made by the directors in the preparation of the financial statements, and of whether the accounting policies are appropriate to the company's circumstances, consistently applied and adequately disclosed.

We planned and performed our audit so as to obtain all the information and explanations which we considered necessary in order to provide us with sufficient evidence to give reasonable assurance that the financial statements are free from material misstatement, whether caused by fraud or other irregularity or error. However, the evidence available to us was limited because we were appointed auditors on .... and for the year to .... the financial statements of the company were not audited as the company was exempt from the audit requirement as a very small company within the meaning of [section ..... of the Companies Act 1985 / Regulation ..... of the .... Regulations ....]. Because of this we were unable to carry out auditing procedures necessary to obtain adequate assurance regarding the amounts and descriptions of items appearing in the balance sheet at .... Any adjustment to those figures may have a consequential effect on the [profit / loss] for the year to ....

In forming our opinion we also evaluated the overall adequacy of the presentation of information in the financial statements.

Qualified opinion arising from limitation in audit scope

In our opinion the financial statements give a true and fair view of the state of the company's affairs as at .... and, except for any adjustments that might have been found to be necessary had we been able to obtain sufficient evidence concerning the balance sheet as at .... , of its [profit / loss] for the year then ended and have been properly prepared in accordance with the Companies Act 1985.

In respect alone of the limitation on our work relating to the balance sheet as at ....:

- we have not obtained all the information and explanations which we considered necessary for the purposes of our audit; and
- we were unable to determine whether proper accounting records had been kept.

2.10.5 Companies in Ireland

This subsection deals briefly with auditors' reports on companies in both geographical parts of Ireland.

Northern Ireland is not part of Great Britain, but is part of the United Kingdom. The Companies Act 1985 does not generally extend to Northern Ireland [s 745]. Northern Ireland has its own legislation governing companies and auditors, the provisions of which are very similar to GB law.

The Republic of Ireland is not part of the United Kingdom. Guidance on audit reports in the Republic of Ireland is included in Auditing Standards because the Institute of Chartered Accountants in Ireland is a member of CCAB Limited, which controls the Auditing Practices Board. While many Auditing Standards provide a framework that is common to the UK and the Republic of Ireland, audit reports are heavily dependent on the requirements of legislation.

2.10.5.1 Northern Ireland

Until there is a consolidation, the relevant legislation for Northern Ireland is the Companies (Northern Ireland) Order 1986 as amended. The legislation cited below may be obtained from HMSO Bookshop, 16 Arthur Street, Belfast, BT1 4GD (0232 233451). HMSO will identify all relevant Statutory Rules of Northern Ireland and supply them. In April 1994, the necessary documents they would have supplied were:

- Companies (Northern Ireland) Order 1986 (£18.50)
- Companies (Northern Ireland) Order 1989 (£4.50)
- Companies (Northern Ireland) Order 1990 (£9.60)
- Companies (No. 2) (Northern Ireland) Order 1990 (£11.40)
- Companies (1986 Order) (Amendment of Articles 258 and 259) Regulations (Northern Ireland) 1993 (£1.00)
- Companies (1990 Order) (Commencement No. 5) Order (Northern Ireland) 1994 (£1.10).

The Companies (Northern Ireland) Order 1986 as amended contains provisions similar to those in the Companies Act 1985. The following are the main references relevant to auditors' reports on accounts.

Companies Act 1985	**Northern Ireland Order**
Section 235 — reporting	Article 243
Section 236 — signing	Article 244
Section 237 — specific matters	Article 245

Amendments to the wording of the standard report are few and restricted to the opinion as shown below.

Report 229
STD: Northern Ireland company

Opinion

In our opinion the financial statements give a true and fair view of the state of the company's affairs as at .... and of its [profit / loss] for the year then ended and

> have been properly prepared in accordance with the Companies (Northern Ireland) Order 1986.

2.10.5.2 Republic of Ireland

Company legislation in the Republic of Ireland has lagged behind that in the United Kingdom in implementing EC Directives. The Companies Acts 1963 to 1990 have been followed by EC Regulations such as the European Communities (Companies: Group Accounts) Regulations 1992.

The provisions relating to specific matters to be referred to in a report are complex and not within the scope of this book. The Auditing Guideline 'Reports by auditors under company legislation in the Republic of Ireland' that was issued in June 1989 is now out of date. The Institute of Chartered Accountants in Ireland is working with the APB on a revision that is likely to be issued as non-mandatory guidance (a Practice Note).

Amendments to the wording of the standard report are restricted to the opinion, which includes explicit material dealt with only by exception in GB.

Report 230
STD: Republic of Ireland company

Opinion

> In our opinion the financial statements give a true and fair view of the state of the company's affairs as at .... and of its [profit / loss] for the year then ended and have been properly prepared in accordance with the Companies Acts 1963 to 1990.
>
> We have obtained all the information and explanations we consider necessary for the purposes of our audit. In our opinion, proper books of account have been kept by the company. The financial statements are in agreement with the books of account.
>
> In our opinion, the information given in the directors' report on pages ..... to ..... is consistent with the financial statements.
>
> The net assets of the company, as stated in the balance sheet on page ....., are more than half of the amount of its called up share capital and, in our opinion, on that basis there did not exist at .... a financial situation which, under section 40(1) of the Companies (Amendment) Act 1983, would require the convening of an extraordinary general meeting of the company.

The paragraphing of this opinion is odd. It may have seemed reasonable to give each opinion or statement its own paragraph but the drafter obviously felt that some matters that could be dealt with in a line or two did not merit a paragraph to themselves.

If the auditors are based in GB they may wish to follow a suggestion in the Auditing Guideline 'Reports by auditors under company legislation in the Republic of Ireland' and add the words 'in the Republic of Ireland' after the two references to legislation. This may be appropriate where the accounts are used in the Republic of Ireland and in GB.

2.10.6 And finally

This section does not deal with some matters that might have featured in this book had size and time constraints been fewer. Two matters that ought perhaps to be mentioned in passing are:

- reporting in Welsh
- reporting on accounts in ECUs.

It is possible for auditors to report in Welsh in appropriate circumstances. An example report is not given in this book because auditors reporting in Welsh ought to be fluent in the language and so capable of writing their own standard report.

Reporting on accounts in ECUs is likely to be a very rare event. Auditors asked to do so need to be aware that such a report is, despite any initial thoughts to the contrary, extremely difficult in practice and that appropriate expert advice should be sought.

2.11 Other entities

2.11.1 Introduction

This section deals with standard reports for entities other than companies. The approach taken is to explain how a report for a company may be adapted to another entity. This is first done generically, then the approach is illustrated using a pension scheme as an example.

2.11.2 The requirements

SAS 600 applies to all reports issued by auditors that express an opinion in terms of whether financial statements give a true and fair view, or where statutory or other specific requirements prescribe the use of a term such as 'presents fairly' or 'properly prepared in accordance with'.

Auditors draft each section of their report on financial statements to reflect the requirements that apply to the particular audit engagement. However, the use of common language in auditors' reports assists the reader's understanding. This common language may be used for other entities, not just companies. In other words, the report on another entity will look similar to that on a company.

2.11.3 Aspects of a standard report common to many entities

The report below shows the wording of a standard report for a company. Aspects that need not change are shown in normal type. Aspects that may change for another entity are shown in *italic type*.

Report 231
STD: Generic for other entities

AUDITORS' REPORT TO THE *SHAREHOLDERS* OF ....

We have audited the financial statements on pages ..... to ..... which have been prepared under the historical cost convention [as modified by the revaluation of certain fixed assets] and the accounting policies set out on page ..... .

Respective responsibilities of *directors* and auditors

As described on page ..... the *company's directors* are responsible for the preparation of financial statements. It is our responsibility to form an independent opinion, based on our audit, of those statements and to report our opinion to you.

Basis of opinion

We conducted our audit in accordance with *Auditing Standards issued by the Auditing Practices Board.* An audit includes examination, on a test basis, of evidence relevant to the amounts and disclosures in the financial statements. It also includes an assessment of the significant estimates and judgements made by the *directors* in the preparation of the financial statements, and of whether the accounting policies are appropriate to the *company's* circumstances, consistently applied and adequately disclosed.

We planned and performed our audit so as to obtain all the information and explanations which we considered necessary in order to provide us with sufficient evidence to give reasonable assurance that the financial statements are free from material misstatement, whether caused by fraud or other irregularity or error. In forming our opinion we also evaluated the overall adequacy of the presentation of information in the financial statements.

Opinion

In our opinion *the financial statements give a true and fair view of the state of the company's affairs as at .... and of its [profit / loss] for the year then ended and have been properly prepared in accordance with the Companies Act 1985.*

Registered Auditors Address
Date

The main areas of change are the opinion and a statement that is only referred to in the standard report, namely the statement of directors' responsibilities. The above report does not make any change to the mention of 'information and explanations' in the basis of opinion section. Although the words owe their origin to section 237 of the Companies Act 1985, the need for such a statement remains.

The next subsections deal with aspects of the standard report that may change for other entities:

- addressees
- what to call the 'directors'
- directors' responsibilities
- auditing standards
- opinion.

2.11.4 Addressees

2.11.4.1 The requirements

The explanatory material to SAS 600.2 explains that an auditors' report on financial statements of entities other than companies should be addressed to the appropriate person or persons, as defined by statute or by the terms of the individual engagement.

2.11.4.2 Deciding on addressees

For some entities deciding on the addressees of a report is easy because it is laid down in the relevant legislation. Unfortunately this is not always the case. Legal requirements for auditors' reports are often not specific as to the addressees. As an example, SI 1992 No. 2165 The Charities Accounts (Scotland) Regulations 1992 calls for a report on a recognised body in the following terms:

> 7(5) The report of an auditor which shall be annexed to the balance sheet and income and expenditure account shall state: . . .

One possible way out of this problem would be for auditors to avoid choosing addressees and title their report as follows:

AUDITORS' REPORT

That approach is not allowed as it would breach SAS 600.2.

In such circumstances, auditors have to choose an appropriate person or persons as addressees. The choice mainly narrows down to the following categories of addressees:

- the entity
- the members (or beneficiaries) of the entity
- the 'directors' of the entity.

Unless the addressees are stipulated in an entity's own constitution, rules or regulations, auditors may consult the 'directors' to agree suitable addressees.

Because auditors are inherently examining the conduct of the 'directors' it makes little sense for their report to be addressed to those people. This is highlighted by SAS 600.3 which would require the auditors to report to the 'directors' that the 'directors' were responsible for the financial statements. For this reason, in the absence of a requirement, this book recommends addressing the report to the entity.

2.11.5 What to call the 'directors'

Directors are defined in SAS 600 as being *'the directors of a company, the partners, proprietors or trustees of other forms of enterprise or equivalent persons responsible for the reporting entity's affairs, including the preparation of its financial statements'.*

Auditors refer to appropriate legislation or the entity's governing requirements (such as a trust deed) to discover the appropriate term. As the requirement to refer to the responsibilities of the directors was not known before SAS 600, auditors have no precedent to assist them in the first year of operation of the Auditing Standard. Although difficulties should be few, auditors need to keep in mind the possibility that the responsibilities may not be what they seem. For example, a charity whose management is carried out by 'the management committee' may be constituted in such a way that the responsibility for the charity's affairs, including the preparation of its financial statements, actually extends to all committee members; not just those on the management committee.

2.11.6 Directors' responsibilities

2.11.6.1 Companies

The analysis of statements concerning the respective responsibilities of directors and auditors in section 2.5 'Elements and options' of this chapter (subsection 2.5.7) occupy nearly twenty pages. In that subsection, the conclusion is reached that (with certain caveats) for a description to be normally considered adequate it should comply with the following scheme of necessary disclosures:

- basic legal framework
- periods of account (but not balance sheet date)
- requirement to give a true and fair view
- accounting policy selection (reasonable and consistent)
- prudent yet objective ('reasonable') assessments ('judgements and estimates')
- any specific disclosures of adherence to accounting standards
- going concern presumption
- keeping proper accounting records
- safeguarding assets (and preventing fraud etc.).

2.11.6.2 Adaptation to other entities

Adapting this scheme to other entities can be done in two ways. The first way is to decide to take only requirements that are embodied in the legislation or regulations for the entity. The second way is to present a free adaptation allowing the 'directors' to explain their responsibilities more fully.

The ICAEW guidance relevant to pension schemes (see later in this section) favours the former approach, but for some entities the requirements would be remarkably few if that approach was taken. For example, the auditors of an unincorporated association that decides to have an audit would have the following description of responsibilities of 'directors' to consider for adequacy:

This description (i.e. none at all) does not even merit a heading.

The alternative approach is to word the description on more helpful lines without implying that the 'directors' are being forced to do something:

STATEMENT OF DIRECTORS' RESPONSIBILITIES

> The directors prepare financial statements for each financial year which give a true and fair view of the state of affairs of the entity and of the [income and expenditure / surplus / etc.] of the entity for that period. In order that a true and fair view may be given, the directors are required to:
>
> - select suitable accounting policies and then apply them consistently
>
> - make judgements and estimates that are reasonable and prudent

> - prepare the financial statements on the going concern basis unless it is inappropriate to presume that the entity will continue in business
>
> To facilitate the preparation of the financial statements, the directors are responsible for keeping proper accounting records which disclose with reasonable accuracy at any time the financial position of the entity. They are also responsible under common law for safeguarding the assets of the entity and hence for taking reasonable steps for the prevention and detection of fraud and other irregularities.

The above probably represents the other end of the spectrum of possible descriptions. In particular the mention of 'common law' and the degree of emphasis given to the going concern basis could be criticised. The statement does not include further specific requirements that could affect certain entities. The statement is not, therefore, presented as a report in the normal sequence in this book.

Auditors should discuss and agree the description of responsibilities with the directors. If the directors do not wish to go further than their legal responsibilities it is difficult for auditors to criticise that approach. Conversely, auditors should not seek to discourage an open and informative description if that is what the directors want.

2.11.6.3 Pension schemes

The full report on a pension scheme is discussed in subsection 2.11.9 below. This subsection examines the possible text of a description of the responsibilities of the trustees of a scheme.

The ICAEW issued FRAG 22/93 'Occupational Pension Schemes and Other Trusts Statement of Trustees' Responsibilities' in October 1993. The FRAG makes the following points:

- the statutory requirement for pension schemes is contained in section 7 of the Occupational Pension Schemes (Disclosure of Information) Regulations 1986:
  - — the trustees 'shall obtain as soon as reasonably practical and, in any event not more than one year after the end of the scheme year audited accounts for that scheme year'
  - — the trustees are also required to make the accounts and other information available to certain parties such as members
- the specific requirement to prepare accounts and make the judgements associated with their preparation is not applicable to trustees under statute law
- under common law trustees are required to account to scheme members on their stewardship of the trust assets but there is no required format for such reporting
- the trust deed of a particular scheme may lay specific duties on trustees
- the wording of any note on trustees' responsibilities will need to take account of the particular circumstances of each trust
- it may be appropriate to take legal advice.

The ICAEW view, therefore, tends towards a minimalist disclosure.

It is early days for many others to have published differing views. In technical bulletin No. 76 (August 1993) Robson Rhodes published a suggested wording for the statement of pension scheme trustees' responsibilities. They took the view that such a report should be as follows:

STATEMENT OF TRUSTEES' RESPONSIBILITIES

> The Occupational Pension Schemes (Disclosure of Information) Regulations 1986 require the trustees to prepare financial statements for each financial year which give a true and fair view of the financial transactions of the scheme and the disposition of the assets and liabilities of the scheme at the year end. In preparing the financial statements the trustees have:
>
> - selected suitable accounting policies and then applied them consistently;
> - made judgements and estimates that are reasonable and prudent; and
> - followed SORP 1 and applicable accounting standards.
>
> The trustees are responsible for keeping proper accounting records which disclose with reasonable accuracy at any time the financial position of the scheme to enable them to ensure that the financial statements comply with the Regulations. They are also responsible for safeguarding the assets of the scheme and hence for taking reasonable steps for the prevention and detection of error, fraud and other irregularities.

This description is more in keeping with the spirit of SAS 600 and includes a helpful reference to SORP 1.

2.11.7 Auditing standards

The standard report refers to conducting the audit in accordance with *'Auditing Standards issued by the Auditing Practices Board'*. This will continue to be appropriate wording for reports on many entities as Auditing Standards apply to any audit (defined by the APB as *'an examination of and expression of opinion on financial information by an external auditor'*).

In some circumstances, auditors are required by statute to follow other comparable standards, such as the Code of Audit Practice for Local Authorities and the National Health Service in England and Wales or the requirements of the Scottish Accounts Commission. If so, the wording of the report is changed so that the relevant standards replace those of the APB.

2.11.8 Opinion

The opinion will normally refer to the true and fair view (or equivalent) and the relevant legislation. A problem can arise, however, if auditors are not required to report on whether the accounts give a true and fair view. If a true and fair view is not given because of special circumstances (which require or permit the adoption of policies or accounting bases that are incompatible with a true and fair view) this should be made clear.

The matter may be included in a separate statement given by the directors. If it is not, paragraph 28 of SAS 600 suggests that auditors can refer to the circumstances in the respective responsibilities of directors and auditors section, or in the basis of opinion section of their report.

2.11.9 A standard auditors' report for a pension scheme

This section uses a pension scheme as an example of a entity for which auditors may develop a standard report.

The legal requirements relevant to the report are contained in paragraph 7(5) of the Occupational Pension Schemes (Disclosure of Information) Regulations 1986 (SI 1986 No. 1046) as amended.[23]

The auditor's report shall include:

(a) a statement whether or not in his opinion the requirements of paragraph (4)(a) are satisfied;
(b) a statement whether or not in his opinion contributions payable to the scheme during the scheme year have been paid in accordance with the scheme rules or contracts under which they were payable, and with the recommendation of the actuary, if appropriate; and
(c) if the statement under sub-paragraph (a) or (b) or both is negative or qualified, a statement of the reasons.

The requirements of paragraph (4)(a) are that the accounts shall:

(i) contain the information specified in Schedule 3 (so however that any such information which is immaterial for the purposes of head (ii) below may be omitted), and
(ii) show a true and fair view of the financial transactions of the scheme during the scheme year and of the disposition, at the end of the scheme year, of the assets, not including [insurance policies which are specifically allocated to the provision of benefits for, and which provide all the benefits payable under the Scheme to, particular members or other persons in respect of particular members or both], and liabilities, other than liabilities to pay pensions and benefits after the end of the scheme year.

---

[23] The most recent amendment was effected by SI 1994 No. 1062 The Occupational and Personal Pension Schemes (Consequential Amendments) Regulations 1994, which came into force on 12 May 1994. The Regulations made under the Pension Schemes Act 1993 substitue references to repealed legislation. There are no alterations of substance.

The relevant professional requirements are contained in the Auditing Standard 102 'The Audit Report' as interpreted by Auditing Guideline 306 'Pension schemes in the United Kingdom. That Guideline gives an example report on a scheme as follows:

AUDITORS' REPORT TO THE TRUSTEES AND MEMBERS OF ....

> We have audited the accounts on pages ..... to ..... in accordance with approved Auditing Standards.
>
> In our opinion the accounts give a true and fair view of the financial transactions of the scheme during the year ended ..... and of the disposition at that date of its assets and liabilities and contain the information specified in Regulation 7 of and Schedule 3 to the Occupational Pension Schemes (Disclosure of Information) Regulations 1986.
>
> In our opinion the contributions payable to the scheme during the year ended ..... have been paid in accordance with the scheme rules and with the recommendation of the actuary.

The Guideline was issued in November 1988 whereas the Auditing Standard was revised in March 1989. That revision removed the need to refer to 'approved' Auditing Standards. The Guideline's example report is arguably flawed because it does not refer directly to the matters legally required.

An example of a modern auditors' report given in the authoritative Butterworths book *Accounts and Audit of Pension Schemes* (2nd edition) is:

AUDITORS' REPORT TO THE TRUSTEES OF THE TRAMP PENSION SCHEME

> We have audited the financial statements on pages x to x in accordance with Auditing Standards.
>
> In our opinion the financial statements show a true and fair view of the disposition of the net assets of the Scheme at 31st December 1992 and of its transactions and cash flows for the year then ended and comply with the requirements of Regulation 7 paragraph 4(a) of the Occupational Pension Schemes (Disclosure of Information) Regulations 1986.
>
> In our opinion the contributions payable to the scheme during the year have been paid in accordance with the scheme rules and with the recommendation of the actuary.

There is no statutory or professional body monitoring auditors' reports on pension schemes. Neither are there definitive requirements directly affecting the detailed wording of such reports. There is no right or wrong wording for a pension scheme auditors' report so long as the legislation and Auditing Standard are complied with.

2.11.9.2 Addressees and 'directors'

The auditors' report should be addressed in accordance with the trust deed. Where the deed is silent, the report should be addressed to the trustees and members. This approach was recommended by the Auditing Guideline.

The 'directors' should normally be called the 'trustees' unless the trust deed uses some other description.

2.11.9.3 Trustees' responsibilities

The trustees' description of their responsibilities was discussed in subsection 2.11.6.3 above.

2.11.9.4 Auditing standards and opinion

The audit of a pension scheme is carried out under ordinary Auditing Standards. The opinion refers to the relevant requirements of SI 1986 No. 1046 as shown at the start of this subsection.

2.11.9.5 A model SAS 600 report for a pension scheme

Report 232
STD: Model, pension scheme

AUDITORS' REPORT TO THE TRUSTEES AND MEMBERS OF ....

We have audited the financial statements on pages ..... to ..... which have been prepared under the historical cost convention [as modified by the revaluation of certain fixed assets] [and] [as modified by the carrying of investments at market value] and the accounting policies set out on page ..... .

Respective responsibilities of trustees and auditors

As described [on page ..... / in the trustees' report] the trustees are responsible for the preparation of financial statements. It is our responsibility to form an independent opinion, based on our audit, on those statements and to report our opinion to you.

Basis of opinion

We conducted our audit in accordance with Auditing Standards issued by the Auditing Practices Board. An audit includes examination, on a test basis, of evidence relevant to the amounts and disclosures in the financial statements. It also includes an assessment of the significant estimates and judgements made by the trustees in the preparation of the financial statements, and of whether the accounting policies are appropriate to the scheme's circumstances, consistently applied and adequately disclosed.

We planned and performed our audit so as to obtain all the information and explanations which we considered necessary in order to provide us with sufficient evidence to give reasonable assurance that the financial statements are free from material misstatement, whether caused by fraud or other irregularity or error. In forming our opinion we also evaluated the overall adequacy of the presentation of information in the financial statements.

Opinion

In our opinion the financial statements give a true and fair view of the financial transactions of the scheme during the year ended .... and of the disposition at that date of its assets and liabilities and contain the information specified in Regulation 7 of and Schedule 3 to the Occupational Pension Schemes (Disclosure of Information) Regulations 1986.

In our opinion the contributions payable to the scheme during the year ended .... have been paid in accordance with the scheme rules and with the recommendation of the actuary.

Statement of Recommended Practice 1 'Pension Scheme Accounts' requires the carrying amount of investments to be their market value at the balance sheet date. The reference to this may be expanded in the report.

2.11.10 Professional guidance

2.11.10.1 Auditing Practices Board

At the time of writing, the APB had decided to start a project to prepare a Practice Note giving guidance on the application of SAS 600 to entities other than companies registered under the Companies Act 1985. The Practice Note is likely to cover wording in the areas of:

- statements of responsibilities of directors or equivalent persons
- statements of auditors' responsibilities
- basis of opinion sections[24].

Example reports should be included for the following entities:

- building societies
- charities (which may be affected by the timing of issue of draft regulations on the content and audit of charities' financial statements to be issued by the Home Office, once expected in the last quarter of 1993)
- friendly societies
- housing associations
- partnerships
- pension schemes (guidance in the context of present legislation, i.e. before any implementation of the Goode Report's recommendations)
- public sector bodies, such as local authorities and health authorities
- sole traders
- unit trusts.

[24] The APB agenda paper considered at their October 1993 meeting did not state that guidance would be given on 'opinion sections' but these too ought to be in the eventual Practice Note.

2.11.10.2 ICAEW

In late October 1993 the ICAEW issued guidance on the statement of trustees' responsibilities for occupational pension schemes and other trusts. FRAG 22/93 is a very brief document. Its purpose seems to be to alert auditors to the fact that they should not use the responsibilities of company directors for trusts. This strikes the writer of this book as an insult to the intelligence of auditors.

The document contains no example wordings and merely warns auditors to take account of the particular circumstances of each trust and consider taking legal advice. An opportunity was lost, therefore, to achieve a consensus on wording of trustees' responsibilities that would be acceptable for the generality of pension schemes.

2.12 Signing and dating

2.12.1 Introduction

SAS 600 included a requirement that changed existing guidance on other information issued with audited financial statements (Auditing Guideline 411). The requirement generated a fair amount of heat (for example an exchange of letters between the ICAEW and the APB) because many auditors considered that it also imposed impossible timing constraints on approving the accounts and signing their report. In fact, the requirement was not really new, the SAS just brought it to the fore.

2.12.2 The requirements

The relevant requirements are found in SAS 600, the law, and SSAP 17 'Accounting for Post Balance Sheet Events'.

2.12.2.1 SAS 600.9

Auditors should not express an opinion on financial statements until those statements and all other financial information contained in a report of which the audited financial statements form a part have been approved by the directors, and the auditors have considered all necessary available evidence.

The date of an auditors' report on a reporting entity's financial statements is the date which the auditors signed their report expressing an opinion on those statements.

2.12.2.2 Companies Act 1985

Section 233 requires a company's annual accounts to be approved by the board of directors and signed on behalf of the board (on the company's balance sheet) by a director of the company. Every copy of the balance sheet which is laid before the company in general meeting, or which is otherwise circulated, published or issued, is required to state the name of the person who signed the balance sheet on behalf of the board.

Section 236 (which is dealt with in detail in section 2.2 'Statutory requirements' of this chapter) requires the auditors' report to state the names of the auditors and be signed by them.

2.12.2.3 SSAP 17

The date on which the financial statements are approved by the board of directors should be disclosed in the financial statements [paragraph 26].

2.12.3 Analysis

Ideally, the accounts are approved by the directors and the auditors sign their report on the same day having completed all audit procedures.

The problem foreseen by auditors was that they would not be able to sign their report when the accounts were approved and would be forced to:

- sign at a later date, increasing their possible liability
- perform further procedures including updating representations from the directors that they would still have approved the accounts at that later date.

The delay could arise through:

- lack of organisation of smaller clients
- postal delays (not all clients have faxes)
- difficulty of co-ordinating the approval of accounts of companies in large groups.

These are practical problems that must be overcome. In this context it is worth considering:

- what the accounts are
- the significance of signing by the directors
- the effect on the auditors' report.

2.12.3.1 The accounts

The accounts approved by the directors may be in the form of final drafts. So long as the auditors are able to assess the overall accounts presentation. There should be no significant matter remaining undecided or unaudited.

There is no need for auditors to have the exact copy approved by the directors in their possession before signing. So long as they have sufficient evidence that the directors have approved the accounts the auditors' report may be signed.

Obviously a copy of the accounts duly signed by the directors is good evidence, especially if handed to the auditors during the board meeting. Auditors may be prepared to accept other evidence depending on their evaluation of risk. This could include faxed or oral representation.

2.12.3.2 Signing by the directors

The approval of the accounts is a separate matter from their signing by the directors though the two often go together. The provisions of the Companies Act 1985 relating to the directors' signing are contrasted with those for the auditors' signing their report. Auditors do not approve their own report, they merely sign it.

It is, therefore, not necessary for auditors to have the signed accounts before signing their own report.

2.12.3.3 The effect on the auditors' report

If auditors sign their report after the accounts are approved the obvious effect is that its date no longer agrees to that of the accounts (and possibly the directors' report or other material unless that was the reason for the delay in signing the auditors' report). Auditors may simply accept this and make no further modification to their report (the date is part of their report). If auditors wish to make some comment in their report they may do so but the modification is outside the scope of SAS 600. Such matters are dealt with in detail in chapter 3 'Modified Reports'.

2.12.4 Related Auditing Standards

2.12.4.1 Post balance sheet events

The date that the auditors sign their report is the key date for post balance sheet events. The proposed SAS 150 'Subsequent events' does not refer to the date of approval of the financial statements. It proposes responsibilities for auditors to perform procedures to provide evidence that material subsequent events have been properly accounted for up to the date of the auditors' report.

2.12.4.2 Other information

The proposed SAS 160 'Other information in documents containing audited financial statements' is destined to replace the Auditing Guideline 'Financial information issued with audited financial statements'. The new SAS will not deal with circumstances where information is not made available until after the date of the auditors' report. This is because of the requirement in SAS 600.9 dealt with above. SAS 600 superseded the paragraphs in the Auditing Guideline that dealt with dating.

2.13 What if I got it wrong?

2.13.1 Introduction

The auditors' nightmare is the audit report that is wrong. Obviously **some** reports will be wrong, but that is just the penalty society pays for limiting the audit to what is economically justifiable to add value to the financial information.

This section is not really concerned with the undiscovered error, even if it is eventually discovered when the client fails, is taken over, or hits one of the many trigger points for a statement of claim to land in the office letterbox.

The only wrong reports that auditors can do something about are those discovered by the auditors after they have signed their report, but before the next accounts are issued.

2.13.2 The requirements

There used to be no statutory recognition of the fact that accounts could be wrong. If an error was discovered, the accounts could be amended and refiled at Companies House. This is still the case for incorrect auditors' reports.

The Companies Act 1989 introduced provisions allowing the directors to revise the accounts and directors' report. Perhaps more importantly it also provided for compulsory revision if ordered by the court. There are Regulations[25] governing voluntary revision but if the court orders a revision, the court decides on the form of revision and associated matters. At the time of writing, there had been no applications to the court, and the material below assumes that revisions, if any, are voluntary.

The Auditing Guideline 'Events after the balance sheet date' predates the defective accounts provisions. It contains extensive guidance on dating of the report and on the responsibilities of the auditors towards events after the balance sheet date. Its dating provisions have been superseded by SAS 600 as discussed elsewhere in this chapter. The proposed SAS 150 'Subsequent events' will replace the Guideline in due course.

The Auditing Practices Committee issued an exposure draft of an Auditing Guideline dealing with 'Auditors' reports on revised annual accounts and directors' reports'. The document was issued in May 1991 only four months after the regulations came into force. Although it includes some guidance on auditors' responsibilities towards events after the balance sheet date, it is mainly concerned with the opinion required on revised accounts.

---

[25] SI 1990 No. 2570 The Companies (Revision of Defective Accounts and Reports) Regulations 1990.

2.13.3 Action

After auditors sign their report the accounts may pass through the following stages:

- finalised
- issued to shareholders
- laid at the AGM and available to other parties (i.e. filed at Companies House)

This list does not extend to the use of the figures in the accounts as comparatives (or 'corresponding amounts') in the next annual accounts, as it is more realistic to treat that as a problem of the next year's audit.

2.13.3.1 Before the accounts are issued

If an auditors' report is discovered to be incorrect before it is issued with the accounts (either because the accounts are discovered to be incorrect or the report itself contains an error) the auditors should withdraw their report and issue a corrected report. In other words, refinalise their audit. The eventual corrected report need not (but may) mention those circumstances.

If the directors issue the original report auditors should take steps to prevent reliance on it. Such action is outside the scope of this book and should not be undertaken without appropriate legal advice.

2.13.3.2 After the accounts are issued

If, once they have been issued, the accounts are discovered to be incorrect the directors may wish to prepare revised accounts or to issue a supplementary note dealing with an isolated matter. In such circumstances the defective accounts regulations are relevant.

Auditors cannot control the distribution of a revised auditors report if the directors do not want to revise the accounts. The possible courses of action for auditors are:

- making a statement at the AGM
- resigning in order to make use of the right to communicate with the members or creditors in writing.

Such action is outside the scope of this book and should not be undertaken without appropriate legal advice.

2.14 Keeping quiet

2.14.1 Introduction

This section deals with two circumstances that might, except for professional guidance, lead to modified auditors' reports: reliance on other auditors and experts. In some cases, custom in other countries, or in the UK in earlier years, has perhaps prompted auditors to mention certain things in their reports that are not now necessary. The matters discussed in this section are normally properly omitted from a report. The underlying circumstances ought, nevertheless, to be considered for possible effects on reporting or other aspects of an audit. For example, if other firms audit a significant part of the assets and profits of a group, some would question whether the risk of acting as group auditors is adequately rewarded.

2.14.2 Other auditors

In the US it is possible to refer to other auditors. If the auditors are satisfied with the other auditors' work (perhaps done by an international associate firm) they may make no reference. If the auditors are unable to carry out work to become satisfied with the work of the other auditors they may refer to the work of the other auditors in their report. However, the auditors may decide to refer to the work of the other auditors simply because those auditors are responsible for a significant part of the audit.

In the US auditors are required to be specific in their report about the division of responsibilities. They must disclose the magnitude of the portion of the accounts audited by other firms.

The relevant international Auditing Standard (ISAS 5 'Using the Work of Another Auditor' and its proposed revision) allows reports to include reference to reliance on the work of other auditors where that is permitted in the country concerned.

Both the above Standards were issued before the UK professional material. In the early 1980s, perhaps as a result of developments outside the UK, some auditors had taken to mentioning reliance on the work of other auditors. The APC Auditing Guideline 'Group financial statements — reliance on the work of other auditors', which was issued in the middle of the 1980s, took the stance that the principal auditors could not delegate any responsibility for their opinion and that readers might be misled by any reference in their report to the other auditors. The guideline took a visionary approach to the disclosure of the fact that material secondary companies were audited by other auditors. It suggested that an indication of that fact might be given in the notes to the accounts.

Now that we have the 1993 version of the Audit Reports SAS we are perhaps better placed to interpret the word 'indication'. The circumstances are still unusual. Instead of the accounts disclosing uncertainty, they are also asked to disclose what might otherwise be mentioned in the auditors' report. This imposition of disclosure standards by a body other than an accounting standard setting one seems destined to continue.

Proposed SAS 510 'The relationship between principal auditors and other auditors' contains the following relevant explanatory paragraphs:

> 23. When the principal auditors are satisfied that the work of the other auditors is adequate for the purposes of their audit, no reference to the other auditors is required in the principal auditor's report.
>
> 24. The principal auditors have sole responsibility for their audit opinion and a reference to the other auditors in the principal auditors' report may be misunderstood and interpreted as a qualification of their opinion or a division of responsibility, neither of which is appropriate.

The proposed SAS is likely to change before it is issued in final form (if only to remove the reference to *'an emphasis of matter'* in paragraph 26!), but the above principals should remain. Auditors may still choose to refer to other auditors. The practical approach for the principal auditors is, however, to keep quiet about other auditors unless repeating a modification on a material subsidiary or where the other auditors cause a scope limitation.

2.14.3 Reliance on experts

The APC Auditing Guideline 'Reliance on other specialists' was issued in May 1986, at about the same time as the Guideline dealing with reliance on other auditors. Not surprisingly it took the same line. Auditors were not to mention in their report any specialist relied upon because such a reference might be misunderstood (as a qualification or a division of responsibilities).

International Auditing Standard 18 'Using the Work of an Expert' had been issued slightly more than a year earlier. Its contents were remarkably similar to the eventual UK Guideline. It too did not support reference to an expert in an unqualified opinion.

The US professional standards had taken the same stance for over a decade. So, why were specialists ever mentioned in standard reports?

It is difficult to separate cause and effect but the APC Auditing Guideline 'Audit report examples', which was issued in 1980, contained an example report for small businesses (that became known as the 'Example 6 report'). That report referred to accepting assurances from the directors. Such a reference is not far from wording such as *'stock has been valued by the directors'* or *'we have accepted a stock valuation provided by independent stocktakers'*.

Proposed SAS 520 'Using the work of an expert' contains the following explanatory paragraph:

> 23. When the auditors are satisfied that the work of an expert provides appropriate audit evidence, reference is not required to the work of the expert in the audit report. Such a reference may be misunderstood and interpreted as a qualification of the auditors' opinion or a division of responsibility, neither of which is appropriate.

It would seem therefore that the current and future positions are clear; whatever the temptations of the past, it is not acceptable to refer to experts (or other specialists) in the auditors' report. In practice, this must be the recommended approach for auditors.

There is, however, a problem with the position taken by proposed SAS 520. The risk of a misunderstanding, such that a reference to the work of an expert might be interpreted as a qualification of the auditors' opinion or a division of responsibility, is surely very low if a SAS 600 auditors' report is properly drafted. Indeed, the basis of opinion section of the report would arguably benefit from the inclusion of suitable explanation (as allowed by paragraph 29 of SAS 600) in appropriate circumstances. Where accounts include substantial property valuations or brand valuations, readers of the auditors' report may appreciate an explanation of the valuer's and auditors' roles. The directors may also wish to consider disclosing (in the accounts or their responsibilities statement) the way that they have used the expert.

3 MODIFIED REPORTS

3.1 Introduction

Any auditors' report that is not a standard auditors' report is a modified one. Modified auditors' reports can include an opinion that is qualified or unqualified. This chapter deals mainly with single modifications.

This chapter:

- gives an overview of the way that SAS 600 attempts to codify auditors' reports
- investigates the prescribed alternatives [SAS 600.6 to 600.8] and some modifications that the SAS does not address
- gives guidance on the first decision: whether to modify and what form of modification [SAS 600.5]
- provides extensive help on writing an effective modification
- briefly considers the consequences of a qualified report and circumstances where reporting is prevented.

Chapter 4 'Multiple Modifications' explores combining modifications to form complex reports and chapter 5 'Illustrative Modifications' provides a large number of examples of modifications.

The structure of this chapter is such that it can be read from front to back. It is, however, primarily designed to be dipped into as required. To make this sort of access easier, the text mainly gives the whole of the information for a particular type of modification in one place. This is not exactly logical for the linear reader, who will have to skip material to avoid getting drawn too deeply into interesting byways.

3.2 Types of modification

The following circumstances can result in a modification:

- a restriction on the scope of the audit
- a disagreement with the accounting treatment or disclosure of a matter in the accounts
- the need to draw attention to a fundamental inherent uncertainty in order to ensure that users appreciate fully the context in which the opinion was formed
- a deficiency in a matter that requires the auditors to report if certain specific statutory requirements are not met (e.g. failure to keep proper accounting records)
- an inadequate statement, in the accounts or accompanying information, of the responsibilities of the directors
- a need to include a matter not within the scope of SAS 600.

The first two circumstances result in a modification that is a qualified opinion. A qualified opinion is significant because it can affect a company's ability to make a distribution or to convert to a public limited company.

The following sections discuss each of the above types of modified report in turn. Some sections are divided into subsections where there is more than one report that could be required within a category. These sections or subsections share a common format. They cover:

- statutory and professional requirements
- typical wording:
  - — a generic skeleton (or outline) of the modification
  - — a generic 'word picture' (describing each section of modified wording)
  - — a specific example
- analysis of the requirements (including further examples)
- links to other modifications
- typical circumstances.

To avoid complicating the discussions, modifications for group accounts have a section to themselves.

The typical wording for modifications and other illustrations given in this chapter do not reproduce material that would be the same as the standard report. Extracts concentrate on the changed headings and paragraphs.

Reports in this book, whether full or extract, are numbered for ease of reference and have a heading that indicates their type and nature. The headings use the following abbreviations:

1 Main abbreviations

STD standard report (mainly found in chapter 2 'The Standard Report')
SL scope limitation
D disagreement
FU fundamental uncertainty
— e except for opinion
— a adverse opinion
— d disclaimer of opinion.

2 Abbreviations for statutory requirements and other matters

I&E information and explanations
AR accounting records
BR branch returns
AARR agreement with accounting records and returns
DR directors' report not consistent with accounts
Sch 6 omission of disclosures required by Schedule 6
RofD responsibilities of directors
OTS outside the scope of SAS 600.

The following text conventions are used:

- a series of dots indicates that information should be filled in. Typical information is: the company's name, the pages referred to, and the balance sheet date
- plain text enclosed by square brackets [ ] should be included in appropriate circumstances
- two or more words in plain text separated by a slash and enclosed by square brackets [..... / .....] are alternative wordings. The most common example is [profit / loss].

In the skeletons and word pictures, modifications are indicated by THE USE OF SMALL CAPITALS and, in the skeletons, a new line indicates the start of a new paragraph.

3.3 Scope limitation

3.3.1 The requirements

Auditors are required by SAS 600.7 to modify their report when a limitation on the scope of their work occurs. That limitation must be significant enough to prevent them from obtaining sufficient evidence to express an unqualified opinion. The modification should include:

- a description of the factors leading to the limitation in the opinion section of their report
- a disclaimer of opinion when the possible effect of a limitation is so material or pervasive that they are unable to express an opinion on the financial statements
- a qualified opinion when the effect of the limitation is not so material or pervasive as to require a disclaimer, and the wording of opinion should indicate that it is qualified as to the possible adjustments to the financial statements that might have been determined to be necessary had the limitation not existed.

An unqualified opinion is one that does not include a disagreement with the treatment or disclosure of a matter in the accounts [SAS 600.8] or a scope limitation [SAS 600.7]. For example, an explanatory paragraph about a fundamental uncertainty does not constitute a qualified opinion.

The Companies Act 1985 recognises that a scope limitation may require a modification of the auditors' report even if the ability to express an unqualified opinion is not affected. This 'statutory scope limitation' is confined to two matters, both of which are to be judged in relation to the needs of the audit. These are dealt with in detail later in this chapter:

- absence of proper returns from branches not visited
- not obtaining all necessary information and explanations.

For example, auditors may not obtain all necessary information and explanations about directors' transactions. If the matter is not material it does not affect the true and fair view but auditors may not be able to include appropriate amounts in their report as required by section 237 of the Companies Act 1985.

3.3.2 Typical wording

There are two sets of three reports, giving illustrations of disclaimers as well as the more common except for opinions for scope limitations as defined by SAS 600.7.

The illustrative reports include wording for the common associated matters required by law: accounting records, and information and explanations. The wording for matters required by law is derived from the examples in appendix 2 to SAS 600 and is challenged in the later section of this chapter dealing with matters required by law. It should not be regarded as the preferred approach.

Report 300
SL — e: Generic skeleton

Basis of opinion

Compliance with Auditing Standards EXCEPT THAT SCOPE WAS LIMITED.

Description of an audit.

Evidence AND A DESCRIPTION OF LIMITATION.

Evaluation of presentation.

QUALIFIED OPINION ARISING FROM LIMITATION IN AUDIT SCOPE

EXCEPT FOR OPINION.

FURTHER MATTER REQUIRED BY LAW.

Report 301
SL — e: Generic word picture

Basis of opinion

We conducted our audit in accordance with Auditing Standards issued by the Auditing Practices Board, EXCEPT THAT THE SCOPE OF OUR WORK WAS LIMITED AS EXPLAINED BELOW.

An audit includes examination, on a test basis, of evidence relevant to the amounts and disclosures in the financial statements. It also includes an assessment of the significant estimates and judgements made by the directors in the preparation of the financial statements, and of whether the accounting policies are appropriate to the company's circumstances, consistently applied and adequately disclosed.

We planned and performed our audit so as to obtain all the information and explanations which we considered necessary in order to provide us with sufficient evidence to give reasonable assurance that the financial statements are free from material misstatement, whether caused by fraud or other irregularity or error. HOWEVER, THE EVIDENCE AVAILABLE TO US WAS LIMITED BECAUSE [MATTER]. THERE WAS NO SYSTEM OF CONTROL OVER [MATTER] ON WHICH WE COULD RELY FOR THE PURPOSES OF OUR AUDIT AND THERE WERE NO OTHER SATISFACTORY AUDIT PROCEDURES THAT WE COULD ADOPT TO CONFIRM THAT [ACCOUNTING FOR MATTER] WAS CORRECT.

In forming our opinion we also evaluated the overall adequacy of the presentation of information in the financial statements.

QUALIFIED OPINION ARISING FROM LIMITATION IN AUDIT SCOPE

EXCEPT FOR ANY ADJUSTMENTS THAT MIGHT HAVE BEEN FOUND TO BE NECESSARY HAD WE BEEN ABLE TO OBTAIN SUFFICIENT EVIDENCE CONCERNING [MATTER], in our opinion the financial statements give a true and fair view of the state of the company's affairs as at .... and of its [profit / loss] for the year then ended and have been properly prepared in accordance with the Companies Act 1985.

IN RESPECT ALONE OF THE LIMITATION ON OUR WORK RELATING TO [MATTER]:

- WE HAVE NOT OBTAINED ALL THE INFORMATION AND EXPLANATIONS THAT WE CONSIDERED NECESSARY FOR THE PURPOSES OF OUR AUDIT; AND

- WE WERE UNABLE TO DETERMINE WHETHER PROPER ACCOUNTING RECORDS HAD BEEN KEPT.

Report 302
SL — e: Cash sales

Basis of opinion

We conducted our audit in accordance with Auditing Standards issued by the Auditing Practices Board except that the scope of our work was limited as explained below.

An audit includes examination, on a test basis, of evidence relevant to the amounts and disclosures in the financial statements. It also includes an assessment of the significant estimates and judgements made by the directors in the preparation of the financial statements, and of whether the accounting policies are appropriate to the company's circumstances, consistently applied and adequately disclosed.

We planned and performed our audit so as to obtain all the information and explanations which we considered necessary in order to provide us with sufficient evidence to give reasonable assurance that the financial statements are free from material misstatement, whether caused by fraud or other irregularity or error. However, the evidence available to us was limited because £ ..... of the company's recorded turnover comprises cash sales. There was no system of control over such sales on which we could rely for the purposes of our audit and there were no other satisfactory audit procedures that we could adopt to confirm that cash sales were properly recorded.

In forming our opinion we also evaluated the overall adequacy of the presentation of information in the financial statements.

Qualified opinion arising from limitation in audit scope

Except for any adjustments that might have been found to be necessary had we been able to obtain sufficient evidence concerning cash sales, in our opinion the financial statements give a true and fair view of the state of the company's affairs as at .... and of its [profit / loss] for the year then ended and have been properly prepared in accordance with the Companies Act 1985.

In respect alone of the limitation on our work relating to cash sales:

- we have not obtained all the information and explanations that we considered necessary for the purposes of our audit; and

- we were unable to determine whether proper accounting records had been kept.

Report 303
SL — d: Generic skeleton

Basis of opinion

Compliance with Auditing Standards EXCEPT THAT SCOPE WAS LIMITED.

Description of an audit.

Evidence AND A DESCRIPTION OF LIMITATION.

Evaluation of presentation.

OPINION: DISCLAIMER ON VIEW GIVEN BY FINANCIAL STATEMENTS

DISCLAIMER OF OPINION.

FURTHER MATTER REQUIRED BY LAW.

Report 304
SL — d: Generic word picture

Basis of opinion

We conducted our audit in accordance with Auditing Standards issued by the Auditing Practices Board EXCEPT THAT THE SCOPE OF OUR WORK WAS LIMITED AS EXPLAINED BELOW.

An audit includes examination, on a test basis, of evidence relevant to the amounts and disclosures in the financial statements. It also includes an assessment of the significant estimates and judgements made by the directors in the preparation of the financial statements, and of whether the accounting policies are appropriate to the company's circumstances, consistently applied and adequately disclosed.

We planned and performed our audit so as to obtain all the information and explanations which we considered necessary in order to provide us with sufficient evidence to give reasonable assurance that the financial statements are free from material misstatement, whether caused by fraud or other irregularity or error. HOWEVER, THE EVIDENCE AVAILABLE TO US WAS LIMITED BECAUSE [MATTER]. THERE WAS NO SYSTEM OF CONTROL OVER [MATTER] ON WHICH WE COULD RELY FOR THE PURPOSES OF OUR AUDIT AND THERE WERE NO OTHER SATISFACTORY AUDIT PROCEDURES THAT WE COULD ADOPT TO CONFIRM THAT [ACCOUNTING FOR MATTER] WAS CORRECT.

In forming our opinion we also evaluated the overall adequacy of the presentation of information in the financial statements.

OPINION: DISCLAIMER ON VIEW GIVEN BY FINANCIAL STATEMENTS

BECAUSE OF THE POSSIBLE EFFECT OF THE LIMITATION IN EVIDENCE AVAILABLE TO US, WE ARE UNABLE TO FORM AN OPINION AS TO WHETHER THE FINANCIAL STATEMENTS GIVE A TRUE AND FAIR VIEW OF THE STATE OF THE COMPANY'S AFFAIRS AS AT .... OR OF ITS [PROFIT / LOSS] FOR THE YEAR THEN ENDED. IN ALL OTHER RESPECTS, IN OUR OPINION THE FINANCIAL STATEMENTS HAVE BEEN PROPERLY PREPARED IN ACCORDANCE WITH THE COMPANIES ACT 1985.

IN RESPECT ALONE OF THE LIMITATION ON OUR WORK RELATING TO [MATTER]:

- WE HAVE NOT OBTAINED ALL THE INFORMATION AND EXPLANATIONS THAT WE CONSIDERED NECESSARY FOR THE PURPOSES OF OUR AUDIT; AND

- WE WERE UNABLE TO DETERMINE WHETHER PROPER ACCOUNTING RECORDS HAD BEEN KEPT.

Report 305
SL — d: Opening stocks

Basis of opinion

We conducted our audit in accordance with Auditing Standards issued by the Auditing Practices Board except that the scope of our work was limited as explained below.

An audit includes examination, on a test basis, of evidence relevant to the amounts and disclosures in the financial statements. It also includes an assessment of the significant estimates and judgements made by the directors in the preparation of the financial statements, and of whether the accounting policies are appropriate to the company's circumstances, consistently applied and adequately disclosed.

We planned and performed our audit so as to obtain all the information and explanations which we considered necessary in order to provide us with sufficient evidence to give reasonable assurance that the financial statements are free from material misstatement, whether caused by fraud or other irregularity or error. However, the evidence available to us was limited because we were appointed auditors on .... and in consequence were unable to carry out auditing procedures necessary to obtain adequate assurance regarding the quantities and condition of stock and work in progress, appearing in the balance sheet at .... Any adjustment to this figure would have a consequential effect on the profit for the year.

In forming our opinion we also evaluated the overall adequacy of the presentation of information in the financial statements.

Opinion: disclaimer on view given by financial statements

Because of the possible effect of the limitation in evidence available to us, we are unable to form an opinion as to whether the financial statements give a true and fair view of the state of the company's affairs as at .... or of its [profit / loss] for the year then ended. In all other respects, in our opinion the financial statements have been properly prepared in accordance with the Companies Act 1985.

In respect alone of the limitation on our work relating to stock and work-in-progress (sic):[1]

- we have not obtained all the information and explanations that we considered necessary for the purposes of our audit; and
- we were unable to determine whether proper accounting records had been kept.

3.3.3 Analysis of the requirements

3.3.3.1 Introduction

SAS 600 deals only with scope limitations that prevent the expression of an unqualified opinion (as defined in the SAS). Because of this, the following terminology has been employed consistently in this book; the second two terms refer to aspects of the first term:

[1] This example is based on example 9 in appendix 2 to SAS 600. That example uses the words 'work in progress' and 'work-in-progress'. Schedule 4 to the Companies Act 1985 uses the form 'work in progress' which should be preferred (consistently).

1 'Scope limitation'

A restriction on the auditors' work that prevents them from obtaining sufficient evidence about a matter relevant to, or potentially relevant to, their report or the proper performance of their duties as auditors.

2 'A SAS 600 limitation of audit scope'

A scope limitation preventing the expression of an unqualified opinion within the meaning of SAS 600.

3 'Statutory scope limitation'

A restriction on the auditors' work that prevents them from obtaining sufficient evidence concerning two matters referred to in law:

- absence of proper returns from branches not visited
- not obtaining all necessary information and explanations.

A statutory scope limitation is normally accompanied by a SAS 600 limitation of audit scope and the remainder of this section deals with such circumstances. The statutory scope limitation alone is considered later in this chapter in section 3.6 'Required by law'.

There is a third potential category of scope limitation for which no special term is used. It includes all scope limitations that are neither a SAS 600 limitation of audit scope, nor a statutory scope limitation. Examples of such scope limitations might be those relating to aspects of fundamental uncertainties. The argument runs that if a scope limitation merely prevents auditors from obtaining evidence about a matter that does not lead to a qualified opinion (here only a possible modification for fundamental uncertainty) then there ought to be some way of reporting it. For practical purposes, this third category should be ignored. Potential candidates for inclusion may be analysed instead into two categories:

- matters so insignificant that they need not be mentioned in the auditors' report
- limitations concerning adequacy of disclosure (of uncertainty) which are, therefore, potential SAS 600 limitations of audit scope.

The following subsections of this analysis of the requirements examine:

- the interaction between scope limitation and inherent uncertainty
- a description of the factors leading to the limitation
- quantification
- the decision between an except for opinion or a disclaimer
- distinguishing between imposed limitations and those outside the control of the auditors and directors.

3.3.3.2 Scope limitation and inherent uncertainty

Inherent uncertainties are dealt with in detail in section 3.5 'Fundamental uncertainty' of this chapter. For the purposes of the following analysis an inherent uncertainty is simply a matter for which the accounting has to be imprecise because it is impossible, at the time of preparing the accounts, to know all the relevant facts. For example, the cost of a legal claim may not be known with any precision until the claim is eventually settled.

When reporting a scope limitation auditors are required to distinguish between limitations imposed on them and those that are outside their and the directors' control. Obviously, by its nature, an inherent uncertainty restricts the availability of evidence. If there are scope limitations in connection with inherent uncertainties, they are normally imposed. In other words, the directors withhold relevant evidence. Auditors consider:

- whether it is reasonable that relevant evidence should be available, and
- whether that evidence exists.

Directors may impose a limitation in two ways. They may:

- prevent access to existing evidence, or
- prevent the existence of evidence by:
  — failing to obtain it, or
  — destroying it.

1 An example

As an example of the above, consider a possible permanent diminution in value of a property occupied and used by a company. It was valued some years ago when the property market was generally higher than at the balance sheet date. Auditors are looking for evidence to decide whether or not there is:

1 actual permanent diminution in value that should be recognised in the accounts by writing the value of the property down, or
2 inherent uncertainty in the value, such that, if the uncertainty is adequately accounted for and disclosed in the accounts, the auditors are required by SAS 600.6 to modify their report by including a paragraph describing a fundamental uncertainty, or
3 inherent uncertainty as in (2) that is not adequately accounted for and disclosed in the accounts, for which a qualification or disclaimer of opinion is appropriate.

The first stage is for auditors to consider whether it is reasonable that relevant evidence should be available. In practice, some evidence is already available through the auditors' knowledge of the business, so the question is really whether further evidence should be available. For example the existence, book value and general condition of the property may be known along with the general state of the property market and management's intention to continue to use the property (for example, no bank pressure to realise a security). If the property market is stable or rising that evidence may be sufficient to convince the auditors that there is no need to obtain further evidence. If property values are known to have fallen generally (as is the case in this example) the auditors may consider that more evidence is necessary.

The second stage, if further evidence is considered necessary, is to obtain and evaluate it or, as is relevant here, ascertain why it is not available. Here, the further necessary evidence is a current valuation of the property and any evidence concerning the property value in the long-term.

The following are some reasons why an acceptable current valuation may not be available:

- the directors have not considered the need for such a valuation
- the directors have decided, as a matter of policy, not to seek a valuation (because it is too costly, or is unnecessary, or would not affect the long-term view anyway)
- the directors have decided that valuations will be obtained regularly every so many years and the regular valuation is due next year
- a valuation has been obtained but it is concealed from the auditors (the auditors may not know that there is a valuation)
- the directors have made their own unsupported valuation
- the directors have made a valuation supported by a letter from external valuers dealing only with the general state of the property market
- a valuation was obtained but it has been lost and the valuer has been struck by lightning (which caused a fire destroying all his or her records).

These circumstances are judged against the criteria above to decide whether a scope limitation exists or whether the imprecision arises only because of the underlying inherent uncertainty.

SAS 600 contains no ranking of modifications. It is not possible to regard a fundamental uncertainty as a minor scope limitation, despite any temptation to the contrary.

3.3.3.3 Description of the factors

The exact wording of the first requirement of SAS 600.7, is worth studying, if only because the examples in appendix 2 to the SAS do not seem to comply with it! The requirement is that the auditors include in their report *'a description of the factors leading to the limitation in the opinion section of their report'*.

A plain reading of this is that the opinion section (not the basis of opinion section) has to contain a description of the factors leading to the limitation. An alternative construction, which is not a plain reading, but is necessary to allow the example reports to comply with SAS 600.7, is that *'the limitation in the opinion section of their report'* has to be described. The examples put this description only[2] in the basis of opinion section.

This inclusion of a description of the limitation in the basis of opinion section seems logical as that is the right place to discuss evidence. The wording of SAS 600.7 is perhaps ambiguous; better wording was included in the exposure draft of SAS 600. This book, therefore, takes the line that (however unlikely it appears from a plain reading of SAS 600.7) the description of a scope limitation may be in the basis of opinion section of a report.

3.3.3.4 Quantification

Although it is a little unfair to compare this modification with one dealt with later in the chapter, it is necessary to do so. When auditors report on a disagreement they are required to refer to the implications for the accounts and quantify if practicable. Those requirements are absent for limitations of audit scope.

Nevertheless, the examples of scope limitations in appendix 2 to SAS 600 include some quantification and some mention of the effect on the accounts. Example 8 (SL — e) gives a figure for the amount of turnover that is cash sales. Example 9 (SL — d) not only states that stock and work in progress amount to a certain sum, but also states that any adjustment to that figure would have a consequential significant effect on the profit for the year.

Either the APB got it wrong in the appendix or, when interpreting a requirement to give a description of the factors leading to the limitation, auditors should attempt to include quantified implications for the accounts. It would appear to be sufficient, however, to give only the wording required by SAS 600.7.

3.3.3.5 Except for or disclaimer

The difference between an except for qualification and a disclaimer depends on the judgement as to whether the possible effect of a limitation is so material or pervasive that an opinion on the financial statements cannot be expressed. This is one of the more difficult decisions auditors have to make.

Direct guidance in SAS 600 is limited to example 9 in appendix 2. That example deals with appointment as auditors after the balance sheet date which, because of uncertainty over stocks, conveniently affects both the balance sheet and the profit and loss account. The wording of the example includes the words *'consequential*

[2] 'Only' is an important word here. The SAS does not prevent the addition of further material so long as the clarity of a report is not impaired. The description is, therefore, allowed in the basis of opinion section. The apparent problem is that the description is not also in the opinion section.

significant effect'; these words are not the same as *'so material or pervasive'* but they convey something of the auditors' thoughts.

In the absence of other direct guidance, what should auditors do to make the decision as to whether to give an except for opinion or disclaimer?

There is a risk-averse line of reasoning that says that a disclaimer is less likely to attract litigation. This line of thought only pays financial dividends if retaining the client is not an issue. Certainly, auditors have to balance natural prudence (tending towards a disclaimer) against the tendency towards the normal (an except for qualification) when exercising judgement.

Obviously, to necessitate a disclaimer a matter must be larger than simply material. How much larger is a matter of personal judgement. Two criteria may be considered in this context:

- the magnitude of the uncertainty
- whether the profit and loss account, or the balance sheet, or both are affected.

As a disclaimer is on the view given by the accounts as a whole it is easier for a matter affecting both the profit and loss account and the balance sheet to give rise to such a report. Obviously, an uncertainty over the profit and loss account is likely to affect the closing balance sheet because of the effect on the net assets. Similarly, unless the matter is one only of allocation (or a prior year adjustment), a matter affecting the closing balance sheet also affects the profit and loss account (or the statement of total recognised gains and losses — which is mentioned here without exhaustive analysis of its place in the great scheme of things).

There are exceptions to the above linking. For example, the profit and loss account alone may be affected if uncertainty is present in the opening balance sheet (and the closing balance sheet is audited satisfactorily) or the uncertainty is only over allocation between account balances.

Assuming that it is possible to choose an amount above which a matter is material, the following guidelines seem sensible for these different cases, to decide whether a matter is so material or pervasive that an opinion on the financial statements cannot be expressed:

- matters affecting both the profit and loss account and the balance sheet — the amount of the potential adjustment (if any) to the accounts is five times materiality
- matters affecting only the profit and loss account (and the closing balance sheet is audited satisfactorily) or only the balance sheet — ten times materiality.

Also relevant is the guidance in the explanatory material to SAS 600.6, dealt with above in the section about the interaction between scope limitations and fundamental uncertainty. The 'rule' is that a disclaimer may be appropriate for a SAS 600 limitation of audit scope (in relation to an inherent uncertainty) only where the uncertainty is fundamental. This guidance implies that, when deciding whether a disclaimer is required, auditors may use similar criteria to those used to decide whether an inherent uncertainty is fundamental.

The decision about whether an inherent uncertainty is fundamental is discussed in detail later in this chapter in the section dealing with fundamental uncertainties. In essence, an inherent uncertainty is fundamental if the accounts are imagined without clear disclosure of the nature and implications of the uncertainty and the view given by the imaginary accounts is 'seriously misleading'. The word 'seriously' narrows the field to where the magnitude of the possible adjustments is very material or very likely (without being so likely that, for example accrual is required).

To use a similar thought process, to decide whether a disclaimer is necessary rather than a lesser qualification for a SAS 600 limitation of audit scope, auditors can:

- imagine the accounts and their report together without clear disclosure of the nature and implications of the SAS 600 limitation of audit scope
- decide whether the view given by the imaginary accounts and report is 'seriously misleading'.

It would seem that to be so serious a problem as to be 'seriously misleading' requires almost an earthquake. Not only must the user know that the matter is unaudited, it also has to be so significant that an error in it (that may be present because it is unaudited) could seriously distort the view given by the accounts.

3.3.3.6 Nature of scope limitation

SAS 600 distinguishes between limitations imposed on the auditors and those that are outside their and the directors' control. The wording of the auditors' report should enable the reader not only to understand the reasons for the limitation, but also to distinguish between these two categories to which the limitation may belong.

The generic word picture for a scope limitation (report 302) is a neutral form of report. Auditors may choose to:

1 use a neutral form of report for a limitation that is not imposed and restrict specific wording (such as referring to the directors' imposing a limitation) to those reports for which it is appropriate, or

2 use specific wording for any scope limitation so that the report explicitly makes clear whether the limitation is imposed or not.

Examples 8 and 9 in appendix 2 to SAS 600 deal respectively with limitations relating to cash sales and late appointment as auditors. Their wording is neutral: requiring the reader to understand in each case that the reasons for the limitation are outside the control of the directors and auditors. Because of the persuasive quality of the examples it is likely that the majority of auditors will adopt alternative (1) above.

Apart from generally increasing the clarity of reports where the limitation is outside the control of the directors and auditors, there are specific circumstances in which auditors may want to make an explicit reference. Directors may welcome such wording where they might otherwise feel that the report could be interpreted as being critical of them. For example, a charitable company may be unable to be certain that its donation income is complete. Explicit wording from the auditors about this being outside the control of the directors may make an except for opinion more palatable, especially where uncertainty was the reason for a 'subject to' in a year before the adoption of SAS 600. A report illustrating this wording is given in chapter 5 'Illustrative Modifications'.

The following basis of opinion section illustrates the changes (in bold type) that may be made to the generic word picture for a scope limitation (report 301) to reveal that a limitation was imposed by the directors:

Report 306
SL — e: Generic word picture, limitation imposed by directors

Basis of opinion

We conducted our audit in accordance with Auditing Standards issued by the Auditing Practices Board, EXCEPT THAT THE SCOPE OF OUR WORK WAS LIMITED AS EXPLAINED BELOW.

An audit includes examination, on a test basis, of evidence relevant to the amounts and disclosures in the financial statements. It also includes an assessment of the significant estimates and judgements made by the directors in the preparation of the financial statements, and of whether the accounting policies are appropriate to the company's circumstances, consistently applied and adequately disclosed.

We planned and performed our audit so as to obtain all the information and explanations which we considered necessary in order to provide us with sufficient evidence to give reasonable assurance that the financial statements are free from material misstatement, whether caused by fraud or other irregularity or error. HOWEVER, THE EVIDENCE AVAILABLE TO US WAS LIMITED BECAUSE **THE DIRECTORS DID NOT ALLOW [RESTRICTION] RELATING TO** [MATTER]. THERE WAS NO SYSTEM OF CONTROL OVER [MATTER] ON WHICH WE COULD RELY FOR THE PURPOSES OF OUR AUDIT AND THERE WERE NO OTHER SATISFACTORY AUDIT PROCEDURES THAT WE COULD ADOPT TO CONFIRM THAT [ACCOUNTING FOR MATTER] WAS CORRECT.

In forming our opinion we also evaluated the overall adequacy of the presentation of information in the financial statements.

If it is considered necessary to include specific reference to the fact that the limitation is outsider the directors' control the report can be modified as follows. The new wording is in bold type:

Report 307
SL — e: Generic word picture, limitation outside directors' control

Basis of opinion

We conducted our audit in accordance with Auditing Standards issued by the Auditing Practices Board, EXCEPT THAT THE SCOPE OF OUR WORK WAS LIMITED AS EXPLAINED BELOW.

An audit includes examination, on a test basis, of evidence relevant to the amounts and disclosures in the financial statements. It also includes an assessment of the significant estimates and judgements made by the directors in the preparation of the financial statements, and of whether the accounting policies are appropriate to the company's circumstances, consistently applied and adequately disclosed.

We planned and performed our audit so as to obtain all the information and explanations which we considered necessary in order to provide us with sufficient evidence to give reasonable assurance that the financial statements are free from material misstatement, whether caused by fraud or other irregularity or error. HOWEVER, THE EVIDENCE AVAILABLE TO US WAS LIMITED BECAUSE [MATTER]. **THIS LIMITATION WAS NOT IMPOSED BY THE DIRECTORS WHO [MITIGATING CIRCUMSTANCES].** THERE WAS NO SYSTEM OF CONTROL OVER [MATTER] ON WHICH WE COULD RELY FOR THE PURPOSES OF OUR AUDIT AND THERE WERE NO OTHER SATISFACTORY AUDIT PROCEDURES THAT WE COULD ADOPT TO CONFIRM THAT [ACCOUNTING FOR MATTER] WAS CORRECT.

In forming our opinion we also evaluated the overall adequacy of the presentation of information in the financial statements.

SAS 600 (paragraph 71) refers to limitations being *'outside the control of the directors'*. This wording is not used in the illustrative report because it could be interpreted as indicating that the directors should have controlled the matter but did not (colloquially it was *'out of control'*).

The mitigating circumstances for late appointment as auditors could for example indicate that the directors did not just change auditors to prevent the attendance at stocktake:

> However, the evidence available to us was limited because we were appointed auditors on .... and in consequence we were unable to attend the year-end stocktaking. This limitation was not imposed by the directors who appointed us to act as auditors when the previous auditors resigned as a consequence of their decision to cease to be Registered Auditors. There was no system of control over stock on which we could rely for the purposes of our audit and there were no other satisfactory audit procedures that we could adopt to confirm that . . .

It can be difficult to decide whether a lack of accounting records (or systems on which the auditors might rely) arises because of an undeclared intention of the directors to limit the scope of the audit. If auditors are suspicious of the directors' motives the whole area of client relations can flare up and affect other aspects of the audit.

One possibility not specifically addressed by SAS 600 is reporting where the limitation is imposed by the auditors (human error); hopefully this will not be a common occurrence. Such circumstances could arise where the auditors fail to carry out a vital procedure at the only time it can be performed. The most obvious failing would be not attending the stocktaking. Bearing in mind the obvious potential for alerting readers to the opportunity to make a professional complaint, auditors could be expected to be reluctant to include wording in their report that advertises the problem.

Paragraph 26 of SAS 600 deals with a departure from Auditing Standards where that is appropriate to fulfil the objectives of a specific audit more effectively. In such circumstances auditors are to explain the reasons for that departure in their report. The paragraph asserts that, other than in exceptional and justifiable circumstances, a departure from an Auditing Standard is a limitation on the scope of work undertaken by the auditors. Unfortunately the paragraph does not deal further with the causes of departures and the effect (if any) on the auditors' report. It merely suggests that, where there is a departure from Auditing Standards auditors should assess whether a qualified opinion or disclaimer of opinion is required, as set out in SAS 600.7.

The SAS does not therefore 'require' an explanation of the reasons for a departure from Auditing Standards that is due to human error; reasons are necessary only if the departure is deliberate in order to fulfil the objectives of a specific audit more effectively.

The following illustrative wording is for a scope limitation due to human error by the auditors. The reasons for the limitation are not given as a minimal disclosure seems preferable. Auditors should not keep quiet about a problem of this nature because they would then fail in their duty to the client. It would be possible for auditors to resign rather than issue a self-condemning report but that should be regarded as a potentially more dangerous option. Undoubtedly, auditors should consult, consider taking legal advice and notify their professional indemnity insurers before issuing a report containing wording such as the following:

Report 308
SL — d: Auditors' error (stocktake not attended)

Basis of opinion

We conducted our audit in accordance with Auditing Standards issued by the Auditing Practices Board except that the scope of our work was limited as explained below.

An audit includes examination, on a test basis, of evidence relevant to the amounts and disclosures in the financial statements. It also includes an assessment of the significant estimates and judgements made by the directors in the preparation of the financial statements, and of whether the accounting policies are appropriate to the company's circumstances, consistently applied and adequately disclosed.

We planned and performed our audit so as to obtain all the information and explanations which we considered necessary in order to provide us with sufficient

evidence to give reasonable assurance that the financial statements are free from material misstatement, whether caused by fraud or other irregularity or error. However, we did not attend the stocktaking at .... and in consequence were unable to carry out all the auditing procedures necessary to obtain adequate assurance regarding the quantities and condition of stock and work in progress, appearing in the balance sheet at .... Any adjustment to this figure would have a consequential effect on the profit for the year.

In forming our opinion we also evaluated the overall adequacy of the presentation of information in the financial statements.

Opinion: disclaimer on view given by financial statements

Because of the possible effect of the limitation in evidence available to us, we are unable to form an opinion as to whether the financial statements give a true and fair view of the state of the company's affairs as at .... or of its [profit / loss] for the year then ended. In all other respects, in our opinion the financial statements have been properly prepared in accordance with the Companies Act 1985.

In respect alone of the limitation on our work relating to stock and work in progress:

- we have not obtained all the information and explanations that we considered necessary for the purposes of our audit; and

- we were unable to determine whether proper accounting records had been kept.

The above extract shows that the matters required by law (in the opinion paragraph) are not affected by the reasons for the scope limitation.

The minimal disclosure, which omits any reasons for the auditors' error, could easily be mistaken for a scope limitation that is outside the control of the directors and auditors. The report could thus be open to criticism that it does not give a clear expression of opinion and so may not comply with SAS 600.1.

3.3.4 Links to other modifications

SAS 600 makes it clear that an inherent uncertainty does not arise from, or give rise to, a scope limitation (paragraph 70).

There are some matters that auditors are required to report on that can accompany a scope limitation. Without dwelling on cause and effect, these are:

- failure to keep proper accounting records
- lack of all the information and explanations considered necessary for the purposes of the audit
- inadequate returns from branches not visited by the auditors
- the company's individual accounts do not agree with the accounting records and returns
- omission of disclosures required by Schedule 6 to the Companies Act 1985 concerning emoluments of and transactions with directors.

The first two matters are much more common than the others, some of which, as explained elsewhere in this book, are only theoretical possibilities. The common matters are also likely to occur together.

3.3.5 Typical circumstances

The following two lists of examples cover some of the more common circumstances that fall into the two categories of scope limitation:

- imposed on the auditors
- outside the control of the auditors and directors.

3.3.5.1 Limitations imposed on the auditors

- some of the accounting records are withheld from the auditors
- directors prevent an audit procedure from being carried out
- directors will not prepare cash flow forecasts to support the going concern basis of preparation of accounts
- directors will not disclose details of 'material interest' transactions
- an up-to-date valuation is not made or obtained
- sufficiently up-to-date actuarial information is not obtained.

3.3.5.2 Limitations outside the control of the auditors and directors

- appointment as auditors only after stocktaking and no practicable alternative evidence available of the existence and condition of stock
- cash sales and no practicable alternative evidence available of the completeness of income
- natural disaster
  - — results of stocktake stolen
  - — books and records in custody of police
- information about an associate not available
- preceding year not audited.

3.4 Disagreement

3.4.1 The requirements

If auditors disagree with the accounting treatment or disclosure of a matter in the accounts and they believe that the effect of that disagreement is material they are required by SAS 600.8 to modify their report. The modifications that are required are all in the opinion section of the report:

- a description of all substantive factors giving rise to the disagreement
- their implications for the accounts
- whenever practicable, a quantification of the effect
- a qualified opinion.

The qualification should be an adverse opinion when the auditors conclude that the effect of the matter giving rise to disagreement is so material or pervasive that the accounts are seriously misleading. For other material disagreements, the auditors should issue a qualified opinion indicating that it is expressed except for the effects of the matter giving rise to the disagreement.

3.4.2 Typical wording

The illustrative reports for disagreements are presented in two sets of three reports, giving illustrations of adverse as well as the more common except for opinions. Only the opinion sections are modified:

Report 309
D— e: Generic skeleton

QUALIFIED OPINION ARISING FROM DISAGREEMENT ABOUT . . .

OPINION OF AUDITORS AS TO CORRECT TREATMENT.

EXCEPT FOR THE ABOVE, opinion.

Report 310
D— e: Generic word picture

QUALIFIED OPINION ARISING FROM DISAGREEMENT ABOUT [ACCOUNTING TREATMENT / DISCLOSURE]

AS MORE FULLY EXPLAINED IN NOTE ..... [MATTER] [WHY MATTER IS A PROBLEM]. IN OUR OPINION [REASON FOR DISAGREEMENT] [QUANTIFICATION].

EXCEPT FOR [NOT FOLLOWING OUR VIEW], in our opinion the financial statements give a true and fair view of the state of the company's affairs as at .... and of its [profit / loss] for the year then ended and have been properly prepared in accordance with the Companies Act 1985.

Report 311
D— e: Bad debt not provided

Qualified opinion arising from disagreement about accounting treatment

As more fully explained in note ..... included in the debtors shown on the balance sheet is an amount of £ ..... due from a company which has ceased trading. .... has no security for this debt. In our opinion the company is unlikely to receive any payment and full provision of £ ..... should have been made, reducing profit before tax and net assets by that amount.

Except for the absence of this provision, in our opinion the financial statements give a true and fair view of the state of the company's affairs as at .... and of its [profit / loss] for the year then ended and have been properly prepared in accordance with the Companies Act 1985.

Report 312
D — a: Generic skeleton

ADVERSE OPINION

OPINION OF AUDITORS AS TO CORRECT TREATMENT.

ADVERSE OPINION.

Report 313
D — a: Generic word picture

ADVERSE OPINION

AS MORE FULLY EXPLAINED IN NOTE ..... [MATTER] [REASON FOR DIRECTORS' TREATMENT]. IN OUR OPINION, [PROPER TREATMENT] AS REQUIRED BY [STATEMENT OF STANDARD ACCOUNTING PRACTICE ..... / FINANCIAL REPORTING STANDARD .....]. [QUANTIFICATION].

IN VIEW OF THE EFFECT OF THE FAILURE TO [ACCOUNT PROPERLY] REFERRED TO ABOVE, IN OUR OPINION THE FINANCIAL STATEMENTS DO NOT GIVE A TRUE AND FAIR VIEW OF THE STATE OF THE COMPANY'S AFFAIRS AS AT .... AND OF ITS [PROFIT / LOSS] FOR THE YEAR THEN ENDED. IN ALL OTHER RESPECTS, IN OUR OPINION THE FINANCIAL STATEMENTS HAVE BEEN PROPERLY PREPARED IN ACCORDANCE WITH THE COMPANIES ACT 1985.

Report 314
D — a: Long-term contract losses not provided

Adverse opinion

As more fully explained in note ..... no provision has been made for losses expected to arise on certain long-term contracts currently in progress, as the directors consider that such losses should be off-set against amounts recoverable on other long-term contracts. In our opinion, provision should be made for foreseeable losses on individual contracts as required by Statement of Standard Accounting Practice 9 'Stocks and long-term contracts'. If losses had been so recognised the effect would have been to [reduce the profit / increase the loss] before and after tax for the year and the contract work in progress at .... by £..... .

In view of the effect of the failure to provide for the losses referred to above, in our opinion the financial statements do not give a true and fair view of the state of the company's affairs as at .... and of its [profit / loss] for the year then ended. In all other respects, in our opinion the financial statements have been properly prepared in accordance with the Companies Act 1985.

The word pictures for adverse and except for opinions differ simply because of the likely nature of the matters that could give rise to an adverse opinion.

3.4.3 Analysis of the requirements

3.4.3.1 Introduction

Accounting matters over which there may be disagreement are unlikely to be simple. Disagreements are most likely over accounting estimates or the selection of accounting policies. In many cases auditors feel unable to disagree with a treatment that is acceptable but not best practice, especially in an area not covered by accounting standards. John Roques of Touche Ross & Co. is quoted in his firm's 1993 Business Review as saying *'I don't think that I have ever felt able to qualify a set of accounts where somebody complied with all the standards. I would sometimes say to a finance director or chief executive: "I don't think you are getting the right reputation, and it would be better if you chose another route." But so long as they followed the rules, I do not believe an auditor could do more or should do more.'*

This may change over time as experience with the Financial Reporting Review Panel develops. As every auditors' report qualified for disagreement is a candidate for the attention of those looking out for defective accounts, directors may be wise to avoid that possibility. According to *Audit Report* magazine for August 1992, except for qualifications made up five percent of its sample of modified reports; it will be interesting to see if the absolute number falls (as SAS 600 reports replace the earlier regime 'subject to' reports will vanish, distorting the percentages).

The explanatory material for SAS 600.8 is limited to one paragraph, the implication being that, once decided upon, a modification for disagreement is relatively easy. Unfortunately, it is not clear whether part of that explanatory material is a mere restatement of the requirements, or goes beyond them. The explanatory material 'requires' the modified report to include:

- a description of the reasons for qualification
- a description of the effects on the accounts
- a sufficient description of the circumstances so that a reader can appreciate the principal points at issue and their implications for an understanding of the accounts.

The explanatory material explicitly permits a reference to the relevant notes to the accounts so long as the 'requirements' are still met by the report.

Rather than getting bogged down in semantics, the following analysis assumes that the explanatory material is intended to be a restatement of the requirements of SAS 600.8, together with clarification that a cross-reference to the note in the accounts is not, of itself, sufficient. Interestingly, some of the wording of the examples in appendix 2 to SAS 600 can be justified more easily by reference to the 'requirements' of the explanatory material than those of SAS 600.8.

The following analysis deals with:

- positioning a modification
- describing all substantive factors giving rise to the disagreement (describing the reasons for qualification)
- describing implications (describing the effects on the accounts)
- quantifying effects
- deciding whether an except for or adverse opinion is necessary

- paragraph 36A of Schedule 4 to the Companies Act 1985 and its interaction with UITF 7.

3.4.3.2 Positioning a modification

The whole of the modification is required to be within the opinion section of the report. It is logical to deal with the problem in one or more paragraphs before the qualified opinion itself.

3.4.3.3 Describing the reasons for qualification

It is interesting to contrast the detailed wording of SAS 600.8 with that of SAS 600.7. What is the difference in meaning between *'a description of the factors'* for a limitation of audit scope (SAS 600.7) and *'a description of all substantive factors'* for a disagreement (SAS 600.8)? To avoid semantic argument about completeness and when a factor becomes substantive, it is probably safe to assume that both phrases mean *'a description of the important factors'*.

The important factors may include:

1 the facts of the problem
2 (if relevant) the directors' reasons for the accounting treatment or disclosure in the accounts
3 the auditors' view as to why it is wrong, which may include stating the correct accounting treatment or disclosure
4 (if relevant) a reference to the accounting standard or company law provision breached.

The SAS does not prescribe the detailed contents of the description and the relevant examples in its appendix 2 provide no consistent guide.

1 The facts and the directors' reasons

Describing the facts (and directors' reasons if relevant) might be thought to be relatively easy but the relevant examples in appendix 2 to SAS 600 adopt different approaches:

> Included in the debtors shown on the balance sheet is an amount of £ ..... due from a company which has ceased trading. .... has no security for this debt. (example 7)

> As more fully explained in note ..... no provision has been made for losses expected to arise on certain long-term contracts currently in progress, as the directors consider that such losses should be off-set against amounts recoverable on other long-term contracts. (example 10)

> As explained in note ..... the financial statements do not contain a statement of cash flows as required by Financial Reporting Standard 1. (example 12)

The examples vary as to the following matters:

- quantification
- identification of the account balances affected
- degree of reliance on noted disclosures
- inclusion of reasons for treatment adopted by the directors
- immediate reference to the requirements of accounting standards (rather than mentioning it in the qualified opinion).

There is little that can be deduced from the above except that the facts and the reasons may be stated in many different ways depending on the particular circumstances encountered.

There is no requirement to quantify the description. SAS 600.8 only requires quantification of the effect. Amounts may be given, however, and it is convenient to do so where that simplifies the prose of the whole modification.

If the notes do not provide information auditors will not refer to them but will include sufficient material in their reports. There are further implications if there is any material departure from applicable accounting standards because paragraph 36A of Schedule 4 to the Companies Act 1985 requires the reasons to be given in the accounts. This matter is dealt with further in section 3.4.3.6 below.

2 The auditors' view and cross-references

The relevant examples in appendix 2 to SAS 600 describe the auditors' disagreement in the following ways:

> in our opinion the company is unlikely to receive any payment and full provision of £ ..... should have been made (example 7)
>
> in our opinion, provision should be made for foreseeable losses on individual contracts as required by Statement of Standard Accounting Practice 9 (example 10)
>
> in our opinion information about the company's cash flows is necessary for a proper understanding of the company's state of affairs and [profit / loss] (example 12)

The use of the words *'in our opinion'* does not promote the clarity of the report as a whole as it detracts from the main opinion. It would have been better to use the more direct *'we believe that'*, but the words in the examples are likely to gain common acceptance.

The extent of justification for the auditors' view increases, from example 7, through example 10, to example 12 as follows:

- the failure to provide against a bad debt is simply contradicted with no mention of the requirement to have regard to prudence embodied in accounting standards and the law

- the incorrect treatment of netting long-term contracts rather than treating them individually is rebutted by a statement of the correct treatment and mention that the correct treatment is prescribed by a particular SSAP
- omission of a cash flow statement prompts a mention that such statements are required by a named FRS and a further opinion that such a statement is necessary for a proper understanding of the state of affairs and [profit / loss].

The cash flow statement omission is a special case. The wording of the example (although flawed) will probably be copied by auditors because such circumstances do not change in essence from company to company.

In the absence of consistent guidance, the following guidelines are proposed for deciding on the wording to describe the auditors' disagreement where the problem is not the omission of a cash flow statement. They are based on established practice as well as the examples in appendix 2 to SAS 600:

- where the disagreement could be interpreted as one of fact (a debt is either good or bad) rather than accounting or disclosure — there is no need to mention the legal or accounting requirements; only the auditors' opposing view need be stated
- where the disagreement does involve accounting or disclosure matters — there should be a statement of the correct treatment and a reference to that treatment being required by a named accounting standard (or legal requirement)
- where an accounting standard and a legal requirement are both concerned — it is sufficient, but not best practice, to mention just the former. This is considered further below.

The omission of a reference to the Companies Act 1985 from a description that mentions an accounting standard cannot be challenged because it is not specifically required by SAS 600.8. The failure to comply with the law is, in any case, covered by the except for or adverse opinion paragraph that follows the descriptive material. However, the following paragraphs examine the case for 'best practice'.

When a disagreement occurs over accounting or disclosure that is clearly in breach of specific provisions of an accounting standard and company law there is considerable pressure of precedent to mention both. For example, because depreciation has not been charged, auditors may refer both to SSAP 12 'Accounting for depreciation' and to Schedule 4 to the Companies Act 1985. The relevant requirements are in paragraph 15 of SSAP 12 and paragraph 18 of Schedule 4. In such circumstances, *Audit Report* magazine provides many examples of reports (pre-SAS 600) that include both references. The magazine also criticises some auditors for failing to include a reference to the Companies Act 1985.

The examples in appendix 2 to SAS 600 do not, however, include circumstances where there is a direct and obvious breach of a specific company law requirement. Example 10 in appendix 2 to SAS 600 refers to the requirement of Statement of Standard Accounting Practice 9 that provision should be made for foreseeable losses on individual contracts. The specific requirement is in paragraph 28 of SSAP 9, which states that *'Long-term contracts should be assessed on a contract by contract basis . . . '*. This could be interpreted as defining such contracts as separate items for the purposes of paragraph 5 of Schedule 4 to the Companies Act 1985, which prohibits the setting off of *'amounts in respect of items representing assets or income . . . against amounts in respect of items representing liabilities or expenditure (as the case may be), or vice versa'*. If this view is taken, example 10 is of an indirect but obvious breach of a specific company law requirement and does not, therefore, follow 'best practice' set out above.

A practical approach for auditors is perhaps to consider the desirability of a reference to company law in all cases but normally only give such a reference in the descriptive material when a disagreement occurs over accounting or disclosure that is clearly in breach of specific provisions of company law that are mirrored in an accounting standard.

This section has not discussed the form or precision of cross-references. Such matters are dealt with in this chapter in section 3.11 'Writing a modification'.

3.4.3.4 Describing the effects on the accounts

The specific requirement of SAS 600.8 are that auditors should state the implications for the accounts of all substantive factors giving rise to the disagreement and, whenever practicable, include a quantification of the effect on the accounts. The explanatory material to SAS 600.8 interprets this simply as a requirement to describe the effects on the accounts. This avoids semantic argument, so it is worth examining how the examples in appendix 2 to SAS 600 describe the effects on the accounts:

> reducing profit before tax and net assets by that amount (example 7)
>
> If losses had been so recognised the effect would have been to reduce the profit before and after tax for the year and the contract work in progress at .... by £ ..... (example 10)
>
> (example 12)

The rather short extract from example 12, which deals with the omission of a cash flow statement, pinpoints the fact that it contains no description of the effects on the accounts (outside the final qualified opinion paragraph).

The following paragraphs consider:

- the general approach (including quantification)
- which primary statements are affected
- taxation.

1 General approach

In common with other professional writing, it is important for auditors to consider the objective of describing the effects and to consider the needs of readers. Readers have already been informed that there is a problem and that the auditors believe that a different presentation or accounting treatment should have been adopted. They will now be in a 'so what?' mode: waiting to find out exactly the effect of the auditors' disagreement. Auditors should not let the moment slip from their grasp. It is important to communicate fully the impact on the accounts.

The general approach to describing the effects on the accounts is to concentrate on matters that readers will consider important. These are likely to be:

- the legality of the dividend
- the reported profit
- the net assets
- the ability of the company to continue as a going concern.

The first matter above is so important that section 271 of the Companies Act 1985 requires a further statement from auditors.

Readers should be given information about the effects of the disagreement so that they may notionally adjust the key elements of the accounts to accord with the auditors' view of the correct treatment, rather than the one actually used by the directors. Some disagreements are, however, less easy to explain in terms of the above. For example, if the directors insist on calling turnover 'money for nothing' the effect on the accounts is only one of faulty disclosure. All the auditors can do is describe the effect in terms of the confusion caused. This perhaps explains why the description of the effect of the omission of a cash flow statement (in example 12 in appendix 2 to SAS 600) is so short.

Readers are in a better position to notionally adjust the key elements of the accounts if the auditors quantify the effects on the accounts. SAS 600.8 calls for quantification 'whenever practicable'. The semantic discussion of these words may be found in subsection 3.5.3.6 'Quantifying the effects' in this chapter. There is no requirement to make any statement about quantification if it is not practicable to quantify the effects. However, if this is the case, it ought to be best practice to make such a statement. Where auditors disagree with a failure to depreciate assets but have no accurate estimate of economic life and residual value they can choose between:

- not quantifying
- stating that it is not practicable to quantify the effect
- stating only that certain amounts in the accounts are overstated (or understated as the case may be)
- illustrating the possible effect by, for example quantifying on the basis of stated assumptions.

Experience of how auditors have reported shows that auditors do not normally comment on matters outside the profit and state of affairs (net assets). Where it is obvious that one particular balance sheet account only is affected (e.g. stocks) it is common to describe the effect on that account and leave readers to form their own view of the effect on the net assets.

2 Which primary statements are affected

Many disagreements over accounting treatment affect both the profit and loss account and balance sheet. The effects of some may, however, be confined to just one of these primary statements. This section examines the wording of auditors' reports where that is the case.

Some auditors choose to report on further primary statements, such as the cash flow statement. This section also examines, therefore, the interaction between primary statements.

Profit and loss account and balance sheet

A disagreement over accounting treatment affecting the profit and loss account normally also affects the balance sheet. This is because the retained profit feeds through to the reserves shown in the balance sheet. Auditors may, however, decide that the balance sheet still gives a true and fair view if:

- the matter is only one of allocation that does not affect the reported profit, for example incorrect netting of a cost of sale against turnover
- the matter arises in connection with a prior year and the opening balance sheet is affected, not the year end balance sheet
- the effect is material to the profit and loss account but not to the balance sheet.

Opinions where the balance sheet is unaffected might use words such as:

> In our opinion the financial statements give a true and fair view of the state of the company's affairs as at .... and except for [NOT FOLLOWING OUR VIEW] of its [profit / loss] for the year then ended and have been properly prepared in accordance with the Companies Act 1985.

A disagreement over accounting treatment affecting the balance sheet normally also affects the profit and loss account. This is because a change in net assets is normally represented by a movement in the profit or loss for the year. Auditors may, however, decide that the profit and loss account still gives a true and fair view if:

- the matter is only one of allocation that does not affect the reported net assets, for example incorrect classification between cash and debtors
- the matter arises in connection with a prior year and the opening balance sheet is affected, not the profit and loss account
- the matter affects shareholders' funds other than the profit and loss account, for example a disagreement about a revaluation affecting only the property concerned and the revaluation reserve
- the effect is material to the balance sheet but not to the profit and loss account.

Opinions where the profit and loss account is unaffected might use words such as:

> In our opinion the financial statements give a true and fair view of the company's [profit / loss] for the year to .... and except for [NOT FOLLOWING OUR VIEW] of its state of its affairs as at that date and have been properly prepared in accordance with the Companies Act 1985.

Because the normal order of primary statements is not followed the prose looks odd. It would be possible to split the sentence into two as follows:

> In our opinion the financial statements give a true and fair view of the company's [profit / loss] for the year to .... Except for [NOT FOLLOWING OUR VIEW] in our opinion the financial statements give a true and fair view of the state of the company's affairs as at .... and have been properly prepared in accordance with the Companies Act 1985.

Further primary statements — general

Reporting on further primary statements is discussed in detail in chapter 2 'The Standard Report'. An understanding of that section is necessary for a proper appreciation of the material that follows. Auditors choosing to report on further primary statements must consider the possible ramifications of any disagreement for each primary statement (and for comparatives given in them).

The following matters can be asserted with reasonable confidence for disagreements:

- disagreements concerning only disclosure are normally confined to the primary statement that is directly affected
- disagreements over accounting treatment affecting the balance sheet normally also affect the profit and loss account and vice versa (but there are exceptions as discussed immediately above)
- if the disagreement is that no cash flow statement is presented the views given by the balance sheet and profit and loss account are both affected (as is compliance with the Companies Act's requirement for proper presentation).

Further primary statements — omission

The explanatory material accompanying example 12 in appendix 2 to SAS 600 (which is for the omission of a cash flow statement) states that *'Omission of a primary statement normally results in the issue of an opinion qualified as to the effect on the view given by the financial statements and the compliance with the Companies Act's other specific requirements because the Act requires additional information to be included in financial statements when necessary to give a true and fair view.'*

This reasoning can presumably be extended to the other primary statements introduced by FRS 3 'Reporting Financial Performance':

- the statement of total recognised gains and losses
- the reconciliation of movements in shareholders' funds (where presented as a primary statement).

Paragraph 59 of the explanatory material to FRS 3 gives the reconciliation of movements in shareholders' funds a choice of whether to be a primary statement or a note and defines its position if the former: *'If included as a primary statement, the reconciliation should be shown separately from the statement of total recognised gains and losses.'* It is, therefore, an optional primary statement. As a result, auditors faced with modifying their opinion on accounts because the reconciliation of movements in shareholders' funds has been omitted are in an impossible position. If the directors are not willing to represent whether the hole in the accounts would have been a note or a primary statement, auditors either have to guess (choosing between an 'except for' relating to the profit and loss account and balance sheet, and other possibilities) or instead modify their report also for a SAS 600 limitation of audit scope because of the lack of representation. It can only be hoped that such circumstances never occur!

If the view is taken that an omitted reconciliation of movements in shareholders' funds is not a primary statement, but is a material (but not fundamental) omission, auditors might give an opinion that, after appropriate explanation, concludes as follows:

> In our opinion the financial statements give a true and fair view of the state of the company's affairs as at .... and of its [profit / loss] for the year then ended and except for the omission of a note reconciling movements in shareholders' funds have been properly prepared in accordance with the Companies Act 1985.

Other auditors might conclude that the reconciliation was pertinent to the balance sheet but not the profit and loss account. According to FRS 3, the purpose of the reconciliation of movements in shareholders' funds is to highlight important changes in the financial position of an entity that do not feature in the profit and loss account or the statement of total recognised gains and losses. A report modified as shown above for opinions where the profit and loss account is unaffected would be issued if this view was taken.[3]

This almost concludes the discussion of omission of further primary statements. Before leaving the topic it is worth considering what effect the omission of the profit and loss account or the balance sheet has on the opinion. The following theoretical discussion ignores the related problems of required notes that may or may not be present and breaches of specific disclosure requirements of the Companies Act 1985.

For the purposes of their reports on financial statements, auditors have for many years considered there to be no automatic link between the profit and loss account and the balance sheet. Matters affecting one statement have not affected the other except by reason of the normal mechanism of double entry and drawing up accounts. Under the status quo, a qualification because one statement is omitted would only refer to that and to the breach of the requirements of the Act. This practice was common even where the matter was considered to be fundamental. Example 10 in the Auditing Standard 'The audit report' that SAS 600 superseded went so far as to explain that its adverse opinion on the accounts as a whole was only appropriate where *'the impact of the disagreement is fundamental in relation to the company's balance sheet, profit and loss account and funds statement.'*

A major unheralded change (or at least a confirmation) introduced by SAS 600 is that adverse opinions must now be on the accounts as a whole, not any particular financial statement.

---

[3] Auditors whose house style includes reporting on the total recognised gains and losses have to decide what to do if no such primary statement is present. In such cases the only realised profit (or loss) is the one in the profit and loss account. The author has seen only two reports where this has happened. In both cases the auditors, nevertheless, reported as if the primary statement had been present.

FRS 3 does not explicitly require a profit and loss account. Its provisions do, however, relating to the form and content of the profit and loss account. Paragraph 13 of FRS 3 (which is really concerned with gains and losses) requires *'All gains and losses recognised in the financial statements for the period* (to be) *included in the profit and loss account or the statement of total recognised gains and losses.'* Omission of a profit and loss account is arguably a breach of at least the spirit, if not the letter, of FRS 3.

Any distinction between the profit and loss account and the balance sheet on the basis of whether they are required by accounting standards as well as company law is lost, however, in the form of qualification. An omitted statement gives no view of the profit or state of affairs. This argues strongly that, in the terms used by SAS 600.8, the matter giving rise to a disagreement is so material or pervasive that the financial statements are seriously misleading. In such circumstances auditors should issue an adverse opinion. An adverse opinion extends to the whole financial statements.

This might have ensured consistency of treatment for all primary financial statements under SAS 600 but, unfortunately, the omission of a cash flow statement is treated by SAS 600 not as an adverse opinion but only as an 'except for'.

Perhaps the only conclusion that can be drawn is that the ASB, in trying to promote new aspects of financial reporting within the constraints of the Companies Act 1985, has succeeded in evading the APB's attempts to prescribe how auditors should report.

Further primary statements — disagreements

Auditors who choose to report on further primary statements must consider the interaction of those statements and the need to report accordingly. For example, the cash flow statement is dependent on the opening and closing balance sheets; the statement of total recognised gains and losses includes the profit or loss before dividends, and changes in asset valuations.

A modified opinion where auditors normally report on all primary statements may, for example include a disagreement affecting the balance sheet, the statement of total recognised gains and losses and the reconciliation of movements in shareholders' funds but not the profit and loss account or the cash flow statement. Such an opinion is constructed by putting the references to the primary statements in appropriate order and inserting the 'except for' at the appropriate point in the sequence.

3 Taxation

Example 7 in appendix 2 to SAS 600 refers to reducing profit before tax and net assets by a particular amount. There are questions as to whether auditors should be reporting on profit before tax, or profit after tax, or both.

Obviously some matters have no tax effects and the choice of reference point is not, on the face of it, important. However, consider the following variations based around example 7 in appendix 2 to SAS 600:

> Included in the debtors shown on the balance sheet is an amount of £ ..... due from a company which has ceased trading. .... has no security for this debt. In our opinion the company is unlikely to receive any payment and full provision of £ ..... should have been made, reducing **profit before tax** and net assets by that amount. (example 7)
>
> Included in the debtors shown on the balance sheet is an amount of £ ..... due from a company which has ceased trading. .... has no security for this debt. In our opinion the company is unlikely to receive any payment and full provision of £ ..... should have been made, reducing **profit after tax** and net assets by that amount.
>
> Included in the debtors shown on the balance sheet is an amount of £ ..... due from a company which has ceased trading. .... has no security for this debt. In our opinion the company is unlikely to receive any payment and full provision of £ ..... should have been made, reducing **profit before and after tax** and net assets by that amount.

Would a reader interpret these opinions differently? Obviously a reader skilled in accountancy would conclude from the first opinion that the matter did not affect the tax charge or else the net assets would have been affected to a different degree to that stated. A less well versed reader would find the third example more informative but might be satisfied with the second example.

Example 10 in appendix 2 to SAS 600 uses the approach in the third example above, so it is clearly acceptable to do so.

Given that there may be complications introduced by disagreements having a tax effect and circumstances where a pre tax profit or loss becomes a post tax loss or profit, what general approach should auditors adopt to taxation when reporting the effects on the accounts?

There is little precedent that can assist auditors. For example, the Auditing Standard 'The audit report' that SAS 600 superseded provided an example of a before and after tax description, but other examples were not helpful. Perhaps as a result, wordings such as *'a provision of £ ..... should have been made'* have been prevalent in practice. It is probably still acceptable to use that approach but it may be better to give explicit information. However, doing so can result in a long modification as the following extract shows.

Report 315

D— e: Tax effect explicitly explained (extract)

Qualified opinion arising from disagreement about income recognition

(Extract) Included in turnover are amounts invoiced to customers for goods supplied to site but not yet fitted on short-term contracts to refit shops. In our opinion such invoices were not issued in accordance with the expectations of the other parties to such contracts and payment will not be received by the company until the contracts are complete. In our opinion, turnover and debtors are overstated by £ ..... , work in progress is understated by £ ..... and profit before tax is overstated by £ ..... . Taxation of £ ...... attributable to the overstated profit should not have been provided for and as a result the profit after tax and net assets of the company are overstated by the net amount of £ ..... .

3.4.3.5 Except for or adverse opinion

The difference between an except for and an adverse opinion depends on the judgement as to whether the effect of the matter giving rise to disagreement is so material or pervasive that the financial statements are seriously misleading.

SAS 600 is not very forthcoming about the decision. The only guidance it provides is in example 10 in appendix 2. That example deals with a lack of provision against losses expected to arise on certain long-term contracts. The wording of the example gives no clue at all as to the magnitude to the provisions being disputed and readers are left wondering whether 'note .....' would have been of any further help.

An adverse opinion is perhaps less likely to attract litigation but it is an extreme measure that ought to be reserved for the minority of disagreements where it is appropriate. Auditors have to balance natural prudence (tending towards an adverse opinion) against the tendency towards the normal (an except for qualification) when exercising judgement.

Obviously, to necessitate an adverse opinion a disagreement must be larger than simply material. How much larger is a matter of personal judgement. Two criteria may be considered in this context:

- the magnitude of the disagreement
- whether the profit and loss account, or the balance sheet, or both are affected.

As an adverse opinion is on the view given by the accounts as a whole it is easier for a matter affecting both the profit and loss account and the balance sheet to give rise to such a report.

Assuming that it is possible to choose an amount above which a matter is material, the following guidelines seem sensible for these different cases, to decide whether a matter is so material or pervasive that the financial statements are seriously misleading:

- matters affecting both the profit and loss account and the balance sheet — the amount of the proposed adjustment (if any) to the accounts is five times materiality
- matters affecting only the profit and loss account (and the closing balance sheet is audited satisfactorily) or only the balance sheet — ten times materiality.

If draft SAS 130 progresses to a SAS without significant changes, reporting on going concern will not obey these general rules.

3.4.3.6 Paragraph 36A of Schedule 4 to the Companies Act 1985

This section and the one that follows dealing with UITF 7 examine the nature of disclosures that ought to be made where there is a breach of accounting or disclosure requirements. Problems with these further disclosures may also affect the auditor's report.

Paragraph 36A of Schedule 4 to the Companies Act 1985 requires the accounts to include a statement that they have been prepared in accordance with applicable accounting standards. If there has been a departure from applicable accounting standards, however, particulars and the reasons for the departure are to be given in a note. The law refers to 'material departures', but this is implicit, as accounting standards need not be applied to immaterial items. The section applies only to larger companies as, by virtue of section 246(1)(a), small and medium-sized companies are exempt from the requirements of paragraph 36A.

The provisions are designed to deal with the exceptional circumstances where departure from the requirements of an accounting standard is necessary for accounts to give a true and fair view. They may, however, be relevant where the auditors' view is that an accounting standard has been breached. In such circumstances, the disclosures for a departure required by paragraph 36A are unlikely to be in the accounts and a further modification to a report expressing disagreement will be necessary to refer to the lack of disclosure (but see the discussion after the illustrations below). There is also the possibility that an inappropriate paragraph 36A disclosure itself will cause a modification. The potential effects on the auditors' report are summarised in the table below. The modification where the accounts do not comply with an accounting standard could be an 'except for' or an adverse opinion. It is assumed that any problem with a disclosure required by paragraph 36A is not itself likely to affect the true and fair view. Auditors should, nevertheless, assess whether a problem is significant and document their decision.

Accounting Standards	Paragraph 36A disclosure	Effect on auditors' report
Accounts comply.	Compliance disclosed.	Standard report.
Accounts comply.	Disclosure omitted.	Modification: true and fair but 'except for' on proper preparation.
Accounts comply.	Notes state that accounts do not comply.	Unlikely circumstances, modification: true and fair but 'except for' on proper preparation.
Accounts do not comply.	Notes state that accounts do not comply.	Modification: 'except for' on true and fair and on proper preparation.
Accounts do not comply.	Disclosure omitted.	Modification: 'except for' on true and fair and on proper preparation because of p36A disclosure.
Accounts do not comply.	Notes incorrectly state that accounts do comply.	Modification: 'except for' on true and fair and on proper preparation because of p36A disclosure.

There is a complication to the above where the accounting standard that is breached itself relies on the true and fair override, for example, a breach of Statement of Standard Accounting Practice 19 'Accounting for investment properties'. This is considered further below when discussing UITF 7.

The following illustrations are of a paragraph 36A modification alone (two versions depending on whether the true and fair view is thought to be affected) and such a modification together with a disagreement over accounting treatment.

Report 316

D— e: Paragraph 36A disclosure omitted, no effect on the true and fair view

Qualified opinion arising from disagreement about disclosure

The financial statements do not disclose that they have been prepared in accordance with applicable accounting standards as required by paragraph 36A of Schedule 4 to the Companies Act 1985.

In our opinion the financial statements give a true and fair view of the state of the company's affairs as at .... and of its [profit / loss] for the year then ended and except for the absence of the above disclosure, have been properly prepared in accordance with the Companies Act 1985.

Report 317

D— e: Paragraph 36A disclosure omitted, considered to affect the true and fair view

Qualified opinion arising from disagreement about disclosure

The financial statements do not disclose that they have been prepared in accordance with applicable accounting standards as required by paragraph 36A of Schedule 4 to the Companies Act 1985.

Except for the absence of this disclosure, in our opinion the financial statements give a true and fair view of the state of the company's affairs as at .... and of its [profit / loss] for the year then ended and have been properly prepared in accordance with the Companies Act 1985.

Report 318
D — e: Long-term contract losses not provided and paragraph 36A disclosure omitted, separate opinions

Qualified opinion arising from disagreement about accounting treatment

No provision has been made for losses expected to arise on certain long-term contracts currently in progress, as the directors consider that such losses should be off-set against amounts recoverable on other long-term contracts. In our opinion, provision should be made for foreseeable losses on individual contracts as required by Statement of Standard Accounting Practice 9 'Stocks and long-term contracts'. If losses had been so recognised the effect would have been to [reduce the profit / increase the loss] before and after tax for the year and the contract work in progress at .... by £ ..... .

The financial statements do not disclose particulars of this material departure from applicable accounting standards and the reasons for it as required by paragraph 36A of Schedule 4 to the Companies Act 1985.

Except for the failure to account correctly for losses on long-term contracts and except for the lack of disclosure of the material departure from accounting standards, in our opinion the financial statements give a true and fair view of the state of the company's affairs as at .... and of its [profit / loss] for the year then ended and have been properly prepared in accordance with the Companies Act 1985.

The last example above is, in effect, a multiple qualification for disagreement. Combining modifications in this way is dealt with in the next chapter. In this instance the failure to disclose the breach of the accounting standards is considered by the auditors to be significant (and hence affects the true and fair view) because there was a material breach that the accounts, through failing to comply with p36A, contrived to hide.

The third example above and the discussion about the consequences of a p36A breach are valid but auditors have frequently not issued such reports. Modifications for breaches of accounting standards would be expected, in most instances, to arise with a failure to make an appropriate p36A disclosure but evidence of auditors referring to the further disagreement is limited. This may be because of conscious judgements made when combining modifications or because the requirement has been overlooked. The Auditing Guideline 'Reports by auditors under company legislation in the United Kingdom' was last revised in February 1991 and includes some guidance on p36A (the most significant being that omission normally requires a modification for *'not properly prepared'*). It did not, however, include any examples of relevant qualified opinions. SAS 600 should promote more knowledge of the matter.

The examples in appendix 2 to SAS 600 do provide some guidance on appropriate wording for a modification but readers also have to assume that examples 10 and

12 were based on circumstances where full disclosure of the breach was made. Example 11 combines a qualified opinion and a fundamental uncertainty but it is only the former that is of interest here. The relevant text is highlighted in bold.

Report 319
D— e: Finance leases accounted for as operating and paragraph 36A disclosure omitted (based on SAS 600 example 11)

Qualified opinion arising from disagreement about accounting treatment

The company leases plant and equipment which have been accounted for in the financial statements as operating leases. In our opinion, these leases should be accounted for as finance leases as required by Statement of Standard Accounting Practice 21. If this accounting treatment were followed, the finance leases would be reflected in the company's balance sheet at £ ..... and the profit for the year would have been reduced by £ ..... . **The financial statements do not include an explanation for this departure from an applicable accounting standard as required by the Companies Act 1985**.

Except for the failure to account for the leases referred to above as required by SSAP 21, in our opinion the financial statements give a true and fair view of the state of the company's affairs as at .... and of its [profit / loss] for the year then ended and have been properly prepared in accordance with the Companies Act 1985.

Paragraph 48 of SAS 600 states that *'Where no explanation is given for a departure from accounting standards, its absence may of itself impair the ability of the financial statements to give a true and fair view of the company's state of affairs and profit or loss. When auditors conclude that this is so, a qualified or adverse opinion on the view given by the financial statements is appropriate, in addition to a reference (where appropriate) to the non-compliance with the specific requirement of company law referred to in paragraph 42 above.'* (i.e. p36A).

Example 11 shows the 'additional reference' (in bold) but the wording of the qualification refers only to the breach of SSAP 21. Had the internal cross-reference been less specific the qualification could have been seen to refer to the p36A problem as well as the breach of SSAP 21. Because of the persuasive impact of the examples in appendix 2 to SAS 600, the probability is that auditors who follow example 11 will not attract professional criticism. The existence of the example also argues towards making cross-references to disagreements less specific. This could be done for one of the illustrative reports above to achieve perhaps the best compromise — a report that includes the words from SAS 600's example 11 and also wording for the two disagreements. The example below continues to refer to paragraph 36A, not just the Companies Act 1985. The precision of cross-references is just a matter of house style and is discussed later in this chapter in the section dealing with writing a modification.

Report 320
D — e: Long-term contract losses not provided and paragraph 36A disclosure omitted, combined opinions

Qualified opinion arising from disagreement about accounting treatment

No provision has been made for losses expected to arise on certain long-term contracts currently in progress, as the directors consider that such losses should be off-set against amounts recoverable on other long-term contracts. In our opinion, provision should be made for foreseeable losses on individual contracts as required by Statement of Standard Accounting Practice 9 'Stocks and long-term contracts'. If losses had been so recognised the effect would have been to [reduce the profit / increase the loss] before and after tax for the year and the contract work in progress at .... by £..... . The financial statements do not include an explanation for this departure from an applicable accounting standard as required by paragraph 36A of Schedule 4 to the Companies Act.

Except for the failure to account correctly for the matter referred to above, in our opinion the financial statements give a true and fair view of the state of the company's affairs as at .... and of its [profit / loss] for the year then ended and have been properly prepared in accordance with the Companies Act 1985.

Paragraph 36A of Schedule 4 to the Companies Act 1985 has to be considered in the light of the Urgent Issues Task Force Abstract 7 'True and Fair View Override Disclosures' (UITF 7). However, before that document is discussed it is necessary to deal with the exemptions available to small and medium-sized companies.

1 Exemptions for small and medium-sized companies

By virtue of section 246 of the Companies Act 1985, small and medium-sized companies are exempt from the requirements of paragraph 36A. All companies do, however, have to comply with UITF Abstract 7 'True and Fair View Override Disclosures' because the UITF 'forgot' to exempt small and medium sized companies. At least, that is one view. A more practical approach, backed up by a reading of the ASB's Foreword to UITF Abstracts, is that the legal exemption extends to the UITF pronouncement. Paragraph 12 of the Foreword states that *'Where UITF Abstracts prescribe information to be contained in financial statements, such requirements do not override exemptions from disclosure given by law to, and utilised by, certain types of entity.'* A similar paragraph is in the ASB's 'Foreword to Accounting Standards'. That has, in the past, been relevant to banks and insurance companies and continues to be relevant for small companies taking advantage of exemptions introduced by SI 1992 No. 2452 The Companies Act 1985 (Accounts of Small and Medium-sized Enterprises and Publication of Accounts in ECUs) Regulations 1992. Applying the logic of paragraph 12, therefore, small and medium-sized companies need not comply with UITF Abstract 7.

3.4.3.7 UITF Abstract 7 'True and Fair View Override Disclosures'

UITF 7 was issued in December 1992 in an attempt to prevent companies understating, rather than emphasising, the significance of what they had done. In some cases the UITF noted that it was not clear from notes to the accounts whether or not the true and fair view override was being invoked.

The term 'true and fair override' refers to the requirement of section 226(5) of the Companies Act 1985 that the directors must depart from the other specific provisions of the Act if in special circumstances compliance with them is inconsistent with the requirement to give a true and fair view. The departure must only be to the extent necessary to give a true and fair view and particulars must be given in a note to the accounts. An equivalent provision for group accounts is in section 227(6).

The UITF consensus was that where the true and fair view override was being invoked that should be stated clearly and unambiguously. The following disclosures should either be included, or cross-referenced, in the note required under paragraph 36A of Schedule 4:

- the treatment that the Act would normally require in the circumstances
- why that would not give a true and fair view
- the treatment actually adopted
- a description of how the accounts are different as a result of the departure.

The description is normally with quantification except if that is not relevant (e.g. the departure involves presentation not measurement) or is not practicable, in which case that fact ought itself to be explained.

Where a departure continues in subsequent years, the disclosures (including corresponding amounts) should be made in all such accounts. When the departure affects only the corresponding amounts, the disclosures should still be given.

UITF 7 also states that its interpretation of the expression *'particulars of any such departure, the reasons for it and its effect'* may be applied to its use in:

- departures from the specified statutory accounting principles:
  — paragraph 15 of Schedule 4
  — paragraph 22 of Schedule 9
- inconsistent accounting rules for an undertaking included in group accounts — paragraph 3(2) of Schedule 4A.

The true and fair override normally involves breaching an accounting standard but some accounting standards rely on the true and fair override themselves. For example SSAP 19 'Accounting for investment properties' requires investment properties to be at valuation, not depreciated historical cost, which breaches the general depreciation rule in paragraph 18 of Schedule 4 to the Companies Act 1985. The disclosure required by paragraph 36A of Schedule 4 to the Companies Act 1985 in such cases is simply that applicable accounting standards have been followed. That disclosure would also refer to the disclosure required by UITF 7.

3.4.3.8 Paragraph 36A and UITF 7

If a p36A disclosure is made concerning the true and fair override when an accounting standard is breached auditors consider whether that disclosure complies with UITF 7. If it does, it is reasonable to consider that the disclosure is properly made for the purpose of assessing compliance with p36A. If it does not comply, not only does the disclosure not comply with p36A, but there is also a breach of UITF 7. This itself requires a modification if it is considered to be a material departure from a UITF Abstract.

This further modification for disagreement is less easy to combine with the disagreement about the accounting treatment than is the p36A modification as the following opinion illustrates. The p36A modification is assumed in this case to affect the true and fair view.

Report 321

D— e: Long-term contract losses not provided and paragraph 36A disclosure breaching UITF 7, combined opinions

Qualified opinion arising from disagreement about accounting treatment

> No provision has been made for losses expected to arise on certain long-term contracts currently in progress, as the directors consider that such losses should be off-set against amounts recoverable on other long-term contracts. In our opinion, provision should be made for foreseeable losses on individual contracts as required by Statement of Standard Accounting Practice 9 'Stocks and long-term contracts'. If losses had been so recognised the effect would have been to [reduce the profit / increase the loss] before and after tax for the year and the contract work in progress at .... by £...... .
>
> The financial statements do not include an adequate explanation for this departure from an applicable accounting standard as required by paragraph 36A of Schedule 4 to the Companies Act. The explanation does not give details of [the treatment that the accounting standard would normally require in the circumstances / why that would not give a true and fair view / a description of how the accounts are different as a result of the departure] as required by UITF Abstract 7 'True and Fair View Override Disclosures'.
>
> Except for the failure to account correctly for long-term contracts and except for the breach of UITF 7 and the requirements of paragraph 36A of Schedule 4 to the Companies Act, in our opinion the financial statements give a true and fair view of the state of the company's affairs as at .... and of its [profit / loss] for the year then ended and have been properly prepared in accordance with the Companies Act 1985.

UITF 7 is effective for accounts for periods ending on or after 23 December 1992 and so predates SAS 600. As it is not acknowledged in SAS 600 it is likely that many auditors will not consider it when drawing up modified reports. Is there any interpretation of its scope (other than that it does not apply to small and medium-sized companies) that can be used to argue that it is not relevant?

The Abstract is clearly designed to improve disclosure of the use of the true and fair override (of which breach of accounting standards is just one part). Should it, therefore, be applied if the directors do not make any disclosure because they believe that they have complied with an accounting standard and it is only the auditors' view that they have not?

The Abstract applies *'in cases where the true and fair view override is being invoked'*. This is not just cases where there is a disclosure to that effect; the test examines the underlying facts. On the other hand, whether it can be said that an error or a different view constitutes 'invoking' is a moot point. 'Invoking' is a strong word. In practice, it is probably currently acceptable for auditors to mention UITF 7 only where they are concerned about a deficient disclosure of the true and fair override.

3.4.4 Links to other modifications

There are no direct links to other modifications. Sometimes it can be difficult to decide, however, whether a modification is required for a disagreement or an uncertainty. Imagine, for example, that the directors do not write down the book value of a fixed asset that has suffered a permanent diminution in value. They may acknowledge that a lower value is correct but not want to put a figure on it and so do not make any write down. Auditors have to decide whether this is an inherent uncertainty or a disagreement that is difficult to quantify.

Uncertainty may be inherent and only capable of resolution through the passage of time, or it may arise because of a scope limitation. The above example is probably one of the more difficult areas in which to come to a decision. In practice, with such circumstances auditors will probably have to 'settle' for a modification describing a fundamental uncertainty.

Other matters may be easier to assess. For example, a common problem is where the split of property costs between land and buildings is not known. If depreciation is not charged the amount may be uncertain but (so long as it is material) the auditors' report ought to point out the lack of compliance with SSAP 12 'Accounting for depreciation' and Schedule 4 to the Companies Act 1985.

3.4.5 Typical circumstances

Disagreements may occur in relation to:

- accounting standards:
  - FRSs
  - UITF Abstracts
  - SSAPs
- company law:
  - sections of the Companies Act 1985
  - paragraphs of Schedule 4 to the Companies Act 1985
  - Statutory Instruments
- accounting where there is no inherent uncertainty:
  - insufficient provision for losses (e.g. bad debts)

— incorrect classification
— incorrect allocation to accounting period
— insufficient disclosure (e.g. concerning an inherent uncertainty).

3.5 Fundamental uncertainty

3.5.1 The requirements

If auditors consider that an inherent uncertainty is fundamental then, if it is adequately accounted for and disclosed in the financial statements, they are required by SAS 600.6 to modify their report by including an explanatory paragraph referring to it. The paragraph should be included in the section of their report setting out the basis of their opinion. Auditors should use words which clearly indicate that their opinion on the financial statements is not qualified because of the matter referred to in the explanatory paragraph.

3.5.2 Typical wording

Three illustrative reports for fundamental uncertainty are shown below. The modification affects only the basis of opinion section.

Report 322
FU: Generic skeleton

Basis of opinion

Compliance with Auditing Standards and description of an audit.

Evidence and evaluation of presentation.

HEADING

DESCRIPTION OF FUNDAMENTAL UNCERTAINTY.

Report 323
FU: Generic word picture

Basis of opinion

We conducted our audit in accordance with Auditing Standards issued by the Auditing Practices Board. An audit includes examination, on a test basis, of evidence relevant to the amounts and disclosures in the financial statements. It also includes an assessment of the significant estimates and judgements made by the directors in the preparation of the financial statements, and of whether the accounting policies are appropriate to the company's circumstances, consistently applied and adequately disclosed.

We planned and performed our audit so as to obtain all the information and explanations which we considered necessary in order to provide us with sufficient evidence to give reasonable assurance that the financial statements are free from material misstatement, whether caused by fraud or other irregularity or error. In forming our opinion we also evaluated the overall adequacy of the presentation of information in the financial statements.

FUNDAMENTAL UNCERTAINTY

IN FORMING OUR OPINION, WE HAVE CONSIDERED THE ADEQUACY OF THE DISCLOSURES MADE IN THE FINANCIAL STATEMENTS CONCERNING [MATTER]. [EFFECT ON FINANCIAL STATEMENTS WHEN MATTER IS RESOLVED] [QUANTIFICATION]. DETAILS OF THE CIRCUMSTANCES RELATING TO THIS FUNDAMENTAL UNCERTAINTY ARE DESCRIBED IN NOTE ..... . OUR OPINION IS NOT QUALIFIED IN THIS RESPECT.

Report 324
FU: Litigation

Basis of opinion

We conducted our audit in accordance with Auditing Standards issued by the Auditing Practices Board. An audit includes examination, on a test basis, of evidence relevant to the amounts and disclosures in the financial statements. It also includes an assessment of the significant estimates and judgements made by the directors in the preparation of the financial statements, and of whether the accounting policies are appropriate to the company's circumstances, consistently applied and adequately disclosed.

We planned and performed our audit so as to obtain all the information and explanations which we considered necessary in order to provide us with sufficient evidence to give reasonable assurance that the financial statements are free from material misstatement, whether caused by fraud or other irregularity or error. In forming our opinion we also evaluated the overall adequacy of the presentation of information in the financial statements.

Fundamental uncertainty

In forming our opinion, we have considered the adequacy of the disclosures made in the financial statements concerning the possible outcome to litigation against B Limited, a subsidiary of the company, for an alleged breach of environmental regulations. The future settlement of this litigation could result in additional liabilities and the closure of B Limited's business, whose net assets included in the consolidated balance sheet totals £ ..... and whose profit before tax for the year is £ ..... . Details of the circumstances relating to this fundamental uncertainty are described in note ..... . Our opinion is not qualified in this respect.

3.5.3 Analysis of the requirements

3.5.3.1 Introduction

The wording of a paragraph about a fundamental uncertainty is not prescribed by SAS 600.6. All the paragraph is required to do is refer to the fundamental uncertainty and to clearly indicate that the auditors' opinion on the financial statements is not qualified in respect of the contents of the paragraph.

The following wording apparently and alarmingly complies with the letter of the SAS:

Fundamental uncertainty

Our opinion is not qualified in respect of the contents of this paragraph. A fundamental uncertainty is described in note ..... to the financial statements.

The explanatory material to SAS 600.6 includes further 'requirements', namely to:

- describe the matter giving rise to the fundamental uncertainty
- describe its possible effects on the financial statements
- where practicable, quantify the possible effects
- if it is not possible to quantify the potential effects of the resolution of the uncertainty, include a statement to that effect.

It seems odd that these reasonable matters were relegated to the explanatory material. Auditors would do well to regard them as if they were part of the standard.

These extended 'requirements' merit close examination together with the examples given in appendix 2 to SAS 600 in order to see how they have been implemented. The following analysis deals with:

- deciding whether an uncertainty is fundamental
- positioning and heading
- introductory wording
- what is meant by 'referring' to the fundamental uncertainty:
  — referring and cross-referring
  — quantifying the effects
- statement that opinion is not qualified.

3.5.3.2 Fundamental?

If an inherent uncertainty is properly accounted for and disclosed auditors need not modify their report unless the matter is considered to be a 'fundamental uncertainty'. This decision is, therefore, very important. The guidance material following SAS 600.6 gives some clues but uses inconsistent language and leaves auditors guessing about the decision and going concern in particular.

Paragraph 64 has been interpreted by some (including the working party drawing up the proposed SAS on going concern) as giving a definition rather than amplifying what paragraph 63 has to say about the factors auditors should consider. Essentially, paragraph 63 advises auditors to consider:

- the risk that the estimate included in financial statements may be subject to change
- the range of possible outcomes, and
- the consequences of those outcomes on the view shown in the financial statements.

Paragraph 64 then says that *'Inherent uncertainties are regarded as fundamental when they involve a significant level of concern about the validity of the going concern basis or other matters whose potential effect on the financial statements is unusually great.'* Paragraph 64 suggests the outcome of major litigation as a common example of fundamental uncertainty.

There are two schools of thought about going concern. Either inherent uncertainty over going concern is always fundamental or it is only fundamental when the potential effect on the financial statements is unusually great. Whatever the 'right' answer is, auditors must wait for, and comply with the final version of SAS130.

For other inherent uncertainties auditors are only provided with a circular test to apply. Where resolution of an inherent uncertainty could affect the view given by the financial statements to the degree that the auditors conclude that it is to be regarded as fundamental then it is a fundamental uncertainty.

The explanatory material seems to use the words 'unusually great' to mean 'very great' and auditors are, therefore, left to decide when 'great' becomes 'very great'.

The definitions section of SAS 600 gives a definition of 'fundamental uncertainty'. *'An inherent uncertainty is fundamental when the magnitude of its potential impact is so great that, without clear disclosure of the nature and implications of the uncertainty, the view given by the financial statements would be seriously misleading.'* The magnitude of an inherent uncertainty's potential impact is to be judged by reference to the matters dealt with above shown in connection with paragraph 63.

The definition implies that auditors should be able to judge the adequacy of disclosure (in case there should be a modification of their report for disagreement) and whether the inherent uncertainty is fundamental by:

- imagining the financial statements without clear disclosure of the nature and implications of the inherent uncertainty
- deciding whether the view given by the imaginary financial statements is 'seriously misleading'.

This is a matter of judgement and auditors who properly document reaching a decision that is not prima facie unreasonable should have few professional worries. It is, nevertheless, possible to use some rules of thumb to decide whether a matter ought to be considered as possibly fundamental. The following guidelines are similar to those suggested for assessing whether a disagreement gives rise to the more extreme adverse opinion.

To be fundamental an inherent uncertainty must be larger than simply material. How much larger is a matter of personal judgement. Two criteria may be considered in this context:

- the magnitude of the inherent uncertainty
- whether the profit and loss account, or the balance sheet, or both are affected.

As the definition is in terms of *'the view given by the financial statements'* it is easier for an inherent uncertainty affecting both the profit and loss account and the balance sheet to be fundamental.

Assuming that it is possible to choose an amount above which a matter is material, the following guidelines seem sensible for these different cases, to decide whether an inherent uncertainty is fundamental:

- matters affecting both the profit and loss account and the balance sheet — the amount of the potential effect (if any) on the accounts is five times materiality
- matters affecting only the profit and loss account (and the closing balance sheet is audited satisfactorily) or only the balance sheet — ten times materiality.

If draft SAS 130 progresses to a SAS without significant changes, reporting on going concern will not obey these general rules.

3.5.3.3 Positioning and heading

SAS 600.6 requires the explanatory paragraph referring to a fundamental uncertainty to be in the section of the auditors' report setting out the basis of their opinion. Examples 4 and 11 in appendix 2 to SAS 600 both have the explanatory paragraph at the end of the 'basis of opinion' section under the subheading 'fundamental uncertainty'.

As the wording of the paragraphs would not easily commence the basis of opinion section, and as there would otherwise have to be a further subheading, this approach seems reasonable. Auditors are likely, therefore, to position explanatory paragraphs in the way illustrated by the examples in appendix 2 to SAS 600.

Those examples use the bare subheading 'fundamental uncertainty'. There are already indications that some auditors consider these words to be too emotive and prefer a heading that merely indicates the nature of the uncertainty. It is too early for SAS 600 reports to have established a pattern in this and, for the present, it is safer for auditors to use the headings shown in the examples in appendix 2. The examples provided by the exposure draft of SAS 130 head the paragraphs dealing with going concern, *'Fundamental uncertainty: going concern'*.

3.5.3.4 Introductory wording

The relevant examples in appendix 2 to SAS 600 commence with the words:

> In forming our opinion, we have considered the adequacy of the disclosures made in the financial statements concerning the possible outcome of . . .

This wording is neither required by SAS 600.6 nor suggested by the explanatory material. Why then is it in the examples?

The intention is clear, to justify the inclusion of the fundamental uncertainty paragraph within the 'basis of opinion', rather than as a separate paragraph, perhaps below the opinion. Perhaps unfortunately, the words are separated only by a title from the normal concluding sentence of the basis of opinion, which also refers to the adequacy of presentation of information in the financial statements.

There is a further problem with this wording that it is perhaps unfair to mention now, namely that when multiple modifications for fundamental uncertainty occur the wording is repetitious. It may not be possible to combine the paragraphs dealing with fundamental uncertainties as SAS 600.6 requires 'an explanatory paragraph' for each. Whether anyone will worry if auditors combine such modifications or split their description of a single fundamental uncertainty into two or more paragraphs remains to be seen.[4] Bearing in mind that fundamental uncertainties are likely to be rare (except for those affecting the going concern basis) any concerns are probably hypothetical.

Auditors who do not feel bound to follow the wording of the examples in appendix 2 to SAS 600 may decide to make a cleaner and quicker start, and also solve any problem of cross-referring, by commencing:

> As described in note ....

3.5.3.5 Referring to the fundamental uncertainty

What is meant by 'referring to the fundamental uncertainty'? Examples 4 and 10 in appendix 2 to the SAS use the following wording close to the end of the explanatory paragraphs:

> Details of the circumstances relating to this fundamental uncertainty are described in note ..... .

This contributes to the thought that 'referring' and 'cross-referring' are closely related.

'Refer' ought to be interpreted in terms of the explanatory material. In other words, the auditors refer (i.e. direct attention to the fundamental uncertainty) by giving a quantified description. The auditors may enhance their description by cross-referring to a note to the accounts giving further information.

Although a cross-reference is not necessary, auditors may well follow the wording of the examples in appendix 2 to SAS 600 and provide one. Given that this will happen, is the wording in the examples to be followed?

---

[4] It would appear that so long as there is 'a' paragraph dealing with a fundamental uncertainty it is acceptable for there to be further paragraphs also dealing with it.

The sentence has a Flesch Reading Ease of only 29.5. The first seven words add little to the meaning of the cross-reference. It is taken for granted that a cross-reference would not be made unless further detail was given there, so the following wording would be sufficient:

> This matter is described in note ..... .

This alternative raises the Flesch Reading Ease to 91.

The only way to make a shorter reference is to put it before the bulk of the paragraph:

> As described in note ..... , . . .

That approach is difficult if auditors wish to start their paragraphs similarly to those in the relevant examples in appendix 2 to SAS 600.

3.5.3.6 Quantifying the effects

Quantifying the effects should be a simple procedure, at least if the figures are available, but SAS 600 uses very complex language which, therefore, requires examination.

The explanatory material (e.g. paragraph 61) uses two different wordings to refer to quantifying. The auditors are to *'describe its possible effects', and 'where practicable, quantify the possible effects'*. These words are consistent. The next wording possibly poses potential problems.

The auditors are required, '*if it is not possible to quantify the potential effects of the resolution of the uncertainty,* (to) *include a statement to that effect*'. The words to contrast are: 'practicable' and 'possible' (single underline), and 'possible' and 'potential' (double underline).

Is there any real reason for using the second form of words other than variety in prose (or 'elegant variation')? Was there any reason for not using the word 'probable' in connection with the effects of the resolution of the uncertainty?

1 'Practicable' and 'possible'

The dictionary definitions of 'practicable' and 'possible' both include 'feasible', so they are largely synonymous. To most readers, 'possible' is the more definite. Something may be possible so long as it is not impossible. For example, it is possible to juggle four balls using only one hand. 'Possible' has meanings involving things existing or happening, not just things being done. 'Practicable' is less widely used as its meanings are more confined to things that can be done or routes that can be followed. It is close to 'practical' though the distinction between the words is reasonably clear as a 'practical solution' is one adapted to actual conditions whereas a 'practicable solution' is merely one that is feasible.

This brings us back to the wording used in SAS 600. Either 'practicable' and 'possible' were intended to be synonymous or 'practicable' was used in error when 'practical' was intended. If exactly the same meaning was intended it would have been better to have used the same word. Nevertheless the following is based on the assumption that it is correct to substitute 'possible' for 'practicable' in the explanatory material.

2 'Possible' and 'potential'

The search for meaning not only includes the words 'possible' and 'potential', but also the difference, if any, between 'effects' and 'effects of the resolution of the uncertainty'. Is there any difference, given that the resolution of the uncertainty does not affect the current accounts, only those of the future?

The interpretation is not helped by the examples in appendix 2 to SAS 600. Although example 4 seems to comply, in example 10 a paragraph describing circumstances relevant to the going concern basis deals with the 'effect' on the current accounts, not the effects of the resolution of the uncertainty (which would be either that the company ceases to trade or that adequate finance is obtained). It could be argued that the description has to include such matters to properly explain the going concern basis. This does not, however, excuse the lack of description of the effects of the resolution of the uncertainty or any quantification (or a statement that it is not possible to quantify the potential effects of the resolution of the uncertainty).

If the examples were carefully considered by the APB and so comply with SAS 600.6 auditors apparently have significant scope for ignoring the explanatory material.

When providing quantification auditors may look for guidance to the examples in appendix 2 to SAS 600. Figures are given for matters such as:

- the amount of a loan that is being renegotiated
- the net assets of a subsidiary
- the profit before tax for the year contributed by a subsidiary.

The first sum indicates the degree of financial flexibility available to the company to achieve other solutions to a problem of necessary refinancing. It does not, however, give any quantification of the possible effects on the financial statements.

The second two amounts indicate the size of the contribution the subsidiary makes to the group accounts. A well informed reader will infer that these will be removed if the business of the subsidiary is closed. However, there is no explicit confirmation of this. Example 4 does refer to 'additional liabilities' that may arise but neither quantifies them nor states that it is not possible to quantify the potential effects.

Auditors could well conclude that the examples could have been more explicit and better focused on the possible effects.

3.5.3.7 Statement that opinion is not qualified

The examples in appendix 2 to SAS 600 use the following wording at the end of the explanatory paragraph:

> Our opinion is not qualified in this respect.

This wording is commendably brief but phrases such as 'in this respect' are only slightly more modern than 'in this regard'. The blame perhaps lies at the door of SAS 600.6 which uses the words *'. . . is not qualified in respect of the contents of the paragraph'.*

A plain English wording, which auditors are free to adopt, might be:

> Our opinion is not qualified because of this.

3.5.4 Links to other modifications

There are no direct links to other modifications. Sometimes it can be difficult to decide, however, whether a modification is required for a fundamental uncertainty or a disagreement. This is considered in the earlier section of this chapter dealing with disagreement.

Uncertainty can arise from a scope limitation but, if that is the case, a modification referring to a fundamental uncertainty is not appropriate. Paragraph 70 of SAS 600 makes it clear that an inherent uncertainty is separate from a scope limitation.

3.5.5 Typical circumstances

Fundamental uncertainties will not be a normal part of life except perhaps for those involving going concern. It is clear that the potential effect of an uncertainty must be very large for an inherent uncertainty to be classsified as fundamental. SAS 600 gives as an example, the outcome of major litigation. This is the second in the following list of possible circumstances:

- going concern
- major litigation
- major contract losses
- asset realisation in a thin market
- restrictions on foreign assets
- possible legislation affecting trade (e.g. ivory trader).

3.6 Required by law

This section is a little different from the other sections dealing with types of modification. This is because there are several matters that auditors are required to report on by the Companies Act 1985 if they arise. The first of these (failure to keep proper accounting records) is dealt with in full. Other sections refer to this section where common aspects are considered. The relevant circumstances are:

- failure to keep proper accounting records
- lack of all the information and explanations considered necessary for the purposes of the audit
- inadequate returns from branches not visited by the auditors
- the company's individual accounts do not agree with the accounting records and returns
- the information given in the directors' report is not consistent with the accounts
- omission of disclosures required by Schedule 6 to the Companies Act 1985 concerning emoluments of and transactions with directors.

The first two matters above frequently occur together with a SAS 600 limitation of audit scope. Other matters may also be linked to circumstances that give rise to a qualified opinion. Because of this, matters required by law are dealt with in two ways in the later section of this chapter dealing with writing a modification:

- with an associated modification
- alone.

The difference between the two ways is simply that a particular 'event' can result in two or more modifications (including one or more required by law). If so, the modifications can all make use of a single description of the event in the report. It makes sense to group such directly related modifications together if it is necessary to draft a complex report.

3.6.1 Accounting records

3.6.1.1 The requirements

Section 237 of the Companies Act 1985 requires auditors to carry out such investigations as will enable them to form an opinion as to whether proper accounting records have been kept by the company. If auditors are of the opinion that proper accounting records have not been kept they shall state that fact in their report.

SAS 600.5 requires the report to contain a clear expression of opinion on the financial statements and on any further matters required by statute or other requirements applicable to the particular engagement.

3.6.1.2 *Typical wording*

The following illustrations are for the relatively rare case of a modification alone. Wording for the more common case of a problem with accounting records occurring together with a scope limitation is given in the earlier section of this chapter dealing with scope limitation.

The wording given below is not prescribed by SAS 600 and alternative approaches are illustrated and discussed in the next section.

Report 325
AR: Generic skeleton

Opinion

Opinion.

FURTHER MATTERS REQUIRED BY STATUTE OR OTHER REGULATIONS.

Report 326
AR: Generic word picture

Opinion

In our opinion the financial statements give a true and fair view of the state of the company's affairs as at .... and of its [profit / loss] for the year then ended and have been properly prepared in accordance with the Companies Act 1985.

AS MORE FULLY EXPLAINED IN NOTE ..... [MATTER]. IN OUR OPINION, IN THIS RESPECT ALONE, PROPER ACCOUNTING RECORDS HAVE NOT BEEN KEPT.

Report 327
AR: Isolated modification, management fraud

Opinion

In our opinion the financial statements give a true and fair view of the state of the company's affairs as at .... and of its [profit / loss] for the year then ended and have been properly prepared in accordance with the Companies Act 1985.

As more fully explained in note ..... a former director of the company created fictitious purchase invoices to support payments by the company that were diverted to his own use. The original accounting entries for such payments were inaccurate, therefore, and adjustments have been made to correct this when preparing these financial statements. In our opinion, in this respect alone, proper accounting records have not been kept.

3.6.1.3 *Analysis of the requirements*

Historically, auditors have found reporting on accounting records a difficult subject. Often the difficulty was making the connection between a larger problem, such as a scope limitation, and the statutory requirement. Even when auditors did include a reference to accounting records in their report, the wording was likely to be less well considered than the rest of their report. The main reasons for this appear to be the relative lack of professional guidance and uncertainty over the legal requirements.

The following sections examine aspects of the modification and also the judgement about whether proper accounting records have been kept.

1 With a SAS 600 limitation of audit scope

A problem with accounting records normally occurs together with a scope limitation. Illustrative reports for such circumstances are given in the earlier section of this chapter dealing with scope limitation.

The discussion later in this section examines various aspects of the modification on its own. That material may also be relevant to the modification in conjunction with a scope limitation. The following paragraphs examine matters specific to such a multiple modification:

- position and heading
- wording the opinion
- uncertainty as to whether proper accounting records have been kept.

Position and heading

SAS 600.5 requires *'a clear expression of opinion on the financial statements and on any further matters required by statute'*. The former opinion is required by SAS 600.2 to be in a separate, appropriately headed, section of the report. However, SAS 600.2 does not prescribe where the latter opinion should go.

This seems to argue that the opinion on a matter required by statute should be in a section separate from the opinion on the financial statements. This is not, however, the approach adopted by the relevant examples in appendix 2 to SAS 600. In those examples the wording is simply a paragraph following the main opinion. It seems both sensible and professionally defensible, therefore, to put the opinion below the main opinion.

Although an appropriate heading could be used it is probably also acceptable to consider that the 'opinion' heading extends to the opinion on the matter required by statute. It is similarly unnecessary to make 'opinion' plural.

The guidance now in the Auditing Guideline 'Reports by auditors under company legislation in the Republic of Ireland' is to be updated for SAS 600 and issued as a Practice Note. Its revision may assist UK auditors because Irish legislation requires explicit opinions on matters such as whether proper books of account have been kept. A standard report for a Republic of Ireland company is given in chapter 2 'The Standard Report'. It is based on the example in appendix 2 to SAS 600. In that report the heading 'opinion' covers all the opinions given. In due course the Practice Note may cover qualified opinions and any changes to headings.

Section 251 of the Companies Act 1985 deals with summary financial statements of listed companies.[5] In such statements there has to be disclosed whether the auditors' report on the annual accounts contained a statement under:

- section 237(2) (accounting records or returns inadequate or accounts not agreeing with records and returns), or
- section 237(3) (failure to obtain necessary information and explanations).

If such a statement was included it must be set out in full. This is obviously facilitated if all the relevant wording is kept together in the auditors' report.

If the auditors' report on the annual accounts was qualified, section 251 requires the report to be set out in full together with any further material needed to understand the qualification. This would include any statement under section 237 and would remove the need to keep that material together.

Although not required by section 251, auditors could include any further material needed to understand a section 237 statement alone.

Wording the opinion

Where the other modification does not introduce uncertainty into the opinion on accounting records, a brief statement, drawing on the explanation for the other modification is appropriate. This might be worded as follows:

> In our opinion, in respect alone of [matter], proper accounting records have not been kept.

The modification could also involve further explanation or avant-garde wording as discussed below in relation to the modification alone.

If uncertainty is introduced, such that the auditors are unable to be positive about proper accounting records not having been kept, the wording is more contentious.

Uncertainty as to whether proper accounting records have been kept

Auditors may be unable to determine whether proper accounting records have been kept. This can happen when a scope limitation prevents them from obtaining necessary evidence.

The earlier section of this chapter dealing with scope limitation explains that SAS 600 only prescribes the modification when a scope limitation prevents the auditors from expressing an unqualified opinion on the accounts. Other scope limitations

---

[5] Reporting on summary financial statements is outside the scope of this book. The subject is considered only because of its possible influence on the form of a section 237 statement.

may be reported, but there is no requirement to do so except for specific matters required by law. These *'statutory scope limitations'* are:

- absence of proper returns from branches not visited
- not obtaining all necessary information and explanations.

These are discussed in detail in their own sections below.

The choices open to auditors who are unable to determine whether proper accounting records have been kept are to:

- keep silent
- follow the examples in appendix 2 to SAS 600 and report that they were unable to determine whether proper accounting records had been maintained
- include other wording describing the matter (in accordance with paragraph 29 of SAS 600)
- report that they had not obtained all necessary information and explanations.

Keeping silent is probably acceptable given that the positive opinion required by law cannot be given (and no material uncertainty is present over and above that reported by any other modification). However, the fact that the examples in appendix 2 to SAS 600 mention the problem with accounting records is a strong argument against keeping silent.

The wording of the examples in appendix 2 is not universally helpful as the modification is dealt with only in conjunction with a scope limitation. In addition, the wording used does not amount to a positive opinion as to whether proper accounting records have been kept or not. The possible justification in SAS 600 for the wording used in the examples is to consider it as being part of the description of the factors leading to the limitation. This is perhaps being generous to the APB as the alternative interpretation is simply that the relevant examples in appendix 2 were drafted with more regard to similar examples in the previous Auditing Standard than to SAS 600.

Auditors are allowed by SAS 600 to include additional comment in their report. However, paragraph 29 of SAS 600 restricts that comment to the 'basis of opinion' section of the report to *'highlight matters . . . relevant to a proper understanding of the basis of their opinion'*. It is possible to construct appropriate wording on this basis as the following example shows:

Report 328
AR: Scope limitation reported under paragraph 29

Basis of opinion

We conducted our audit in accordance with Auditing Standards issued by the Auditing Practices Board. An audit includes examination, on a test basis, of evidence relevant to the amounts and disclosures in the financial statements. It also includes an assessment of the significant estimates and judgements made by the directors in the preparation of the financial statements, and of whether the accounting policies are appropriate to the company's circumstances, consistently applied and adequately disclosed.

We planned and performed our audit so as to obtain all the information and explanations which we considered necessary in order to provide us with sufficient evidence to give reasonable assurance that the financial statements are free from material misstatement, whether caused by fraud or other irregularity or error. In forming our opinion we also evaluated the overall adequacy of the presentation of information in the financial statements.

Accounting records

We are required by law to carry out such investigations as will enable us to form an opinion as to whether proper accounting records have been kept by the company. If we are of the opinion that proper accounting records have not been kept we are required to state that fact in our report. However, the evidence available to us concerning the keeping of proper accounting records was limited because a small amount of the company's turnover comprises cash sales. There was no system of control over such sales on which we could rely for the purposes of our audit and there were no satisfactory audit procedures that we could adopt to confirm that proper accounting records had been kept for such sales. Accordingly we are unable to express an opinion as to whether, in this respect alone, proper accounting records had been kept. Our opinion on the financial statements is not qualified in this respect because the amounts involved are not material.

The above wording is not recommended. The main reason for preferring a different approach is that the above paragraph is disproportionately long and is hardly going to be welcomed by a reader of the report.

The last alternative is for auditors to report that they have not obtained all necessary information and explanations. This approach was supported by Touche Ross & Co. in the third edition of their excellent *Manual of Financial Reporting and Accounting* (published by Butterworths). Touche argued that *'As the Act requires the auditor to report on the accounting records only when he has formed an opinion that they have not been kept, it would appear inappropriate for the auditor to refer to his inability to be satisfied as to the completeness and accuracy of the accounting records as is done in the example in the standard* (i.e. the Auditing Standard replaced by SAS 600). *Instead it is considered preferable for the auditor to state that he has been unable to obtain all the information and explanations which he considers necessary for the purposes of his audit.'*

It is difficult to fault the above argument and this ought to be regarded as the preferred approach. The difficulty with just dropping any mention of accounting records (which Touche advocated as the alternative) is that readers will assume the reported deficiency relates only to the scope limitation (assuming one is reported). This may be a problem if auditors wish to make it clear that there is also some restriction on their ability to report on accounting records. Appropriate wording might be introduced in that case, or if auditors wish to report on a scope limitation relating only to accounting records.

The following illustration is for a multiple modification and is based on the report given in the scope limitation section of this chapter. It does not show any further wording about auditors' responsibilities that some auditors may wish to give in the appropriate section of their report. It does, however, make it clear that the scope limitation includes the accounting records.

Report 329
AR: I&E: SL — e: Cash sales accounting records uncertainty

Basis of opinion

We conducted our audit in accordance with Auditing Standards issued by the Auditing Practices Board except that the scope of our work was limited as explained below.

An audit includes examination, on a test basis, of evidence relevant to the amounts and disclosures in the financial statements. It also includes an assessment of the significant estimates and judgements made by the directors in the preparation of the financial statements, and of whether the accounting policies are appropriate to the company's circumstances, consistently applied and adequately disclosed.

We planned and performed our audit so as to obtain all the information and explanations which we considered necessary in order to provide us with sufficient evidence to give reasonable assurance that the financial statements are free from material misstatement, whether caused by fraud or other irregularity or error. However, the evidence available to us was limited because £ ..... of the company's recorded turnover comprises cash sales. There was no system of control over such sales on which we could rely for the purposes of our audit and there were no other satisfactory audit procedures that we could adopt to confirm for cash sales that they were properly recorded or that proper accounting records had been kept.

In forming our opinion we also evaluated the overall adequacy of the presentation of information in the financial statements.

Qualified opinion arising from limitation in audit scope

Except for any adjustments that might have been found to be necessary had we been able to obtain sufficient evidence concerning cash sales, in our opinion the financial statements give a true and fair view of the state of the company's affairs as at .... and of its [profit / loss] for the year then ended and have been properly prepared in accordance with the Companies Act 1985.

In respect alone of the limitation on our work relating to cash sales we have not obtained all the information and explanations that we considered necessary for the purposes of our audit.

The remaining parts of this section deal mainly with the modification alone.

2 Explanation

In most instances, the absence of proper accounting records is accompanied by a qualification for limitation in scope. Exceptions to this are rare. One possibility is where proper accounting records have not been kept because of a fraud. Once the fraud is discovered the accounting records are corrected and the accounts prepared from them show a true and fair view. During the year, however, the records were deficient.

As the report includes no explanation about another modification, auditors have to decide how to provide explanation for the accounting records modification alone.

A bare opinion could be given as follows:

Opinion

> In our opinion the financial statements give a true and fair view of the state of the company's affairs as at .... and of its [profit / loss] for the year then ended and have been properly prepared in accordance with the Companies Act 1985.
>
> In our opinion proper accounting records have not been kept.

Although this approach is not adopted for the typical wording of reports illustrated above, it is arguably acceptable as it complies with the law. Its use is rejected, however, because it raises more questions than it answers.

The amount of explanation that should be in the auditors' report is not prescribed. It seems reasonable to refer to the requirement of SAS 600.7 (when dealing with scope limitation) to include a '*description of the factors leading to the limitation*'. The section of this chapter dealing with scope limitation discusses the wording of such descriptions and may be referred to for further information. If the accounts describe the problem it is reasonable for the auditors' report to cross-refer.

The Auditing Standard 'The audit report' issued by the APC contained only three paragraphs dealing with statutory matters. The appendix to that standard did however have an example of a report modified only for an inconsistency between the directors' report and the accounts. An accounting records modification could usefully draw on that precedent.

After the opinion, the example modification continues by describing the circumstances, in other words giving the reasons. That is the first possible approach. The second possible solution is to treat the matter in the same way as a qualification for disagreement. In that case, the matter is described before the opinion, which itself acts as a conclusion. The positioning of the explanation affects the construction of the prose but otherwise is only a matter of house style.

The simple alternatives in generic word picture form (and without complicating matters by including any cross-references) are:

> IN OUR OPINION PROPER ACCOUNTING RECORDS HAVE NOT BEEN KEPT. [REASON], or
>
> [MATTER]. IN OUR OPINION, IN THIS RESPECT ALONE, PROPER ACCOUNTING RECORDS HAVE NOT BEEN KEPT.

The different approaches are seen in the following two opinions. Although this section is primarily about accounting records, the illustrations refer to lack of consistency of the directors' report and the accounts because that wording is given in an example in the Auditing Standard that SAS 600 replaced. The reference to an extraordinary item is only of historical interest following the issue of FRS 3 'Reporting Financial Performance'.

Report 330
DR: In opinion—reason order (pre SAS 600)

Opinion

In our opinion the financial statements give a true and fair view of the state of the company's affairs as at .... and of its [profit / loss] for the year then ended and have been properly prepared in accordance with the Companies Act 1985.

In our opinion, the information given in paragraph ..... of the directors' report is not consistent with these financial statements. That paragraph states without amplification that the company's trading resulted in a profit before tax of £ ..... . The profit and loss account, however, states that the company incurred a loss before tax for the year of £ ..... and, as an extraordinary item, a profit from the sale of land of £ ..... .

Report 331
DR: In matter—opinion order (pre SAS 600)

Opinion

In our opinion the financial statements give a true and fair view of the state of the company's affairs as at .... and of its [profit / loss] for the year then ended and have been properly prepared in accordance with the Companies Act 1985.

Paragraph ..... of the directors' report states without amplification that the company's trading resulted in a profit before tax of £ ..... . The profit and loss account, however, states that the company incurred a loss before tax for the year of £ ..... and, as an extraordinary item, a profit from the sale of land of £ ..... .

In our opinion, in respect alone of the information given in paragraph ..... , the directors' report is not consistent with these financial statements.

The first of the above alternatives uses six fewer words and has a better Flesch Reading Ease (53.7 compared to 46.1). It is, therefore, suggested as the preferred approach.

3 Directors' responsibility

One aspect that is relevant to a SAS 600 limitation of audit scope is the need to make it clear whether or not the directors were responsible for it. This might be considered to be irrelevant for accounting records. There is no doubt that it is the directors' duty to keep accounting records that satisfy the requirements of section 221 of the Companies Act 1985. Indeed appendix 3 to SAS 600 provides an example wording of a description of the directors' responsibilities that states that *'The directors are responsible for keeping proper accounting records which disclose with reasonable accuracy at any time the financial position of the company and to enable them to ensure that the financial statements comply with the Companies Act 1985.'* Any explanation given by the auditors, therefore, need not emphasise that responsibility.

4 *Auditors' responsibility*

The exposure draft of SAS 600 contained example reports that set out the responsibility of auditors to report on the adequacy of accounting records and other matters required by law. In response to pleas for brevity from commentators, such wording was not included in SAS 600.

It would be possible for auditors to include an explanation of their related responsibility only when one of the matters required by law is mentioned in their report. This approach could be adopted consistently, or only when a modification arises without others.

Respective responsibilities of directors and auditors

> As described on page ..... the company's directors are responsible for the preparation of financial statements. It is our responsibility to form an independent opinion, based on our audit, of those statements and to report our opinion to you. We are also required to report to you if certain requirements of the Companies Act 1985 are not met. These requirements include the keeping of proper accounting records.

5 *Heading*

A report on a matter required by statute has to be dealt with in the opinion section of the report and be expressed as an opinion, even if the auditors are only giving disclosures required by Schedule 6 to the Companies Act 1985 that are not material to the true and fair view.

Reporting on these statutory matters does not constitute a qualification for purposes of, for example determining the legality of a distribution. So the heading of the opinion paragraph should not indicate that it is qualified. However, if the heading is to be of use in alerting a reader to modifications (such as the heading relating to a fundamental uncertainty) it might be well to reflect the circumstances in it. Possible headings could include:

Opinion including adequacy of accounting records

Unqualified opinion on financial statements and opinion on accounting records

Opinion on financial statements and other matter[s]

Opinion on financial statements and the keeping of accounting records

6 'Kept' or 'maintained'

The examples in appendix 2 to SAS 600 use the words *'proper accounting records had been maintained'*. This is despite:

- the requirement in section 221 of the Companies Act 1985 being to 'keep' accounting records
- the requirement of section 237 for auditors to report whether proper accounting records have been 'kept'
- commentators on the exposure draft drawing the attention of the APB to the above
- the need to achieve clarity by using plain English.

As SAS 600 does not prescribe the words to be used, either 'kept' or 'maintained' is acceptable. The former should, however, be the preferred term.

7 Director resistance

On the basis that any modified audit report is a Bad Thing, directors (or at least auditors anticipating the reaction of directors) are not in favour of any mention of accounting records. Directors who know their law realise that there is the possibility that an offence under section 221 of the Companies Act 1985 could result in imprisonment or a fine, or both. A failure to comply with section 221 could also be taken into account under section 9 of, and paragraph 4(a) of Schedule 1 to, the Company Directors Disqualification Act 1986 in relation to an application for disqualification of a director.[6] In practice, penalties for breach of section 221 alone are rare, perhaps because of the availability of a statutory defence whereby an officer may show that he or she acted honestly and that in the circumstances in which the company's business was carried on the default was excusable.

Auditors should not let pressure from the directors dissuade them from an appropriate modification. Further wording may be added, however, to go some way to meeting any directors' concerns. Such material is discussed in detail in a later section of this chapter dealing with matters outside the scope of SAS 600.

8 Judging accounting records against the legal requirements

Auditors are required by section 237 of the Companies Act 1985 to carry out such investigations as will enable them to form an opinion as to whether *'proper accounting records have been kept by the company'*.

---

[6] In Re New Generation Engineers Ltd (1993) BCLC 435, in connection with an insolvent liquidation, accounting records were found to be inadequate because they, for example failed to distinguish between transactions of the company and an associated company. The directors were disqualified for three years.

It is reasonable to assume that if the records comply with the requirements of section 221 they are proper. Section 221 specifies what the records must be capable of and what they must contain.

The accounting records must be sufficient to show and explain the company's transactions and be such as to:

- disclose with reasonable accuracy, at any time, the financial position of the company at that time
- enable the directors to ensure that accounts are properly prepared in accordance with the Act.

The above are the main requirements. There are also detailed requirements about what, for all companies, the accounting records should contain:

- entries from day to day of all receipts and payments and their nature
- a record of the assets and liabilities.

For a company dealing in goods the accounting records shall also contain:

- statements of stock held at the end of each financial year
- all statements of related stocktakings
- statements of all goods purchased identifying the goods and the sellers
- (except for ordinary retail sales) statements of all goods sold identifying the goods and the purchasers.

Section 222(5) sets out the requirements for preserving accounting records. These are such that all relevant accounting records should be available to auditors at the time of their audit.

Section 722 of the Companies Act 1985 is of historical interest. It reminds auditors of the golden age of bound ledgers and audit stamps. It also has a bearing on keeping proper accounting records. The section allows companies to keep accounting records (and registers, minute books etc.) in any manner, not just bound books. However, if bound books are not used, adequate precautions must be taken for guarding against falsification and facilitating its discovery.

If section 722 is breached auditors may conclude that the requirements of section 221, in their wider interpretation, have not been met. The law may take a narrower view. The section is, after all, more to do with the proper keeping of proper accounting records rather than just their 'properness'.

Perhaps more important for most businesses are the requirements to keep satisfactory accounting records for VAT purposes. Some specialised industries, such as building societies are also required to keep specific records.

The interpretation of section 221 has caused trouble for many years. Some have sought to interpret the requirements as being very onerous, while others have taken a more pragmatic line. The debate has raged over the heads, and out of the sight, of most auditors who are quite capable of deciding whether, in the particular circumstances of their client, the accounting records are adequate.

Auditors faced with making a decision on whether proper accounting records have been kept need to be aware of the relevant professional literature and justify their decision in writing on their audit file. It is probably fair to say that audit manuals (at least those that are published) have not adequately addressed the work necessary to form an opinion on accounting records. Reference should be made to legal textbooks and the main professional material currently available:[7]

- FRAG 5/92 (published on pages 112 and 113 of the April 1992 edition of *Accountancy* magazine)
- *Accounting Records and the Smaller Company* by Professor Harold Edey.

Essential reading on this topic, FRAG 5/92 was issued in March 1992 by the Council of the Institute of Chartered Accountants in England and Wales for the guidance of members on the obligation of companies to keep accounting records under the Companies Act 1985. FRAG 5/92 is important because it was settled in consultation with Counsel. A Court might disagree with Counsel, but at least auditors have referred to appropriate professional guidance.

Unfortunately, in some instances, the interpretation in FRAG 5/92 appears out of step with what is reasonable for some smaller companies. For example, a seemingly reasonable paragraph 11 starts off by explaining that certain provisions (e.g. depreciation and bad debts) are often made only at the end of an accounting year. However, it goes on in effect to require memorandum records to be made and retained as part of the accounting records when an expected material loss arises.

The document is not legislation and should not be studied as if it were. Some other apparently onerous interpretations in it are probably matters of drafting rather than intent. For example, the FRAG notes that *'Details must therefore be included of all the company's assets and liabilities such as debtors, creditors, properties and plant.'* This could be taken as supporting the interpretation that there should be recorded control over every pencil in use, but in practice this cannot be the case.

The ICAEW has also put its name to a booklet by Professor Harold Edey, published in 1992, called *Accounting Records and the Smaller Company*. The introduction to the booklet is by the then president of the ICAEW (now the Chair

[7] Issue No. 6 (Winter 1977/78) of the APC bulletin *True and Fair* was the previous authoratitive source. It gave guidance on interpreting section 12 of the Companies Act 1976 dealing with accounting records.

of the APB). In it, Ian Plaistowe expresses the view that '. . . *I am sure that smaller companies and their advisers will find it* (the booklet) *particularly helpful.*' This may not be the case. The booklet is a mixture of advice for the businessperson and interpretation of the law. It is unclear whether it has been considered by Counsel. The booklet goes beyond the interpretations in FRAG 5/92 and, if accepted as authoritative by the profession, could increase either auditors' or directors' potential liabilities and the number of auditors' reports modified in respect of deficient accounting records.

3.6.1.4 Links to other modifications

A modification for failure to keep proper accounting records is frequently associated with a SAS 600 limitation of audit scope. There is no question of cause and effect; the two modifications simply arise from the same circumstances. However, the need to modify the auditors' report for accounting records is likely to be considered after the main modification.

Where the modification for accounting records is discovered first, auditors should consider the need for modifications for:

- a SAS 600 limitation of audit scope
- failure to obtain all necessary information and explanations.

There need be no effect on the accounts. Accounts can still be true and fair even if the accounting records are less than perfect. This can arise, for example where records are reconstituted.

If the problem with accounting records is considered to be a SAS 600 limitation of audit scope the report should also be modified to refer to a failure to obtain all necessary information and explanations.

If the problem with accounting records is not also a SAS 600 limitation of audit scope it may still require modification for a failure to obtain all necessary information and explanations. Accounting records are judged against statutory criteria based on accounting; whereas information and explanations are judged against what auditors consider necessary for the purposes of their audit.

3.6.1.5 Typical circumstances

Deficiencies in accounting records can occur in any area of a company's operations. The more common areas affected are:

- cash sales
- stocktaking
- fraudulent transactions
- computer system failures.

3.6.2 Information and explanations

For a full understanding of this form of modification it is necessary to read the earlier section dealing with modifications arising because of deficiencies in accounting records.

The modification discussed in this section results from auditors' failure to obtain all the information and explanations which, to the best of their knowledge and belief, are necessary for the purposes of their audit. For obvious reasons, where possible, this is abbreviated in this book to the 'I&E modification'.

3.6.2.1 The requirements

If auditors fail to obtain all the information and explanations which, to the best of their knowledge and belief, are necessary for the purposes of their audit, section 237 of the Companies Act 1985 requires them to state that fact in their report.

SAS 600.5 requires the auditors' report to contain a clear expression of opinion on the financial statements and on the above as a matter required by statute.

3.6.2.2 Typical wording

The following illustrations are for the relatively rare case of a modification alone. Wording for the more common case of an I&E modification occurring together with a scope limitation is given in the earlier section of this chapter dealing with scope limitation.

The wording given below is not prescribed by SAS 600 and alternative approaches are illustrated and discussed in the next section.

A generic skeleton report is not given, as one suitable for matters required by law may be found in the accounting records section.

Report 332
I&E: Generic word picture

Opinion

> In our opinion the financial statements give a true and fair view of the state of the company's affairs as at .... and of its [profit / loss] for the year then ended and have been properly prepared in accordance with the Companies Act 1985.
>
> AS MORE FULLY EXPLAINED IN NOTE ..... [MATTER]. IN OUR OPINION, IN THIS RESPECT ALONE, WE HAVE NOT OBTAINED ALL THE INFORMATION AND EXPLANATIONS THAT WE CONSIDERED NECESSARY FOR THE PURPOSES OF OUR AUDIT.

Report 333
I&E: Isolated modification, inadequate information about Schedule 6 disclosures

Opinion

In our opinion the financial statements give a true and fair view of the state of the company's affairs as at .... and of its [profit / loss] for the year then ended and have been properly prepared in accordance with the Companies Act 1985.

As more fully explained in note ..... sums were paid to a company controlled by a director of this company. That company has not provided information on the extent to which such sums were consideration for making available the services of the director as a director of this company, or while a director of this company, that are required to be disclosed in the accounts by virtue of paragraph 9 of Schedule 6 to the Companies Act 1985. Because of this we are not able to include in our report a statement giving the required particulars. In our opinion, in this respect alone, we have not obtained all the information and explanations that we considered necessary for the purposes of our audit.

3.6.2.3 Analysis of the requirements

If Auditing Standards did not exist, scope limitations would be reported by an I&E modification. The modification alone may still be used for scope limitations that are not SAS 600 limitations of audit scope.

The following sections examine aspects of the modification including its interaction with other modifications required by law.

1 With a SAS 600 limitation of audit scope

Where auditors do not obtain all necessary information and explanations a scope limitation is present. In normal circumstances a SAS 600 limitation of audit scope (as defined in the earlier section of this chapter dealing with scope limitations) occurs and the wording of the modification draws on the description of the reason for that qualification.

The discussion later in this section examines various aspects of the modification on its own. That material may also be relevant to the modification in conjunction with a scope limitation. The following paragraphs examine (or cross-refer to an examination of) matters specific to such a multiple modification:

- position and heading — see equivalent discussion for accounting records
- wording the opinion.

Wording the opinion
The modification could involve further explanation or avant-garde wording as discussed below in relation to the modification alone. Examples of wording for the opinion are given in examples 8 and 9 in appendix 2 to SAS 600. The examples use a form of words as follows:

> We have not obtained all the information and explanations that we considered necessary for the purpose (sic) of our audit.

This wording is subtly different to that used in section 237 of the Companies Act 1985, which is *'If the auditors fail to obtain all the information and explanations which, to the best of their knowledge and belief, are necessary for the purposes of their audit, they shall state that fact in their report.'*

Simply paraphrasing the Act would produce a modification as follows:

> We have failed to obtain all the information and explanations which, to the best of our knowledge and belief, were necessary for the purposes of our audit.

The two modifications differ in the following ways (neither couched as opinions):

SAS 600 examples	**Paraphrase of the Act**
Readability: 19 words Flesch Reading Ease 40.6 comparative readability 1.2 times	Readability: 27 words Flesch Reading Ease 47.8 used as basis for comparative readability
'not obtained'	*'failed to obtain'*
'that'	*'which, to the best of our knowledge and belief,'*
'purpose'	*'purposes'*

The first conclusion is that the examples in appendix 2 to SAS 600 do not comply with the requirements of the law or SAS 600. They use different wording to the Act and are not couched as opinions as required by SAS 600.5. In mitigation it ought to be mentioned that SAS 600.5 is at fault in requiring opinions when the Act requires a statement of fact.

Leaving this aside, as it has little practical effect, it is clear that the brevity of the SAS 600 examples give them the edge in comparative readability (as defined in section 2.7 of chapter 2 'The Standard Report' of this book).

It is understandable that auditors might wish to avoid using the words 'failed to obtain', because readers might assume that it was their fault. That impression could be avoided if the report distinguished between limitations imposed on the auditors and those outside their and the directors' control as discussed in the earlier section of this chapter dealing with scope limitation.

The use of 'that' instead of the longer 'which, to the best of our knowledge and belief,' has the merit of shortening the modification. The paraphrase of the Act, as well as complying with the statutory requirement, does however retain a more positive appearance of judgement being applied.

There is no justification for the use, in the examples in appendix 2 to SAS 600, of 'purpose' in the singular. It is a simple error. Unless the word is plural the requirements of the Act are not met. Having said that, the error has no practical effect. There are no obvious penalties for auditors using the singular and most readers of the report would not notice any difference. Compliance with the wording of the examples in appendix 2 to SAS 600 is likely, therefore, to be the norm.

The remaining parts of this section deal mainly with the modification alone.

2 *Explanation*

In most instances, the I&E modification is accompanied by a qualification for limitation in scope. Exceptions to this are rare. In such cases, as the report includes no explanation about another modification, auditors have to decide how to provide explanation for the I&E modification alone.

As discussed in the accounting records section, the use of a bare opinion is rejected because it raises more questions than it answers. Reference should be made to that section for a discussion of the explanation that should be in the auditors' report.

3 *Directors' responsibility*

One aspect that is relevant to a SAS 600 limitation of audit scope is the need to make it clear whether or not the directors were responsible for it. It seems consistent to use equivalent wording where the limitation is an I&E modification. Suitable wording is discussed in the earlier section of this chapter dealing with scope limitation.

4 *Auditors' responsibility*

The exposure draft of SAS 600 contained example reports that set out the responsibility of auditors to report on I&E and other matters required by law. In response to pleas for brevity such wording was not included in SAS 600.

It would be possible for auditors to include an explanation of their related responsibility only when one of the matters required by law is mentioned in their report. This approach could be adopted consistently, or only when a modification arises without others.

Respective responsibilities of directors and auditors

> As described on page ..... the company's directors are responsible for the preparation of financial statements. It is our responsibility to form an independent opinion, based on our audit, of those statements and to report our opinion to you. We are also required to

> report to you if certain requirements of the Companies Act 1985 are not met. These requirements include reporting if we have not obtained all the information and explanations that we considered necessary for the purposes of our audit.

I&E are also mentioned in the 'basis of opinion' section of the standard report as shown by the following extract from a standard report. The material is highlighted by the use of bold text.

Basis of opinion

> We conducted our audit in accordance with Auditing Standards issued by the Auditing Practices Board. An audit includes examination, on a test basis, of evidence relevant to the amounts and disclosures in the financial statements. It also includes an assessment of the significant estimates and judgements made by the directors in the preparation of the financial statements, and of whether the accounting policies are appropriate to the company's circumstances, consistently applied and adequately disclosed.
>
> We planned and performed our audit **so as to obtain all the information and explanations which we considered necessary** in order to provide us with sufficient evidence to give reasonable assurance that the financial statements are free from material misstatement, whether caused by fraud or other irregularity or error. In forming our opinion we also evaluated the overall adequacy of the presentation of information in the financial statements.

The remainder of the sentence after the bold text could be interpreted as the APB's attempt to describe the 'purposes of the audit'. The wording in the examples in appendix 2 to SAS 600 is inconsistent as 'which' is used in the 'basis of opinion' while 'that' is used in the 'opinion'. As discussed in the elements and options section of chapter 2 'The Standard Report', 'that' is to be preferred but 'which' is apparently prescribed. Neither is actually prescribed by SAS 600.4; the examples in appendix 2 to SAS 600 go beyond the SAS. Perhaps the last word in the debate should, however, go to Price Waterhouse. This is an extract from their report on The Intercare Group PLC for the year to 31 October 1993. In it the problem is solved by perhaps applying the maxim *'if in doubt, leave it out'*.

Basis of opinion

> We conducted our audit in accordance with Auditing Standards issued by the Auditing Practices Board. An audit includes examination, on a test basis, of evidence relevant to the amounts and disclosures in the financial statements. It also includes an assessment of the significant estimates and judgements made by the directors in the preparation of the financial statements, and of whether the accounting policies are appropriate to the company's circumstances, consistently applied and adequately disclosed.
>
> We planned and performed our audit so as to obtain all the information and explanations we considered necessary in order to provide us with sufficient evidence to give reasonable assurance that the financial statements are free from material misstatement, whether caused by fraud or other irregularity or error. In forming our opinion we also evaluated the overall adequacy of the presentation of information in the financial statements.

5 *Heading*

See the equivalent discussion for accounting records. A statement about failure to obtain necessary information and explanations alone is not a qualification.

6 *Director resistance*

See the equivalent discussion for accounting records. Directors are likely to be less concerned about an I&E modification than one for accounting records because there is no offence involved.

Under section 389A of the Companies Act 1985 auditors are entitled to require from the company's officers such information and explanations as they think necessary for the performance of their duties as auditors. An officer commits an offence only if he or she knowingly or recklessly makes a statement that is misleading, false or deceptive in a material particular. There is no sanction against officers who simply refuse to provide information and explanations.

7 *Deciding whether to modify the report*

In view of the wording of section 389A, auditors could conclude that they need only include a statement about their failure to obtain necessary information and explanations when that section was breached. There are, however, other reasons that can prevent auditors obtaining information and explanations:

- refusal of directors to provide
- circumstances outside of the control of the directors and auditors
- error by the auditors.

These matters are discussed in detail in the earlier section of this chapter dealing with scope limitation.

The correct interpretation of the requirement of section 237(3) is that all the above reasons could necessitate an I&E modification. This is supported by the examples in appendix 2 to SAS 600 and earlier pronouncements. For example, the superseded Auditing Standard 'Qualifications in audit reports' (circa 1980 and birthplace of the 'Example 6' small company report) gave an example (No. 5) in which the absence of a physical stocktake is commented upon as constituting lack of necessary information and explanations.

Obviously some matters are more significant than others. The law does not intend auditors to report every non-reply to a circularisation of debtors.

There is no direct materiality test in section 237 where the I&E modification originates. An indirect test would be whether an immaterial matter could be necessary for the purposes of the audit. Immaterial matters are not relevant to the true and fair view; so, if the possible I&E modification is related to a SAS 600 limitation of audit scope, the two would either be reported together or not at all.

There are more purposes of an audit than simply giving an opinion on the proper preparation and truth and fairness of the accounts. The further responsibilities of auditors under section 237 may also be subject to limitation of scope. For such matters the question of a threshold of disclosure cannot be solved simply by looking at accounts materiality. Instead auditors may look towards the language of section 389A to determine the degree of significance of a particular scope limitation that should be reported. That section uses terms such as *'is misleading, false or deceptive in a **material** particular'* and *'such information and explanations as they may **reasonably** require'.*

Such language argues towards auditors taking a reasonable view of the significance of scope limitations affecting section 237 matters. It is not necessary to report every matter irrespective of significance because each matter has to be judged against what the auditors feel is necessary for the purposes of their audit. Obviously auditors cannot be unreasonable in their assessments, but it would be difficult to challenge a judgement properly made and documented.

3.6.2.4 *Links to other modifications*

Events that give rise to a SAS 600 limitation on the scope of the audit 'automatically' require an I&E modification.

There is no direct link between I&E and the other matters required to be included in the auditors' report by section 237 (including perhaps I&E itself). The interaction of the modification with other matters required by law is as follows:

- failure to keep proper accounting records is judged against accounting criteria and is not directly related to I&E, though the two may occur together
- failure to obtain proper branch returns is judged against the needs of the auditors, as is I&E
- agreement of individual accounts to accounting records is unlikely to be a problem in practice if accounting records exist. A related I&E problem will therefore be rare.

1 Interaction with returns from branches

If a problem occurs that relates to returns from branches it may be sufficient to modify the auditors' report only for that rather than also for information and explanations. This is because the law seems to treat the two matters as mutually exclusive. However, auditors wishing to be prudent can modify their reports for both matters and that approach is used in the later section of this chapter dealing with returns from branches.

3.6.2.5 *Typical circumstances*

Typical circumstances in which an I&E modification may be necessary are set out in the earlier section of this chapter dealing with scope limitation.

3.6.3 Returns from branches

For a full understanding of this form of modification it is necessary to read the earlier section dealing with modifications arising because of deficiencies in accounting records.

3.6.3.1 The requirements

Section 237 of the Companies Act 1985 requires auditors to carry out such investigations as will enable them to form an opinion as to whether proper returns adequate for their audit have been received from branches not visited by them. If auditors are of the opinion that proper returns adequate for their audit have not been received from branches not visited by them they shall state that fact in their report.

SAS 600.5 requires the report to contain a clear expression of opinion on the financial statements and on any further matters required by statute or other requirements applicable to the particular engagement.

3.6.3.2 Typical wording

Because the requirement relating to returns from branches includes a test of relevance to the audit the modification occurs only together with a scope limitation. This is in contrast to accounting records, which just have to be proper, i.e. they are judged only for accounting relevance. The illustrations below are therefore, for multiple modifications. For the purpose of these illustrations the other modification is assumed to be a SAS 600 limitation of audit scope.

Report 334
BR: SL — e: Skeleton

Basis of opinion

Compliance with Auditing Standards EXCEPT THAT SCOPE WAS LIMITED.

Description of an audit.

Evidence AND A DESCRIPTION OF LIMITATION.

Evaluation of presentation.

QUALIFIED OPINION ARISING FROM LIMITATION IN AUDIT SCOPE

EXCEPT FOR OPINION.

FURTHER MATTER REQUIRED BY LAW.

Report 335
BR: SL — e: Generic word picture

Basis of opinion

We conducted our audit in accordance with Auditing Standards issued by the Auditing Practices Board, EXCEPT THAT THE SCOPE OF OUR WORK WAS LIMITED AS EXPLAINED BELOW.

An audit includes examination, on a test basis, of evidence relevant to the amounts and disclosures in the financial statements. It also includes an assessment of the significant estimates and judgements made by the directors in the preparation of the financial statements, and of whether the accounting policies are appropriate to the company's circumstances, consistently applied and adequately disclosed.

We planned and performed our audit so as to obtain all the information and explanations which we considered necessary in order to provide us with sufficient evidence to give reasonable assurance that the financial statements are free from material misstatement, whether caused by fraud or other irregularity or error. HOWEVER, THE EVIDENCE AVAILABLE TO US WAS LIMITED BECAUSE [MATTER]. THERE WAS NO SYSTEM OF CONTROL OVER [MATTER] ON WHICH WE COULD RELY FOR THE PURPOSES OF OUR AUDIT AND THERE WERE NO OTHER SATISFACTORY AUDIT PROCEDURES THAT WE COULD ADOPT TO CONFIRM THAT [ACCOUNTING FOR MATTER] WAS CORRECT.

In forming our opinion we also evaluated the overall adequacy of the presentation of information in the financial statements.

QUALIFIED OPINION ARISING FROM LIMITATION IN AUDIT SCOPE

EXCEPT FOR ANY ADJUSTMENTS THAT MIGHT HAVE BEEN FOUND TO BE NECESSARY HAD WE BEEN ABLE TO OBTAIN SUFFICIENT EVIDENCE CONCERNING [MATTER], in our opinion the financial statements give a true and fair view of the state of the company's affairs as at .... and of its [profit / loss] for the year then ended and have been properly prepared in accordance with the Companies Act 1985.

IN RESPECT ALONE OF THE LIMITATION ON OUR WORK RELATING TO [MATTER]:

- WE HAVE NOT OBTAINED ALL THE INFORMATION AND EXPLANATIONS THAT WE CONSIDERED NECESSARY FOR THE PURPOSES OF OUR AUDIT; AND

- WE HAVE NOT RECEIVED PROPER RETURNS ADEQUATE FOR OUR AUDIT FROM BRANCHES NOT VISITED BY US.

Report 336
BR: SL — e: Branch expenditure not analysed

Basis of opinion

We conducted our audit in accordance with Auditing Standards issued by the Auditing Practices Board except that the scope of our work was limited as explained below.

An audit includes examination, on a test basis, of evidence relevant to the amounts and disclosures in the financial statements. It also includes an assessment of the significant estimates and judgements made by the directors in the preparation of the financial statements, and of whether the accounting policies are appropriate to the company's circumstances, consistently applied and adequately disclosed.

We planned and performed our audit so as to obtain all the information and explanations which we considered necessary in order to provide us with sufficient

evidence to give reasonable assurance that the financial statements are free from material misstatement, whether caused by fraud or other irregularity or error. However, the evidence available to us was limited because £ ..... of the company's expenditure was incurred through its branches, the returns from which did not identify the nature of the expenditure. There was no system of control over such expenditure on which we could rely for the purposes of our audit and there were no other satisfactory audit procedures that we could adopt to confirm that expenditure was properly analysed.

In forming our opinion we also evaluated the overall adequacy of the presentation of information in the financial statements.

Qualified opinion arising from limitation in audit scope

Except for any adjustments that might have been found to be necessary had we been able to obtain sufficient evidence concerning expenditure through branches, in our opinion the financial statements give a true and fair view of the state of the company's affairs as at .... and of its [profit / loss] for the year then ended and have been properly prepared in accordance with the Companies Act 1985.

In respect alone of the limitation on our work relating to branch expenditure:

- we have not obtained all the information and explanations that we considered necessary for the purposes of our audit; and
- we have not received proper returns adequate for our audit from branches not visited by us.

3.6.3.3 Analysis of the requirements

A modification because of inadequate branch returns is a rare event. Self-accounting branches are not common and the facilities for communications are now so good that, unless the branch is in Atlantis, data may be transmitted electronically from anywhere in the World.

In view of the above, the following sections are relatively brief. Much of the material in the earlier section dealing with accounting records also applies to branch returns.

1 With a SAS 600 limitation of audit scope

The test that auditors apply when deciding on a modification for inadequate branch returns is whether they are adequate for their audit. Where the particular purpose that the auditors are concerned about is their ability to express an opinion on the truth and fairness of the accounts the modification coincides with a SAS 600 limitation of audit scope.

There is no room for uncertainty about branch returns. Unless auditors can be positive that the branch returns are adequate for their audit then they have to form the view that the returns are not adequate. Possible difficulties of reporting uncertainty, such as is done in the examples in appendix 2 to SAS 600 for accounting records, do not therefore occur.

2 Directors' responsibility

Directors are responsible for keeping accounting records that satisfy the requirements of section 221 of the Companies Act 1985. The example wording of a description of the directors' responsibilities in appendix 3 to SAS 600 specifically refers to the fact that that '*The directors are responsible for keeping proper accounting records . . .* '

The Companies Act 1985 contains no requirements relevant to accounts for branch returns. The topic only surfaces because of the requirement in section 237 for auditors to report. It would be possible for auditors to suggest extending the wording of the description of the responsibilities of directors to cover branch returns if that was considered to be helpful to users of the accounts but the responsibility could only be a general one.

3.6.3.4 Links to other modifications

The obvious link to another modification is shared with 'accounting records', which has a similar link. If the returns from branches are inadequate, there is likely to have been a scope limitation and a failure to obtain all the 'information and explanations'.

A major question to answer is whether branch returns are an identifiable part of the accounting records or are separate from them. The former seems more logical as, if the latter applies, in theory a company could conduct all its activities through branches and have no accounting records (except for share capital).

If they are part of the accounting records then any modification for inadequate branch returns is likely to be accompanied by an accounting records (as well as a scope limitation) modification. This fact argues for regarding accounting records as different from branch returns because readers of the auditors' report would gain nothing from the double reporting. This is supported by the wording of the legislation. Section 237 requires auditors to report concerning '*whether the company's individual accounts are in agreement with the accounting records and returns*'.

The typical wording shown in this subsection, therefore, links inadequate branch returns to a scope limitation (with I&E) but is silent about accounting records. Auditors could also choose to include a modification for accounting records if that was considered appropriate (the judgement is not related to adequacy for the purposes of the audit).

3.6.4 Agreement with accounting records and returns

For a full understanding of this form of modification it is necessary to read the earlier section dealing with modifications arising because of deficiencies in accounting records.

3.6.4.1 The requirements

Section 237 of the Companies Act 1985 requires auditors to carry out such investigations as will enable them to form an opinion as to whether the company's individual accounts are in agreement with the accounting records and returns. If the company's individual accounts are not in agreement with the accounting records and returns the auditors shall state that fact in their report.

SAS 600.5 requires the auditors' report to contain a clear expression of opinion on the financial statements and on the above as a matter required by statute.

3.6.4.2 Typical wording

With one important exception, a modification because accounts are not in agreement with the accounting records and returns will be highly unusual. The reasons for this are explained in the analysis that follows. No generic skeleton report is given, as one suitable for all matters required by law may be found in the accounting records section.

Report 337
AARR: Generic word picture

Opinion

In our opinion the financial statements give a true and fair view of the state of the company's affairs as at .... and of its [profit / loss] for the year then ended and have been properly prepared in accordance with the Companies Act 1985.

AS MORE FULLY EXPLAINED IN NOTE ..... [MATTER]. IN OUR OPINION, IN THIS RESPECT ALONE, THE ACCOUNTS ARE NOT IN AGREEMENT WITH THE ACCOUNTING RECORDS [AND RETURNS].

Report 338
AARR: Accounts do not include marking to market in accounting records

Opinion

In our opinion the financial statements give a true and fair view of the state of the company's affairs as at .... and of its [profit / loss] for the year then ended and have been properly prepared in accordance with the Companies Act 1985.

As more fully explained in note ..... the accounts do not reflect the changes in value of investments recorded in the accounting records by virtue of the linking of the company's accounting systems to the trading data emanating from the .... exchange. In our opinion, in this respect alone, the accounts are not in agreement with the accounting records [and returns].

3.6.4.3 Analysis of the requirements

This analysis begins and ends by examining whether the modification is likely to occur at all, given the recognition of the role of 'memorandum records'. For simplicity the following introductory analysis ignores returns.

Proper accounting records must, according to section 221 of the Companies Act 1985, be such as to enable the directors to ensure that accounts are properly prepared in accordance with the Act. There is, therefore a link between the accounts, their agreement to the accounting records, and the accounting records themselves. This is shown in the following diagram:

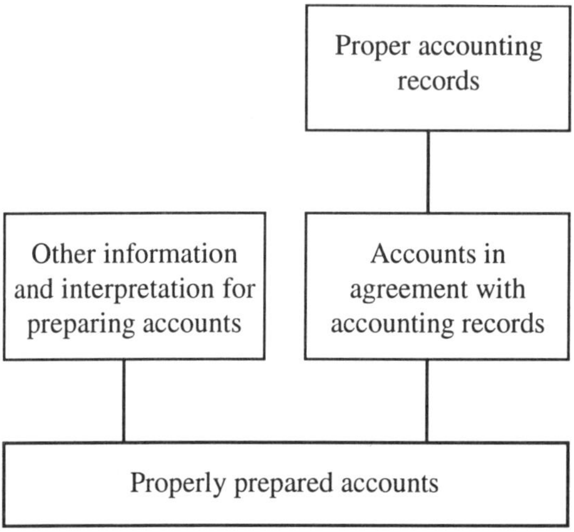

The difference between accounting records and 'other information' is a matter of interpretation. Professor Edey subdivides accounting records into 'articulated records' and 'memorandum records'. The latter could be interpreted as including much that might be thought by some accountants to be 'other information', i.e. outside of the accounting records entirely.

A qualified auditors' report on the accounts may have as its cause (ignoring auditors' error!):

1 accounting records not proper in a manner affecting the accounts
2 accounts not in agreement with proper accounting records
3 incorrect other information or interpretation, (e.g. inappropriate accounting policy)
4 combinations of (1) to (3), (e.g. accounts not in agreement with accounting records that are not proper).

If the accounting records are not proper in a manner potentially affecting the accounts, theoretically the problem may be addressed by ensuring that the accounts do not agree to the accounting records. In reality, this is a remote possibility as the 'memorandum records' created when preparing the accounts will 'repair' the accounting records in time for them to agree to the accounts.

Professor Edey states that *'Any adjustments made to the figures in the accounting records in the process of drawing up the true and fair accounts at the year-end will be part of the accounting records . . .'*

In any case, most qualifications for disagreement arise from incorrect other information or interpretation and there is no question of whether the accounts are in agreement with the accounting records.

The conclusion is that, in practice, auditors will not need to modify their reports for accounts not being in agreement with the accounting records and returns.

3.6.5 Directors' report not consistent with the accounts

For a full understanding of this form of modification it is necessary to read the earlier section dealing with modifications arising because of deficiencies in accounting records.

3.6.5.1 The requirements

Auditors are required by section 235(3) to consider whether the information given in the directors' report for the financial year for which the annual accounts are prepared is consistent with those accounts. If they are of the opinion that it is not they are required to state that fact in their report.

SAS 600.5 requires the auditors' report to contain a clear expression of opinion on the financial statements and on the above as a matter required by statute.

3.6.5.2 Typical wording

A generic skeleton report is not given, as one suitable for all matters required by law may be found in the accounting records section.

Report 339
DR: Generic word picture

Opinion

In our opinion the financial statements give a true and fair view of the state of the company's affairs as at .... and of its [profit / loss] for the year then ended and have been properly prepared in accordance with the Companies Act 1985.

IN OUR OPINION, THE INFORMATION GIVEN IN PARAGRAPH ..... OF THE DIRECTORS' REPORT IS NOT CONSISTENT WITH THESE FINANCIAL STATEMENTS. THAT PARAGRAPH STATES THAT [INCONSISTENT MATTER]. [THE PROFIT AND LOSS ACCOUNT / THE BALANCE SHEET / NOTE ..... TO THE ACCOUNTS] STATES, HOWEVER, THAT [MATTER] [EXPLANATION OF INCONSISTENCY].

Report 340
DR: Profit inconsistently reported

Opinion

In our opinion the financial statements give a true and fair view of the state of the company's affairs as at .... and of its [profit / loss] for the year then ended and have been properly prepared in accordance with the Companies Act 1985.

In our opinion the information given in the directors' report in the paragraph headed 'This year's results' is not consistent with these financial statements. That paragraph states, without giving any further details, that the profit for the year was £ ..... . The profit and loss account states that there was a loss after taxation for the year of £ ..... . The figure in the directors' report is stated before deduction of interest payable of £ ..... .

3.6.5.3 Analysis of the requirements

Inconsistencies may arise between:

- actual figures or narrative appearing in both the accounts and the directors' report
- the bases of preparation of related items appearing in the accounts and the directors' report, where the figures themselves are not directly comparable and the different bases are not disclosed
- figures in the accounts and a narrative interpretation of the effect of those figures in the directors' report.

The first potential inconsistency above is rare because it is most likely to arise from simple error. Once discovered the error will be corrected. Continuing problems are more likely to arise from intentional distortions or ambiguities.

1 Position and heading

See the equivalent discussion for accounting records. A modification for inconsistency between the directors' report and the financial statements is not a qualification.

2 Cross-referring

As the directors' report is normally short it is probably acceptable to refer readers to 'the directors' report' without having to give page numbers. Obviously, a more precise reference may be given. It is rare for paragraphs in the directors' report to be numbered so, in the examples in this section, references are to matters under a particular named heading.

3 Explanation

In most instances, the modification is not accompanied by a qualification that is directly related. Auditors have to decide, therefore, how to provide explanation for the modification alone.

As discussed in the accounting records section, the use of a bare opinion is rejected because it raises more questions than it answers. In this instance a bare opinion would read:

Opinion

In our opinion the financial statements give a true and fair view of the state of the company's affairs as at .... and of its [profit / loss] for the year then ended and have been properly prepared in accordance with the Companies Act 1985.

In our opinion the information given in the directors' report is not consistent with the financial statements.

Reference should be made to the accounting records section for a discussion of the explanation that should be in the auditors' report. For inconsistencies it is suggested that, as well as identifying the inconsistent matter, the reason for the inconsistency is given. Where two figures that should be the same are different the explanation is trivial. If the inconsistency is one of interpretation the explanation may need to be longer as illustrated below. This illustration assumes that there is not also a fundamental uncertainty.

Report 341
DR: Suppression of contingency

Opinion

In our opinion the financial statements give a true and fair view of the state of the company's affairs as at .... and of its [profit / loss] for the year then ended and have been properly prepared in accordance with the Companies Act 1985.

In our opinion the information given in the directors' report in the paragraph headed 'Environmental improvements' is not consistent with these financial statements. That paragraph states that provision has been made for any future costs that may arise from the chemical spill at the Attenborough facility. Note 42 to the financial statements states that there is a contingent liability arising from that incident that it is not possible to quantify. The financial statements do not, therefore, give the view that the matter cannot have any further financial effect on the company.

4 Directors' responsibility

The directors' statement of responsibility does not normally include any mention of the directors' report. In view of the title of the report, even where a modification arises, it seems unnecessary to refer to the fact that the directors are responsible for it.

5 Auditors' responsibility

The exposure draft of SAS 600 contained example reports that set out the responsibility of auditors to report on inconsistencies and other matters required by law. In response to pleas for brevity such wording was not included in SAS 600.

It would be possible for auditors to include an explanation of their responsibility to report inconsistencies between the directors' report and the financial statements.

Respective responsibilities of directors and auditors

> As described on page ..... the company's directors are responsible for the preparation of financial statements. It is our responsibility to form an independent opinion, based on our audit, of those statements and to report our opinion to you. We are also required to report to you if we consider that the information given in the directors' report is not consistent with these financial statements.

The above wording is different to wording used for other matters required by law because it omits the sentence:

> We are also required to report to you if certain requirements of the Companies Act 1985 are not met.

The reason for the omission is that there is no direct requirement for the directors' report to be consistent with the financial statements. That is implied by section 235(3), but it is only the auditors who have a legal obligation to consider whether the two documents are consistent.

6 Deciding whether to modify the report

Section 235(3) includes no explicit test of materiality or significance in its requirement. However materiality is relevant to the financial statements and this introduces an indirect test as it is difficult to see how an immaterial matter could create an inconsistency. The directors' report itself is not generally required to deal with matters that are also in the accounts unless they are 'significant'. For example, significant changes in fixed assets and significant differences between market and book values of land and buildings. In any case, the law does not intend auditors to report every insignificant inconsistency.

Such matters argue towards auditors taking a reasonable view of the significance of inconsistencies when deciding whether to modify their report.

7 What is information?

The statutory requirement refers to the 'information' in the directors' report. The possibility that certain aspects of the directors' report might not be 'information' for this purpose is considered in detail in chapter 2 'The Standard Report'. That analysis concludes that the word 'information' is used to describe only two disclosures required by Schedule 7 to the Companies Act 1985 but, nevertheless, it is probably untenable to divide the directors' report into 'information' and other material.

The analysis also investigates the highly improbable possibility of inconsistency between a description of the directors' responsibilities in the directors' report and a similar description in the accounts.

3.6.5.4 Links to other modifications

There is no direct link between a modification for inconsistency and other modifications.

There is a theoretical possibility that a scope limitation could affect the auditors' ability to form an opinion on the existence or significance of an inconsistency. Possibilities that are discussed below are:

- scope limitation relating to valuation of land and buildings
- directors' report not presented.

Scope limitation relating to valuation of land and buildings

If a scope limitation that results in a modification to the auditors' report relates to the valuation of land and buildings it is possible that auditors may feel limited in their ability to form an opinion on any related disclosures in the directors' report.

Paragraph 1(2) of Schedule 7 to the Companies Act 1985 requires the directors to indicate, in certain circumstances, the difference between market value (as at the end of the financial year) and the amount at which interests in land are included in the balance sheet. That must be done if the difference is substantial and, in the directors' opinion, of such significance as to require that the attention of members of the company or of holders of its debentures should be drawn to it. The report should indicate the difference with such degree of precision as is practicable.

There is no mechanism within the SAS 600 limitation of audit scope to report in relation to the directors' report. It is sufficient for auditors to focus on whether the directors' report is inconsistent with the financial statements. It is not relevant to users of the auditors' report whether the auditors are also uncertain as to the accuracy of the matters in the directors' report.

Directors' report not presented

If a directors' report is not presented there is potentially a scope limitation that prevents the auditors from forming the opinion required by section 235(3). However, SAS 600.9 prevents auditors from expressing an opinion on financial statements until those statements and all other financial information contained in a report of which the audited financial statements form a part have been approved by the directors. To issue a report auditors would either have to be convinced that:

- the omitted report is not *'financial information contained in a report of which the audited financial statements form a part'*, or
- they are prepared to breach SAS 600.9 in order to report (their report would also have to explain their breach of Auditing Standards).

Although normally considered to be linked documents that are bound, laid and filed together, the Companies Act 1985 treats the accounts and directors' report separately. The directors could decide to prepare their report after the accounts and exclude it from the *'report of which the audited financial statements form a part'*. If auditors choose to report in such circumstances, the following report might be appropriate. It uses a modification reporting the absence of necessary information and explanations.

As the directors' report is not attached to the accounts the report also changes the way that the respective responsibilities of directors and auditors are described. If the directors' responsibilities are not described in the report of which the audited financial statements form a part it will be necessary to include them in the auditors' report. A cross-reference to a future directors' report is not acceptable.

Report 342
I&E: Directors' report not presented

AUDITORS' REPORT TO THE SHAREHOLDERS OF ....

We have audited the financial statements on pages ..... to ..... which have been prepared under the historical cost convention [as modified by the revaluation of certain fixed assets] and the accounting policies set out on page ..... .

Respective responsibilities of directors and auditors

As described on page ..... the company's directors are responsible for the preparation of financial statements. It is our responsibility to form an independent opinion, based on our audit, of those statements and to report our opinion to you. We are also required to report to you if certain requirements of the Companies Act 1985 are not met. These requirements include reporting if we have not obtained all the information and explanations that we considered necessary for the purposes of our audit. We are further required to consider whether the information given in the directors' report for the financial year for which these financial statements are prepared is consistent with these financial statements and, if we are of opinion that it is not, to state that fact in our report.

Basis of opinion

We conducted our audit in accordance with Auditing Standards issued by the Auditing Practices Board. An audit includes examination, on a test basis, of evidence relevant to the amounts and disclosures in the financial statements. It also includes an assessment of the significant estimates and judgements made by the directors in the preparation of the financial statements, and of whether the accounting policies are appropriate to the company's circumstances, consistently applied and adequately disclosed.

We planned and performed our audit so as to obtain all the information and explanations which we considered necessary in order to provide us with sufficient evidence to give reasonable assurance that the financial statements are free from material misstatement, whether caused by fraud or other irregularity or error. In forming our opinion we also evaluated the overall adequacy of the presentation of information in the financial statements.

Opinion

In our opinion the financial statements give a true and fair view of the state of the company's affairs as at .... and of its [profit / loss] for the year then ended and have been properly prepared in accordance with the Companies Act 1985.

The directors' report for the financial year for which these financial statements are prepared has not been approved by the directors. Because of this we are not able to consider, as required by section 235(3) of the Companies Act 1985, whether the information given in the directors' report for the financial year for which these financial statements are prepared is consistent with these financial statements. In our opinion, in this respect alone, we have not obtained all the information and explanations that we considered necessary for the purposes of our audit.

3.6.5.5 Typical circumstances

It is rare for the directors' report to be inconsistent with the accounts. Circumstances where inconsistency may be introduced are confined to those matters appearing in both documents. Required disclosures in the directors' report are mainly confined to those required by section 234 of and Schedule 7 to the Companies Act 1985.

3.6.6 Schedule 6 disclosures

3.6.6.1 The requirements

If any of the requirements of Schedule 6 to the Companies Act 1985 concerning emoluments and other benefits of directors and others are not complied with in the annual accounts, section 237(4) requires the auditors to include in their report a statement giving the required particulars, but only so far as they are reasonably able so to do.

SAS 600 does not refer directly to this legal requirement. The whole area of *'further matters required by statute or other regulations'* being relegated to two paragraphs of guidance relating to SAS 600.5 (or not, depending on one's reading of the format of the SAS!). There is no guidance in the SAS on appropriate wording except those examples in appendix 2 relating to other matters required by law, such as accounting records.

3.6.6.2 Typical wording

The wording shown below includes optional explanatory material in the section dealing with the respective responsibilities of directors and auditors.

Report 343
Sch 6: Skeleton

Respective responsibilities of directors and auditors

Responsibilities of directors and of auditors.

DUTY TO INCLUDE A STATEMENT GIVING THE REQUIRED PARTICULARS IF THE REQUIREMENTS OF SCHEDULE 6 ARE NOT COMPLIED WITH.

Basis of opinion

Compliance with Auditing Standards and description of an audit.

Evidence and evaluation of presentation.

Opinion

Opinion.

REQUIRED PARTICULARS.

Report 344
Sch 6: Generic word picture

Respective responsibilities of directors and auditors

As described on page ..... the company's directors are responsible for the preparation of financial statements. It is our responsibility to form an independent opinion, based on our audit, on those statements and to report our opinion to you.

IF THE REQUIREMENTS OF SCHEDULE 6 TO THE COMPANIES ACT 1985 CONCERNING THE DISCLOSURE OF EMOLUMENTS AND OTHER BENEFITS OF DIRECTORS AND OTHERS ARE NOT COMPLIED WITH, SO FAR AS WE ARE REASONABLY ABLE SO TO DO WE ARE REQUIRED TO INCLUDE IN OUR REPORT A STATEMENT GIVING THE REQUIRED PARTICULARS.

Basis of opinion

We conducted our audit in accordance with Auditing Standards issued by the Auditing Practices Board. An audit includes examination, on a test basis, of evidence relevant to the amounts and disclosures in the financial statements. It also includes an assessment of the significant estimates and judgements made by the directors in the preparation of the financial statements, and of whether the accounting policies are appropriate to the company's circumstances, consistently applied and adequately disclosed.

We planned and performed our audit so as to obtain all the information and explanations which we considered necessary in order to provide us with sufficient evidence to give reasonable assurance that the financial statements are free from material misstatement, whether caused by fraud or other irregularity or error. In forming our opinion we also evaluated the overall adequacy of the presentation of information in the financial statements.

Opinion

In our opinion the financial statements give a true and fair view of the state of the company's affairs as at .... and of its [profit / loss] for the year then ended and have been properly prepared in accordance with the Companies Act 1985.

THE FINANCIAL STATEMENTS DO NOT DISCLOSE [OMITTED REQUIREMENTS OF SCHEDULE 6 TO THE COMPANIES ACT 1985].

Report 345
Sch 6: Nature of non-cash compensation for loss of office

Respective responsibilities of directors and auditors

As described on page ..... the company's directors are responsible for the preparation of financial statements. It is our responsibility to form an independent opinion, based on our audit, on those statements and to report our opinion to you.

If the requirements of Schedule 6 to the Companies Act 1985 concerning the disclosure of emoluments and other benefits of directors and others are not complied with, so far as we are reasonably able so to do we are required to include in our report a statement giving the required particulars.

Basis of opinion

We conducted our audit in accordance with Auditing Standards issued by the Auditing Practices Board. An audit includes examination, on a test basis, of evidence relevant to the amounts and disclosures in the financial statements. It also includes an assessment of the significant estimates and judgements made by the directors in the preparation of the financial statements, and of whether the accounting policies are appropriate to the company's circumstances, consistently applied and adequately disclosed.

We planned and performed our audit so as to obtain all the information and explanations which we considered necessary in order to provide us with sufficient evidence to give reasonable assurance that the financial statements are free from material misstatement, whether caused by fraud or other irregularity or error. In forming our opinion we also evaluated the overall adequacy of the presentation of information in the financial statements.

Opinion

In our opinion the financial statements give a true and fair view of the state of the company's affairs as at .... and of its [profit / loss] for the year then ended and have been properly prepared in accordance with the Companies Act 1985.

The financial statements do not disclose that the nature of the compensation paid .... for loss of office as a director of the company was the estimated money value of the company's freehold interest in ....

3.6.6.3 Analysis of the requirements

Schedule 6 has been under review by the Government but at the time of writing no definite proposals for reform have emerged despite a consultative document issued in October 1991. Eventual clarification of the requirements is more likely than their removal.

The disclosure requirements are dealt with in many accounting text books and are included in companies' accounts checklists, such as those published as part of the Accountants Digest series (e.g. number 305). The requirements are not straightforward and guidance on interpretation is frequently necessary.

Directors cannot avoid making a disclosure. If the matter is not dealt with in the accounts it appears in the auditors' report, arguably with greater prominence. As a result the accounts are likely to be identified as defective and the directors may have to correct them or face legal sanction. Because of this, Schedule 6 modifications are rare. They can arise, however, in conjunction with other modifications and so should not be overlooked.

Schedule 6 does not contain any general provision whereby amounts that are not material may be disregarded (in contrast to paragraph 86 of Schedule 4). Where a matter is not specifically exempted from disclosure its omission requires the auditors to give the required particulars, irrespective of the significance. It is possible for an omission to arise, therefore, that does not affect the true and fair view.

The following aspects of the reporting requirements are dealt with further below:

- whether to include explanatory material in the report
- where to include the required particulars
- the extent to which the disclosure should explain itself
- the meaning of the phrase 'so far as they are reasonably able to do so'.

The first two above are in common with other matters required by law and the arguments in the earlier section dealing with accounting records are not reproduced here. In summary; the inclusion of explanatory material is optional (it is preferred in this book), and the required disclosure should follow the main opinion if it does not affect it.

1 The extent to which the disclosure should explain itself

The disclosure can either simply give the omitted facts or state that those facts were omitted. The difference can mean the inclusion or exclusion of perhaps one sentence, as shown within the square brackets at the start of the following extract:

> [The financial statements do not disclose that nature of the non-cash compensation paid to Ms. J. Smith for loss of office as a director of the company as required by paragraph 8(3) of Schedule 6 to the Companies Act 1985.] The compensation paid to Ms. J. Smith for loss of office was the estimated money value of the company's freehold interest in .... , London, WC1.

Alternatively, the statement may be written in an integrated way:

> The financial statements do not disclose that the compensation paid to Ms. J. Smith for loss of office as a director of the company was the estimated money value of the company's freehold interest in .... , London, WC1.

This second, integrated version is shorter and so preferred in this book. It does not mention Schedule 6, as the explanatory material would have done that earlier in the report. It is assumed that the amount of compensation is disclosed and that the omission is only of its nature.

If the auditors do not give the explanatory material earlier in their report, the statement can include more explanation.

2 'So far as they are reasonably able to do so'

Auditors are not required to include a statement giving the required particulars if they cannot reasonably do so. This leads to two questions:

- in what circumstances are auditors reasonably able to give the required particulars?
- if they are not so able, is their report affected in any way?

This second question is also complicated by the possible links to other modifications which are dealt with further below.

The requirement means that if auditors know what the required particulars should be they are required to give them. If they do not know the required particulars, the guidance in Auditing Guideline 413 'Reliance on other specialists' (which is repeated in the exposure draft of SAS 520 'Using the work of an expert') is useful in interpreting the law. In essence, auditors are not required to obtain information if the cost of doing so is unreasonable. For example, if the client does not disclose the value of a classic car included in a payment for loss of office, the auditors need not hire an expert valuer to give a figure.

If the auditors are prevented from giving the required particulars because of a scope limitation they consider modifying their report to refer to lack of necessary information and explanations. This form of modification is discussed earlier in this chapter.

3.6.6.4 Links to other modifications

As well as a possible scope limitation, auditors may consider Schedule 6 disclosures in connection with other modifications. There are no direct links to modifications for fundamental uncertainty or disagreement.

The disclosure requirements of Schedule 6 are such that failure to comply is unlikely to be as a result of the existence of an inherent uncertainty. If the directors do not know the facts it follows that the accounting records are deficient (or there has been an equivalent problem with group companies). If there are no further matters necessitating modification, the auditors' report is likely to be modified primarily for the accounting records matter.

An intentional omission of a known fact is a disagreement but there is no need for the auditors to qualify their opinion unless the matter is material.

3.7 Responsibilities of directors

3.7.1 The requirements

There is no requirement in company law for auditors to report on the adequacy of the directors' description of their responsibilities.

If the accounts or accompanying information, such as the directors' report, do not include an adequate description of directors' relevant responsibilities, auditors are required by SAS 600.3 to include a description of those responsibilities in their report.

3.7.2 Typical wording

If there is no description of the directors' responsibilities outside the auditors' report, the inclusion of a description in the auditors' report is treated in this book as a variation of the standard report. The wording is dealt with in detail in section 2.5 'Elements and options' of chapter 2 'The Standard Report'.

The illustrations below are for circumstances where the auditors find part of the directors' description inadequate. Different approaches are discussed in the next part of this section.

Report 346
RofD: Generic skeleton

Respective responsibilities of directors and auditors

Responsibilities of directors. FURTHER DESCRIPTION. Responsibilities of auditors.

Report 347
RofD: Generic word picture

Respective responsibilities of directors and auditors

As described on page ..... the company's directors are responsible for the preparation of financial statements. THOSE RESPONSIBILITIES INCLUDE [MATTER]. It is our responsibility to form an independent opinion, based on our audit, on those statements and to report our opinion to you.

Report 348
RofD: Omission of reference to judgements and estimates

Respective responsibilities of directors and auditors

As described on page ..... the company's directors are responsible for the preparation of financial statements. Those responsibilities include making judgements and estimates that are reasonable and prudent. It is our responsibility to form an independent opinion, based on our audit, of those statements and to report our opinion to you.

3.7.3 Analysis of the requirements

3.7.3.1 Introduction

This subject is discussed at length in section 2.5 'Elements and options' of chapter 2 'The Standard Report'. That section includes a framework for assessing the adequacy of the directors' description.

SAS 600 is not very helpful in circumstances where some description is given, but part of that description may be inadequate. The following analysis concentrates on such circumstances.

3.7.3.2 Two main approaches

There are two possible approaches:

- ignore the directors' description and give the 'correct' version in the auditors' report
- overtly correct the directors' description in the auditors' report.

The first approach is used in the illustrations given earlier in this section. It is more appropriate for an omission. The approach may lead to confusion for readers if the directors say one thing and the auditors another.

The second approach is more informative for readers but, if implemented rigorously, it can unbalance what would otherwise be an unmodified report.

The following illustrations show how the same circumstances may be treated using the above methods. The first example is taken from a published annual report; the second example has been written using the same directors' description but is more explicit. The statement of directors' responsibilities is outside the auditors' report.

Report 349
RofD: Extra material included in auditors' report, Bass PLC, 30 September 1993, Ernst & Young

STATEMENT OF DIRECTORS' RESPONSIBILITIES IN RELATION TO FINANCIAL STATEMENTS

The following statement, which should be read in conjunction with the Report of the Auditors set out below, is made with a view to distinguishing for shareholders the respective responsibilities of the Directors and of the auditors in relation to the financial statements.

The Directors are required by the Companies Act 1985 to prepare financial statements for each financial year which give a true and fair view of the state of affairs of the Company and the Group as at the end of the financial year and of the profit or loss for the financial year.

Following discussions with the auditors, the Directors consider that, in preparing the financial statements on pages 30 to 58 inclusive, the Company has used appropriate accounting policies, consistently applied and supported by reasonable and prudent judgements and estimates, and that all applicable accounting standards have been followed. The financial statements have been prepared on a going concern basis.

The Directors have responsibility for ensuring that the Company keeps accounting records which disclose with reasonable accuracy the financial position of the Company and which enable them to ensure that the financial statements comply with the Companies Act 1985.

The Directors have general responsibility for taking such steps as are reasonably open to them to safeguard the assets of the Group and to prevent and detect fraud and other irregularities.

REPORT OF THE AUDITORS TO THE MEMBERS OF BASS PLC

We have audited the financial statements on pages 30 to 58, which have been prepared under the historical cost convention as modified by the revaluation of certain fixed assets and on the basis of the accounting policies set out on pages 30 to 32.

Respective responsibilities of directors and auditors

As described above, the Company's Directors are SOLELY responsible for the preparation of the financial statements INCLUDING THE SELECTION OF SUITABLE ACCOUNTING POLICIES. It is our responsibility to form an independent opinion, based on our audit, on those financial statements and to report our opinion to you.

The extra wording is identified above by the use of small capitals (the actual report used plain text).

Report 350
RofD: Extra material included in auditors' report and inadequacy explained

STATEMENT OF DIRECTORS' RESPONSIBILITIES IN RELATION TO FINANCIAL STATEMENTS

Statement as shown above in report 349.

REPORT OF THE AUDITORS TO THE MEMBERS OF BASS PLC

Introductory paragraph.

Respective responsibilities of directors and auditors

As described above, the company's directors are responsible for the preparation of the financial statements. It is our responsibility to form an independent opinion, based on our audit, on those statements and to report our opinion to you. We are also required to consider the description of directors' relevant responsibilities and, where that description is not adequate, include a description of those responsibilities in our report. We consider that, without amplification, the reference in the third paragraph of the description, to discussions with the auditors may be misleading. Such discussions take place so that we make an assessment of the accounting policies for the purposes of our audit as described further under the heading 'Basis of opinion' below. The directors alone are responsible for the selection of suitable accounting policies.

The illustration not only provides an explanation of the problem, it first sets out the auditors' related responsibility. This increases the length of the section dramatically but it could arguably be even longer. There is no reason why auditors should not also provide a subheading, refer to the specific requirement of SAS 600.3, and state that their opinion is not qualified in this respect.

Auditors have a free choice between the two approaches above. It seems likely that the first alternative will be adopted in practice. The second alternative could be criticised for unbalancing the auditors' report by devoting too many words to a matter that is, after all, less important to users of the accounts than the opinion on truth and fairness. This is not to say that the first alternative is above criticism. It would be interesting to survey users of the Bass PLC annual report to ask whether they noticed that the auditors had judged the description of the directors' responsibilities to be inadequate. The influential *Company Reporting* magazine,[8] which analysed the accounts and published the auditors' report in full in its February 1994 issue, did not draw attention to this unusual wording.

3.7.3.3 Wording the modification

As indicated above, auditors may modify their report by including further explanation and references. General guidance on such matters may be found in earlier sections of this chapter. As there are no specific rules, auditors have significant scope for adopting a house style that is consistent with, for example, the way they approach modifications for matters required by law.

3.7.4 Links to other modifications

Unless the directors' statement is in the accounts or directors' report it cannot interact with any modifications that arise in relation to those documents. The statement is, in any case, logically separate from other SAS 600 modifications so the potential for a link is low. For practical purposes it is reasonable to assume that there are no direct links to other modifications.

One matter that might be considered before being dismissed is whether there can be an associated scope limitation. If auditors are allowed to read the statement then they have sufficient evidence to form an opinion on its adequacy. If they are potentially prevented from seeing the statement before signing their report the circumstances are governed by SAS 600.9. As discussed in section 12 'Signing and dating' of chapter 2 'The Standard Report', auditors should not express an opinion on financial statements until those statements and all other financial information contained in a report of which the audited financial statements form a

[8] A monthly subscription magazine published by Company Reporting Limited, 68 Dundas Street, Edinburgh EH3 6QZ (031 558 1400).

part have been approved by the directors, and the auditors have considered all necessary available evidence. So long as auditors consider the statement of directors' responsibilities to be 'financial information' (which, given its subject, appears reasonable) they either do not sign their report or include a description in it instead. The directors are required by law to lay and deliver accounts and reports so the situation must be resolved in some way in due course.

The directors may not issue the directors' report (containing a description) at the time the accounts are approved. An appropriate response from the auditors is to include a description of the directors' responsibilities in their own report and modify their report because of the lack of all necessary information and explanations. A suggested auditors' report in such circumstances is provided earlier in this chapter.

3.7.5 Typical circumstances

The wording of a directors' statement of responsibilities is likely to be based on one of the models that are available, for example that given in appendix 3 to SAS 600. Unless the directors are being perverse there is little that auditors will find inadequate. Problems may arise over the wording of the Law Society model or matters referred to in the corporate governance Code of Best Practice. These are dealt with in detail in the appropriate part of section 2.5 'Elements and options' of chapter 2 'The Standard Report'. The most common problems may be:

- omission of reference to 'going concern'
- inclusion of reference to discussions with the auditors.

The wording of the description may also prove to be controversial where group accounts are presented.

3.8 Outside the scope of SAS 600

3.8.1 The requirements

It goes without saying that there are normally no legal or professional requirements relating to matters outside the scope of SAS 600. Putting words into an auditors' report is not, however, something that should be done lightly. Auditors must always remember that the qualified privilege that their report normally enjoys may not extend to further material included in it that is outside of their statutory or professional obligations. Consequently, particularly if the further material is controversial, it may be sensible to seek legal advice before issuing such a report.

Although there are normally no legal or professional requirements for matters outside the scope of SAS 600, some matters may be prescribed. For example, draft SAS 130 'The going concern basis in financial statements' proposes a requirement for an explanatory paragraph if the accounts are prepared on a basis other than going concern.

3.8.2 Typical wording

Before dealing with typical wording it is necessary to consider what matters may give rise to a modification outside the scope of SAS 600. Some changes to typical wording for the standard report are dealt with as variations of the standard report and not as modifications, for example the extension of the normal opinion for small companies taking advantage of the disclosure exemptions available under SI 1992 No. 2452.

Some modifications dealt with elsewhere in this chapter may be accompanied by extra wording outside the scope of SAS 600. For example, auditors may extend the description of their and the directors' responsibilities when modifying their report for a matter required by law, such as inadequate branch returns. The extra wording is discussed in the section dealing with the related modification and not below.

This section is, therefore, confined to two types of modification:

- explanatory material that is not a fundamental uncertainty, for example the presence of a proforma statement, or a change in ownership of the company
- opinions on matters considered relevant by the directors, for example the adequacy of a provision against fraudulent matters perpetrated by former directors.

Report 351
OTS: Generic skeleton (explanation)

Basis of opinion

Compliance with Auditing Standards and description of an audit.

Evidence and evaluation of presentation.

Heading

EXPLANATION.

Report 352
OTS: Generic word picture (explanation)

Basis of opinion

We conducted our audit in accordance with Auditing Standards issued by the Auditing Practices Board. An audit includes examination, on a test basis, of evidence relevant to the amounts and disclosures in the financial statements. It also includes an assessment of the significant estimates and judgements made by the directors in the preparation of the financial statements, and of whether the accounting policies are appropriate to the company's circumstances, consistently applied and adequately disclosed.

We planned and performed our audit so as to obtain all the information and explanations which we considered necessary in order to provide us with sufficient evidence to give reasonable assurance that the financial statements are free from material misstatement, whether caused by fraud or other irregularity or error. In forming our opinion we also evaluated the overall adequacy of the presentation of information in the financial statements.

MATTER

[MATTER]. OUR OPINION IS NOT QUALIFIED IN THIS RESPECT.

Report 353
OTS: Change in ownership (explanation)

Basis of opinion

We conducted our audit in accordance with Auditing Standards issued by the Auditing Practices Board. An audit includes examination, on a test basis, of evidence relevant to the amounts and disclosures in the financial statements. It also includes an assessment of the significant estimates and judgements made by the directors in the preparation of the financial statements, and of whether the accounting policies are appropriate to the company's circumstances, consistently applied and adequately disclosed.

We planned and performed our audit so as to obtain all the information and explanations which we considered necessary in order to provide us with sufficient evidence to give reasonable assurance that the financial statements are free from material misstatement, whether caused by fraud or other irregularity or error. In forming our opinion we also evaluated the overall adequacy of the presentation of information in the financial statements.

Change in ownership

The whole of the issued ordinary share capital of the company was acquired by .... on .... The new owners of the company have expressed their intention in due course to review the carrying values of assets and the appropriateness of accounting policies included in these financial statements. Our opinion is not qualified in this respect.

Report 354
OTS: Generic skeleton (further opinion)

Opinion

Opinion.

HEADING

FURTHER OPINION.

Report 355
OTS: Generic word picture (further opinion)

Opinion

In our opinion the financial statements give a true and fair view of the state of the company's affairs as at .... and of its [profit / loss] for the year then ended and have been properly prepared in accordance with the Companies Act 1985.

Matter

Further explanation.

In our opinion [matter] [opinion].

Report 356
OTS: Value of consideration (further opinion)

Opinion

In our opinion the financial statements give a true and fair view of the state of the company's affairs as at .... and of its [profit / loss] for the year then ended and have been properly prepared in accordance with the Companies Act 1985.

Sale of freehold property

As described in note ..... the company sold three timber centres to a company controlled by a former director of this company. We have been asked by the directors to carry out such work as we consider necessary to report to the shareholders of this company on the fairness and reasonability of the sale price.

In our opinion the sale price was equivalent to that which the company would have expected to receive on the open market.

3.8.3 Analysis of the requirements

3.8.3.1 Including extra wording

Auditors wishing to incude extra wording in their reports should ensure that the clarity of their main opinion is not impaired. Although further explanation and opinions are discussed here under the heading 'Outside the scope of SAS 600', the SAS does contain some provisions relevant to extra wording.

SAS 600 does not prescribe the inclusion of explanatory material except for a fundamental uncertainty. However, explanatory paragraph 29, following SAS 600.4, suggests the possible optional inclusion of further material. That material should be in the basis of opinion section to highlight matters that are *'relevant to a proper understanding of the basis of* (the auditors') *opinion.'*

Such matters should, therefore, relate to the basis of opinion (i.e. what an audit is and what the auditors did) and be 'highlighted'. It is difficult to highlight something that is not there (as users of highlight pens will testify). The explanatory material to SAS 600.4 could have used the words 'draw attention to' instead of highlight, with almost the same meaning. Words were not used however that explicitly allowed reference to matters excluded from the accounts.

Not all matters that auditors may wish to include in their report will, prima facie, be relevant to a proper understanding of the basis of their opinion. There would be no other types of information in the basis of opinion section if it were not for SAS 600.6. SAS 600.6 requires explanatory paragraphs dealing with fundamental uncertainties to be in the basis of opinion section. The examples in appendix 2 to SAS 600 use wording clearly intended to justify the inclusion of the fundamental uncertainty paragraph within the 'basis of opinion', rather than as a separate paragraph, perhaps below the opinion. They commence with the words:

> In forming our opinion, we have considered the adequacy of the disclosures made in the financial statements concerning the possible outcome of . . .

Auditors will either have to adopt a loose interpretation of paragraph 29, perhaps using similar introductory wording to that immediately above, or accept that some wording they wish to include in their report is completely outside the scope of SAS 600.

SAS 600 deals with further opinions, such as might be requested by the directors, only in connection with opinions on further primary statements. Such opinions are supposed to be clearly identified as not detracting from the main opinion but auditors have so far shown no inclination to include appropriate wording to make that fact clear.

Any auditors including explanatory material relating to a matter included in the accounts would be wise to document on file why that approach is taken in preference to a modification within the scope of SAS 600. The main point at issue is the adequacy of disclosure. If a matter is adequately disclosed no modification is necessary (except for fundamental uncertainty). If it is not adequately disclosed, a qualification is in order disagreeing with the presentation (or lack of it).

3.8.3.2 Positioning of explanation

Explanation that is outside the scope of SAS 600 may be included anywhere in the auditors' report. Two preferred positions are:

- at the end of the basis of opinion section
- at the end of the report.

The former is used in the illustrations shown in the 'typical wording' section above. It is favoured because it is more in the spirit of SAS 600. SAS 600.6 requires explanatory paragraphs dealing with fundamental uncertainties to be in the section of the auditors' report setting out the basis of their opinion.

This seems to be a reasonable approach for other explanatory paragraphs that are not prescribed by SAS 600. In such cases, the term 'fundamental uncertainty' should not be used, either in a heading or the body of the text, because of the risk of readers interpreting the explanatory material incorrectly as a modification required by SAS 600.6.

There are two other reasons why the explanation should not be at the end of the main report. The first is that, unless there is a strong heading, readers could interpret the explanation as being part of the opinion. The second (tongue in cheek) reason is that the JMU may well eventually be on the lookout for auditors who still issue 'emphasis of matter' paragraphs commencing *'Without qualifying our opinion above, we draw attention to . . . '* as this would hark back to the pre SAS 600 auditors' report.[9]

3.8.3.3 *Positioning of opinions*

It would be convenient if auditors could be persuaded to adopt a simple rule that further information is dealt with in the basis of opinion section and further opinions are dealt with in the opinion section of their report. Unfortunately for readers, auditors seem unlikely to maintain such a division. Indeed the APB proposes in draft SAS 130 'The going concern basis in financial statements' to include in the basis of opinion section, opinions (disguised by unfamiliar words such as 'we consider') such as

> . . . on the basis of our discussions with the directors and other information of which we have become aware during our audit we consider that it is appropriate for the directors to prepare financial statements drawn up on the going concern basis.

If further opinions are not to be confined to the opinions section of the auditors' report, a further possibility is for auditors to report to the directors who then note their opinion in the accounts. For example:

Note ..... (extract)

> In the opinion of the auditors the sale price was equivalent to that which the company would have expected to receive on the open market.

3.8.3.4 *Wording of explanation*

The wording of explanation depends on the matter concerned. Auditors have to decide house style such as:

- whether to use a heading
- whether a heading should indicate the nature of the explanation or just that an explanation is being given
- whether to use an introductory phrase such as *'In forming our opinion . . . '*
- whether to include wording that their opinion is not qualified in respect of the explanation.

The house style adopted for modifications for fundamental uncertainty may provide a suitable starting point.

---

[9] The JMU criticised auditors for including reference to the historical cost convention before such wording was rehabilitated by SAS 600.

3.8.3.5 Wording of opinions

The wording of further opinions depends on the matter concerned and on the position of the opinion. Once the position is decided the main area of flexibility in drafting is the extent to which a bare opinion is expanded.

Auditors may include, in addition to a bare opinion:

- a heading
- a description of the respective responsibilities of the directors and auditors in respect of the subject of the further opinion
- the basis of their opinion.

The expansion of the bare opinion may take place next to it or may be distributed throughout the remainder of the auditors' report.

Auditors are already giving further opinions on compliance with the corporate governance Code of Best Practice. In such instances, the opinions are being given, together with their related explanatory material, in a separately headed section below the main opinion. This approach seems simpler than attempting to extract the explanatory material to put it into other sections of the report. Where auditors are giving further opinions on matters that are not directly related to the accounts this separate display seems suitable. Where the opinion is closely related to the accounts (e.g. on the level of a provision) it is more likely that auditors will simply integrate it as closely as possible into the main report.

3.8.4 Links to other modifications

There are no direct links to other modifications. Some matters on which a further opinion is given may, however, arise because of a modification. For example, the directors may want an opinion from the auditors that a provision mentioned in a fundamental uncertainty modification is neither excessive nor imprudent.

3.8.5 Typical circumstances

3.8.5.1 Explanation

SAS 600 has gone a long way towards removing the need for explanatory material as many potential emphasis of matter paragraphs would be about circumstances that are now classified as fundamental uncertainties. In any case, emphasis of matter under the preceding Auditing Standard was becoming unfashionable. For example, the fifth edition of the *Coopers & Lybrand Manual of Auditing* gives only one example of the 'rare circumstances' where emphasis of matter might be appropriate and even then the circumstances (illegal transactions with directors) would have to be 'exceptional' to merit such treatment.

There should be few circumstances about which auditors feel that further explanation is necessary. The need to give explanation is more likely to arise because the events do not have accounting recognition. For example, auditors might wish to mention a change in ownership if the future trade of the company will be markedly changed.

3.8.5.2 Opinions

Auditors may be requested to give opinions to confirm the director's views on such matters as:

- the view given by proforma financial statements
- the appropriateness of accounting policies
- the value of consideration
- the accuracy of provisions
- the likely outcome of tax or VAT disputes
- the valuation of purchased goodwill
- compliance with debt covenants
- reasonableness of assumptions
- independence of third parties (e.g. pension scheme trustees)
- the proper preparation of reconciliations of results and financial position to that which would have been reported under US or other non-UK GAAP.

Auditors of listed companies will also consider reporting on the directors' statement of compliance with the corporate governance Code of Best Practice.

3.9 Groups

3.9.1 Introduction

Auditors' reports on group accounts are different because auditors report on the group results and the balance sheets of the group and the company (the parent undertaking of the group). These matters are dealt with in detail in section 2.9 'Groups' of chapter 2 'The Standard Report'.

Modifications affecting group accounts are normally worded similarly to modifications affecting the accounts of a single company. Problems arise where the balance sheet of the parent undertaking is affected (or not affected) differently. This is a slight simplification, as modifications that are not for a SAS 600 limitation of audit scope or a disagreement can be affected by whether the accounts are of a group or of a single company. For example, a modification concerning agreement of accounts to accounting records is only relevant to individual accounts and cannot relate to a group balance sheet or profit and loss account.

This section assumes a detailed knowledge of the individual modifications dealt with in earlier sections of this chapter. The material below therefore concentrates on:

- highlighting those aspects of individual modifications that may be different where group accounts are presented
- providing illustrative wording for modifications relating only to the group or only to the company.

3.9.2 Group aspects of individual modifications

The existence of a group can itself increase the possibilities for a modified auditors' report. The following sections illustrate some of the items that may arise.

3.9.2.1 Scope limitation

Evidence may be restricted because:

- the directors of the parent undertaking do not arrange for directors and auditors of subsidiary undertakings to assist the auditors
- the results of a subsidiary undertaking up to the date of disposal are not available because the new owners refuse to provide information.

3.9.2.2 Disagreement

Group accounts may give rise to disagreement because of:

- failure to prepare group accounts as required by section 237 (wilfully or through misapplication of an exemption)
- group accounts not in accordance with Schedule 4A
- failure to include all subsidiary undertakings
- problems with accounting for associated undertakings
- company's individual profit and loss account not presented but section 230 not complied with
- failure to comply with Part II (not Part I) of Schedule 5 for related undertakings
- errors in the consolidation process, such as inclusion of results of subsidiary undertakings for incorrect periods
- accounting policies not uniform throughout the group.

3.9.2.3 Fundamental uncertainty

There are normally no further fundamental uncertainties arising only because of the existence of a group.

3.9.2.4 *Required by law*

Some matters required by law are only in relation to the company, not the group accounts. Conversely, some matters occur only for a group, though these are, in practice, confined to Schedule 6 disclosures, some of which relate to subsidiary undertakings.

The application of matters required by law to groups is a difficult topic. It is discussed in this book primarily in relation to the description of directors' responsibilities. Uncertainty over the legal requirements may, however, be accommodated by adopting a form of wording for the auditors' report that may be interpreted in more than one way. This is discussed further below.

3.9.2.5 *Description of directors' responsibilities*

The framework given earlier in this chapter may be used to assess whether the directors' description of their responsibilities is adequate. For a group there are some possible additions to that framework:

- a true and fair view has to be given by the company balance sheet as well as the group accounts
- going concern may be relevant to the company and the group
- the requirement to keep proper accounting records is only in relation to the company
- the responsibility to safeguard assets and so on may be reported in relation to the group and the company, or only for the group.

As the example given in appendix 3 to SAS 600 does not deal with a group there are no authoritative sources to which auditors may refer. The matters are not clear cut and auditors will, therefore, be influenced by what other auditors are accepting as adequate. The annual reports of listed companies normally include group accounts but a diversity of practice seems to be emerging from that source. This is dealt with in detail in section 2.9 'Groups' of chapter 2 'The Standard Report'. The practical conclusion from studying current practice is that auditors are accepting all reasonable statements of directors' responsibilities for groups as adequate and are not modifying their report for any matters related to the existence of a group. Prudent auditors, should however, consider the possible benefits of following the majority, rather than the minority practice.

3.9.3 Wording modifications for groups

Modifications where group accounts are presented should refer to either the 'group', or the 'company', or both as appropriate. The type of modification is more likely to be assessed in relation to the group accounts. The remainder of this section looks at group aspects of some elements of the auditors' report.

3.9.3.1 True and fair view

Some modifications may affect only the company or only the group. Auditors may make this clear or adopt ambiguous wording. It is unlikely that most readers of the report will understand the distinction in a modification, so ambiguous wording may be as effective in communicating its message as the theoretically correct approach.

Matters affecting the company normally also affect the group because the company is part of the group. Exceptions to this are where a matter is material to the company but not the group, or where the matter relates to account balances that are eliminated on consolidation, for example the investments in group companies.

Matters affecting the group (unless they originate in the company) only affect the company where they are transmitted to it through the intercompany balances. For example, uncertainty over the net assets of subsidiary undertakings may give rise to uncertainty in the value of the company's investment. Some parent undertakings have a policy of revaluing their investments in group companies to the underlying net asset value. Other parent undertakings keep their investments at historical cost (less amounts written off). The latter companies are less likely to be affected by adverse financial change in the subsidiary undertakings.

3.9.3.2 Proper preparation

Auditors are required by section 235 of the Companies Act 1985 to report on the proper preparation of the annual accounts. The meaning of annual accounts for a parent undertaking is explained in section 262. The term refers to:

1 the individual accounts of the parent undertaking required by section 226, and
2 the group accounts required by section 227.

Section 262 also refers to section 230. If the appropriate conditions are met, section 230(3) allows the company profit and loss account to be omitted from the company's annual accounts.

It follows from the above that the auditors' opinion on proper presentation refers to the group and company. It is not possible to 'split' the opinion.

3.9.3.3 Disclaimer of opinion

If auditors disclaim an opinion they do so on the financial statements as a whole. In theory, auditors would have to consider that a matter affected the view given by the group accounts and the individual company balance sheet in order to disclaim an opinion on the annual accounts of a parent undertaking that prepared group accounts.

Before SAS 600 some auditors issued disclaimers restricted to one or more primary statements. This fact, coupled with the knowledge that arguments could be found for interpreting SAS 600 differently, point to the likelihood that disclaimers will continue to be issued on, for example the group accounts but not the parent company's balance sheet.

The preferred option must be, however, to issue disclaimers on the annual accounts as a whole. Auditors will take into consideration the fact that the annual accounts include group and individual accounts when deciding whether a disclaimer or an except for modification is appropriate. This factor should not, however, significantly reduce the number of disclaimers issued. This is because the presence of a balance sheet of the parent undertaking is of little relevance to most users of the financial statements except for determinig the level of distributable reserves. This conclusion is supported by the fact that the profit and loss account of the parent undertaking is considered to be so irrelevant that section 230 of the Companies Act 1985 allows it to be omitted entirely.

3.9.3.4 Adverse opinion

Similar arguments to those given immediately above for disclaimers apply equally to adverse opinions.

3.9.4 Example wordings

This section gives just two example wordings. The first is for a modification affecting only the group, the second for a more pervasive matter.

Report 357

D— e: Bad debt not provided by subsidiary undertaking

Qualified opinion arising from disagreement about accounting treatment

Included in the debtors shown on the group balance sheet is an amount of £ ..... due to a subsidiary undertaking from a company that has ceased trading. The group has no security for this debt. In our opinion the group is unlikely to receive any payment and full provision of £ ..... should have been made, reducing group profit before tax and net assets by that amount.

In our opinion the financial statements give a true and fair view of the state of affairs of the company as at .... Except for the absence of the above provision, in our opinion the financial statements give a true and fair view of the state of affairs of the group as at .... and of its [profit / loss] for the year then ended and have been properly prepared in accordance with the Companies Act 1985.

The following modification for a group is loosely based on example 12 in appendix 2 to SAS 600 which is for a single company. The link between the cash flow statement and the view given by the balance sheets and group profit and loss account is not rigid. Because of this, it is possible for auditors to decide that:

- only the view given by the group profit and loss account is affected, or
- the views given by the group balance sheet and profit and loss account are both affected, or
- the view given by the company balance sheet is affected along with the group balance sheet and profit and loss account.

The arguments to support the above alternatives are not important to this discussion. Rather than focus their attention on what might be considered by some to be the more logical consequence, in similar circumstances auditors have frequently just modified their report on all the primary statements. This form of wording is illustrated below:

Report 358

D— e: Omission of cash flow statement from group accounts

Qualified opinion arising from omission of cash flow statement

As explained in note ..... the financial statements do not contain a statement of cash flows as required by Financial Reporting Standard No. 1 'Cash Flow Statements'. Net cash flows for the year ended .... amounted to £ ..... and in our opinion information about the group's cash flows is necessary for a proper understanding of the group's state of affairs and [profit / loss].

Except for the failure to provide information about the group's cash flows, in our opinion the financial statements give a true and fair view of the state of affairs of the company and of the group as at .... and of its [profit / loss] for the year then ended and have been properly prepared in accordance with the Companies Act 1985.

3.10 Deciding on a modification

3.10.1 Introduction

Anything other than a standard report raises questions in the minds of users of accounts (at least those who read the auditors' report). The difference between a standard and a modified report is arguably more important than the form of the modification itself. However, the length of the standard SAS 600 report is such that it is more difficult to spot a modification.

SAS 600.1 calls for a clear expression of opinion, based on review and assessment of the conclusions drawn from evidence obtained in the course of the audit.[10] The correct expression of an opinion depends on auditors selecting the right

[10] SAS 600.5 echoes this and also calls for a clear expression of opinion on any further matters required by statute or other requirements applicable to the particular engagement.

modification for the conclusions drawn and wording it properly. This section explores a methodology for deciding whether, and in what way, to modify the auditors' report. The next section of this chapter looks at the detail of the writing.

This section makes use of the following circumstances presented as a file note to an imaginary reporting partner:

'The freehold properties are not depreciated. This is contrary to SSAP 12 and the Companies Act 1985. They were valued 4 years ago and the property market has fallen substantially. The client will not get an independent valuation so we do not know the current value, nor the amount attributable to buildings as the accounting records do not record this. At least half of the properties are to be disposed of despite a contrary statement in the draft directors' report; they are still shown in fixed assets. One significant property is heavily polluted and requires reclamation work. The client will not obtain an expert's report on this and contends that the surplus of valuation above cost is sufficient to cover any associated expenses.'

The following circumstances can result in a modification:

- a restriction on the scope of the audit (a SAS 600 limitation of audit scope)
- a disagreement with the accounting treatment or disclosure of an item in the accounts
- the need to draw attention to a fundamental inherent uncertainty in order to ensure that users appreciate fully the context in which the opinion was formed
- a deficiency in a matter that requires the auditors to report if certain specific statutory requirements are not met (e.g. failure to keep proper accounting records)
- an inadequate statement, in the accounts or accompanying information, of the responsibilities of the directors
- a need to include a matter not within the scope of SAS 600.

Each of the above types of modified report have been discussed in earlier sections of this chapter

Assuming, as ever, that audit procedures are appropriate and discover all relevant facts, the decision to modify the auditors' report should be capable of resolution into a series of analytical steps. These steps are:

- state the problem(s)
- analyse the problem(s) into discrete 'events'
- analyse the events into categories of possible modification
- decide whether the matters are significant (i.e. material or otherwise meet the criteria for inclusion in the auditors' report)
- set aside any events that are not judged to be significant

- for the remaining significant matters, decide whether they are linked to other modifications
- tabulate the proposed auditors' report.

At the tabulation stage, when the modifications can be considered together, auditors consider whether an adverse opinion or disclaimer of opinions arises.

Stating the problem(s) is perhaps self-explanatory. Perhaps because of the way auditors organise their work, problems are normally collected on an account-by-account basis. It is also normal to record proposed journal entries in support of the narrative.

Further steps are dealt with in the subsections below. Once the form of report is decided it is necessary to write it. This process itself has two main aspects:

- writing individual modifications (see section 3.11 below)
- combining modifications (see chapter 4 'Multiple Modifications').

It is, of course, of paramount importance that auditors document their decisions on file. This is not only important for modifications in a report, it is perhaps even more important for potential modifications that are not eventually included.

3.10.2 Analyse the problem(s) into discrete 'events'

This step recognises that when it comes to writing modifications, multiple modifications may be able to draw upon one description of an event. It is, therefore, worthwhile to split the problem into 'events'. Once the step passes from theory to practice it becomes synonymous with the initial stating of the problem.

The events in the example are:

1 failure to depreciate properties
2 possible permanent diminution in value of properties
3 properties held for disposal despite disclosure to the contrary
4 pollution of a property.

Although the events may affect each other, for example the lack of a current valuation hampers the assessment of the materiality of depreciation, they are essentially separate.

3.10.3 Analyse the events into categories of possible modification

To continue the analysis it is essential to ask questions designed to point to the right form of modification (if any). At this stage no distinction is drawn between matters that are just material and those that may be fundamental. That decision is left until it is possible to consider the financial statements after any later adjustments that the directors may make because of the consultation process.

Because some events can give rise to linked modifications it is better initially just to assume that every problem is a primary one. After that has been done the guidance in sections 3 to 7 of this chapter may be referred to, to check that all possible links have been considered. The questions to ask are:

1 has the scope of our work been limited (a SAS 600 limitation of audit scope)?
2 do we disagree with an accounting treatment or disclosure of an item in the accounts?
3 is there an inherent uncertainty (that may be fundamental)?
4 does the problem involve any matter that we are required by law to report on:
   a have proper accounting records been kept?
   b have we received all the information and explanations we considered necessary for the purposes of our audit ?
   c are returns from branches that we have not visited inadequate for our audit?
   d do the company's individual accounts not agree with the accounting records and returns?
   e is the information given in the directors' report inconsistent with the accounts?
   f has there been any omission of disclosures required by Schedule 6 to the Companies Act 1985 concerning emoluments of and transactions with directors?
5 is the statement of the responsibilities of the directors inadequate?
6 do matters not falling within the above nevertheless need mentioning in our auditors' report?

In practice, question 4b is closely connected to question 1. The two questions may be combined into an inquiry that first looks for scope limitation and then analyses that between SAS 600 limitation of audit scope and the I&E modification.

The analysis of problems can take some answers to the above questions almost for granted. There is no need to clutter up audit files with negative statements, for example about the lack of any effect of the circumstances on the statement of the responsibilities of the directors. Auditors are free to develop a checklist along these or similar lines. It is essential, however, that any such analysis is comprehensive.

Using the above questions to analyse the example, the following might emerge. It is not vital at this stage for the analysis to be perfect. This is, in fact, one of the strengths of this method of analysis. To save space the questions have not been answered four times, once for each event; instead, the answers for each event are shown underneath the relevant questions. If an event is not shown it means that there is no problem with that particular question.

Has the scope of our work been limited?— Have we received all the information and explanations we considered necessary for the purposes of our audit?

- no analysis of depreciable amounts available (1)
- independent valuation not obtained by directors (2)
- no expert report on costs of reclamation work (4).

The scope limitations in this instance, as in most common circumstances, involve only potential SAS 600 limitations of audit scope.

Do we disagree with an accounting treatment or disclosure of an item in the accounts?

- freeholds not depreciated (1)
- no disclosure of uncertainty in carrying value of freehold properties (2)
- properties held for disposal shown as fixed assets (3)
- costs of reclamation work not provided for (client seems to want to charge any costs against revaluation reserve) (4).

Is there an inherent uncertainty?

- amount of permanent diminution, if any, of property values (2)
- reclamation costs of polluted land (4).

Although there is uncertainty over the amount of depreciation that ought to have been charged against freehold buildings that uncertainty is not regarded as an inherent one because it will not be resolved by future events. This is perhaps just a convenient (and conventional) way of regarding depreciation. A case could also be made out for treating it as a further inherent uncertainty.

Have proper accounting records been kept?

- accounting records do not show depreciable amounts of buildings (1)
- records could be deficient in not recording on timely basis:
  - — appropriate write down of properties (if any) (2)
  - — change of status of fixed assets to current (3)
  - — provision for reclamation (4).

Are returns from branches that we have not visited inadequate for our audit?
No problems.

Do the company's individual accounts not agree with the accounting records and returns?
No problems.

Is the information given in the directors' report inconsistent with the accounts?
Report is consistent with accounts but neither is consistent with the fact that half the properties are held for disposal (see below).

Has there been any omission of disclosures required by Schedule 6 to the Companies Act 1985 concerning emoluments of and transactions with directors?
No problems.

Is the statement of the responsibilities of the directors inadequate?
No problems.

Do matters not falling within the above nevertheless need mentioning in our auditors' report?
Directors' report as it stands is misleading because it says all properties will be retained although we know half are held for disposal.

3.10.3.1 Decide whether the matters are significant

Each of the above matters should be assessed to decide whether it is material or meets other relevant criteria for inclusion in the auditors' report.

Deciding what is material and what is not is one of those matters that experienced auditors reserve to their own judgement. There are endless sources of guidance on the topic and in all probability a book could be written on the subject. The following brief discussion should, therefore, be regarded only as an introduction to the topic.

1 Materiality

One of the greatest shocks to trainee accountants, fresh from an arts degree at university, is that accounts are not precise. The neat columns of figures hide underlying uncertainty from such factors as:

- the need to produce the accounts economically and to a deadline
- choices between equally valid accounting bases
- difficulty in measuring some items (such as stocks)
- uncertainty over the outcome of future events.

Science graduates may be equally shocked: but only because the accounts do not actually disclose their uncertainty as a matter of course. No scientist would dream of giving the result of an experiment without indicating the possible error in measurement (i.e. plus or minus some amount). To see a bald profit figure or revaluation surplus without such an indication is a scientific joke.

Materiality is, therefore, one of the great secrets that accountants hide from users of accounts. To avoid getting buried in technical jargon, accountants would do well to remember that, for users of accounts who are not in on the secret, the word 'material' means fabric or cloth.

2 *Definitions*

Although auditors deal with materiality it is really an accounting concept. The Accounting Standards Board refers to it in the draft statement 'The Objective of Financial Statements and the Qualitative Characteristics of Financial Information'. The ASB refers to materiality as a 'threshold quality'. In other words, a quality that needs to be considered before other qualities. If any information does not pass the test of the threshold quality, it need not be considered further.

For companies, although materiality features in the Companies Act 1985, there is no statutory definition.

The ASB proposes that information is material if its omission or misstatement could influence the economic decisions of users taken on the basis of the financial statements. Materiality depends on the size of the item or error judged in the particular circumstances of its omission or misstatement.

The definition in SAS 600 is similar but different. According to the SAS, a matter is material if its omission or misstatement would reasonably influence the decisions of a user of the financial statements. The SAS goes further and indicates that materiality may be considered in the context of the financial statements as a whole, any individual primary statement within the financial statements or individual items included in them.

The two definitions seem to differ in terms of degree: the ASB uses the test *'could influence'*, the APB prefers *'would reasonably influence'*. The semantic argument is probably not worth pursuing. Academic studies have concluded that auditors are generally very good at agreeing whether a matter is material or not. This means that auditors should not attempt to treat matters as immaterial as an alternative to modifying their report. If the report became the subject of a court case, any number of expert witnesses could be found to assert that the matter really was material.

3 *Practical guidelines*

In practice, auditors use guidelines to help in the decision as to whether something is material. Such guidelines address:

- which amounts in the accounts should be used as benchmarks
- whether such amounts may be taken at face value
- how to relate matters to the benchmarks.

For the profit and loss account, most auditors regard turnover and profit on ordinary activities before taxation as appropriate benchmarks. For the balance sheet, shareholders' funds (otherwise known as net assets, i.e. heading K of format 1) is a popular choice, but total assets (i.e. headings A, B, C and D of format 1) may also be used.

The purpose of using benchmarks is to find a figure that allows one set of accounts to be compared to another. For example, if all the benchmarks for company A are twice the amount as for company B it is reasonable to expect a similar relationship between materialities for each company. This breaks down if there are reasons why the benchmarks for company A are not directly comparable with those for company B. This can be because:

- the year in question is not a typical year for one of the companies
- the basis of the figures is different between the companies.

A year may not be typical, for example if, after a history of profits, a loss is incurred.

There could be many reasons why different bases arise:

- one company could pay high directors' remuneration, another could use dividends to reward the owner/managers
- a company in a group could be forced to distribute all its realised profits, another may retain such profits
- one company could have revalued its assets, another might keep them at historical cost.

Auditors may choose to remeasure the benchmark figures or simply make allowance for the above factors when deciding on the materiality level.

Matters are related to the benchmarks by considering their relative size. It is broadly accepted that matters are material if they exceed:

- 10% of profit on ordinary activities before taxation
- 1% of turnover
- 2% of net assets.

Matters are generally considered to be immaterial if they do not exceed half of the above amounts. In other words, are below:

- 5% of profit on ordinary activities before taxation
- 1/2 % of turnover
- 1% of net assets.

Between these limits judgement has to be used more carefully to decide whether a matter is material or not. This is particularly true for errors that affect critical points, as they may be more important than their absolute size would indicate. Critical points in accounts may include:

- the availability of accounting exemptions (e.g. as a small company)
- achieving milestones (e.g. turnover just over £10,000,000)

- having sufficient profits to cover dividends
- breaches of debt covenants
- a change from profit to loss (or vice versa)
- a change from solvency to insolvency
- achieving profits forecast to the public (or bank)
- statutory disclosures, such as loans to directors.

Materiality, quantification and deciding whether matters are fundamental are considered for individual categories of modification in sections 3 to 7 of this chapter.

4 Significant but not material

Some matters are not material in the sense that they affect the view of the profit or the state of affairs. They may, nevertheless, be so significant that they ought to result in a modified auditors' report. These could include problems with:

- non-financial disclosures
- proforma information
- proper accounting records (where the problem has been rectified).

Significance may be left to the auditors' judgement entirely or guidelines may be used. Such guidelines may refer to the normal guidelines for materiality. For example, in judging the significance of an error in a proforma balance sheet auditors may consider it to be significant if it exceeds two percent of the proforma net assets.

3.10.3.2 Set aside any events that are not judged to be significant

If, as a result of considering some events, it is decided that they are not material or otherwise significant they may be set aside. The decision is normally made for events because it is based on significance. The significance of individual potential modifications arising from an event is unlikely to differ one from another.

Auditors will, nevertheless, consider whether there is a need to communicate matters set aside formally to management or others outside the auditors' report.

If proposed audit adjustments to the accounts are judged to be immaterial they should be considered with other similarly immaterial adjustments to decide whether, taken together, the combined potential effect is material. This is unlikely to be a common event but could occur if, for example, management and auditors disagree on the level of provisions and write downs in some account balances. If management is not being objective when making accounting estimates but is motivated by a desire to achieve a certain profit figure the proposed audit adjustments could all have the same sort of effect on reported profit (e.g. increasing it). Auditors keep this in mind when assessing individual accounting estimates as an overall trend may emerge and influence their willingness to accept any particular estimate.

Often the process of assessing significance will result in negotiation with the directors that may remove the need for a modification. This may be because the directors agree to remove a scope limitation or make an appropriate adjustment to the accounts. Alternatively, the process may allow auditors to be more precise with their assessment of significance than in their initial (prudent) statement of the problem. This stage of the process should be used therefore to challenge the assessment of significance. If no matter has been set aside, are the remaining aspects truly significant?

It may seem odd to ask this question again now, but the experience of the author is that too often reporting partners become caught up in the problem at hand and persist in believing that something is material when it plainly is not.

At this point in the continuing example shown above, one aspect is set aside as not material. The event initially identified was that *'The freehold properties are not depreciated. This is contrary to SSAP 12 and the Companies Act 1985.'* Without also giving a full set of accounts, showing the proportion of net assets that are freehold properties, this may be difficult to justify but the following arguments might be used to arrive at the assumed conclusion:

- the properties were valued four years ago so depreciation would only run for four years
- a 'normal' depreciation rate for freehold property is only say two per cent per annum
- the value of land (which is not depreciated) is likely to be a considerable proportion of the total (say at least a quarter).

The annual depreciation charge would be only one and a half per cent of the book value and the accumulated depreciation charge against the book value of the freehold properties would be only six per cent of that total.

As well as the calculation above, auditors will be aware of the associated problems with the properties. Users will be alerted to the fact that there may have been a permanent diminution in value and so should not be much influenced in their decisions by any depreciation effect on the unadjusted carrying value.

It is stressed that this conclusion is only for the purposes of the continuing example. It should not be applied generally to such circumstances.

As a result of the discussions with the directors during this phase it is assumed that the following further facts have emerged for the purposes of the continuing example:

- the properties are usually revalued on a five-year cycle. The directors accept that the current value is less than the book value but contend that the change is not a permanent diminution in value (even though they are trying to sell half the properties). Since the year end two properties have been sold, both at a considerable loss against book value. The directors claim that the other properties (which have remained on the market at higher prices and have not sold) will realise close to their book values. The directors agree to disclose the uncertainty in the valuation and to write down the two properties to the amount they realised
- the possible provision for reclamation is material but not more precisely quantifiable. The directors did not obtain an expert's report because they were mistaken about the accounting effects and thought it would have no effect on the profits. They are planning to sell the property in the hopes that the sale price would not be affected by the pollution problem. They continue to refuse to obtain an expert's report because of the cost.

3.10.3.3 Decide whether significant potential modifications are linked to other modifications

This stage of the process takes into account information that may have come to light during the assessment of significance. It:

- acts as a check on the accuracy of the earlier stages
- prepares the ground for an accurate tabulation of the proposed auditors' report by helping to decide:
  - — which modification is the primary one for each event
  - — what secondary modifications are linked to each primary modification.

If the earlier stages have been completed accurately this stage should produce no new conclusions. However, after the significance of possible modifications has been assessed and further information may have been come to light, it is important for auditors to revisit the first assessments.

The links for individual modifications are discussed in detail in sections 2 to 7 of this chapter. The most common simple links are between scope limitations and the statutory matters: adequacy of accounting records, and receipt of information and explanations. Any links in the continuing example would be shown in the tabulation below. Probably the most difficult area to analyse is where there appears to be a potential scope limitation, disagreement or fundamental uncertainty all stemming from the same event. For example, in the continuing example, the auditors have been alerted to the fact that there is a possible need for reclamation work on polluted land. In the absence of an expert's report they are unable to quantify the cost of such work. It may, in any case, be impossible even for an expert to predict the cost accurately. Is this just a scope limitation or are the directors refusing to obtain a valuation because they fear the effect on the accounts? The auditors' response is also affected by the nature of the disclosure (if any) concerning the matter in the accounts. These difficult topics are discussed at length in sections 2 to 7 of this chapter. A further practical example is given in the section of chapter 5 dealing with 'Stock and work in progress'.

For the purposes of the continuing example, information revealed during the assessment of significance allows a decision to be made.

Possible permanent diminution in value of properties (event 2)

Primary modification	**Secondary modifications**
Inherent uncertainty (if fundamental)	None

The failure to disclose uncertainty in the carrying value of freehold properties identified as a possible disagreement was removed when the directors agreed to make appropriate disclosure. This also removed the need to consider whether the accounting records should have recorded the write down of properties.

On the basis of the available evidence the auditors conclude that they have not suffered a scope limitation and are therefore left with only an inherent uncertainty that may require a modification if it is decided that it is fundamental.

Properties held for disposal despite disclosure to the contrary (event 3)

Primary modification	**Secondary modifications**
Disagreement	None

The directors have not agreed to change the presentation in the accounts or the directors' report (other than writing down two properties that were sold). On the basis of the available evidence the auditors believe that the misclassification of the properties in the balance sheet is material. They have also thought whether there is a discontinued operation as defined by FRS 3 'Reporting Financial Performance' but decided that there is not. The auditors' decision on the classification of properties as other than fixed assets was reached after consultation and with proper consideration of the individual circumstances. The circumstances are not covered by an accounting standard or directly by a statutory provision so a different conclusion might be appropriate in other circumstances.

The auditors decide that, on the facts available, the directors' report is consistent with the accounts and that there is no point in referring to it separately in a modification as being misleading as there is no chance that a reader of the financial statements will have their understanding undermined by it.

The auditors considered the possibility of a secondary modification concerning accounting records. Transfers from the 'fixed asset register' had not been made but inclusion in that subledger was not conclusive evidence of an asset's status. The properties would not have been transferred to 'trading stock' so there was no account in the articulated accounting records immediately suitable. The minutes of the directors' meeting concerning the decision to dispose of the properties were accepted by the auditors as constituting a memorandum accounting record and accordingly there was no need for a modification as proper accounting records had indeed been kept.[11] Unfortunately this conclusion introduces a further possible modification that was not anticipated during the earlier analysis. The accounts are not in accordance with the memorandum accounting records, even though they agree with the articulated accounting records. The auditors judge this to be too confusing for users and so decide not to modify their report for this matter.

Pollution of a property (event 4)

Primary modification	**Secondary modifications**
None	None

The auditors believe that there will be a material cost for reclaiming polluted land but are unable to say whether the cost will fall on the company because it may not affect the selling price. Unless there had been a permanent diminution in value the cost would not be recognised by writing down the value of the asset. It might instead be appropriate to capitalise it or charge it through the profit and loss account but the directors have no present intention of carrying out the work.

After due consideration of the information gained during the earlier phases of the analysis the auditors conclude that they cannot be sufficiently certain that a permanent diminution has occurred to disagree with the absence of a provision. The property is, in any case, included in other possible modifications concerning its value. An independent valuation should include such matters as the pollution in its scope and accordingly the auditors conclude that a separate modification is not necessary. If the potential impact of the pollution was a relatively large factor in the valuation it might be appropriate to explain that in the modification. For the purposes of this continuing example it is not.

1 Comparatives and other secondary potential modifications

The discussions above have included some potential modifications that were rejected. The rejections arose only because the matter was much less significant than another modification arising from the same event. This phenomenon has also been seen in earlier sections of this chapter when examining the individual types of modification.

---

[11] The terms used for accounting records are explained earlier in the chapter. They derive from a book by Professor H. Edey.

Examples of this have included:

Event	Primary modification	Modification rejected
Auditors unable to obtain sufficient evidence about going concern basis (see chapter 5 section 5.2 'Going concern').	Scope limitation.	Fundamental uncertainty over going concern basis.
Directors describe assets held for disposal as being held for long-term.	Disagreement.	The accounts are not in accordance with the memorandum accounting records.
Directors describe assets held for disposal as being held for long-term (same event as above).	Disagreement.	Directors' report is misleading.

There is no particular theoretical justification for ignoring the secondary matters other than the overriding requirement for a clear expression of opinion. This practical approach by auditors has been in evidence for many years before SAS 600. Auditors who want to adopt a 'belt and braces' approach to reporting can hardly be criticised for their rigour but the resulting reports are likely to consume many more 'column inches'.

Despite their exclusion from the above examples, the most common instances of practical report shortening occur in relation to comparative figures. This has not been discussed earlier in this chapter and so a brief discussion is given in this subsection.

The existing Auditing Guideline is due to be replaced by proposed SAS 450 'Opening balances and comparatives' but there is no sea change in the professional material. Proposed SAS 450 contains the following reporting requirements (abbreviated):

- if auditors are unable to obtain sufficient appropriate audit evidence concerning opening balances and appropriate consistent application of accounting policies (or properly accounted and disclosed changes) they need to *'consider the implications for their report'*. (SAS 450.2)
- if auditors are unable to obtain sufficient appropriate audit evidence concerning the appropriateness of comparatives they need to *'consider the implications for their report'*. (SAS 450.3)
- if comparatives are unaudited auditors need to *'consider the implications for their report'*. (SAS 450.4)

The thrust of the SAS is that if any of the normal problems are rooted in comparatives, they ought to be reported as such. For example, there may be a scope limitation relating to opening stocks because the auditors were not appointed until after the date of stocktaking (the subject of report 305 in this chapter). This is all well and good but it does not address the circumstances where both the current year and comparative amounts are affected. For example, if auditors do not agree that matters disclosed as discontinued activities are properly discontinued they may qualify their report for disagreement. Assuming that the comparatives have been presented in accordance with FRS 3, the auditors will also consider that amounts have been incorrectly described as discontinued activities of the previous year.

If the current year had no problem the comparative amounts would:

- not be correct
- not be comparable to the current year figures.

As, in this example, there is a problem in the current year, the comparative figures are comparable, but they are still incorrect. What, if anything should the auditors report.

Proposed SAS 450 states the auditors responsibilities towards comparatives are *'to ensure that they are the amounts which appeared in the preceding period's financial statements or, where appropriate, have either been properly restated to achieve consistency and comparability with the current period's amounts, or have been restated due to a change in accounting policy or a correction of a fundamental error as required by Accounting Standards'.*

Unfortunately, if the comparatives fail to meet these criteria, proposed SAS 450 only examines the consequences where there is a scope limitation. Paragraph 20 of proposed SAS 450 ends an excursion through the possible defects in comparative amounts with the already familiar words *'the auditors need to consider the implications for their report'.*

There are three possible responses for auditors where a modification also affects comparative amounts:

- ignore comparatives
- mention comparatives outside the normal wording of modifications
- extend the wording of modifications to encompass comparatives.

The above is slightly simplified as the comparatives can be simple comparatives or comparatives that are also opening balances. Errors in the latter affect the profit and loss account for the year. There is a weight of precedent in favour of the first option and no imperative in proposed auditing standards to do other than *'consider the implications for the report'.* In practice, auditors are unlikely to venture into the complications of wording that could follow from a mention of comparatives. The extra complications in the report could arguable also detract from the clear expression of opinion required by SAS 600.1.

This is not to say that no modifications should refer to comparatives. Where opening balances are involved a problem can affect the allocation of results between financial years, for example if a long-standing fraud is discovered and it is not feasible to allocate the associated loss between years.

3.10.3.4 Tabulate the proposed auditors' report

The purpose of tabulating the proposed report is to document exactly what the auditors wish to say in their report about each event without having to worry about the wording that will be in the report. If auditors go directly to the writing stage they increase the risk of generating a report that does not say exactly what it should. If there is only one modification, auditors may dispense with this stage or set out the tabulation as a skeleton report.

The tabulation takes the decisions made for the individual events and combines them by type of modification (in preparation for writing the report). A complex tabulation may also be used to record which primary statements and account balances are affected, the practicality of quantification (and amounts), whether or not comparative figures are to be referred to, and so on.

At this stage auditors must consider whether the modifications involve fundamental matters. The tabulation may prompt auditors to decide that a matter initially treated as a fundamental uncertainty is not so serious. Conversely, except for opinions may, taken together, give rise to an adverse or disclaimer of opinion. Decisions made should, of course, be properly justified and documented.

For the purposes of the continuing example the simple tabulation below confirms that the inherent uncertainty is fundamental and the disagreement is not considered to be such as to require an adverse opinion:

1 Fundamental uncertainty

Possible permanent diminution in value of properties (event 2)

2 Disagreement (not adverse)

Properties held for disposal despite disclosure to the contrary (event 3)

Writing an appropriate report based on this tabulation is not dealt with in this chapter as multiple modifications are the subject of chapter 4.

3.11 Writing a modification

3.11.1 Introduction

There is little case law that is relevant to auditors' reports, but the Court of Appeal judgement in Newton v BSA ([1906] 2 Ch 378) underlies the current professional requirements. In that case, the auditor had formed the view that certain loans were uncollectable. His report merely stated, however, that *'the value of the assets as shown is dependent upon realisation'*. The Court decided that this was a truism that did not give the members sufficient information: *'A person whose duty it is to convey information to others does not discharge that duty by simply giving them so much information as is calculated to induce them, or some of them, to ask for more'*. The auditor was held liable to repay dividends paid by the company relying on his report. When writing modifications, auditors have a duty, therefore, to communicate clearly and without omission of relevant information.

This section does not stand alone. Auditors must have decided on the modification to their report before starting on its drafting. This process is covered in section 3.10 of this chapter. Earlier sections of this book have included guidance on the options available when drafting elements of the standard report and modifications. That guidance is not repeated here. Instead the section:

- sets out the golden rules of drafting
- deals with reports as prose
- identifies common types of error
- examines house style and wording variations in cross-references
- sets out the golden rules of signing (final review).

This section looks at single modifications but its principles may be applied to the less frequent reports that are discussed in chapter 4 'Multiple Modifications'. That chapter gives further guidance on drafting complex reports.

The following material does not refer explicitly to the likely event that the partner will be assisted by audit staff. Firms will put in place their own quality control procedures to ensure, for example that a report drafted by a newly qualified person in charge of the audit fieldwork will be reviewed by a more experienced manager and/or partner.

3.11.2 Golden rules of drafting

Drafting a single modification when that modification has been decided is a matter of following a series of logical steps. It is not at all like the blank piece of paper (or screen) that faces the creative writer. It is a relatively easy task but one that has to be done competently because an error will be spotted by other auditors. By contrast, creative writers hardly ever have to face criticism from their peers or a negligence claim from users of their work.

The golden rules of drafting are:

1 start from the right place:
   - your firm's proforma standard report (perhaps developed with the aid of this book)
   - the client's house style (if any)
   - the basic tailoring facts (client name, year end etc.)
2 tailor the standard report for the related matters in (1) above
3 ensure that there is a useable tabulation of the proposed modification
4 select a generic word picture from within this chapter that is:
   - appropriate to the proposed modification
   - in accordance with your firm's preferred approach (if any) for a modification
5 if possible, select an illustrative modification dealing with the matter of the modification from within this book (or elsewhere)
6 review the accounts against the proposed modification to determine the extent to which the disclosures in the accounts may be referred to from the auditors' report
7 draft a modified report based on the tailored standard report using the information referred to in items 3 to 6 above and any legal or professional material from which vocabulary will be taken
8 make use of computer-assisted spelling and grammar checking
9 review the draft and amend as necessary.

During this process auditors will consult in accordance with their firm's quality control procedures and, in appropriate circumstances, consider taking legal advice.

The client will also be consulted because:

- the client may correct errors of fact (or simple drafting)
- the client may decide, at the last minute, to change the accounts to avoid the need for the modified auditors' report.

Obviously, step 7 above (drafting) is lightly described in comparison to the time and effort that can be spent on it. However, if the earlier steps are followed, the actual drafting is less hazardous than if an unstructured approach is taken with no reference to detailed guidance (as set out in this book).

The review of the draft (step 9) should include all the matters discussed in the subsection that follows dealing with signing the report. Ideally the review here should be done by someone other than the partner signing the report. As part of the review of a complex report it may be helpful to 'reverse engineer' the report, in other words constructing a detailed tabulation of the modifications. If that tabulation does not agree to the tabulation on which the report is supposedly based there is a problem. The review should be 'effective reading' where the reviewer actively thinks about the prose and anticipates the errors that might be present.

3.11.3 Modified reports as prose

Writing auditors' reports is a very specialised form of writing but there is still a need for auditors to be able to produce effective and correct prose. Accountants as a group are often happier with figures that they are with words. Even so, the ability to produce good professional prose can be learnt. Auditors are qualified professional people who have had to pass written exams demonstrating a good command of language, so many of the requisite skills should already be in place.

Auditors drafting modified reports should ensure that they have access to appropriate reference material and make use of computer spelling and grammar checking programs where they are available. Company law and the original professional pronouncements are essential sources to ensure that the words used are correct. For example, SSAP 9 should be consulted to decide whether to write about 'stocks' or 'stock', or about 'work in progress' or 'work-in-progress'. A good dictionary is essential and auditors should also consider having access to books on grammar, usage and the rules of typesetting (such as hyphenation).[12]

This book does not set out to teach auditors how to write prose. There are many courses and text books dealing with the subject.[13] Instead, the next subsection examines the errors that can affect modified reports.

3.11.4 Don't make mistakes

The introductory chapter to this book highlighted some of the more entertaining mistakes made by auditors. Those were related to:

- confusion over dates
- failure to adjust references to deleted paragraphs
- confusing similar words
- computer-induced errors.

This subsection gives some more examples of the types of error that can arise. The errors that writers ought to be most alert for are those that can evade computer checking:

- incorrect punctuation
- selecting the wrong word
- typing slips (or voice recognition errors) that generate a valid word
- inconsistency.

---

[12] *Collins Cobuild English Grammar, Fowler's Modern English Usage* and *Hart's Rules for Compositors and Readers* are recommended.

[13] The *Business Guide to Effective Writing* by Fletcher & Gowing (published by Kogan Page, £7.99) is recommended.

3.11.4.1 Punctuation

Cynically, the most common punctuation error in auditors' reports is the omission of full stops. Sentences tend to grow too long for clear communication. A computer check will detect some punctuation errors (such as unmatched parentheses) but not all. For example, the first extract below passed computer scrutiny. In it two apostrophes are missing (A&P Computers Ltd., 28 February 1991):

> . . . the stock valuation has been calculated based on the previous months (sic) purchases. We have therefore relied on the directors (sic) representations . . .

3.11.4.2 Selecting the wrong word

The wrong word may appear in a report through a simple error or because the writer thought it was correct. Some simple errors arise because many words can be made plural simply by adding the letter 's'. If the plural is used in the wrong place it may not be picked up by a computer check. The following was seen in the auditors' report on the Willenhall Tube and Forging Co. Ltd.:

> . . . Statements (sic) of standard accounting practice No. 12 . . .

Some words are so familiar to auditors that they can be accepted in the wrong place. For example, the word 'companies' in the following phrase:

> . . . the companies profit for the year . . .

Sometimes the wrong choice is made from similar words. The following was in a report on Shop Fittings and Interiors Ltd., 31 January 1992:

> . . . is dependant on the close control of the directors . . .

'Dependant' (noun) means a person who depends on another (e.g. a child depends on its parent). The word used in the report should have been 'dependent' (adjective).[14] Some computer checking may highlight commonly confused words (such as 'from' and 'form', or 'effect' and 'affect'), but auditors ought to be alert for those that the computer does not detect. The confusion may be visible as well as logical. Anticipation, as discussed below for typing errors, may help detect both these types of problems.

3.11.4.3 Typing slips

Simple typing slips usually produce a world that a computer spelling check will detect and correct. Others, such as the one in the previous sentence, are left for human beings to discover.

[14] Some dictionaries allow the other spellings as rare variants.

One thing that auditors can do is to anticipate likely problems. Imagine that SI 1993 No. 3135 The Severn Bridges Tolls Order 1993, is being written about (not in an auditors' report). The obvious errors that could be anticipated are:

- The Severn Brides Tolls Order 1993
- The Severn Bridges Trolls Order 1993.

Anticipation is nearly impossible in some circumstances. Errors may arise over the little words in a report. The following error was in the report on Nippon Steel Computer PLC, 31 December 1991, Ernst & Young:

> The accounts have been prepared on the going concern basis. This basis in (sic) not appropriate because . . .

Alternatives for all short words should, perhaps be given special attention. The following list shows some of the potential problems:

- a — an
- an — as / and
- from — form
- is — in / it
- of — or / on
- so — do / to
- that — than
- the — he
- to — do.

Short words are also more likely to be omitted or included twice when they should not be. The latter problem will be detected by a computer check but if the error arises from a late change there is a danger that, because it has been done once already, the computer check is not carried out when it is most needed.

3.11.4.4 Inconsistency

Sometimes a report is internally inconsistent in its wording. Example 9 in appendix 2 to SAS 600 has been criticised elsewhere in this book because it includes both 'work in progress' and 'work-in-progress'. Hyphenation itself can also cause problems. Inconsistency in hyphenation is more likely to be visible when comparing two reports from the same firm rather than looking at just one.

Hyphenation is one of the more quirky aspects of the language, for example both 'year-end' and year end' can be correct depending on the context. In some instances, reference books are of no help and auditors have to decide their own treatment of hyphenated words. Those seeking the protection of the flock should adopt the majority view, where one is known. For example, although some auditors use 'mis-statement', most auditors prefer 'misstatement'.

3.11.4.5 Computer help

The subsections above have looked in particular at errors that can escape normal computer checking. As well as increasing human vigilance, the effectiveness of computer help can also be improved.

The spelling and grammar checking facilities of the 'top end' word processing programs are generally customisable. If auditors want to invest the time to do so, the programs may be tailored to the specific task of checking the auditors' report. If this is coupled with the use of boilerplate (or 'autotext' or 'glossary') text during the writing phase, the chance of human error may be greatly reduced.

For example, if house style is always to use the full name of an accounting standard, the 'autotext' facility of one major program could be used to prevent an abbreviated form from being accepted (if 'SSAP' is typed the computer changes it to 'Statement of Standard Accounting Practice').

3.11.5 Preferences for modifications

House style is discussed in chapter 2 for the standard report. Auditors may choose to use different words to express the same meaning, such as:

- state of the company's affairs — state of affairs of the company
- financial statements — accounts
- profit — results.

House style is generally of little consequence. The only reason for revisiting the topic in this chapter is because modified reports present greater opportunities for variation, in such matters as:

- forms of cross-reference
- quantification
- paragraphing
- order of inclusion of matters.

The preferred approaches to these and similar matters determine the form of report that is produced for a particular modification. In other words, in the same circumstances, two firms may produce very different modified reports.

The basic reason for developing a house style for modifications is to reduce the likelihood of a simple error in any modified report, because there are less things that can go wrong if the writer starts from the right place. For larger firms, a preferred form of modification helps to ensure that modified reports achieve a consistently excellent presentation. For a sole practitioner, this step in writing a particular modification may not be separate from writing the individual report; but once one report has been drafted it can act as a precedent to save time in the future.

The house style for modified reports ought to be consistent with the choices made when deciding on a standard report. The writer may have to follow their firm's preferred approach or may, for example choose to:

- stay close to the examples in appendix 2 to SAS 600
- give more information to users
- write as little as possible
- be avant-garde.

The earlier sections of this chapter dealing with the different types of modification include explanation of the possible alternative wordings. The following subsection gives guidance on an aspect of reporting that is common to many modifications.

3.11.6 Cross-referencing

3.11.6.1 Introduction

Modified reports frequently refer to other material. This is either contained in the accounts or accompanying information, or is a professional or legal requirement.

Obviously, the first requirement is to get the cross-reference right. No computer spelling check is going to right an incorrect reference, so the auditor has only him or herself to rely on to spot such an error. The following extract was reported by *Audit Report* magazine in its May 1993 issue (report on Ancaster Investments Ltd, 31 December 1991):

> Freehold property has not been depreciated in accordance with SSAP 16 . . .

While this is undoubtedly true (after all SSAP 16, before it was withdrawn, was concerned with current cost accounting), the person who signed this report would probably have noticed the error if the title of the SSAP had also been given.

There are three other aspects of cross-referencing that deserve exploring:

- how much information to give in the report itself
- how to word the cross-reference
- how precise to be.

These are considered below in sections dealing with cross-referring to the accounts and referring to external material.

3.11.6.2 Cross-referring to the accounts

1 Giving information in the auditors' report

The relevant requirements of SAS 600 are:

- for a fundamental uncertainty — *an explanatory paragraph referring to the fundamental uncertainty* [SAS 600.6]
- for a limitation of audit scope — *a description of the factors leading to the limitation* [SAS 600.7]
- for a disagreement on accounting treatment or disclosure:
  - *a description of all substantive factors giving rise to the disagreement*
  - *their implications for the financial statements*
  - *whenever practicable, a quantification of the effect on the financial statements* [SAS 600.8].

The explanatory material to SAS 600.8 confirms that a reference to relevant notes in the financial statements is not a substitute for sufficient description of the circumstances in the auditors' report. A reader must be able to appreciate the principal points at issue and their implications for an understanding of the financial statements. This wording is repeated in the explanatory material to SAS 600.6 dealing with fundamental uncertainties.

Conversely, the report need not give all the information that readers could possibly want. That is the function of the accounts. The report may cross-refer to such information simply to help interested readers find it. The examples in appendix 2 to SAS 600 contain cross-references to notes when dealing with:

- an adverse opinion concerning no provision for losses on certain long-term contracts (example 10)
- a fundamental uncertainty (example 11)
- a disagreement over the omission of a cash flow statement (example 12).

No such cross-references are provide, however, for three other modifications:

- a disagreement over the recoverability of debtors (example 7)
- a limitation on the auditors' work on cash sales (example 8)
- a disclaimer of opinion because the auditors were unable to attend stocktaking (example 9).

The only general rule that might be developed from the above is that there should always be a cross-reference for a fundamental uncertainty. Logically the accounts must contain an adequate disclosure of the circumstances or else the modification would be a disagreement, not a fundamental uncertainty.

2 *A practical approach*

Auditors have to judge whether to include all the explanation in their report, or to include some information but also cross-refer to a relevant note to the accounts. Obviously, if the accounts do not have any relevant information, the material must be wholly provided by the auditors' report.

Where a real choice exists, auditors may use the following approach to drafting their report. Sometimes auditors are concurrently advising the directors on appropriate wording for the notes to the accounts. The suggested approach also helps in that work. The steps should be:

1 draft the report as if no explanation was given in the accounts
2 if there is further information in the accounts, add a note to the report cross-referring to it
3 stop! (if advising on the wording of the notes to the accounts do not be tempted to revise the auditors' report by deleting anything put into a note).

This approach forces auditors to include sufficient material in the report to meet the main professional risk. The lesser risk, of providing too much information and so impairing the clear expression of opinion required by SAS 600.5, is not so pressing. The method also indirectly encourages auditors to be brief in what they say.

The basic question remaining is how to carry out step (1) above. The answers are provided, for each of the types of modification, in the appropriate earlier sections of this chapter.

3 *Wording the cross-reference*

The cross-reference to the accounts or accompanying information should be made in appropriate terms to direct the reader's attention to the matter concerned. This is normally done in terms of the relevant page or note number, or both.

3.11.6.3 Referring to external material

Auditors give their opinion as to whether the accounts have been properly prepared in accordance with the Companies Act 1985. In a modified report they may also refer to non-compliance with the law. The way that auditors make such references has developed over many years and the following are examples of the most usual forms of reference:

- Schedule 4 to the Companies Act 1985
- section 221 of the Companies Act 1985.

Alternative methods of referring to the legal requirements extend to:

- company law
- the Companies Act 1985
- a specific paragraph or sub-paragraph within the Act or a Schedule to it.

There is no reason why auditors should not be more precise than the normal reference, but less precision could be open to criticism. Increased precision brings its own risks, namely that further opportunity for error is introduced. This may be the simple error of quoting an incorrect reference or the more complex error of quoting a specific reference when the full picture can only be given by considering related matters not directly referred to.

In contrast to company law, references to accounting standards in published reports show a large degree of apparent divergence. However, many of the different forms of reference are simply matters of house style. Most auditors agree on the basic precision of the reference, which is to refer to the accounting standard but not the specific paragraph within it. The following words may be used to refer to an accounting standard:

- SSAP 12
- Statement of Standard Accounting Practice 12
- Statement of Standard Accounting Practice 12 'Accounting for depreciation'.

The examples in SAS 600 favour the second wording. The last reference is, however, not only more informative for readers, but the use of words as well as numbers may assist in preventing errors such as that illustrated above in relation to Ancaster Investments Ltd.

It is purely a matter of house style as to whether the reference includes the following forms:

- 12
- No. 12
- number 12
- number twelve.

SAS 600 favours the first form but the second is used by many auditors (with or without the stop in the abbreviation for number). The last two forms are relatively rare. Whether it is better to use 'No. 12', or 'No 12', or to have no preference is of minor consideration as there is little scope for misunderstanding. For those who are interested; 'No' is the normal abbreviation for 'Nobelium', which is a transuranic element having an atomic number of 102. It was discovered in 1957 and is named (like the prize) after Alfred B. Nobel (1833-96), the Swedish inventor of dynamite. Auditors are unlikely to encounter it, or be able to verify it, as it is unstable and decays in a few seconds. 'No.' is, therefore, the preferred form.[15] With the advent of desk-top publishing, even accounts that are not printed can now give as an alternative the more familiar printer's version 'N°'.

1 Being helpful

Readers of a report can be assumed to know that the Companies Act 1985 is an Act of Parliament which can be obtained from sources such as Her Majesty's Stationery Office. A minority of auditors reasonably consider that it is helpful to refer also to the main amending Act, but many statutory instruments and Acts have also amended the Companies Act 1985. No such certainty attaches, however, to accounting standards, or to UITF pronouncements, or to *'standard accounting practice'* (a term favoured in the fifth edition of the *Coopers & Lybrand Manual of Auditing*).

Few non-accountant readers of the auditors' report will know, for example that Statement of Standard Accounting Practice 12 is a pronouncement issued by the Accounting Standards Committee and adopted by the Accounting Standards Board. Of course, readers could always look at section 256 of the Companies Act 1985 to discover that 'accounting standards' means statements of standard accounting practice issued by such body or bodies as may be prescribed by regulations. Readers could then discover the relevant statutory instrument and so on. Given that many readers of this book would be hard pressed to find the right SI, it may be easier for auditors simply to give the phone number of a supplier of copies of the relevant SSAP!

Some auditors have objected to the first sentence of the 'basis of opinion' in the standard report given in appendix 2 to SAS 600 because it defines Auditing Standards as those issued by the Auditing Practices Board. They argue that the examples of modified reports do not do the same for accounting standards, so the reference to the APB is superfluous. SAS 600.4 only requires auditors to including in their report a statement *'as to their compliance or otherwise with Auditing Standards . . . '*, so auditors who omit the relevant words do not breach the Standard.

Auditors who favour this minimum disclosure approach will not support the alternative avant-garde approach to external cross-references illustrated below, which aims to give readers access to the means to understand a modification. It would, of course, only be necessary if the accounts did not provide this information. The illustration side-steps the issue of whether accounts should actually be understandable to readers who are not accountants (cynically this class of readers includes financial analysts). This area of debate includes: plain English, 'health warnings' about uncertainty, and better explanation of what the figures mean. An auditors' report is not really the ideal place to explain, for example what depreciation is.

---

[15] Other variations are even less correct, for example, 'n.o.' is used by cricket scorers to denote 'not out'.

The following is a typical modified opinion where the client has failed to depreciate fixed assets:

> As explained in note ..... , no depreciation has been provided on freehold properties. In our opinion, a provision for depreciation is required in accordance with the requirements of Statement of Standard Accounting Practice 12 'Accounting for depreciation' and of paragraph 18 of Schedule 4 to the Companies Act 1985. It is not practicable to quantify the effects of the absence of depreciation.

The avant-garde auditor might add the following wording which is based on the ASB's explanatory foreword to accounting standards:

> SSAP 12 is one of a number of authoritative professional statements, recognised in law, of how particular types of transaction and other events should be reflected in financial statements. Compliance with such accounting standards is normally necessary for financial statements to give a true and fair view. Copies may be purchased from Accountancy Books, PO Box 620, Central Milton Keynes, MK9 2JX (0908 248000).[16]

The phone number will, of course, change when all numbers are updated by the inclusion of a further digit. Any auditors issuing such a report should check the validity of the phone number by testing it and enquiring about any planned change in at least the next year.

3.11.7 Golden rules of signing (effective review)

It seems a shame to throw away all the effort put into drafting a report. But that is what can happen if the auditor signing the report does not check that the document is as expected and is correct. This need for checking applies equally to the report sent out with the accounts to the members. Slips such as omitting the name of the firm can cause a lot of embarrassment at that stage.

The following discussion assumes that the person signing the report is in a position to do so. That is, the accounts are approved and all necessary audit evidence has been received and considered. Most firms have some sort of audit completion checklist. The following review ought perhaps to be evidenced in such a way.

Perhaps the first golden rule should be to assume that the report presented for signature is wrong. Finding out the error is the job of the partner concerned. So rule one is:

1 Read what you are signing

This does not mean just scan the page and if it seems about the right length uncap the pen. It means read it as closely as the small print on a contract with the Devil. It does not take long, even at a partner's charge out rate. Companies House has

---

[16] Since FRS 5, accounting standards have been available from ASB Publications, PO Box 939, Central Milton Keynes, MK9 2HT (0908 230344).

seen many instances of auditors failing to observe rule 1. In years gone by the JMU was not even a glint in the eye. A similar failure today could be seriously damaging to a Registered Auditor's health.

The reading should ensure that the report makes sense, that there are no obvious errors, and that it agrees to the evidence and decisions on the audit file. The report should implement the proposed modifications that have been tabulated.

The next few rules are based on an analysis of report failures over the years. The things to check seem simple. They are. They have, nevertheless, all frequently been the subject of error.

2 Check that the client's name is correct in every way

This extends to noticing the difference between 'PLC' and 'plc' but also includes the basic name.[17] Danger is probably most present when several reports are being signed on group companies having similar names.

3 Check the page numbers of the accounts

At least one of the SAS 600 reports issued by a 'Big Six' firm mentioned elsewhere in this book gave an incorrect page reference. Even if the 'real' report that was signed was not the printed one, auditors should ensure that printing errors do not slip into later versions.

4 Check any references to notes or legislation etc.

It is vital to 'tick' across internal references and to verify external ones. The following extract comes from a report on James Timms Transport Ltd for the year to 31 March 1992:

> In our opinion proper accounting records have not been kept as required by section 237 (sic) of the Companies Act 1985. (should be section 221)

5 Check the date of the balance sheet

6 Check that the reporting period or year is accurately stated

7 Check if profit or loss (or results) and check if further primary statements referred to are actually present

8 Check that the firm is properly described— name and address and as required by Audit Regulations

The last two rules below are not based on an analysis of errors. They are designed to reduce risk and portray the auditors in the best possible light.

---

[17] In this book 'PLC' is used throughout, to simplify references to companies.

9 Look the writer in the eye and ask yourself do we both believe in this report?

10 Sign with a good fountain pen and a confident and legible signature

3.12 Consequences of a modification

3.12.1 Introduction

This section deals briefly with some of the possible consequences of a proposed modification. Potential modifications may be divided first into two categories:

- where a report is not issued
- where a modified report is issued.

The first category is, thankfully, very rare. Auditors may have to deal, however, with directors who refuse to let them report, or try to appoint other auditors, or even issue a forged report. Where such circumstances are encountered, auditors should refer to relevant legislation and to professional and ethical guidance and consider taking legal advice.

Assuming that a modified report is actually issued it may affect the ability of the company to:

- make a distribution
- file abbreviated accounts
- gain exemption from the need to prepare group accounts
- re-register as a public limited company
- gain or retain a Stock Exchange listing.

The reason for these potential effects is the uncertainty in the audited accounts. This means that the various circumstances share common characteristics. These are dealt with after subsections below dealing with the individual circumstances. The Inland Revenue confirmed in discussions with the ICAEW (technical release TAX 4/94) that guidance on SAS 600 was to be issued to Inspectors. The new report would not itself lead to enquiries (e.g. because it highlighted the estimates in accounts) but Inspectors would *'continue to take careful note of the wording of audit certificates* (sic) *in deciding whether or not to raise enquiries'.*

Interestingly, a modified report does not affect the directors' ability to take advantage of accounting exemptions allowed by SI 1992 No. 2452 for small companies. This is because the auditors do not have to give a report on the availability of the exemptions. There is, however, an effect on the auditors' report on the accounts. If the accounts are prepared utilising exemptions that are not (in the auditors' view) available, the auditors may conclude that they have not been properly prepared in accordance with the Companies Act 1985 and so may not give a true and fair view.

3.12.2 Distributions

Section 263 of the Companies Act 1985 states that a distribution shall not be made except out of profits available for the purpose. There are further restrictions for public and investment companies. These are in sections 264 and 265 respectively. The measurement of distributable profits is dealt with in sections 270 to 276. If a company can justify a distribution based on its last annual accounts the matter ends there.

If the auditors' opinion on those accounts is qualified, a distribution cannot be made unless the auditors have stated in writing whether, in their opinion, the qualification is material for determining realised profits and a copy of the statement must have been laid before the company in general meeting. The statement may be made either at the time of the auditors' report or subsequently. The statement must be conclusive; either that the qualification is material, or the qualification is not material.

'Qualified' in this context is defined by section 262 as meaning that *'the report does not state the auditors' unqualified opinion that the accounts have been properly prepared in accordance with this Act'*. In other words, modifications, such as the inclusion of explanatory material or reporting on whether proper accounting records have been kept, are not qualifications.

The removal by SAS 600 of 'subject to' qualifications for uncertainty means that some dividends that previously could not go ahead without an auditors' statement are now permitted as there is no qualification, just explanatory material.

3.12.3 Abbreviated accounts

Provided that a company falls within the definitions of small or medium-sized, the directors may file abbreviated accounts taking advantage of exemptions in Section A or Section B of Part III of Schedule 8 to the Companies Act 1985.

Auditors are required to report to the directors on the availability of the facility to file abbreviated accounts and to issue a special report for inclusion with such accounts. In practice, if auditors are unable to issue a satisfactory first report, the need for a second report is removed because abbreviated accounts cannot be filed without a satisfactory report.

3.12.4 Exemptions for small and medium-sized groups

A parent company need not prepare group accounts if the group of which it is the parent meets the criteria set out in sections 248 and 249 of the Companies Act 1985 as a small or medium-sized group. The exemption does not apply if any member of the group is:

- a public company
- an authorised institution under the Banking Act 1987
- an insurance company
- an authorised person under the Financial Services Act 1986.

If the directors propose to take advantage of the exemption, it does not apply unless:

- a report by the auditors, addressed to the directors, provides an opinion that the company is entitled to the exemption, and
- the report is attached to the individual accounts of the parent company.

3.12.5 Re-registration of a private company as a public company

If a private company wishes to re-register as a public company, certain documents must be sent to the registrar, including reports from the auditors:

- a copy of the relevant balance sheet, together with a copy of an unqualified report (defined in section 46) by the company's auditors
- a statement by the auditors that in their opinion the relevant balance sheet shows that at the balance sheet date the amount of the company's net assets (within the meaning given to that expression by section 264(2)) was not less than the aggregate of its called-up share capital and undistributable reserves.

The relevant balance sheet is one prepared as at a date not more than seven months before the date of the application to re-register. This is usually as part of the statutory accounts.

A report is unqualified for this purpose if:

- it is a standard report, or
- it is modified but not qualified, or
- it is qualified but the qualification is not material for this purpose.

For a qualification to be not material the auditors must state that the matter giving rise to the qualification is not material for the purpose of determining (by reference to the company's balance sheet) whether at the balance sheet date the amount of the company's net assets was not less than the aggregate of its called up share capital and undistributable reserves.

3.12.6 Listing

A qualified auditors' report may affect a company's ability to obtain or retain a Stock Exchange listing. Paragraph 3.3(e) of the Listing Rules, in conjunction with paragraphs 12.1(d) and 12.4, stipulates that admission may not be appropriate if a qualified report is issued on the relevant accounts.

A less usual circumstance is where the continuation of a listing is affected. Paragraph 1.21 of the Listing Rules refers to the existence of special circumstances which preclude normal regular dealings in the securities. The importance of the auditors' report was confirmed in the case of R v International Stock Exchange of the UK and the Republic of Ireland Ltd, ex parte Else (1982) Ltd & Anor. [1993] BCC 11.

In that case, shareholders applied for judicial review of the decision to delist the shares of Titaghur PLC. The announcement made by the Stock Exchange after the meeting of the relevant committee, read as follows:

> At a meeting held on Friday, 7 December 1990 the Committee on Quotations of The International Stock Exchange ('the committee') decided to cancel the listing of the securities of Titaghur PLC.
>
> The auditors' report on the accounts of Titaghur PLC for the year ended 31 March 1990 contains numerous qualifications. In the opinion of the committee therefore there is inadequate financial information available concerning this company.
>
> Following the committee decision, Titaghur PLC's listing will be cancelled on Thursday, 13 December 1990.

Mr. Legge-Bourke, a member of the committee, expressed views apparently shared by other members. In an affidavit he said:

> I have seldom seen a set of company accounts with such a combination of qualifications in them. With such qualifications it would be very difficult for there to be an orderly market in the shares because investors would not have adequate information to form a judgement as to the company's real financial position and prospects.

3.12.7 Common aspects

If the auditors' report is modified, the accounts may give a picture of net assets, or turnover or distributable reserves that is uncertain. If auditors have concerns about whether such matters exceed the benchmarks imposed by legislation they may not be able to issue the reports required.

A modified report need not be a qualification. The presence of a fundamental uncertainty may be as significant as a qualification except where distributions are concerned. Distributions are only affected by qualified reports.

Uncertainties do not necessarily affect a benchmark adversely. For example a potential distribution is not affected by uncertainty that relates to irrelevant matters or to a potential overstatement of distributable reserves, for example:

- overprudent accounting
- a matter not affecting distributable reserves (e.g. valuation of investment properties)
- where there are already no distributable reserves disclosed in the accounts (and any distribution would be illegal)
- only affecting disclosure
- a modification only relating to group accounts, not the distributable reserves of the holding company.

It may also be possible to limit uncertainty. For example, uncertainty in the value of an asset is usually limited to its book value (which may be reduced to £nil).

3.12.8 Reporting to regulators

Auditors should assess whether the matter giving rise to the modification is such as to require notification to a regulator. Reference should be made to SAS 620 'The Auditors' Right and Duty to Report to Regulators in the Financial Sector' and Practice Notes issued by the APB dealing with the specific requirements in individual regulated industries, for example Practice Note 5 'The Auditors' Right and Duty to Report to SIB and Other Regulators of Investment Businesses'.

4 MULTIPLE MODIFICATIONS

4.1 Introduction

This chapter explains how to write a report with two or more modifications. Combining two modifications is relatively easy, whether they are of the same type or different. Complex reports, with many potential modifications, can be very difficult indeed. This chapter suggests a general approach that may be applied to all modified reports to simplify even the most complex.

This chapter does not stand alone. The guidance in chapter 3 'Modified Reports' concerning the writing of individual modifications should first be understood. For example, the section in this chapter about combining two scope limitations does not repeat warnings about possible failure to comply with an interpretation in paragraph 71 of SAS 600. That is, to distinguish between imposed limitations and those outside the control of the auditors and directors.

4.2 Types of modification and combination

The modifications analysed in chapter 3 are dealt with under the following headings:

- scope limitation
- disagreement
- fundamental uncertainty
- required by law
- responsibilities of directors
- outside the scope of SAS 600.

The above list ignores, for the moment, the diversity of modification that comes under the heading of 'outside the scope of SAS 600'. Scope limitation may be divided into:

- except for qualifications
- disclaimers of opinion.

Disagreement may be divided into:

- except for qualifications
- adverse opinions.

The following analysis looks at combining the essential aspects of individual modifications. The analysis does not extend to combining additional or avant-garde wording that is discussed in chapters 2 and 3. Such wording is not essential and those auditors choosing to go beyond the requirements of SAS 600 must accept that combining additional wording introduces further risk into the process of report writing. Where a complex report is to be issued, auditors have to balance the benefit of additional or avant-garde wording against the need to issue a clear (and short) report.

4.2.1 Linked modifications

As discussed in chapter 3, some modifications required by law arise from the same event as other modifications that may involve a qualified audit report. For example, a modification for failure to receive all necessary information and explanations arises together with a SAS 600 limitation of audit scope. The wording of such modifications has been dealt with in detail in chapter 3. They are dealt with in this chapter together with the primary modification to which they are linked. For example, discussion about combining two scope limitations also extends to combining the linked modifications for information and explanations.

4.3 General approach

The early parts of this chapter examine combining only two modifications of each type. The methods used may, however, be extended to more complex reports. The general approach to a modified report should be:

- write the individual modifications. If there are primary and linked secondary modifications deriving from the same event these are written together as explained in chapter 3
- combine modifications of the same type
- choose a base (combined) modification (a scope limitation if there is one) and add the other (combined) modifications to it one at a time
- review the resulting report against its objective and amend if necessary to improve clarity.

This method is set out in detail in the section of this chapter dealing with complex reports. That section explains how the method is adapted when an adverse opinion or disclaimer of opinion is present.

Writing the individual modifications is the easy part. Simply follow the guidance earlier in this book to decide on appropriate wording. As a modification will not, in this case, stand alone it is not necessary to write the non-essential parts. For example, the only essential part of a fundamental uncertainty is the headed paragraph itself.

4.4 Two modifications of the same type

The first step in producing a complex report should be to combine modifications of the same type. Many reports do not include this stage in their drafting because only one modification of any type is present. The following subsections examine combining:

- scope limitations
  - except for qualifications
  - disclaimers of opinion
- disagreements
  - except for qualifications
  - adverse opinions
- fundamental uncertainties
- required by law
- responsibilities of directors
- outside the scope of SAS 600.

In some cases the modifications do not affect each other and auditors can effect the combination merely by including the two modification paragraphs in their report. If two modifications are in the same section of the report, auditors have to decide on the order in which to present them. There are no requirements affecting this choice. The following approach is suggested:

- put the more significant modification first, but
- if one modification is about the going concern basis of preparation of the accounts, that modification should be the last one.

The reason for dealing with going concern last is simply that other modifications may contribute to the doubt about the continuation of the business. It seems reasonable, therefore, to place the consequence last. An alternative approach is to put the modifications in decreasing order of importance. Using this approach, going concern would usually come before other modifications.

4.4.1 Scope limitation — except for qualification

4.4.1.1 Introduction

Qualifications due to a SAS 600 limitation of audit scope are relatively simple to combine. Such qualifications affect the basis of opinion as well as the opinion itself and so the wording is slightly more complex than for a qualification arising from a disagreement about accounting treatment or disclosure.

The discussion below also deals with combining wording in the linked modifications that may be present for information and explanations and accounting records.

4.4.1.2 Summary of the approach

The following skeletons show first one modification then a combination of two modifications.

Report 400
SL — e: Generic skeleton

Basis of opinion

Compliance with Auditing Standards EXCEPT THAT SCOPE WAS LIMITED.

Description of an audit.

Evidence AND A DESCRIPTION OF LIMITATION.

Evaluation of presentation.

QUALIFIED OPINION ARISING FROM LIMITATION IN AUDIT SCOPE

EXCEPT FOR OPINION.

FURTHER MATTER REQUIRED BY LAW.

Report 401
SL — e: SL — e: Generic skeleton

Basis of opinion

Compliance with Auditing Standards EXCEPT THAT SCOPE WAS LIMITED.

Description of an audit.

Evidence.

DESCRIPTION OF LIMITATION 1.

DESCRIPTION OF LIMITATION 2.

Evaluation of presentation.

QUALIFIED OPINION ARISING FROM LIMITATIONS IN AUDIT SCOPE

EXCEPT FOR OPINIONS.

FURTHER MATTERS REQUIRED BY LAW.

The basis of opinion paragraphs are combined by dealing with each limitation in scope in a separate paragraph. The opinion paragraphs are combined by eliminating the duplicated wording after their introductory phrases. This produces a single opinion paragraph in the combined report. A similar elimination of duplicated wording is carried out for the further matters required by law. The heading of the basis of the opinion section also indicates that there is more than one scope limitation.

4.4.1.3 Typical wording

The illustrative reports include wording for the common associated matters required by law: accounting records, and information and explanations. The wording for matters required by law is derived from the examples in appendix 2 to SAS 600 and is challenged in the relevant section of chapter 3. It should not be regarded as the preferred approach.

Report 402
SL — e: SL — e: Generic word picture

Basis of opinion

We conducted our audit in accordance with Auditing Standards issued by the Auditing Practices Board, EXCEPT THAT THE SCOPE OF OUR WORK WAS LIMITED AS EXPLAINED BELOW.

An audit includes examination, on a test basis, of evidence relevant to the amounts and disclosures in the financial statements. It also includes an assessment of the significant estimates and judgements made by the directors in the preparation of the financial statements, and of whether the accounting policies are appropriate to the company's circumstances, consistently applied and adequately disclosed.

We planned and performed our audit so as to obtain all the information and explanations which we considered necessary in order to provide us with sufficient evidence to give reasonable assurance that the financial statements are free from material misstatement, whether caused by fraud or other irregularity or error. HOWEVER, THE EVIDENCE AVAILABLE TO US WAS LIMITED BECAUSE OF THE MATTERS REFERRED TO BELOW.

[MATTER 1]. THERE WAS NO SYSTEM OF CONTROL OVER [MATTER 1] ON WHICH WE COULD RELY FOR THE PURPOSES OF OUR AUDIT AND THERE WERE NO OTHER SATISFACTORY AUDIT PROCEDURES THAT WE COULD ADOPT TO CONFIRM THAT [ACCOUNTING FOR MATTER 1] WAS CORRECT.

[MATTER 2]. THERE WAS NO SYSTEM OF CONTROL OVER [MATTER 2] ON WHICH WE COULD RELY FOR THE PURPOSES OF OUR AUDIT AND THERE WERE NO OTHER SATISFACTORY AUDIT PROCEDURES THAT WE COULD ADOPT TO CONFIRM THAT [ACCOUNTING FOR MATTER 2] WAS CORRECT.

In forming our opinion we also evaluated the overall adequacy of the presentation of information in the financial statements.

QUALIFIED OPINION ARISING FROM LIMITATIONS IN AUDIT SCOPE

EXCEPT FOR ANY ADJUSTMENTS THAT MIGHT HAVE BEEN FOUND TO BE NECESSARY HAD WE BEEN ABLE TO OBTAIN SUFFICIENT EVIDENCE CONCERNING [MATTER 1] AND [MATTER 2], in our opinion the financial statements give a true and fair view of the state of the company's affairs as at .... and of its [profit / loss] for the year then ended and have been properly prepared in accordance with the Companies Act 1985.

IN RESPECT ALONE OF THE LIMITATIONS ON OUR WORK RELATING TO [MATTER 1] AND [MATTER 2]:

- WE HAVE NOT OBTAINED ALL THE INFORMATION AND EXPLANATIONS THAT WE CONSIDERED NECESSARY FOR THE PURPOSES OF OUR AUDIT; AND

- WE WERE UNABLE TO DETERMINE WHETHER PROPER ACCOUNTING RECORDS HAD BEEN KEPT.

Report 403
SL — e: SL — e: Opening stocks and cash sales

Basis of opinion

We conducted our audit in accordance with Auditing Standards issued by the Auditing Practices Board except that the scope of our work was limited as explained below.

An audit includes examination, on a test basis, of evidence relevant to the amounts and disclosures in the financial statements. It also includes an assessment of the significant estimates and judgements made by the directors in the preparation of the financial statements, and of whether the accounting policies are appropriate to the company's circumstances, consistently applied and adequately disclosed.

We planned and performed our audit so as to obtain all the information and explanations which we considered necessary in order to provide us with sufficient evidence to give reasonable assurance that the financial statements are free from material misstatement, whether caused by fraud or other irregularity or error. However, the evidence available to us was limited because of the matters referred to below.

We were appointed auditors on .... and in consequence were unable to carry out auditing procedures necessary to obtain adequate assurance regarding the quantities and condition of stock and work in progress, appearing in the balance sheet at .... Any adjustment to this figure would have a consequential effect on the profit for the year.

£ ..... of the company's recorded turnover comprises cash sales. There was no system of control over such sales on which we could rely for the purposes of our audit and there were no other satisfactory audit procedures that we could adopt to confirm that cash sales were properly recorded.

In forming our opinion we also evaluated the overall adequacy of the presentation of information in the financial statements.

Qualified opinion arising from limitations in audit scope

Except for any adjustments that might have been found to be necessary had we been able to obtain sufficient evidence concerning stock and work in progress and cash sales in our opinion the financial statements give a true and fair view of the state of the company's affairs as at .... and of its [profit / loss] for the year then ended and have been properly prepared in accordance with the Companies Act 1985.

In respect alone of the limitations on our work relating to stock and work in progress and cash sales:

- we have not obtained all the information and explanations that we considered necessary for the purposes of our audit; and
- we were unable to determine whether proper accounting records had been kept.

The reports combined above were given as typical wording in the scope limitation section of chapter 3. They do not, therefore accord exactly with the generic skeleton. The modification concerning the opening stock and work in progress was presented in chapter 3 as a disclaimer of opinion. It is assumed for the purposes of this illustration that the matter is simply material and so the more normal except for opinion is appropriate.

4.4.1.4 Elements and options

1 Basis of opinion — degree of integration

The basis of opinion sections in the typical wording above use independent paragraphs for the two modifications. This option is preferred because it allows the modifications to be written separately and combined easily. The following is an alternative approach which could be adopted if there was less difference between the wording of the modifications. As will be seen from this generic word picture, the modification is potentially complex unless that is the case.

Report 404

SL — e: SL — e: Generic word picture, alternative basis of opinion

Basis of opinion

We conducted our audit in accordance with Auditing Standards issued by the Auditing Practices Board, EXCEPT THAT THE SCOPE OF OUR WORK WAS LIMITED AS EXPLAINED BELOW.

An audit includes examination, on a test basis, of evidence relevant to the amounts and disclosures in the financial statements. It also includes an assessment of the significant estimates and judgements made by the directors in the preparation of the financial statements, and of whether the accounting policies are appropriate to the company's circumstances, consistently applied and adequately disclosed.

We planned and performed our audit so as to obtain all the information and explanations which we considered necessary in order to provide us with sufficient evidence to give reasonable assurance that the financial statements are free from material misstatement, whether caused by fraud or other irregularity or error. HOWEVER, THE EVIDENCE AVAILABLE TO US WAS LIMITED BECAUSE [MATTER 1] AND [MATTER 2]. THERE WAS NO SYSTEM OF CONTROL OVER [MATTER 1] OR OVER [MATTER 2] ON WHICH WE COULD RELY FOR THE PURPOSES OF OUR AUDIT AND THERE WERE NO OTHER SATISFACTORY AUDIT PROCEDURES THAT WE COULD ADOPT TO CONFIRM THAT [ACCOUNTING FOR MATTER 1] AND [ACCOUNTING FOR MATTER 2] WERE CORRECT.

In forming our opinion we also evaluated the overall adequacy of the presentation of information in the financial statements.

The following is an example of two modifications combined in the basis of opinion section without using independent paragraphs. It is not the preferred approach.

Report 405
SL — e: SL — e: Fire and flood, alternative basis of opinion

Basis of opinion

We conducted our audit in accordance with Auditing Standards issued by the Auditing Practices Board, except that the scope of our work was limited as explained below.

An audit includes examination, on a test basis, of evidence relevant to the amounts and disclosures in the financial statements. It also includes an assessment of the significant estimates and judgements made by the directors in the preparation of the financial statements, and of whether the accounting policies are appropriate to the company's circumstances, consistently applied and adequately disclosed.

We planned and performed our audit so as to obtain all the information and explanations which we considered necessary in order to provide us with sufficient evidence to give reasonable assurance that the financial statements are free from material misstatement, whether caused by fraud or other irregularity or error. However, the evidence available to us was limited because a fire at the company's data processing centre destroyed the sales records for the month of August and the fixed asset register was lost in a flood in September. There were no alternative systems of control over sales in August or over fixed assets on which we could rely for the purposes of our audit and there were no other satisfactory audit procedures that we could adopt to confirm that the amount included in turnover for August sales and the cost and depreciation of fixed assets shown in the balance sheet at .... were correct.

In forming our opinion we also evaluated the overall adequacy of the presentation of information in the financial statements.

Combining modifications in the basis of opinion section is easier if the two modifications have similar wording. Taken to its logical conclusion, two modifications may be merged into one at the point where the distinctions between the events giving rise to them break down. This leads to a discussion of the exact nature of a SAS 600 limitation of audit scope. This is really only relevant to circumstances where more than one limitation of audit scope may be reported.

The limitation of audit scope may be defined either by the event or its accounting consequences. For example, during the year fire may destroy records that cannot be reconstituted. The following theoretical possibilities may arise:

- one fire affects one aspect of the accounting records (e.g. *'a fire in September destroyed the company's sales records for the month of August'*)
- one fire affects two aspects of the accounting records (e.g. *'a fire in September destroyed the company's sales records for the month of August and the fixed asset register'*)

- two fires affect one aspect of the accounting records (e.g. *'two fires in September destroyed the two halves of the company's sales records for the month of August'*)
- two fires affect two aspects of the accounting records (e.g. *'two fires in September separately destroyed the company's sales records for the month of August and the fixed asset register'*).

There are, of course, many more combinations of fires and aspects of the accounting records that could occur.

Auditors may decide that the fires or the accounting records are the focus of their modification. They may combine modifications into one where either; one fire affects two aspects of the accounting records, or one aspect of the accounting records is affected by two fires. In such cases the basis of opinion would have to explain matters accordingly but the modification would be a single one. Thus, not all potential combinations of modifications are, in fact, combinations; some are simply the realisation that there was only one modification in the first place.

2 Opinion — degree of integration

In contrast to the separate paragraph approach in the basis of opinion, the suggested opinion combines the two modifications as much as possible. The following extract shows how unreadable a combined paragraph (one sentence of some 94 words) would be if the duplicated wording was not eliminated.

Qualified opinion arising from limitations in audit scope

> Except for any adjustments that might have been found to be necessary had we been able to obtain sufficient evidence concerning stock and work in progress and except for any adjustments that might have been found to be necessary had we been able to obtain sufficient evidence concerning cash sales in our opinion the financial statements give a true and fair view of the state of the company's affairs as at .... and of its [profit / loss] for the year then ended and have been properly prepared in accordance with the Companies Act 1985.

3 Matters required by law — degree of integration

The degree of integration depends on the presence of similar matters. Both limitations of audit scope may be accompanied by a modification resulting from a failure to obtain necessary information and explanations. If so, the two are combined by eliminating duplicate wording and inserting an 's' at the end of the word 'limitation'. The relevant section of the report, therefore, commences:

> In respect alone of the limitations on our work relating to stock and work in progress and cash sales:

The opening words *'in respect alone'* might be considered to be out of place as there are two matters and so by definition they are together rather than alone. The words have been retained in the illustrations as they are used in examples 8 and 9 in appendix 2 to SAS 600.

Auditors who decide not to use wording referring to their uncertainty about accounting records may turn the material around and perhaps use wording such as:

> We have not obtained all the information and explanations that we considered necessary for the purposes of our audit in respect of the limitations on our work relating to stock and work in progress and cash sales.

4 Disclaimer

If two except for opinions are being combined, the overall effect may cause the auditors to reassess their report. It may be that, taken together, the circumstances may influence the auditors into forming a view that, instead, a disclaimer of opinion is appropriate.

4.4.2 Scope limitations — disclaimers of opinion

4.4.2.1 Introduction

Much of the guidance in the section above, dealing with the except for qualification due to a SAS 600 limitation of audit scope, remains relevant to disclaimers of opinion. This section concentrates on the special aspects of combining disclaimers of opinion with each other.

The difference between an except for qualification and a disclaimer depends on the judgement as to whether the possible effect of a limitation is so material or pervasive that an opinion on the financial statements cannot be expressed.

4.4.2.2 Summary of the approach

Where both modifications are disclaimers, auditors just combine the two basis of opinion sections and express the disclaimer of opinion in relation to both matters.

4.4.2.3 Typical wording

Report 406

SL — d: SL — d: Generic word picture

Basis of opinion

> We conducted our audit in accordance with Auditing Standards issued by the Auditing Practices Board, EXCEPT THAT THE SCOPE OF OUR WORK WAS LIMITED AS EXPLAINED BELOW.
>
> An audit includes examination, on a test basis, of evidence relevant to the amounts and disclosures in the financial statements. It also includes an assessment of the significant estimates and judgements made by the directors in the preparation of the financial statements, and of whether the accounting policies are appropriate to the company's circumstances, consistently applied and adequately disclosed.
>
> We planned and performed our audit so as to obtain all the information and explanations which we considered necessary in order to provide us with sufficient

evidence to give reasonable assurance that the financial statements are free from material misstatement, whether caused by fraud or other irregularity or error. HOWEVER, THE EVIDENCE AVAILABLE TO US WAS LIMITED BECAUSE OF THE MATTERS REFERRED TO BELOW.

[MATTER 1]. THERE WAS NO SYSTEM OF CONTROL OVER [MATTER 1] ON WHICH WE COULD RELY FOR THE PURPOSES OF OUR AUDIT AND THERE WERE NO OTHER SATISFACTORY AUDIT PROCEDURES THAT WE COULD ADOPT TO CONFIRM THAT [ACCOUNTING FOR MATTER 1] WAS CORRECT.

[MATTER 2]. THERE WAS NO SYSTEM OF CONTROL OVER [MATTER 2] ON WHICH WE COULD RELY FOR THE PURPOSES OF OUR AUDIT AND THERE WERE NO OTHER SATISFACTORY AUDIT PROCEDURES THAT WE COULD ADOPT TO CONFIRM THAT [ACCOUNTING FOR MATTER 2] WAS CORRECT.

In forming our opinion we also evaluated the overall adequacy of the presentation of information in the financial statements.

OPINION: DISCLAIMER ON VIEW GIVEN BY FINANCIAL STATEMENTS

BECAUSE OF THE POSSIBLE EFFECTS OF THE LIMITATIONS IN EVIDENCE AVAILABLE TO US, WE ARE UNABLE TO FORM AN OPINION AS TO WHETHER THE FINANCIAL STATEMENTS GIVE A TRUE AND FAIR VIEW OF THE STATE OF THE COMPANY'S AFFAIRS AS AT .... OR OF ITS [PROFIT / LOSS] FOR THE YEAR THEN ENDED. IN ALL OTHER RESPECTS, IN OUR OPINION THE FINANCIAL STATEMENTS HAVE BEEN PROPERLY PREPARED IN ACCORDANCE WITH THE COMPANIES ACT 1985.

IN RESPECT ALONE OF THE LIMITATIONS ON OUR WORK RELATING TO [MATTER 1] AND [MATTER 2]:

- WE HAVE NOT OBTAINED ALL THE INFORMATION AND EXPLANATIONS THAT WE CONSIDERED NECESSARY FOR THE PURPOSES OF OUR AUDIT; AND
- WE WERE UNABLE TO DETERMINE WHETHER PROPER ACCOUNTING RECORDS HAD BEEN KEPT.

4.4.3 Disagreements — except for qualifications

4.4.3.1 Introduction

Modifications for disagreement affect only the opinion section of the auditors' report. In addition to the qualified opinion, there should be:

- a description of all substantive factors giving rise to the disagreement
- their implications for the accounts
- whenever practicable, a quantification of the effect.

4.4.3.2 Summary of the approach

The following skeletons show first one modification then a combination of two modifications.

Report 407
D— e: Generic skeleton

QUALIFIED OPINION ARISING FROM DISAGREEMENT ABOUT . . .

OPINION OF AUDITORS AS TO CORRECT TREATMENT.

EXCEPT FOR THE ABOVE, opinion.

Report 408
D— e: D— e: Generic skeleton

QUALIFIED OPINION ARISING FROM DISAGREEMENTS ABOUT . . .

OPINION OF AUDITORS AS TO CORRECT TREATMENT 1.

OPINION OF AUDITORS AS TO CORRECT TREATMENT 2.

EXCEPT FOR THE ABOVE, opinion.

The opinion section deals with each disagreement in a separate paragraph. The wording of the final opinion paragraph is arrived at by eliminating the duplicated wording in the two individual except for opinions. The heading of the opinion section may also indicate that there is more than one disagreement.

4.4.3.3 Typical wording

Report 409
D— e: D— e: Generic word picture

QUALIFIED OPINION ARISING FROM DISAGREEMENT(S) ABOUT [ACCOUNTING TREATMENT / DISCLOSURE / ACCOUNTING TREATMENT AND DISCLOSURE]

AS MORE FULLY EXPLAINED IN NOTE ..... [MATTER 1] [WHY MATTER 1 IS A PROBLEM]. IN OUR OPINION [REASON FOR DISAGREEMENT 1] [QUANTIFICATION 1].

AS MORE FULLY EXPLAINED IN NOTE ..... [MATTER 2] [WHY MATTER 2 IS A PROBLEM]. IN OUR OPINION [REASON FOR DISAGREEMENT 2] [QUANTIFICATION 2].

EXCEPT FOR [NOT FOLLOWING OUR VIEW 1] AND EXCEPT FOR [NOT FOLLOWING OUR VIEW 2], in our opinion the financial statements give a true and fair view of the state of the company's affairs as at .... and of its [profit / loss] for the year then ended and have been properly prepared in accordance with the Companies Act 1985.

Report 410
D— e: D— e: Bad debt not provided and investment properties not at valuation

Qualified opinion arising from disagreements about accounting treatment

As more fully explained in note ..... included in the debtors shown on the balance sheet is an amount of £ ..... due from a company which has ceased trading. .... has

> no security for this debt. In our opinion the company is unlikely to receive any payment and full provision of £ ..... should have been made, reducing profit before tax and net assets by that amount.
>
> As more fully explained in note ..... , investment properties are included in the balance sheet at .... [year] valuation of £ ..... . In our opinion, these properties should be included in the balance sheet at their open market value, in accordance with the requirements of SSAP 19 'Accounting for investment properties'. In the absence of a current valuation it is not practicable to quantify the effect, if any, of this failure to comply with the accounting standard.
>
> Except for the absence of an appropriate provision against the unsecured debt and except for the failure to include investment properties at open market value in our opinion the financial statements give a true and fair view of the state of the company's affairs as at .... and of its [profit / loss] for the year then ended and have been properly prepared in accordance with the Companies Act 1985.

4.4.3.4 Elements and options

The above opinion section uses independent paragraphs for the initial aspects of the two modifications. This option is preferred because it allows the modifications to be written separately and combined easily. An alternative wording is not given here as a similar omnibus paragraph is shown in the equivalent discussion of scope limitation earlier in this chapter. The conclusions arrived at in that section about potentially complex wording are also valid for disagreements.

The final paragraph retains specific references to the modifications rather than commencing:

> Except for the above . . .

This is because the earlier paragraphs do not spell out that the qualified opinion is expressed except for the effects of the matter giving rise to the disagreement, as required by SAS 600.8. The specific wording is also retained because it makes it easier to combine disagreements with other modifications affecting the opinion section. As a matter of house style auditors could shorten the opinion by starting:

> Except for the effects of the matters above . . .

There are, however, dangers in the use of such a simple wording. While auditors would immediately comprehend the cross-reference, others may mistake the reference as being to aspects of the report, such as the respective responsibilities of the directors and auditors. This was not so much of a danger prior to SAS 600, as the standard report did not include other material.

4.4.4 Disagreements — adverse opinions

4.4.4.1 Introduction

Modifications arising from disagreements are normally except for qualifications. An adverse opinion is only appropriate if the matter giving rise to a disagreement is so material or pervasive that the financial statements as a whole are seriously misleading.

4.4.4.2 Summary of the approach

In the very rare case where both modifications are adverse opinions, auditors follow the same approach used for combining other disagreements. The opinion section deals with each disagreement in a separate paragraph. The final opinion paragraph is written by eliminating the duplicated wording in the two individual adverse opinions. Skeleton opinions are not shown as they are very similar to those for except for opinions dealt with above.

4.4.4.3 Typical wording

Report 411

D— a: D— a: Generic word picture

ADVERSE OPINION

AS MORE FULLY EXPLAINED IN NOTE ..... [MATTER 1] [REASON FOR DIRECTORS' TREATMENT 1]. IN OUR OPINION, [PROPER TREATMENT 1] AS REQUIRED BY [STATEMENT OF STANDARD ACCOUNTING PRACTICE ..... / FINANCIAL REPORTING STANDARD .....]. [QUANTIFICATION 1].

AS MORE FULLY EXPLAINED IN NOTE ..... [MATTER 2] [REASON FOR DIRECTORS' TREATMENT 2]. IN OUR OPINION, [PROPER TREATMENT 2] AS REQUIRED BY [STATEMENT OF STANDARD ACCOUNTING PRACTICE ..... / FINANCIAL REPORTING STANDARD .....]. [QUANTIFICATION 2].

IN VIEW OF THE EFFECT OF THE FAILURE TO [ACCOUNT PROPERLY 1] AND [ACCOUNT PROPERLY 2] REFERRED TO ABOVE, IN OUR OPINION THE FINANCIAL STATEMENTS DO NOT GIVE A TRUE AND FAIR VIEW OF THE STATE OF THE COMPANY'S AFFAIRS AS AT .... AND OF ITS [PROFIT / LOSS] FOR THE YEAR THEN ENDED. IN ALL OTHER RESPECTS, IN OUR OPINION THE FINANCIAL STATEMENTS HAVE BEEN PROPERLY PREPARED IN ACCORDANCE WITH THE COMPANIES ACT 1985.

A further example of the wording of two adverse opinions is not given in full because the paragraphs dealing with the two matters are entirely independent. It is sufficient, therefore, to illustrate just the final paragraph of the opinion which refers to both modifications (in this case, unprovided losses on long-term contracts and the going concern basis).

Report 412
D— a: D— a: Losses on contracts and going concern (extract)

> In view of the effect of the failure to provide for the losses referred to above and the failure to prepare the financial statements on a basis other than that of a going concern, in our opinion the financial statements do not give a true and fair view of the state of the company's affairs as at .... and of its [profit / loss] for the year then ended. In all other respects, in our opinion the financial statements have been properly prepared in accordance with the Companies Act 1985.

4.4.4.4 Elements and options

The above opinion section uses independent paragraphs for the initial aspects of the two modifications. This option is preferred because it allows the modifications to be written separately and combined easily. An alternative wording is not given here for the reasons discussed and illustrated for except for opinions arising from disagreement in the preceding subsection.

4.4.5 Fundamental uncertainties

Combining two modifications for fundamental uncertainty is easy. The paragraphs, under their appropriate heading in the basis of opinion section are independent of one another. For this reason no skeleton, generic word picture, or other illustration is given in this section. The only decision to take when issuing a report with two such modifications is which to put first. This decision is considered generally when discussing combining modifications of different types elsewhere in this chapter.

4.4.6 Required by law

4.4.6.1 Introduction

Auditors are required to report on the following matters in appropriate circumstances:

- failure to keep proper accounting records
- lack of all the information and explanations considered necessary for the purposes of the audit
- inadequate returns from branches not visited by the auditors
- the company's individual accounts do not agree with the accounting records and returns
- the information given in the directors' report is not consistent with the accounts
- omission of disclosures required by Schedule 6 to the Companies Act 1985 concerning emoluments of and transactions with directors.

In theory, reports could be issued combining two modifications of the same type for each of the above. However, the following matters arguably give rise to only one modification:

- inadequate returns from branches not visited by the auditors
- the company's individual accounts do not agree with the accounting records and returns
- the information given in the directors' report is not consistent with the accounts.

The reasoning is similar for each of the above. Although auditors may cite more than one circumstance giving rise to each modification, the modification is only issued once. For example, it does not matter how returns from branches are inadequate or how many branches the returns are inadequate for; the opinion extends to all of these.

The failure of the accounts to agree to the accounting records and returns may be because one balance does not agree or because many do not. Similarly, one or more pieces of information given in the directors' report may not be consistent with the accounts. There is no multiple modification in these circumstances. Each modification is just explained in terms of more than one deficiency.

The remaining three matters are treated as giving rise to reports where more than one instance may be reported:

- failure to keep proper accounting records
- lack of all the information and explanations considered necessary for the purposes of the audit
- omission of disclosures required by Schedule 6 to the Companies Act 1985 concerning emoluments of and transactions with directors.

The first two matters are likely to occur in conjunction with a SAS 600 limitation of audit scope. Combining such modifications is dealt with in this chapter in relation to the primary modification rather than the linked secondary matters required by law. It is for this reason that they are included in the category of modifications where more than one instance may be reported. It would be possible to argue logically for their inclusion in the earlier category instead.

The only matter required by law dealt with here that may occur two or more times in auditors' reports is, therefore, the omission of disclosures required by Schedule 6 to the Companies Act 1985. A single modification of this type takes the following form:

Opinion

In our opinion the financial statements give a true and fair view of the state of the company's affairs as at .... and of its [profit / loss] for the year then ended and have been properly prepared in accordance with the Companies Act 1985.

THE FINANCIAL STATEMENTS DO NOT DISCLOSE [OMITTED REQUIREMENTS OF SCHEDULE 6 TO THE COMPANIES ACT 1985].

A multiple modification is, therefore, simply effected by including more omitted requirements. Accordingly it is not necessary to give a typical wording.

4.4.7 Responsibilities of directors

If the accounts or accompanying information, such as the directors' report, do not include an adequate description of directors' relevant responsibilities, auditors are required by SAS 600.3 to include a description of those responsibilities in their report.

If the description is absent, auditors simply include a full description in their own report. A multiple modification occurs, therefore, only when a description is given by the directors but it is deficient in two or more ways. The multiple modification is easily constructed by including further matters as shown by the generic word picture below.

Report 413
RofD: RofD: Generic word picture

Respective responsibilities of directors and auditors

As described on page ..... the company's directors are responsible for the preparation of financial statements. THOSE RESPONSIBILITIES INCLUDE [MATTER 1] AND [MATTER 2]. It is our responsibility to form an independent opinion, based on our audit, on those statements and to report our opinion to you.

4.4.8 Outside the scope of SAS 600

Matters that are outside the scope of SAS 600 that are dealt with in chapter 3 are:

- explanatory material that is not a fundamental uncertainty, for example concerning the presence of a proforma statement, or a change in ownership of the company
- opinions on matters considered relevant by the directors, for example the adequacy of a provision against fraud perpetrated by former directors.

Multiple occurrences of such matters are easily combined because they are dealt with in separate, appropriately headed, paragraphs as the following skeleton reports show.

Report 414
OTS: OTS: Generic skeleton (explanations)

Basis of opinion

Compliance with Auditing Standards and description of an audit.

Evidence and evaluation of presentation.

Heading

EXPLANATION 1.

Heading

EXPLANATION 2.

Report 415
OTS: OTS: Generic skeleton (further opinions)

Opinion

Opinion.

HEADING

FURTHER OPINION 1.

HEADING

FURTHER OPINION 2.

4.5 Three or more modifications of the same type

If there are three or more modifications of the same type they may be combined by successively following the methods given above for two modifications. For example, to combine three modifications the first step is to combine two. Having done that, the remaining modification may be combined with the multiple modification of the first two which now behaves effectively as a single modification.

4.6 Two modifications of different types

4.6.1 Introduction

Combining two modifications of different types may be a simple operation if the types do not interact. Other modifications interact and cannot be combined so simply.

This section commences by listing the simple combinations before moving on to deal with the more complex combinations: the qualified opinions for scope limitation and disagreement.

4.6.2 Simple combinations

The majority of modifications may be combined with others easily because, if the methods suggested in this book are used, their wording is confined to a specific part of the auditors' report (often with an appropriate heading). These are:

- fundamental uncertainty
- required by law (alone)
  - — failure to keep proper accounting records
  - — lack of all the information and explanations considered necessary for the purposes of the audit

  - inadequate returns from branches not visited by the auditors
  - the company's individual accounts do not agree with the accounting records and returns
  - the information given in the directors' report is not consistent with the accounts
  - omission of disclosures required by Schedule 6 to the Companies Act 1985 concerning emoluments of and transactions with directors
- responsibilities of directors
- outside the scope of SAS 600
  - explanation
  - opinion.

The matters required by law are also considered later where they occur together with linked primary modifications.

Two of the above modifications may be combined simply by adding to the first modification those aspects of the second modification that are not the same as the first. For example, a modification for a fundamental uncertainty and a further opinion required by the directors that is outside the scope of SAS 600 only affect respectively the basis of opinion and opinion sections of the auditors' report.

Where additions affect the same section of the report, auditors should choose an appropriate order. There are no requirements affecting this choice. The following approach is suggested:

- put the more significant modification first, but
- if one modification is about the going concern basis of preparation of the accounts, that modification should be the last one.

The reason for dealing with going concern last is simply that other modifications may contribute to the doubt about the continuation of the business and it seems reasonable to place the consequence last. An alternative approach is to put the modifications in decreasing order of importance. Using this approach, going concern would usually come before other modifications.

4.6.3 Combining qualifications

The following modifications all affect the opinion paragraph and so combining them is not simple:

- scope limitation
  - except for qualifications (SL — e)
  - disclaimers of opinion (SL — d)
- disagreement
  - except for qualifications (D — e)
  - adverse opinions (D — a).

Combining two modifications of the same type is discussed in the appropriate section above. The combinations that are dealt with below are shown in the following table.

Combine	Combine with		
SL — e	D — e	D — a	SL — d
D — e	SL — d	D — a	
SL — d		D — a	

The following subsections examine each of the six combinations in turn. Subsections involving the rarer disclaimer and adverse opinions draw on material in the first subsection which examines the more likely combination of except for opinions due to scope limitation and disagreement.

4.6.4 'Except for' scope limitation and disagreement

The qualifications have the following skeletons:

Report 416
SL — e: Generic skeleton

Basis of opinion

Compliance with Auditing Standards EXCEPT THAT SCOPE WAS LIMITED.

Description of an audit.

Evidence AND A DESCRIPTION OF LIMITATION.

Evaluation of presentation.

QUALIFIED OPINION ARISING FROM LIMITATION IN AUDIT SCOPE

EXCEPT FOR OPINION.

FURTHER MATTER REQUIRED BY LAW.

Report 417
D — e: Generic skeleton

Basis of opinion

Compliance with Auditing Standards and description of an audit.

Evidence and evaluation of presentation.

QUALIFIED OPINION ARISING FROM DISAGREEMENT ABOUT . . .

OPINION OF AUDITORS AS TO CORRECT TREATMENT.

EXCEPT FOR THE ABOVE, opinion.

A qualification due to scope limitation affects the basis of opinion as well as the opinion itself, whereas a disagreement does not affect the basis of opinion. Combining the basis of opinion sections for the two modifications is therefore achieved by using just the section from the scope limitation.

The word pictures of the opinion paragraphs show how they too may be combined.

Report 418
SL — e: Generic word picture (opinion only)

QUALIFIED OPINION ARISING FROM LIMITATION IN AUDIT SCOPE

EXCEPT FOR ANY ADJUSTMENTS THAT MIGHT HAVE BEEN FOUND TO BE NECESSARY HAD WE BEEN ABLE TO OBTAIN SUFFICIENT EVIDENCE CONCERNING [MATTER], in our opinion the financial statements give a true and fair view of the state of the company's affairs as at .... and of its [profit / loss] for the year then ended and have been properly prepared in accordance with the Companies Act 1985.

IN RESPECT ALONE OF THE LIMITATION ON OUR WORK RELATING TO [MATTER]:

- WE HAVE NOT OBTAINED ALL THE INFORMATION AND EXPLANATIONS THAT WE CONSIDERED NECESSARY FOR THE PURPOSES OF OUR AUDIT; AND

- WE WERE UNABLE TO DETERMINE WHETHER PROPER ACCOUNTING RECORDS HAD BEEN KEPT.

Report 419
D — e: Generic word picture

QUALIFIED OPINION ARISING FROM DISAGREEMENT ABOUT [ACCOUNTING TREATMENT / DISCLOSURE]

AS MORE FULLY EXPLAINED IN NOTE ..... [MATTER] [WHY MATTER IS A PROBLEM]. IN OUR OPINION [REASON FOR DISAGREEMENT] [QUANTIFICATION].

EXCEPT FOR [NOT FOLLOWING OUR VIEW], in our opinion the financial statements give a true and fair view of the state of the company's affairs as at .... and of its [profit / loss] for the year then ended and have been properly prepared in accordance with the Companies Act 1985.

The scope limitation includes wording that expresses uncertainty as to whether proper accounting records have been kept. This derives from the examples in appendix 2 to SAS 600. While it is anticipated that such wording will be widely used it is, nevertheless criticised in chapter 3 and some auditors may wish to exclude it from their reports.

Combining the opinion sections can be done by using the paragraphs from each modification that have no equivalent in the other and merging the 'except for' paragraphs to eliminate the duplicated wording.

The whole operation is illustrated by the following combined modification.

Report 420
SL — e: D — e: Cash sales and bad debt not provided

Basis of opinion

We conducted our audit in accordance with Auditing Standards issued by the Auditing Practices Board except that the scope of our work was limited as explained below.

An audit includes examination, on a test basis, of evidence relevant to the amounts and disclosures in the financial statements. It also includes an assessment of the significant estimates and judgements made by the directors in the preparation of the financial statements, and of whether the accounting policies are appropriate to the company's circumstances, consistently applied and adequately disclosed.

We planned and performed our audit so as to obtain all the information and explanations which we considered necessary in order to provide us with sufficient evidence to give reasonable assurance that the financial statements are free from material misstatement, whether caused by fraud or other irregularity or error. However, the evidence available to us was limited because £ ..... of the company's recorded turnover comprises cash sales. There was no system of control over such sales on which we could rely for the purposes of our audit and there were no other satisfactory audit procedures that we could adopt to confirm that cash sales were properly recorded.

In forming our opinion we also evaluated the overall adequacy of the presentation of information in the financial statements.

QUALIFIED OPINION ARISING FROM DISAGREEMENT ABOUT ACCOUNTING TREATMENT AND LIMITATION IN AUDIT SCOPE

As more fully explained in note ..... included in the debtors shown on the balance sheet is an amount of £ ..... due from a company which has ceased trading. .... has no security for this debt. In our opinion the company is unlikely to receive any payment and full provision of £ ..... should have been made, reducing profit before tax and net assets by that amount.

Except for the absence of this provision, and except for any adjustments that might have been found to be necessary had we been able to obtain sufficient evidence concerning cash sales, in our opinion the financial statements give a true and fair view of the state of the company's affairs as at .... and of its [profit / loss] for the year then ended and have been properly prepared in accordance with the Companies Act 1985.

In respect alone of the limitation on our work relating to cash sales:

- we have not obtained all the information and explanations that we considered necessary for the purposes of our audit; and
- we were unable to determine whether proper accounting records had been kept.

4.6.5 'Except for' scope limitation and adverse opinion

The qualifications have the same skeletons as above except that the adverse opinion replaces the 'except for' disagreement.

Report 421
SL — e: Generic skeleton

Basis of opinion

Compliance with Auditing Standards EXCEPT THAT SCOPE WAS LIMITED.

Description of an audit.

Evidence AND A DESCRIPTION OF LIMITATION.

Evaluation of presentation.

QUALIFIED OPINION ARISING FROM LIMITATION IN AUDIT SCOPE

EXCEPT FOR OPINION.

FURTHER MATTER REQUIRED BY LAW.

Report 422
D — a: Generic skeleton

Basis of opinion

Compliance with Auditing Standards and description of an audit.

Evidence and evaluation of presentation.

ADVERSE OPINION

OPINION OF AUDITORS AS TO CORRECT TREATMENT.

ADVERSE OPINION.

When an adverse opinion is expressed the two opinion paragraphs cannot be combined as simply as two 'except for's.

The following two modification extracts are shown separately then combined.

Report 423
SL — e: Cash sales (opinion only)

Qualified opinion arising from limitation in audit scope

Except for any adjustments that might have been found to be necessary had we been able to obtain sufficient evidence concerning cash sales, in our opinion the financial statements give a true and fair view of the state of the company's affairs as at .... and of its [profit / loss] for the year then ended and have been properly prepared in accordance with the Companies Act 1985.

In respect alone of the limitation on our work relating to cash sales:

- we have not obtained all the information and explanations that we considered necessary for the purposes of our audit; and
- we were unable to determine whether proper accounting records had been kept.

Report 424
D — a: Long-term contract losses not provided for

Adverse opinion

As more fully explained in note ..... no provision has been made for losses expected to arise on certain long-term contracts currently in progress, as the directors consider that such losses should be off-set against amounts recoverable on other long-term contracts. In our opinion, provision should be made for foreseeable losses on individual contracts as required by Statement of Standard Accounting Practice 9 'Stocks and long-term contracts'. If losses had been so recognised the effect would have been to [reduce the profit / increase the loss] before and after tax for the year and the contract work in progress at .... by £..... .

In view of the effect of the failure to provide for the losses referred to above, in our opinion the financial statements do not give a true and fair view of the state of the company's affairs as at .... and of its [profit / loss] for the year then ended. In all other respects, in our opinion the financial statements have been properly prepared in accordance with the Companies Act 1985.

Report 425
SL — e: D — a: Cash sales (opinion only) and long-term contract losses not provided for

Adverse opinion and limitation in audit scope

As more fully explained in note ..... no provision has been made for losses expected to arise on certain long-term contracts currently in progress, as the directors consider that such losses should be off-set against amounts recoverable on other long-term contracts. In our opinion, provision should be made for foreseeable losses on individual contracts as required by Statement of Standard Accounting Practice 9 'Stocks and long-term contracts'. If losses had been so recognised the effect would have been to [reduce the profit / increase the loss] before and after tax for the year and the contract work in progress at .... by £..... .

In view of the effect of the failure to provide for the losses referred to above, in our opinion the financial statements do not give a true and fair view of the state of the company's affairs as at .... and of its [profit / loss] for the year then ended. In other respects, except for any adjustments that might have been found to be necessary had we been able to obtain sufficient evidence concerning cash sales, in our opinion the financial statements have been properly prepared in accordance with the Companies Act 1985.

In respect alone of the limitation on our work relating to cash sales:

- we have not obtained all the information and explanations that we considered necessary for the purposes of our audit; and

- we were unable to determine whether proper accounting records had been kept.

The aspects of the combined opinion section that are considered further are:

- the title
- the absorption of the scope limitation by the adverse opinion
- the need for a specific opinion on other aspects of proper preparation.

4.6.5.2 The title

Where no adverse opinion is present, the title of the opinion section can refer to both qualifications. For example, above, the example wording for a disagreement and a scope limitation was titled *'Qualified opinion arising from disagreement about accounting treatment and limitation in audit scope'*.

If this approach was continued, the title of the current extract might be *'Adverse opinion and qualified opinion arising from limitation in audit scope'*.

The title actually used is not only shorter, it reflects the partial absorption of the scope limitation by the adverse opinion as discussed below.

4.6.5.3 Absorption of the scope limitation by the adverse opinion

An adverse opinion is on the financial statements as a whole. It reflects the auditors' view that the effect of the matter giving rise to disagreement is so material or pervasive that the financial statements are seriously misleading.

An except for qualification for limitation of audit scope does not affect the true and fair view expressed directly. It informs readers that possible adjustments to the financial statements could have been determined to be necessary had the limitation not existed. These adjustments could have affected the true and fair view which (otherwise) the accounts give.

The two opinions therefore address different matters and seem to be mutually exclusive. In theory, the scope limitation could be reported against the background of accounts not giving a true and fair view just as well as accounts that otherwise give a true and fair view.

The adverse opinion illustrated in appendix 2 to SAS 600 deals with what seems to be a well defined area of the accounts: insufficient provision has been made for losses. Users could be expected to adjust the accounts notionally to accord with the auditors' views simply by increasing the provisions. The same users would presumably still want to know if another aspect of the accounts was subject to uncertainty introduced by a scope limitation.

Auditors who agree with this line of thought would not only give an adverse opinion but also seek to report the scope limitation. Unfortunately, the prose then becomes difficult.

This is, however, just one side to the argument. The counter argument runs that because the adverse opinion relates to the accounts as a whole it does not matter what explanation is given for it (lack of provisions). Once an adverse opinion is issued it is meaningless to try to report a scope limitation in relation to it. The analogy from mathematics is that infinity plus or minus one (or one million) is still infinity.

SAS 600 has not really changed the status of the extreme qualifications, many considered that they always were in relation to the accounts as a whole. The practical problem for auditors is that readers of their report will not necessarily understand the special nature of an adverse opinion. This is hardly surprising as before SAS 600, there have been instances of auditors issuing adverse opinions (or disclaimers) on one primary statement and a standard opinion on the other. Indeed, the fifth edition of the *Coopers & Lybrand Manual of Auditing* includes an example of an adverse report on the profit and loss account and balance sheet with a true and fair view being reported for the cash flows.

The illusion that some aspects of the accounts are not affected by an adverse opinion is preserved by the wording of example 10 in appendix 2 to SAS 600. That example uses wording that was also in the Auditing Standard that SAS 600 replaced. After the adverse opinion on truth and fairness the report continues:

> . . . In all other respects, in our opinion the financial statements have been properly prepared in accordance with the Companies Act 1985.

This wording is included in the examples in this book because it is likely to gain general acceptance. It assumes that readers of such a report will be pleased to know that there were no minor disclosure problems. This approach was criticised by Touche Ross & Co. in the third edition of their *Manual of Financial Reporting and Accounting* as being *'too insignificant to be worth saying'.*[1]

Auditors who nevertheless fear that readers of their report will criticise them for not mentioning other matters will look for a reasonable approach to wording a report that complies with SAS 600. On the one hand, the SAS tells auditors that if there is (for example) a limitation of audit scope they have to qualify their opinion accordingly. The SAS also tells auditors to issue a clear opinion. When their opinion is an adverse one any mention of related uncertainty could jeopardise its clarity.

There seems to be no simple answer to this problem. Certainly, SAS 600 does not offer guidance. Two possible answers are discussed below:

- utilise the wording about proper preparation as a vehicle to carry the qualification for limitation of audit scope
- consider the scope limitation to be one of the reasons for the adverse opinion.

1 Utilising proper preparation

The first possibility is the preferred approach in this book. It has been illustrated in the combined report shown above. After the adverse opinion the report goes on to say:

> . . . In other respects, except for any adjustments that might have been found to be necessary had we been able to obtain sufficient evidence concerning cash sales, in our

[1] A new edition of this book is about to be published. It is likely to be a worthwhile addition to the list of essential reference books for auditors. Auditors are also likely to find a new edition of a book by Lean Hopkins (to be published by Butterworths) of interest. The first edition of *Audit Report* dealt with reporting on various entities and gave a history of the development of reporting (this 'highlights' does not do the book justice). Amongst his many other interests, Leon Hopkins has been the moving force behind the subscription magazine *Audit Report* and he is in an ideal position to offer auditors the benefit of his considerable insight into the breadth and diversity of practice.

> opinion the financial statements have been properly prepared in accordance with the Companies Act 1985.

The adverse opinion is properly issued in accordance with explanatory paragraph 34 following SAS 600.5 which stipulates that '. . . *An adverse opinion is expressed by stating that the financial statements do not give a true and fair view.'*

The limitation in audit scope is not expressed in relation to the true and fair view despite the explanatory text in SAS 600 that calls for it (paragraph 37). However the qualified opinion is arguably expressed in accordance with SAS 600.7 which states that '. . . *the wording of the opinion should indicate that it is qualified as to the possible adjustments to the financial statements that might have been determined to be necessary had the limitation not existed.'*

2 Part of the reasons

The alternative approach is to consider the scope limitation to be one of the factors giving rise to the adverse opinion. If the basis of opinion section of the combined report is as shown above, the second and later paragraphs of the opinion might be worded as follows:

> In view of the effect of the failure to provide for the losses referred to above and the limitation on the scope of work, in our opinion the financial statements do not give a true and fair view of the state of the company's affairs as at .... and of its [profit / loss] for the year then ended. In other respects, in our opinion the financial statements have been properly prepared in accordance with the Companies Act 1985.
>
> In respect alone of the limitation on our work relating to cash sales:
>
> - we have not obtained all the information and explanations that we considered necessary for the purposes of our audit; and
> - we were unable to determine whether proper accounting records had been kept.

Auditors taking this 'all inclusive' view would presumably also wish to change the wording beginning *'in other respects . . .'*.

4.6.6 'Except for' scope limitation and disclaimer of opinion

Combining modifications that individually would result from different degrees of scope limitation is done by treating the lesser modification as part of the reason for the disclaimer.

This approach is illustrated by the reports given earlier in this chapter for combining two disclaimers.

This result may occasionally be arrived at when two except for opinions are being combined as, taken together, they may influence the auditors into forming a view that a disclaimer of opinion is appropriate.

4.6.7 'Except for' disagreement and disclaimer of opinion

The qualifications have the following skeletons.

Report 426
D— e: Generic skeleton

Basis of opinion

Compliance with Auditing Standards and description of an audit.

Evidence and evaluation of presentation.

QUALIFIED OPINION ARISING FROM DISAGREEMENT ABOUT . . .

OPINION OF AUDITORS AS TO CORRECT TREATMENT.

EXCEPT FOR THE ABOVE, opinion.

Report 427
SL— d: Generic skeleton

Basis of opinion

Compliance with Auditing Standards EXCEPT THAT SCOPE WAS LIMITED.

Description of an audit.

Evidence AND A DESCRIPTION OF LIMITATION.

Evaluation of presentation.

OPINION: DISCLAIMER ON VIEW GIVEN BY FINANCIAL STATEMENTS

DISCLAIMER OF OPINION.

FURTHER MATTER REQUIRED BY LAW.

When a disclaimer of opinion is expressed the two opinion paragraphs cannot be combined as simply as two 'except for's.

The following two modification extracts are shown separately then combined.

Report 428
D— e: Bad debt not provided

Qualified opinion arising from disagreement about accounting treatment

As more fully explained in note ..... included in the debtors shown on the balance sheet is an amount of £ ..... due from a company which has ceased trading. .... has no security for this debt. In our opinion the company is unlikely to receive any payment and full provision of £ ..... should have been made, reducing profit before tax and net assets by that amount.

Except for the absence of this provision, in our opinion the financial statements give a true and fair view of the state of the company's affairs as at .... and of its [profit / loss] for the year then ended and have been properly prepared in accordance with the Companies Act 1985.

Report 429
SL— d: Opening stocks (opinion only)

Opinion: disclaimer on view given by financial statements

Because of the possible effect of the limitation in evidence available to us, we are unable to form an opinion as to whether the financial statements give a true and fair view of the state of the company's affairs as at .... or of its [profit / loss] for the year then ended. In all other respects, in our opinion the financial statements have been properly prepared in accordance with the Companies Act 1985.

In respect alone of the limitation on our work relating to stock and work in progress:

- we have not obtained all the information and explanations that we considered necessary for the purposes of our audit; and
- we were unable to determine whether proper accounting records had been kept.

Report 430
D — e: SL — d: Bad debts not provided and opening stocks (opinion only)

Opinion: disclaimer on view given by financial statements and disagreement

As more fully explained in note ..... included in the debtors shown on the balance sheet is an amount of £ ..... due from a company which has ceased trading. .... has no security for this debt. In our opinion the company is unlikely to receive any payment and full provision of £ ..... should have been made, reducing profit before tax and net assets by that amount.

Because of the possible effect of the limitation in evidence available to us concerning stock and work in progress, we are unable to form an opinion as to whether the financial statements give a true and fair view of the state of the company's affairs as at .... or of its [profit / loss] for the year then ended. In all other respects, except for the absence of the provision referred to above, in our opinion the financial statements have been properly prepared in accordance with the Companies Act 1985.

In respect alone of the limitation on our work relating to stock and work in progress:

- we have not obtained all the information and explanations that we considered necessary for the purposes of our audit; and
- we were unable to determine whether proper accounting records had been kept.

The aspects of the combined opinion section that are considered further are:

- the title
- the absorption of the disagreement by the disclaimer of opinion
- the need for a specific opinion on other aspects of proper preparation.

4.6.7.2 The title

Where no disclaimer of opinion is present, the title of the opinion section can refer to both qualifications. For example, earlier, the example wording for a disagreement and a scope limitation was titled *'Qualified opinion arising from disagreement about accounting treatment and limitation in audit scope'*.

If this approach was continued, the title of the current extract might be *' Opinion: disclaimer on view given by financial statements and disagreement about accounting treatment'*.

The title actually used is not only shorter, it reflects the partial absorption of the scope limitation by the disclaimer of opinion as discussed below.

4.6.7.3 Absorption of the disagreement by the disclaimer of opinion

A disclaimer of opinion is on the financial statements as a whole. It reflects the auditors' view that the possible effect of a limitation on scope is so material or pervasive that they are unable to express an opinion on the financial statements.

An 'except for' disagreement informs readers that adjustments to the financial statements are necessary in order for them to give, in the auditors' opinion, a true and fair view.

The presence of a disclaimer of opinion, therefore, removes the reference point against which an adjustment to the financial statements could be judged. The auditors may still be of the opinion that a different accounting treatment or disclosure is appropriate. They are no longer able to state, however, that such a change to the accounts is necessary in order that a true and fair view be given.

Auditors may, however, feel that they wish to draw the disagreement to the attention of readers of their report. Arguments in and around a similar desire to communicate have been explored in the section above dealing with combining an adverse opinion and an 'except for' modification because of scope limitation.

The proposed mechanism for auditors to report the disagreement as well as the disclaimer of opinion is to utilise the wording in the opinion about proper preparation in accordance with the Companies Act 1985 as a vehicle.

Using this approach, the opinion section commences with a paragraph that is normal for a disagreement where the auditors' view as to the correct treatment is given. There is no other convenient place in the opinion section for this paragraph.

After the disclaimer of opinion the report goes on to say:

> . . . In all other respects, except for the absence of the provision referred to above, in our opinion the financial statements have been properly prepared in accordance with the Companies Act 1985.

The disagreement is not expressed in relation to the true and fair view despite the explanatory text in SAS 600 that calls for it (paragraph 35). However the qualified opinion is arguably expressed in accordance with SAS 600.8 which states that '*. . . the auditors should issue a qualified opinion indicating that it is expressed except for the effects of the matter giving rise to the disagreement.*'

An alternative approach is to consider the disagreement to be one of the factors giving rise to the disclaimer of opinion. This argument is not pursued here.

4.6.8 'Except for' disagreement and adverse opinion

Combining modifications that individually would result from different degrees of disagreement is done by treating the lesser modification as part of the reason for the adverse opinion.

This approach is illustrated by the reports given earlier in this chapter for combining two adverse opinions.

This result may occasionally be arrived at when two except for opinions are being combined as, taken together, they may influence the auditors into forming a view that an adverse opinion is appropriate.

4.6.9 Disclaimer of opinion and adverse opinion

Disclaimers of opinion and adverse opinions are both rare. To have a report where both are present is something that auditors would not expect to see in their lifetime. This is a comforting thought as, otherwise, auditors would be faced with the problem of reconciling conflicting opinions.

The following model report is offered as a solution to a problem with no right answer. The report includes some avant-garde wording and does not mention uncertainty as to whether proper accounting records have been kept.

Report 431
D — a: SL — d: Generic word picture (limitation outside directors' control)

AUDITORS' REPORT TO THE SHAREHOLDERS OF ....

We have audited the financial statements on pages ..... to ..... which have been prepared under the historical cost convention [as modified by the revaluation of certain fixed assets] and the accounting policies set out on page ..... .

Respective responsibilities of directors and auditors

As described on page ..... the company's directors are responsible for the preparation of financial statements. It is our responsibility to form an independent opinion, based on our audit, of those statements and to report our opinion to you. WE ARE ALSO REQUIRED TO REPORT TO YOU IF CERTAIN REQUIREMENTS OF THE COMPANIES ACT 1985 ARE NOT MET. THESE REQUIREMENTS INCLUDE REPORTING IF WE HAVE NOT OBTAINED ALL THE INFORMATION AND EXPLANATIONS THAT WE CONSIDERED NECESSARY FOR THE PURPOSES OF OUR AUDIT.

Basis of opinion

We conducted our audit in accordance with Auditing Standards issued by the Auditing Practices Board EXCEPT THAT THE SCOPE OF OUR WORK WAS LIMITED AS EXPLAINED BELOW.

An audit includes examination, on a test basis, of evidence relevant to the amounts and disclosures in the financial statements. It also includes an assessment of the significant estimates and judgements made by the directors in the preparation of the financial statements, and of whether the accounting policies are appropriate to the company's circumstances, consistently applied and adequately disclosed.

We planned and performed our audit so as to obtain all the information and explanations which we considered necessary in order to provide us with sufficient evidence to give reasonable assurance that the financial statements are free from material misstatement, whether caused by fraud or other irregularity or error. HOWEVER, THE EVIDENCE AVAILABLE TO US WAS LIMITED BECAUSE [MATTER]. THIS LIMITATION WAS NOT IMPOSED BY THE DIRECTORS WHO [MITIGATING CIRCUMSTANCES]. THERE WAS NO SYSTEM OF CONTROL OVER [MATTER] ON WHICH WE COULD RELY FOR THE PURPOSES OF OUR AUDIT AND THERE WERE NO OTHER SATISFACTORY AUDIT PROCEDURES THAT WE COULD ADOPT TO CONFIRM THAT [ACCOUNTING FOR MATTER] WAS CORRECT.

In forming our opinion we also evaluated the overall adequacy of the presentation of information in the financial statements.

OPINION: DISCLAIMER ON VIEW GIVEN BY FINANCIAL STATEMENTS AND ADVERSE OPINION

BECAUSE OF THE POSSIBLE EFFECT OF THE LIMITATION IN EVIDENCE AVAILABLE TO US, WE ARE UNABLE TO FORM AN OPINION AS TO WHETHER THE FINANCIAL STATEMENTS GIVE A TRUE AND FAIR VIEW OF THE STATE OF THE COMPANY'S AFFAIRS AS AT .... OR OF ITS [PROFIT / LOSS] FOR THE YEAR THEN ENDED.

IF THE EVIDENCE AVAILABLE TO US HAD NOT BEEN LIMITED IN THIS WAY, WE WOULD HAVE CONCLUDED THAT IN OUR OPINION THE FINANCIAL STATEMENTS DO NOT GIVE A TRUE AND FAIR VIEW OF THE STATE OF THE COMPANY'S AFFAIRS AS AT .... AND OF ITS [PROFIT / LOSS] FOR THE YEAR THEN ENDED. THIS IS BECAUSE, AS MORE FULLY EXPLAINED IN NOTE ..... [MATTER] [REASON FOR DIRECTORS' TREATMENT]. IN OUR OPINION, [PROPER TREATMENT] AS REQUIRED BY [STATEMENT OF STANDARD ACCOUNTING PRACTICE ..... / FINANCIAL REPORTING STANDARD .....]. [QUANTIFICATION].

IN ALL OTHER RESPECTS, IN OUR OPINION THE FINANCIAL STATEMENTS HAVE BEEN PROPERLY PREPARED IN ACCORDANCE WITH THE COMPANIES ACT 1985.

IN RESPECT ALONE OF THE LIMITATION ON OUR WORK RELATING TO [MATTER]:

- WE HAVE NOT OBTAINED ALL THE INFORMATION AND EXPLANATIONS THAT WE CONSIDERED NECESSARY FOR THE PURPOSES OF OUR AUDIT.

4.7 Numbering paragraphs

There comes a point in a complex report where it is necessary to resort to paragraph numbers to retain clarity. The use of numbers allows cross-references to be short and unambiguous.

There is a practical reason for avoiding numbers: they are very easy to get wrong because there is no intrinsic sense in them. Auditors should beware of typing errors, late insertion or deletion of paragraphs and changes in paragraph order.

It is a matter of house style as to whether the introductory paragraph is numbered.

When cross-referring using numbers it is important to retain sufficient of the wording that would otherwise be used so that the meaning of the modification is not lost. For example, for a simple scope limitation the cross-reference should be

> Except for any adjustments that might have been found to be necessary had we been able to obtain sufficient evidence concerning the matter referred to in paragraph .....

It is not acceptable to shorten this to:

> Except for the matter referred to in paragraph .....

because SAS 600.7 requires the opinion to indicate that it is qualified as to the possible adjustments to the financial statements that might have been determined to be necessary had the limitation not existed.

4.8 Complex reports

4.8.1 Approach

Earlier sections of this chapter have dealt with combining modification of the same type and two modifications of different types. The combination of dissimilar modifications can involve single modifications or multiple modifications of the same type.

A complex report that does not involve an adverse opinion or a disclaimer of opinion can be constructed by successively combining the individual modifications. First, modifications of the same type are combined. Then, modifications of different types are combined. Many types of modification do not interact with each other. It is really only scope limitations and disagreements that require their opinion paragraphs to be integrated. Because of this, the best order in which to combine modification is:

1 combine modifications of the same type
2 use a scope limitation (except for) modification as the basis for the report (either single or combined) together with any linked modifications required by law
3 combine it with any modifications for disagreement
4 successively combine the remaining types.

If an adverse opinion or a disclaimer of opinion is present the following order is best because of the way that those opinions subsume their 'except for' cousins.

1 combine modifications of the same type
2 combine disclaimer of opinion and 'except for' scope limitations (if any) or combine the adverse opinion and 'except for' disagreements (if any)
3 use the combined disclaimer of opinion or adverse opinion as the basis for the report together with any linked modifications required by law

4 combine it with any remaining 'except for' modifications
5 successively combine the remaining types.

The final stage in writing a complex report is to consider whether it is sufficiently clear. The SAS 600 auditors' report is lengthy even in its standard form. If a modified report extends over many pages readers may lose track of material early in a report (such as further explanatory material concerning auditors' responsibilities). This concern could be addressed by deleting all material that is not essential or adopting an avant-garde approach. For example, a series of 'mini reports' dealing with the basis of each modification and giving the modification itself.

4.8.2 A published example

The following is an extract from a report issued on 7 February 1994.[2] The report deals with:

- a SAS 600 limitation of audit scope
- a linked I&E modification
- fundamental uncertainty over going concern.

The report is interesting because it refers to the potential effect on the statement of total recognised gains and losses. Also worthy of note is the way the I&E modification is explained, while the basis of opinion section of the report does not explicitly state that the evidence available was limited. A neutral wording is used so readers are left guessing whether the limitation was outside the directors' control. The report also supports the view that it is not usual to refer to problems concerning comparative amounts if there are more interesting things to say. A decision has also been taken, in the report, to refer to the going concern basis in relation to the group, rather than the company (or the group and company).

Report 432
SL — e: I&E: FU: Anglia Secure Homes PLC, 30 September 1993, KPMG Peat Marwick

Basis of opinion

We conducted our audit in accordance with Auditing Standards issued by the Auditing Practices Board, except that the scope of our work was limited as explained below. An audit includes examination, on a test basis, of evidence relevant to the amounts and disclosures in the accounts. It also includes an assessment of the significant estimates and judgements made by the directors in the preparation of the accounts, and of whether the accounting policies are appropriate to the Group's circumstances, consistently applied and adequately disclosed.

We planned our audit so as to obtain all the information and explanations which we considered necessary in order to provide us with sufficient evidence to give reasonable

[2] Reported by *Company Reporting magazine* April 1994.

assurance that the accounts are free from material misstatement, whether caused by fraud or other irregularity or error. We were appointed auditors to the Group on 29th October 1993 and as such did not report on the accounts of the Group for the year ended 30th September 1992. In their report on the accounts for the year ended 30th September 1992 the previous auditors reported that they were unable to determine with reasonable certainty whether the freehold reversionary interests included within fixed assets, which had been revalued by the directors, had been stated at open market value. Because of this, we have been unable to satisfy ourselves in this respect as to the Company's and the Group's opening balance sheets at 1st October 1992. Any adjustment to the balance sheets would have a consequential effect on the statement of total recognised gains and losses for the year ended 30th September 1993, but would not affect the loss for the year ended 30th September 1993 or the Company and Group balance sheets at that date.

In forming our opinion we also evaluated the overall adequacy of the presentation of information in the accounts.

Fundamental uncertainty regarding going concern

In forming our opinion we have considered the adequacy of the disclosures made in the accounts concerning the ability of the Group to continue as a going concern for the foreseeable future. The accounts have been prepared on a going concern basis, the validity of which is dependent upon the availability of future funding, and do not include any adjustments that would result were the going concern basis of preparation considered to be inappropriate. Details of the circumstances relating to the fundamental uncertainty are described in note ..... , which also describes the nature of any adjustments that would be necessary if the going concern basis is inappropriate. Our opinion is not qualified in this respect.

Qualified opinion arising from limitation in audit scope

Except for any adjustment that might have been found to be necessary to the statement of total recognised gains and losses had we been able to satisfy ourselves as to the value of freehold reversionary interests appearing in the Company's and the Group's opening balance sheets at 1st October 1992, in our opinion the accounts give a true and fair view of the state of affairs of the Company and the Group as at 30th September 1993 and of the loss of the Group for the year then ended and have been properly prepared in accordance with the Companies Act 1985.

In respect solely of the limitation on our work relating to the value of freehold reversionary interests appearing in the Company's and the Group's opening balance sheets, we have not been able to obtain all the information and explanations that we considered necessary, due to the absence both of a professional valuation and of an active market for these reversionary interests as at 1st October 1992.

The extract's readability (Flesch Reading Ease) is assessed by computer as being 34.1; which is within 4.1 points of being 'very difficult'; but, nevertheless it is an improvement on the SAS 600 standard report. The above report could be analysed further using the earlier sections of this book, but that exercise is left to interested readers.

5 ILLUSTRATIVE MODIFICATIONS

5.1 Introduction

This chapter provides illustrative modifications for typical circumstances that may confront auditors. Many other examples are given in the text of earlier chapters. To save space, such examples have not been repeated or cross-referred in detail from this chapter. Instead, a full table of reports is provided towards the end of this book.

The illustrative modifications are presented in sections dealing with areas of difficulty, such as going concern and the completeness of income in small companies. The sections provide background and discuss the practical problems as well as giving illustrative wordings. The last section of this chapter deals with the reading of reports by auditors at annual general meetings.

Originally, this chapter of the book was planned to be little more than a collection of reports covering as many of the likely modifications as possible. When SAS 600 was issued, and as the writing of this book progressed, it became apparent that auditors had enormous flexibility in wording their modifications. As well as matters of client and house style, there were many alternative approaches to word order, level of detail of explanation, quantification, cross-referencing and so on. Any illustrative report that was used might therefore have to be almost entirely re-engineered before it was issued. This means that, to be of most use, this chapter should be read in conjunction with the first four chapters of this book. Illustrations are, however, still very useful and so they are retained in this chapter. The sections do, however, contain much more analysis than might be expected.

5.1.1 A health warning

There is an obvious need to tailor the illustrative wordings for practical use by inserting such matters as the client's year end and conforming the wording to the auditors' house style. Inevitably, no illustration will be an exact match for the real circumstances that auditors are responding to. It is, therefore, very important that, when using the wording of any illustration, it is treated only as if it were the auditors' own first draft. In other words, it must be reviewed and properly considered for suitability before issue.

The disclaimer at the front of this book applies to all its text but it is particularly relevant when considering the illustrative modifications in this chapter. No matter how much effort has gone into making the illustrations as useful as possible, it is still the auditors' responsibility to ensure that the report they issue is appropriate. This is not just a general warning. There are specific matters that ought to be considered before using any illustrative wording because the passage of time may have made it out-of-date. For example:

- has a matter now become the subject of a Urgent Issues Task Force (UITF) pronouncement or an accounting standard?
- have any references to accounting standards been superseded?
- has a UITF pronouncement been withdrawn (e.g. on the issue of a Financial Reporting Standard (FRS))?
- are company law references still current?
- has there been a change in the basis of the report (e.g. criteria for a company to be classified as small, or to not require an audit)?
- has the Stock Exchange, or a working party set up to consider aspects of the corporate governance Code of Best Practice, issued relevant material?
- has the Auditing Practices Board (APB) issued related guidance?

Some changes may already be anticipated. At the time this book was finalised, the APB had not issued a final version of Statement of Auditing Standards 130 'The going concern basis in financial statements' (SAS 130) nor had the Government decided how the abolition of the small company audit would be implemented.

5.1.2 The illustrations

5.1.2.1 Single and multiple

The modifications shown in this chapter are generally single, rather than multiple, as multiple modifications may always be constructed from the illustrative wordings using the methodology set out in chapter 4 'Multiple Modifications'. Some multiple modifications are included, however, as in certain circumstances their exclusion would have been artificial.

5.1.2.2 'Except for' and adverse or disclaimer of opinion

Modifications for disagreement and scope limitation are normally given as except for opinions, as these are the more common forms of qualification. The wording may be adapted for the extreme adverse or disclaimer of opinion by altering the opinion paragraph in an appropriate manner as set out in chapter 3 'Modified Reports'.

5.1.2.3 Form and numbering

The reports are given in extract form and so exclude material that is unchanged from the standard report. As in other chapters, reports are numbered for ease of reference and have a heading that indicates their type and nature. The first digit of the number refers to the chapter, the other digits form a sequence within each chapter.

Except where they are derived from published reports, the illustrations follow the format of the word pictures for modifications that are given in chapter 3 'Modified Reports'. As a result, the illustrations do not normally include avant-garde or other wording that may be recommended in the earlier chapter in appropriate circumstances.

5.2 Going concern

5.2.1 Introduction

Going concern problems are probably the most difficult faced by auditors. The client's management is likely to be financially and emotionally involved in the problem and the auditors run high risks of failing to warn of impending insolvency or perhaps precipitating that event. The problem of making sure that the audit fee is not a bad debt pales into insignificance.

The most satisfactory way to avoid the business risk is to resign the audit two years before the client 'unexpectedly' fails. But, assuming that most firms do not have a technical update newsletter warning partners of a recession, that approach is only viable for clairvoyant auditors. Alternatively, auditors might look to a change in a recognised indicator of the health of the economy provided by the APB. That indicator is the professional guidance on auditing going concern itself. It seems inevitable that the APB will begin to consider the next revision in time for the next recession and issue it as a marker for the end of it. This was done by the Auditing Practices Committee (APC) in 1985 and the APB are re-exposing the draft SAS 130 at the time this book is being finalised. It is to be hoped that SAS 130 is issued in final form quickly. If not, the promised emergence from recession could falter. However, some influential bodies, such as the Institute of Chartered Accountants in England and Wales (ICAEW) and the Hundred Group of finance directors have publicly condemned the proposed SAS and it may have to undergo further gestation.

The following reporting guidance is based in part on draft SAS 130. In some instances, pointed out below, that document does not seem to agree with SAS 600 or the author of this book's views on reporting. The final SAS 130 could differ from the exposure draft and from suggestions made in this book. Auditors should ensure, therefore, that relevant reports that they issue comply with it. Reporting differences are likely to be confined to matters not prescribed by SAS 600:

- requirements to report in a particular way depending on individual circumstances (e.g. if the break-up basis is used)
- illustrative wordings for modifications.

The material below does not include reporting on statements on going concern made by directors of listed companies in connection with compliance with the corporate governance Code of Best Practice. The working group publishing guidance for directors has not progressed its exposure draft, *'Going concern and financial reporting'*, since its issue in May 1993. Further progress is dependent on the resolution of the question as to what period after the balance sheet date is it appropriate for directors to report on (to the next balance sheet date or one year from approving the accounts). The APB has stated that it will issue a Bulletin to give guidance to auditors. The Bulletin will be separate from SAS 130.

The remainder of this section examines:

- the history of reporting on going concern
- the reporting requirements of draft SAS 130
- scope limitation
- disagreement
- fundamental uncertainty
- outside the scope of SAS 600.

The subsections dealing with the forms of modification that may be encountered in connection with going concern problems contain appropriate illustrative modifications.

5.2.2 History of auditing guidance

This section looks at the relevant reporting guidance in the Auditing Guideline 'The auditor's considerations in respect of going concern'. The guidance is also evident in example 7 in the appendix to the superseded Auditing Standard 'The audit report'.

The reason for considering this history is to explain why going concern seems to have a special place in reporting even though it is essentially no different from any other inherent uncertainty.[1] Also, until SAS 130 is issued, the guidance remains relevant, even though the reports now have to comply with SAS 600.

The Auditing Guideline set out reporting responses for auditors as follows:

Circumstances	**Effect on audit report**
Auditor satisfied going concern basis is appropriate.	No mention in report.
Auditor considers readers will obtain a better understanding if attention is drawn to important matters.	Emphasis of matter paragraph.
Auditor considers that uncertainty about going concern materially affects the view given by the accounts.	'Subject to' opinion.
Uncertainty is fundamental.	Disclaimer of opinion.
Overwhelming evidence that going concern basis is not appropriate.	'Except for' or adverse opinion (depending on extent of adjustments).
Significant uncertainty about ability to continue in business (even if no likely impact on carrying values and classifications) but no disclosure in accounts.[2]	Refer to it in his report.

[1] Similar historical reasons have also affected reporting in connection with cash flow statements.

[2] Note that the need to report if there is no likely impact is only present if the doubt about the going concern basis is not disclosed.

A report complying with the above professional requirements typically included the following explanation and opinion.

> The accounts have been prepared on a going concern basis. This basis may not be appropriate because the company incurred a loss after taxation of £ ..... during the year ended .... and at that date its current liabilities exceeded its current assets by £ ..... . Further, the company is currently negotiating for long-term facilities to replace the loan of £ ..... , which is repayable on .... These factors, which are explained in note ..... , indicate that the company may be unable to continue trading.
>
> Should the company be unable to continue trading, adjustments would have to be made to reduce the value of assets to their recoverable amount, to provide for any further liabilities which might arise, and to reclassify fixed assets and long-term liabilities as current assets and liabilities.
>
> SUBJECT TO THE COMPANY BEING ABLE TO CONTINUE TRADING, in our opinion the accounts give a true and fair view of the state of affairs of the company at .... and of its loss and source and application of funds for the year then ended and have been properly prepared in accordance with the Companies Act 1985.

The words in small capitals above are a form of qualification that was outside the forms of qualification dealt with in the body of the Auditing Standard. 'Subject to' opinions were then normally expressed as being either:

'(a) *subject to any adjustments that he might have found to be necessary if the scope of his work had not been limited; or*

(b) *in the case of an inherent uncertainty, subject to any adjustments that might have been necessary if the outcome of the uncertainty had been known.'*

The special form of qualification could have been perceived as being almost a disclaimer. If so, auditors would be unlikely to issue a disclaimer of opinion at all. If they considered the going concern basis was not appropriate at all they would issue an 'except for' or adverse opinion.

5.2.3 Reporting requirements of (draft) SAS 130

The draft SAS refers to the auditors' report in the following circumstances:

Circumstances	**Effect on audit report**
Auditors unable to obtain written assertion from directors (draft SAS 130.2).	Consider the effect on the report (could be a limitation on the scope of their work or indicate that there is concern about going concern basis) (paragraph 19).
Auditors unable to satisfy themselves regarding the existence and terms of borrowing facilities and the intentions of the lender (draft SAS 130.4).	Consider need for explanatory paragraph or qualified opinion (paragraph 29).
Auditors consider that the disclosures in the accounts of the matters relevant to the appropriateness of the going concern basis are not adequate for the accounts to give a true and fair view (draft SAS 130.9).	Issue an auditors' report including a qualified opinion arising from disagreement with the disclosure of these matters.
Auditors consider that there is a significant level of concern as to the appropriateness of the going concern basis but they do not disagree with its use (draft SAS 130.7).	Include an explanatory paragraph when setting out the basis of their opinion describing the matters giving rise to their concern and should refer to the relevant accounts disclosures.
Auditors disagree with the presumption that the company is a going concern (draft SAS 130.8).	Issue an adverse audit opinion and should provide in their audit report such additional information as they consider necessary.
In rare circumstances, in order to give a true and fair view, the directors may have prepared financial statements on a basis other than that of a going concern. If the auditors consider this other basis to be appropriate in the specific circumstances, and if the financial statements contain the necessary disclosures, the auditors should not qualify their audit report in this respect (draft SAS 130.10).	Include an explanatory paragraph when setting out the basis of their opinion describing the basis of preparation and referring to the notes to the accounts concerning this basis.

Appendix 1 to draft SAS 130 contains example reports for fundamental uncertainty and for 'except for' and adverse opinions arising from disagreement. There is no example of a scope limitation but, to compensate for this, the modification for fundamental uncertainty is accompanied by a further modification that is outside the scope of SAS 600. The proposed requirements of draft SAS 130 are discussed in the following subsections that deal with the forms of modification that may arise.

5.2.4 Scope limitation

Draft SAS 130 refers to two matters that could give rise to a scope limitation:

- auditors unable to obtain a written assertion from directors
- auditors unable to satisfy themselves regarding the existence and terms of borrowing facilities and the intentions of the lender.

The first matter may indicate that there is concern about the going concern basis or it may of itself be a scope limitation. The latter is illustrated below, as is a scope limitation arising because a lender will not confirm borrowing facilities. The accompanying text explores the need to modify the report also for a fundamental uncertainty about the use of the going concern basis.

Report 500
SL — e: No written going concern representation from directors

Basis of opinion

We conducted our audit in accordance with Auditing Standards issued by the Auditing Practices Board, except that the scope of our work was limited as explained below.

An audit includes examination, on a test basis, of evidence relevant to the amounts and disclosures in the financial statements. It also includes an assessment of the significant estimates and judgements made by the directors in the preparation of the financial statements, and of whether the accounting policies are appropriate to the company's circumstances, consistently applied and adequately disclosed.

We planned and performed our audit so as to obtain all the information and explanations which we considered necessary in order to provide us with sufficient evidence to give reasonable assurance that the financial statements are free from material misstatement, whether caused by fraud or other irregularity or error. However, the evidence available to us was limited because the directors have not provided us with an adequate written assertion confirming their view that it is appropriate to adopt the going concern basis in preparing the financial statements. There were no other satisfactory audit procedures that we could adopt to confirm the directors' intention to continue to provide sufficient finance to enable the company to continue in operational existence for the foreseeable future. As explained in note ..... , the company is dependent on the continuing financial support of the directors.

In forming our opinion we also evaluated the overall adequacy of the presentation of information in the financial statements.

Qualified opinion arising from limitation in audit scope

Except for any adjustments that might have been found to be necessary had we been able to obtain sufficient evidence concerning the directors' intention to continue to provide financial support to the company, in our opinion the financial statements give a true and fair view of the state of the company's affairs as at .... and of its [profit / loss] for the year then ended and have been properly prepared in accordance with the Companies Act 1985.

In respect alone of the limitation on our work relating to the availability of continuing finance for the company, we have not obtained all the information and explanations that we considered necessary for the purposes of our audit.

The above report attempts to make it clear that the company is dependent on the continuing financial support of the directors. It is assumed that this is properly disclosed in the financial statements.

The wording draws on the definition of the going concern basis in Statement of Standard Accounting Practice 2 'Disclosure of accounting policies' (SSAP 2) that *'the enterprise will continue in operational existence for the foreseeable future'*. This could be shortened to improve clarity. The scope limitation is expressed in terms directly of the matter to which the evidence that is not available would have related. The alternative, to refer to the going concern basis of preparation of the accounts, is less precise.

There is an argument for coupling the above modification with a modification reporting fundamental uncertainty over the company's ability to continue as a going concern. It is probably sufficient, however, to mention just the scope limitation. This is discussed further after the next illustration.

Report 501
SL — e: No confirmation of borrowing facilities relevant to going concern basis

Basis of opinion

We conducted our audit in accordance with Auditing Standards issued by the Auditing Practices Board, except that the scope of our work was limited as explained below.

An audit includes examination, on a test basis, of evidence relevant to the amounts and disclosures in the financial statements. It also includes an assessment of the significant estimates and judgements made by the directors in the preparation of the financial statements, and of whether the accounting policies are appropriate to the company's circumstances, consistently applied and adequately disclosed.

We planned and performed our audit so as to obtain all the information and explanations which we considered necessary in order to provide us with sufficient evidence to give reasonable assurance that the financial statements are free from material misstatement, whether caused by fraud or other irregularity or error. However, the evidence available to us was limited because, despite the directors' seeking such confirmation, ... Bank would not confirm their intentions with regard to the continuation of the facilities referred to in note ..... . As explained in that note, the company is dependent on the continuing financial support of its bank to continue in operational existence for the foreseeable future.

In forming our opinion we also evaluated the overall adequacy of the presentation of information in the financial statements.

Qualified opinion arising from limitation in audit scope

Except for any adjustments that might have been found to be necessary had we been able to obtain sufficient evidence concerning the availability of continuing finance for the company, in our opinion the financial statements give a true and fair view of the state of the company's affairs as at .... and of its [profit / loss] for the year then ended and have been properly prepared in accordance with the Companies Act 1985.

> In respect alone of the limitation on our work relating to the availability of continuing finance for the company, we have not obtained all the information and explanations that we considered necessary for the purposes of our audit.

The above example aims to make it clear that the scope limitation was outside the directors' and auditors' control.

The example does not include any paragraph referring to a fundamental uncertainty over the application of the going concern basis. Theoretically, such a paragraph is required, whether or not there is a scope limitation, if the auditors form the view that there is (in the terms of draft SAS 130) *'a significant level of concern about the validity of the going concern basis'*. This might happen if the confirmation of the bank facility was important to the auditors' decision as to whether they disagreed with the basis used.

Draft SAS 130 clearly intends the various responses to individual circumstances to be mutually exclusive. This is demonstrated in the explanatory text and in its appendix 3, where a decision chart gives only two consequences for a scope limitation: an 'except for' or disclaimer of opinion.

Unless this is changed when the draft SAS is finalised it would seem that auditors have the option of a single or multiple modification in these unusual circumstances. Given that it is twice as easy to make a mistake in two modifications than it is in one (all things being equal) auditors will probably settle for reporting just the scope limitation.

5.2.5 Disagreement

Auditors considering the adequacy of disclosures are hampered by the lack of specific accounting standards relating to these disclosures. The provisions in proposed SAS 130 aim to encourage fuller disclosures than have so far emerged under current practice.

If the disclosure made is not adequate, the auditors should give an 'except for' or adverse qualification in their audit report and explain the disagreement. Under draft SAS 130, an adverse opinion is required if the auditors disagree with the presumption that the company is a going concern. This seems to be at variance with the requirements of SAS 600 as that SAS applies a test as to whether the matter makes the financial statements 'seriously misleading'.

Nevertheless, draft SAS 130 includes an example of a qualified opinion where the auditors bring themselves to disagree. This forms the basis for the first illustration below.

Report 502
D— e: Going concern (based on draft SAS 130)

Qualified opinion arising from disagreement as to the adequacy of a disclosure in the financial statements

As already announced to the public, the directors are currently negotiating with lenders to the group for new terms for amounts borrowed totalling £ ..... , and have plans for raising funds of approximately £ ..... from a share issue by the company. The directors are currently uncertain as to the outcome of both these matters. The validity of the going concern basis on which the financial statements are prepared depends on the successful conclusion of both these matters. Further details of the circumstances relating to this fundamental uncertainty are described in note ..... .

In our opinion the financial statements should also disclose that the company and certain of its subsidiaries have not complied with covenants relating to certain of their borrowings included in the financial statements. Under the terms of these covenants, the publication of these financial statements gives rise to defaults on covenants relating to certain of the group's borrowings. These defaults result in the related borrowings becoming repayable on demand. Hence the related borrowings should have been reclassified as amounts falling due within one year, which would have reduced the figures recorded in the financial statements for 'net current assets' and 'creditors: amounts falling due after more than one year' by £ ..... .

Except for the absence of the disclosures, and the failure to reclassify the relevant borrowings, referred to in the paragraph above, in our opinion the financial statements give a true and fair view of the state of affairs of the company and the group as at .... and have been properly prepared in accordance with the Companies Act 1985. In our opinion the financial statements give a true and fair view of the profit of the group for the year ended ....

The heading for the opinion section is very long. The examples in appendix 2 to SAS 600 use a shorter heading (referring to accounting treatment) that could be substituted as follows:

Qualified opinion arising from disagreement about disclosure

The above report includes a reference to a fundamental uncertainty as well as the disagreement. However, the wording for the fundamental uncertainty does not comply with the requirements of SAS 600.6. It is not in the basis of opinion section nor does it use words that clearly indicate that the opinion on the financial statements is not qualified in respect of it. Multiple modifications where a fundamental uncertainty might be combined with a limitation of audit scope were discussed above. The conclusions in that section seem equally valid here. In this case, however, auditors have a precedent that includes a fundamental uncertainty (albeit oddly) whereas the earlier precedent excluded such a modification. The safe route, if similar circumstances face auditors before SAS 130 is finalised, would seem to be to follow the precedent for the above disagreement but reposition and reword the modification for a fundamental uncertainty to accord with SAS 600.

The next illustration is also based on draft SAS 130. In this case the disagreement is over the use of the going concern basis and an adverse opinion is given.

Report 503
D — a: Going concern (based on draft SAS 130)

Adverse opinion

> As more fully explained in note ..... , in the second half of the financial year the company was faced with deteriorating conditions in the electronics market and a sharp decline in sales to the Government sector. The directors considered that the prospects for improvement were very poor, and therefore decided to withdraw from computers and network activities. Accordingly heads of agreement have been entered into for the sale of substantially the whole of the trade and net assets of the company. The consideration for the sale has yet to be determined, but it will be at a value considerably less than net book value. As a result, in our opinion, the company cannot be considered to be a going concern and thus the preparation of its financial statements on the going concern basis is inappropriate. In our opinion the financial statements should reflect adjustments to the net book value of assets, reducing them to the amounts expected to be realised, together with additional provisions for future losses up to the date of disposal and other liabilities, such as redundancies, which will arise as a result of disposing of substantially the whole of the company's trade. We are unable to determine the total of the required adjustments and provisions with a reasonable degree of accuracy.
>
> In view of the above, in our opinion the financial statements do not give a true and fair view of the state of the company's affairs as at .... and of its loss for the year then ended. In all other respects, in our opinion the financial statements have been properly prepared in accordance with the Companies Act 1985.

The adverse opinion does not conform to the generic word picture set out in chapter 3 of this book. It ought to set out in the first paragraph what the disagreement is. In this case there is an opinion on going concern and an opinion on adjustments to the net book value of assets. What is missing is a statement telling readers what the directors have or have not done. The auditors could then give their opinion as to what should have been done and the reason for their views. The muddling of the first paragraph is perhaps the reason for the woolly cross-reference at the start of the second paragraph. The example in draft SAS 130 cannot, therefore, be recommended as a model.

One is also left wondering whether note ..... could have more fully explained the matter than the seven and a half lines following the reference to it. Using the same facts as above, and the methods advocated in chapter 3 of this book, the report might instead read as shown below. The new draft assumes that note ..... states that the going concern basis is being used and gives some justification for the directors adopting that basis.

Report 504
D — a: Going concern (model using chapter 3 methods)

Adverse opinion

> As more fully explained in note ..... , the financial statements have been prepared on a going concern basis. In our opinion, the preparation of the company's financial

> statements on that basis is inappropriate. The company cannot be considered to be a going concern because the directors are selling substantially the whole of its trade and net assets at a significant loss, ending the operational existence of the company. Accordingly, the financial statements should reflect adjustments to the net book value of assets, reducing them to the amounts expected to be realised, together with additional provisions for future losses up to the date of disposal and other liabilities, such as redundancies. We are unable to determine the total of the required adjustments and provisions with a reasonable degree of accuracy.
>
> In view of the inappropriate use of the going concern basis, in our opinion the financial statements do not give a true and fair view of the state of the company's affairs as at .... and of its loss for the year then ended. In all other respects, in our opinion the financial statements have been properly prepared in accordance with the Companies Act 1985.

The model report uses the words *'ending the operational existence of the company'*. These are from the definition of going concern in SSAP 2 and are used for that reason.

Despite reusing some prose, the model is demonstrably more readable than the draft SAS 130 example, if only because it is significantly shorter.

5.2.6 Fundamental uncertainty

SAS 600 itself refers to the going concern basis. Paragraph 64, in the explanatory material to SAS 600.6 dealing with fundamental uncertainty, includes a statement that '*Inherent uncertainties are regarded as fundamental when they involve a significant level of concern about the validity of the going concern basis or other matters whose potential effect on the financial statements is unusually great.*'

This wording is quoted in paragraph 25 of draft SAS 130. The quote does not reproduce the wording that commences *'or other matters'*. SAS 130, therefore, interprets the statement as meaning that for there to be a fundamental uncertainty there only has to be a significant level of concern about the validity of the going concern basis. It does not matter whether the potential effect on the financial statements is unusually great or not. This may not be a correct interpretation, as an attempt to extract meaning from paragraph 64 only in relation to other matters (by deleting the reference to going concern) argues that the sentence should be read as a whole.[3]

The apparent interpretation in draft SAS 130 seems to stem from the historical need (see the last item in the table in section 5.2.2 above) to refer to the matter in the auditors' report where there is significant uncertainty about the ability of the company to continue in business (but no disclosure in the accounts) even if there is no likely impact on carrying values and classifications. If this interpretation is used by auditors there will be no need to make decisions about the materiality of

[3] *'Inherent uncertainties are regarded as fundamental when they involve a significant level of concern about ~~the validity of the going concern basis or~~ other matters whose potential effect on the financial statements is unusually great.'*

possible adjustments and the number of modified opinions will be larger than would otherwise be the case.

The first illustration below is based on draft SAS 130.

Report 505
FU: Going concern dependent on renewal of overdraft facility (based on draft SAS 130)

Fundamental uncertainty: going concern

In forming our opinion, we have considered the adequacy of the disclosures made in the financial statements concerning the inherent uncertainty as to the continuation and renewal of the company's bank overdraft facility. The company meets its day to day working capital requirements through this overdraft facility which, in common with all such facilities, is repayable on demand. At the year end the overdraft amounted to £ ..... , which lies within the facility of £ ..... currently agreed with the company's bankers. However, the nature of the company's business is such that there can be considerable variation in the timing of cash inflows.

Details of the circumstances relating to this inherent uncertainty are described in note ..... . We consider that, in view of the matters referred to above and in note ..... , there is a significant level of concern as to the appropriateness of the going concern basis. However, our opinion is not qualified in this respect, and on the basis of our discussions with the directors and other information of which we have become aware during our audit we consider that it is appropriate for the directors to prepare financial statements drawn up on the going concern basis.

The modification goes further than it need. If it was based only on the word picture set out in the appropriate section of chapter 3 of this book it would read as follows.

Report 506
FU: Going concern dependent on renewal of overdraft facility (model using chapter 3 methods)

Fundamental uncertainty: going concern

In forming our opinion, we have considered the adequacy of the disclosures made in the financial statements concerning the inherent uncertainty as to the continuation and renewal of the company's bank overdraft facility. Should the bank overdraft facility not be renewed the company may not be able to continue in operational existence. In such circumstances the use of the going concern basis of preparation of financial statements would not be appropriate. As a consequence, adjustments would have to be made to reduce the value of assets to their recoverable amount, to provide for any further liabilities which might arise, and to reclassify fixed assets and long-term liabilities as current assets and liabilities. It is not possible to quantify these potential effects. Details of the circumstances relating to this inherent uncertainty are described in note ..... . Our opinion is not qualified in this respect.

The reasoning behind the above modification is set out in detail in the appropriate section of chapter 3 'Modified Reports'. It excludes much of the wording used in the first example.

The draft SAS 130 report has the following additional features:

- further information is given that the overdraft facility of the company is *'in common with all such facilities'* repayable on demand
- the auditors make an explicit statement that they consider that *'there is a **significant level of concern** as to the appropriateness of the going concern basis'*
- the auditors give a further opinion that the going concern basis is appropriate (*'we consider that it is appropriate for the directors to prepare financial statements drawn up on the going concern basis'*)
- the basis of the opinion that the going concern basis is appropriate is given (*'on the basis of our discussions with the directors and other information of which we have become aware during our audit'*).

There are two lines of reasoning that can justify such features. Either the auditors take it upon themselves to state the matters because they are true and necessary to their forming an opinion that a modification for fundamental uncertainty (and no other) is appropriate; or, they were feeling kind. Obviously, the directors would welcome three of the statements because they support their views, either by implication — *'in common with all such facilities'* — or explicitly. The inclusion of a statement about a significant level of concern is perhaps motivated by a need to demonstrate that the auditors have read draft SAS 130. Readers who can form a view as to what constitutes 'significant' concern and not just 'concern' might nevertheless be confused to find that the auditors can make a plain and simple statement that the going concern basis is appropriate and DO NOT INDICATE ANY UNCERTAINTY IN THEIR VIEW! Presumably if the directors had done this the auditors would have qualified their opinion for disagreement concerning the inadequacy of disclosure.

Until draft SAS 130 becomes a standard, auditors are faced with a difficult choice. They could comply with the example wording in draft SAS 130, which is seriously flawed, or give a simpler modification that complies with SAS 600.

A partial compromise would be to include a reference to there being *'a significant level of concern as to the appropriateness of the going concern basis'*. This could be achieved by inserting the words as shown below.

Report 507
FU: Going concern dependent on renewal of overdraft facility (model referring to significant level of concern)

Fundamental uncertainty: going concern

In forming our opinion, we have considered the adequacy of the disclosures made in the financial statements concerning the inherent uncertainty as to the continuation and renewal of the company's bank overdraft facility. Should the bank overdraft facility not be renewed the company may not be able to continue in operational existence. There is, therefore, a significant level of concern as to the appropriateness of the going concern basis of preparation of financial statements. As a consequence, adjustments would have to be made to reduce the value of assets to their recoverable amount, to provide for any further liabilities which might arise, and to reclassify fixed assets and long-term liabilities as current assets and liabilities. It is not possible to quantify these potential effects. Details of the circumstances relating to this inherent uncertainty are described in note ..... . Our opinion is not qualified in this respect.

There is a second example modification for fundamental uncertainty in appendix 1 to draft SAS 130 and example 11 in appendix 2 to SAS 600 also relates to the going concern basis.

Report 508
FU: Going concern dependent on major contract (based on draft SAS 130 example 2)

Fundamental uncertainty: going concern

In forming our opinion, we have considered the adequacy of the disclosures made in the financial statements concerning the inherent uncertainty as to the possible outcome of a tender that the company has placed with a current major customer for a two-year contract. If awarded to the company, the contract would comprise approximately 50% of the turnover presently forecast for the two years following the award of the contract. In prior years this customer has awarded the contract to the company before the date on which the directors have approved the financial statements. At the date on which the directors approved the financial statements the customer had not awarded the contract and the company was continuing to trade with the customer on the basis of the most recently agreed contract, with the customer making a monthly decision whether or not to extend the contract for a further month. The directors have a number of alternative plans for utilising the company's resources and generating income should it not be awarded the contract. However the company has yet to submit tenders for several of these alternative contracts.

Details of the circumstances relating to this inherent uncertainty are described in note ..... . We consider that, in view of the matters referred to above and in note ..... , there is a significant level of concern as to the appropriateness of the going concern basis. However, our opinion is not qualified in this respect, and on the basis of our discussions with the directors and other information of which we became aware during our audit we consider that it is appropriate for the directors to prepare financial statements drawn up on the going concern basis.

Comments on the first example based on draft SAS 130 are also valid here as the two modifications have a common structure. Neither accords with the way example 11 in appendix 2 to SAS 600 deals with similar circumstances.

Report 509
FU: Going concern dependent on additional finance (based on SAS 600 example 11)

Fundamental uncertainty

In forming our opinion, we have considered the adequacy of the disclosures made in the financial statements concerning the possible outcome of negotiations for additional finance being made available to replace an existing loan of £ ..... which is repayable on .... The financial statements have been prepared on a going concern basis, the validity of which depends upon future funding being available. The financial statements do not include any adjustments that would result from a failure to obtain funding. Details of the circumstances relating to this fundamental uncertainty are described in note...... Our opinion is not qualified in this respect.

Example 11 fails to describe the possible effects on the financial statements (saying merely that any adjustments are not included) and includes no statement about quantification. Its use is not, therefore, recommended for any reason other than making use of a recognised precedent.

The following extract from a published report shows a multiple modification and illustrates the diversity of introductory wording that may be used.

Report 510
FU: FU: FU: Going concern and uncertainty over asset values and classifications, The Hartstone Group PLC, 31 March 1993, BDO Binder Hamlyn

Going concern and uncertainty over asset values and classifications

In forming our unqualified opinion, we consider that we should draw your attention to the following matters referred to in notes ..... and ..... to the financial statements.

The group is currently in breach of certain of its borrowing covenants and discussions are taking place with the group's lenders with a view to formalising a standstill agreement with short term finance to 31 December 1993 pending the securing of long term financing. Until the plans for the refinancing of the group are fully and satisfactorily completed there could be doubt over the appropriateness of the going concern basis. The financial statements do not include any reclassification of borrowings as falling due within one year rather than after one year as a result of the breach of certain of the group's covenants.

The projected cash flows covering the period to 31 March 1994 indicate that the group has peak seasonal borrowings from May 1993 through October 1993 and that during this period it will exceed the current level of informal borrowing facilities. However, on the basis of discussions with the group's lenders and advisers, the directors consider that sufficient additional facilities will be made available in the short term to enable the group to achieve a satisfactory refinancing.

The directors have carried out a strategic review of the group's businesses and as a result the directors have made a provision for exceptional costs of a fundamental reorganisation as set out in note ..... to the financial statements. As part of the continuing restructuring it is possible that further assets may be disposed of at less than their current net book amounts.

We consider that in view of the matters referred to in the preceding paragraphs, there are doubts which could threaten the appropriateness of the going concern basis and uncertainties regarding the carrying value of assets and classification of liabilities. However, on the basis of our discussions with the directors and other information which we obtained during the course of our audit we consider that it is appropriate for the directors to prepare financial statements drawn up on the going concern basis and that no further provisions to reduce the value of assets or reclassification of liabilities are required.

Our opinion is not qualified in these respects.

The above modifications may better be understood if the following extract from the accounts is also read.

Going concern and asset values

The group is currently in breach of certain of its borrowing covenants and discussions are taking place with the group's lenders with a view to formalising a standstill agreement with short term finance to 31 December 1993 pending the securing of long term financing.

The financial statements have been prepared on a going concern basis which is dependent upon the anticipated successful completion of long term financing of the group. Until the plans for the refinancing of the group are fully and satisfactorily completed there could be doubt over the appropriateness of the going concern basis.

The directors have carried out a strategic review of the group's businesses and as a result the directors have made a provision for exceptional costs of a fundamental reorganisation as set out in note ..... to the financial statements. As part of the continuing restructuring it is possible that further assets may be disposed of at other than their current net book amounts.

The length of the auditors' modifications is initially surprising. The introduction emphasises that the opinion is unqualified. Other features worthy of note are:

- the words 'fundamental uncertainty' do not appear
- the auditors give an explicit opinion on the correctness of the accounting
- the modifications are separately described and are apparently all fundamental.

If the three matters are not all fundamental uncertainties one or more could have been included by the auditors by virtue of paragraph 29 of SAS 600 as *'matters which they regard as relevant to a proper understanding of the basis of their opinion.'*

The last illustration in this subsection is of a modification where the appropriateness of the going concern basis depends on the continuing financial support of the parent undertaking. Arrangements within groups vary as to the demonstrated commitment of the parent to subsidiaries needing support. Auditors will consider, if available, such matters as:

- letters confirming intentions
- board minutes
- legally binding agreements (e.g. to subordinate debt)
- the financial standing of the parent undertaking
- the trading prospects of the subsidiary undertaking.

If sufficient evidence is not available, auditors may consider modifying their report for a scope limitation.

Report 511
FU: Going concern

Fundamental uncertainty: going concern

In forming our opinion, we have considered the adequacy of the disclosures made in the financial statements concerning the inherent uncertainty as to the continuation of the financial support by the company's parent undertaking. If that support were withdrawn the company might not be able to continue in operational existence. There is, therefore, a significant level of concern as to the appropriateness of the going concern basis of preparation of financial statements. As a consequence, adjustments would have to be made to reduce the value of assets to their recoverable amount, to provide for any further liabilities which might arise, and to reclassify fixed assets and long-term liabilities as current assets and liabilities. It is not possible to quantify these potential effects. Details of the circumstances relating to this inherent uncertainty are described in note ..... . Our opinion is not qualified in this respect.

5.2.7 Outside the scope of SAS 600

Draft SAS 130.10 requires the inclusion of an explanatory paragraph in the basis of opinion section of the report if the accounts are prepared on a basis other than that of a going concern. The explanatory paragraph is required to describe the basis of preparation and refer to the notes to the accounts. The paragraph is required even though the auditors consider this other basis to be appropriate in the specific circumstances, and the financial statements contain the necessary disclosures.

The requirement was contained in substantially the same form in the first (May 1992) exposure draft of SAS 130 and so is likely to be retained in the final SAS.

It is an odd requirement for the following reasons:

- it gives the auditors' report a sort of 'super primary financial statement' status because it alone is capable of disclosing the matter adequately
- it is not prescribed by SAS 600 (which allows such material by virtue of paragraph 29 '*Auditors may wish to include additional comment in this part of their report* (basis of opinion) *to highlight matters which they regard as relevant to a proper understanding of the basis of their opinion.*')
- it removes from the auditors any need to exercise judgement about the significance of the other basis of preparation of accounts
- it has not been changed during exposure despite the fact that the final version of SAS 600 includes (in the example reports) a reference to the accounting convention and accounting policies and a reference to an appropriate note. These matters were not present in the exposure draft of SAS 600 issued at the same time that SAS 130 was first exposed
- the requirement does not parallel the requirement of SAS 600 (for explanatory paragraphs dealing with fundamental uncertainties) that it should include words that clearly indicate that the auditors' opinion on the accounts is not qualified in respect of its contents

- there is no suggestion equivalent to that in paragraph 62 of SAS 600 that an appropriate subheading would enhance communication with the reader.

In view of the last two matters above, the following illustrative report includes material suggested by SAS 600, but not actually required by draft SAS 130.10.

Report 512
OTS: Basis other than going concern

Basis of preparation of the financial statements

> The financial statements have been prepared on the [break up / liquidation / discontinuation / termination of business] basis as described in note ..... . This basis of preparation is abnormal as financial statements are usually prepared on the basis that the company will carry on business as a going concern. Under the [break up / liquidation / discontinuation / termination of business] basis, the financial statements include adjustments to the net book value of assets, reducing them to the amounts expected to be realised, together with additional provisions for future losses up to the date of cessation and other liabilities, such as redundancies, which will arise as a result of the company ceasing to trade. Details of the circumstances relating to this are described in note ..... . Our opinion is not qualified in this respect.

SAS 130.10 calls for a 'description' of the basis of preparation. A description is more than just naming, so '*the break up basis*' will not do. The SAS does not use modifying terms, or explain what objective the description is to achieve, so auditors are left to their own devices. Luckily, the main effects of employing a basis other than a going concern basis are described in the wording of the example of an adverse opinion provided with draft SAS 130. This has been used as the basis for the above description.

Auditors whose house style is to commence their reports as follows have no need to fear repetition in their report:

> We have audited the financial statements on pages ..... to ..... .

On the other hand, auditors who follow the house style of the examples in appendix 2 to SAS 600 will start normally their reports as follows:

> We have audited the financial statements on pages ..... to ..... which have been prepared under the historical cost convention [as modified by the revaluation of certain fixed assets] and the accounting policies set out on page ..... .

This wording not only refers to the same area of the accounts as the explanatory paragraph about the basis of preparation, it also seems illogical. There is no good reason to refer at the start of the report to the historical cost convention but not to the unusual basis of preparation. It may have been better for draft SAS 130.10 to have left auditors with an option of giving the explanation outside the basis of opinion section. But, as it stands, auditors can either:

- accept the odd look of the report

- change their normal house style for the introductory paragraph to delete the duplicated information
- give the explanatory material in two places in their report.

As this type of modification should be fairly rare, further illustrative reports are not given.

5.3 Small companies, completeness of income

5.3.1 Introduction

Reporting on owner-managed companies has historically been a problem for auditors. Uncertainty may be introduced into the accounts because there is often a lack of division of duties and, where there is a rigorous system of internal control, management may be able to override it.

This section looks at the history of reporting in such circumstances before setting out some typical SAS 600 reports. As the problem of completeness of income is so common, earlier chapters of this book have used cash sales as a typical example of limitation of audit scope and potential failure to keep proper accounting records.

5.3.2 History of auditing guidance

The Audit Regulations Joint Monitoring Unit (JMU) commented in a review of its first year of operation that auditors were still using the superseded 'Example 6' qualification for small companies. That qualification had its origin in the Auditing Standard 'The audit report' before that document was revised in March 1989. The qualification was by far the most popular reason for a modified audit report: over a fifth of all reports of a sample in 1988 carried the suggested wording.[4] The qualification became so common that it was almost inevitable that reporting guidance would be changed. The 1989 revision included guidance on uncertainty and management representations. In summary that guidance concluded that (where no adverse opinion is concerned):

- if auditors accepted representations there should be no mention of that in their report in case it was misconstrued as a form of qualification
- if representations in specific areas were insufficient to support an unqualified opinion a 'subject to' (or disclaimer) for uncertainty should be reported
- if the uncertainties were pervasive to the financial statements a disclaimer should be considered, but if that is not appropriate a 'subject to' may be issued with regard to the completeness of recording of transactions.

---

[4] 12,000 reports surveyed by *Audit Report* magazine as reported by its December 1988 issue.

The Auditing Standard included an example of a qualified audit report for uncertainty over cash sales (example 5).

Report 513
SL: Cash sales uncertainty (pre SAS 600)

AUDITORS' REPORT TO THE MEMBERS OF ....

We have audited the financial statements on pages ..... to ..... in accordance with Auditing Standards except that the scope of our work was limited by the matter referred to below.

£ ..... of the company's recorded turnover comprises cash sales. There was no system of control over such sales on which we could rely for the purpose of our audit and there were no satisfactory audit procedures that we could adopt to confirm independently that all cash sales were properly recorded. In this respect alone we have not obtained all the information and explanations that we considered necessary for the purpose of our audit and we were unable to satisfy ourselves as to the completeness and accuracy of the accounting records.

Subject to any adjustments that we might have found to be necessary had we been able to satisfy ourselves as to the matter referred to above, in our opinion the financial statements give a true and fair view of the state of the company's affairs as at .... and of its [profit / loss] and source and application of funds for the year then ended and have been properly prepared in accordance with the Companies Act 1985.

Much of the wording of the above report was repeated in the relevant examples in appendix 2 to SAS 600. Note, for example the report's uncertainty over accounting records and the use of 'purpose' in the singular.

5.3.3 Current requirements

In March 1991 the APC produced an exposure draft of an Auditing Guideline 'The audit of small businesses'. This has not been progressed further. The document examines the audit of the completeness assertion and its final words are: *'in the case of many small businesses the auditor will be able to obtain sufficient assurance from various sources . . . the need for a qualification . . . will not arise.'*

This draft Auditing Guideline and SAS 600's removal of the 'subject to' qualification clearly indicate that auditors are being encouraged to choose between a standard report and a scope limitation, the former being the preferred option of the standard setters.

There is no escape route for auditors. There is no fundamental uncertainty about the level of income (in SAS 600 terms) because, to be treated as such, there must be an inherent uncertainty. Inherent uncertainty is defined, by SAS 600, as *'an uncertainty whose resolution is dependent upon uncertain future events outside the control of the reporting entity's directors at the date the financial statements are approved'.* The level of income will not be made certain by future events.

Where a scope limitation is reported, the directors may welcome appropriate wording, as recommended by paragraph 71 of the SAS, making it clear that the scope limitation is outside the control of the auditors and the directors (if that is felt to be the case).

Before SAS 600 an 'emphasis of matter' was allowed but it was only supposed to draw attention to important matters in the accounts. As such, it could not be used to draw readers' attention to such matters as the lack of internal control in a small company.

This did not stand in the way of some auditors who adopted an avant-garde approach that was destined to be vindicated by events. This is illustrated by the extract below (note the Nostradamian reference to the *'basis for our opinion'*!):

Report 514
OTS: Small company, emphasis of matter (pre SAS 600), Hawkins Tiles (Cannock) Ltd., 4 April 1987

> In our opinion the financial statements give a true and fair view of the state of the company's affairs at 4th April 1987 and of its profit and source and application of funds for the period then ended and have been properly prepared in accordance with the Companies Act 1985.
>
> Without qualifying our opinion above, we draw attention to the fact that in common with many businesses of similar size and organisation the company's system of control is dependent on the close involvement of the directors, and as part of the basis for our opinion, we have accepted assurances from the former directors that all the company's transactions have been properly recorded.

Paragraph 29 of SAS 600 suggests that auditors may include additional comment in the basis of opinion section of the report to highlight matters which they regard as relevant to a proper understanding of the basis of their opinion. This could open the door to a new 'small company' report; so an appropriate example is given below.

5.3.4 Example reports

Earlier chapters of this book contain examples of:

- SAS 600 limitation of audit scope for cash sales
- a non-SAS 600 limitation of audit scope (reported under the provisions of paragraph 29) concerning accounting records for cash sales.

This section, therefore, only contains:

- a disclaimer of opinion with an accounting records modification
- a paragraph 29 comment.

Report 515
SL — d: I&E: AR: Small company

Basis of opinion

We conducted our audit in accordance with Auditing Standards issued by the Auditing Practices Board except that the scope of our work was limited as explained below.

An audit includes examination, on a test basis, of evidence relevant to the amounts and disclosures in the financial statements. It also includes an assessment of the significant estimates and judgements made by the director in the preparation of the financial statements, and of whether the accounting policies are appropriate to the company's circumstances, consistently applied and adequately disclosed.

We planned and performed our audit so as to obtain all the information and explanations which we considered necessary in order to provide us with sufficient evidence to give reasonable assurance that the financial statements are free from material misstatement, whether caused by fraud or other irregularity or error. However, the evidence available to us was limited because the director did not maintain accounting records. The accounts have been prepared from primary documents such as returned cheques and invoices issued and received. There was no system of control over the transactions of the company on which we could rely for the purpose of our audit and there were no other satisfactory audit procedures that we could adopt to confirm the completeness of income or liabilities or the valuation of stocks.

In forming our opinion we also evaluated the overall adequacy of the presentation of information in the financial statements.

Opinion: disclaimer on view given by financial statements

Because of the possible effect of the limitation in evidence available to us, we are unable to form an opinion as to whether the financial statements give a true and fair view of the state of the company's affairs as at .... or of its [profit / loss] for the year then ended. We are also unable to form a view as to whether the financial statements have been properly prepared in accordance with the Companies Act 1985.

In our opinion:

- we have not obtained all the information and explanations that we considered necessary for the purpose of our audit, and

- proper accounting records have not been kept.

In the above example, the view on matters required by law is widely expressed and a definite opinion is expressed on accounting records. As there is only one director, the section of the report dealing with the respective responsibilities of the director and auditors should be worded appropriately.

The following illustration of further explanation introduced under paragraph 29 of SAS 600 may seem familiar to auditors with long memories. Under SAS 600 the old wording takes on new acceptability. Here it is offered without recommendation as such an approach could well be regarded as suitable only for avant-garde auditors (or in this case 'arrière-garde'). The words 'system of control' ought really to be modernised, in accordance with SASs, to be 'internal control system'.

Report 516
OTS: Small company further explanation

Basis of opinion

> We conducted our audit in accordance with Auditing Standards issued by the Auditing Practices Board. An audit includes examination, on a test basis, of evidence relevant to the amounts and disclosures in the financial statements. It also includes an assessment of the significant estimates and judgements made by the directors in the preparation of the financial statements, and of whether the accounting policies are appropriate to the company's circumstances, consistently applied and adequately disclosed.
>
> We planned and performed our audit so as to obtain all the information and explanations which we considered necessary in order to provide us with sufficient evidence to give reasonable assurance that the financial statements are free from material misstatement, whether caused by fraud or other irregularity or error. In forming our opinion we also evaluated the overall adequacy of the presentation of information in the financial statements.

System of control

> In common with many businesses of similar size and organisation the company's system of control is dependent on the close involvement of the directors. Where independent confirmation of the completeness of the accounting records was not therefore available we have accepted their assurances that all the company's transactions have been reflected in the financial statements. Our opinion is not qualified in this respect.

5.4 Stock and work in progress

5.4.1 Introduction

The earlier sections of this chapter have dealt with matters that can pervade the financial statements. This section is the first of several that examine modifications that can arise in connection with significant account balances. Although some modifications relate to 'mechanical' errors, most arise from problems with the relevant accounting estimates. For stock and work in progress (whether long-term contract or other) the significant accounting estimates relate to valuation and realisability. These include:

- provision for losses (which may be because management decides to sell at a loss or can do nothing else)
- obsolescence provision (demand falls away because a better competing product is available)
- damaged stock provision (damage may occur through production errors or adverse weather).

Modifications also commonly arise through failures in the costing system or the physical stocktake.

Errors in stock and work in progress normally affect both the balance sheet and the profit and loss account. For auditors, this means that modifications are unlikely to be confined to just one primary statement. As a result of this and the financial significance of stock to many companies, adverse or disclaimer of opinion modifications may be necessary.

When referring to stock problems auditors may pick their words from those used in the Companies Act 1985 or SSAP 9 'Stocks and long-term contracts'. The Companies Act's balance sheet formats use the heading 'stocks'. That heading includes as subheadings 'work in progress', 'raw materials and consumables', 'finished goods and goods for resale', and 'payments on account'. Nowhere is the term 'stock' (singular) used. SSAP 9 lapses into the singular only in the body of its text for 'stock on the shelves' and 'items of stock'. It therefore must come as a shock to auditors that example 9 in appendix 2 to SAS 600 uses the words 'stock and work in progress' (or work-in-progress). The message is clear, it is perfectly acceptable to use the wrong terms (as is done in this book).

5.4.2 Stocktake

Failure by the auditors to attend stocktaking due to the timing of their appointment is the subject of the illustrative report given in chapter 3 as typical wording for a scope limitation. That chapter also contains an appropriate report where the auditors made an error and did not attend. Illustrations are given below for the following circumstances:

- no stocktake, directors have estimated stock
- records of stocktake lost.

These two illustrative modifications use as their basis the wording of example 8 in appendix 2 to SAS 600.

Report 517
SL — d: Stocktake, not carried out

Basis of opinion

We conducted our audit in accordance with Auditing Standards issued by the Auditing Practices Board, except that the scope of our work was limited as explained below.

An audit includes examination, on a test basis, of evidence relevant to the amounts and disclosures in the financial statements. It also includes an assessment of the significant estimates and judgements made by the directors in the preparation of the financial statements, and of whether the accounting policies are appropriate to the company's circumstances, consistently applied and adequately disclosed.

We planned and performed our audit so as to obtain all the information and explanations which we considered necessary in order to provide us with sufficient

evidence to give reasonable assurance that the financial statements are free from material misstatement, whether caused by fraud or other irregularity or error. However, the evidence available to us was limited because the directors did not carry out a physical stocktake at the balance sheet date. There was no system of control over stock and work in progress on which we could rely for the purposes of our audit and there were no other satisfactory audit procedures that we could adopt to obtain adequate assurance regarding the quantities and condition of stock and work in progress, appearing in the balance sheet at .... Any adjustment to this figure would have a consequential effect on the profit for the year.

In forming our opinion we also evaluated the overall adequacy of the presentation of information in the financial statements.

Opinion: disclaimer on view given by financial statements

Because of the possible effect of the limitation in evidence available to us concerning stock and work in progress, we are unable to form an opinion as to whether the financial statements give a true and fair view of the state of the company's affairs as at .... or of its [profit / loss] for the year then ended. In all other respects, in our opinion the financial statements have been properly prepared in accordance with the Companies Act 1985.

In respect alone of the limitation on our work relating to stock and work in progress:

- we have not obtained all the information and explanations that we considered necessary for the purposes of our audit; and

- we were unable to determine whether proper accounting records had been kept.

The report could include further explanation to make it clear that stock was included in the balance sheet at directors' valuation.

Report 518
SL — d: Stocktaking records lost

Basis of opinion

We conducted our audit in accordance with Auditing Standards issued by the Auditing Practices Board except that the scope of our work was limited as explained below.

An audit includes examination, on a test basis, of evidence relevant to the amounts and disclosures in the financial statements. It also includes an assessment of the significant estimates and judgements made by the directors in the preparation of the financial statements, and of whether the accounting policies are appropriate to the company's circumstances, consistently applied and adequately disclosed.

We planned and performed our audit so as to obtain all the information and explanations which we considered necessary in order to provide us with sufficient evidence to give reasonable assurance that the financial statements are free from material misstatement, whether caused by fraud or other irregularity or error. However, the evidence available to us was limited because the records of a physical stocktaking at the balance sheet date were lost. There was no system of control over stocks on which we could rely for the purpose of our audit and there were no other satisfactory audit procedures that we could adopt to obtain adequate assurance regarding the quantities and condition of stocks appearing in the balance sheet at .... Any adjustment to this figure would have a consequential effect on the profit for the year.

In forming our opinion we also evaluated the overall adequacy of the presentation of information in the financial statements.

Opinion: disclaimer on view given by financial statements

Because of the possible effect of the limitation in evidence available to us, we are unable to form an opinion as to whether the financial statements give a true and fair view of the state of the company's affairs as at .... or of its [profit / loss] for the year then ended. In all other respects, in our opinion the financial statements have been properly prepared in accordance with the Companies Act 1985.

In respect alone of the limitation on our work relating to stocks:

- we have not obtained all the information and explanations that we considered necessary for the purposes of our audit; and
- we were unable to determine whether proper accounting records had been kept.

In the above report the term 'stocks' is used as an alternative to 'stock and work in progress'. The shorter term looks more appropriate where reference is also made to the relevant accounting standard as in the next report.

5.4.3 Net realisable value

Illustrations are given below for the following circumstances:

- overheads not allocated to stock value
- inadequate provisions for obsolescence
- uncertainty over the outcome of major contracts.

Report 519

D— e: Stocks, production overheads not allocated to

Qualified opinion arising from disagreement about accounting treatment

Stocks do not include an appropriate element of production overheads. This is contrary to Statement of Standard Accounting Practice 9 'Stocks and long-term contracts' which requires stocks to be included in the financial statements at an amount that reflects the full cost of bringing them to their location and condition at the balance sheet date. In our opinion, production overheads of £ ..... should have been included in the value of stocks.

Except for the failure to include production overheads in stocks, in our opinion the financial statements give a true and fair view of the state of the company's affairs as at .... and of its [profit / loss] for the year then ended and have been properly prepared in accordance with the Companies Act 1985.

The above illustration gives minimal disclosure about the quantified effects. Questions that are not answered by it are:

- is there an effect on profit (before or after tax)?
- how are comparative amounts affected?
- what is the effect on net assets?

The illustration could be expanded to indicate the effects on comparative amounts (which for the profit and loss account are affected by the opening balance sheet of two years earlier) and hence the effects on profit and net assets.

In practice, auditors may find it impossible to arrive at an amount that should have been included in the value of stocks for production overheads.

The language used in the illustration is drawn from SSAP 9. In SSAP 9, 'cost' includes 'cost of purchase' and 'cost of conversion'. The latter includes 'direct labour', 'direct expenses', 'sub-contracted work', 'production overheads' and 'other attributable overheads'.

Report 520
D— e: Stocks, inadequate provision for obsolescence

Qualified opinion arising from disagreement about accounting treatment

Stocks include £ ..... in respect of ....(a) , a material synthesised by the company for inclusion in ....(b) . The production of ....(a) and ....(b) was ceased on .... because of lack of sales following the introduction to the market of a competing product. The directors have disposed of all stocks of ....(b) but consider that the stocks of ....(a) may be used in a process currently the subject of research and so have not made any provision to reduce the carrying value of ....(a) . In our opinion, in the absence of a current planned use for ....(a), for which no external market exists, the value of stocks should have been reduced by £ ..... . Had this been done the profit for the year after taxation would have been £ ..... lower and the net assets of the company reduced by £ ..... .

Except for the absence of a provision against the vale of stocks referred to above, in our opinion the financial statements give a true and fair view of the state of the company's affairs as at .... and of its [profit / loss] for the year then ended and have been properly prepared in accordance with the Companies Act 1985.

The above illustration assumes that the information about the product is available elsewhere in the financial statements or is in the public domain. Information about the disposal of ....(b) is given for the avoidance of doubt.

Report 521
FU: Long-term contracts, uncertain outcome

Fundamental uncertainty

In forming our opinion, we have considered the adequacy of the disclosures made in the financial statements concerning the uncertainty over the eventual profitability of certain substantial long-term contracts. The directors have provided for all losses anticipated to arise but the eventual outcome may prove those provisions to have been inaccurate and profit over or understated as a result. It is not possible to quantify the potential effects of the resolution of this matter. Details of the circumstances relating to this fundamental uncertainty are described in note ..... . Our opinion is not qualified in this respect.

5.5 Fixed assets and depreciation

5.5.1 Introduction

This section mainly gives examples of reports modified because of problems with depreciation. Except for investment properties, fixed assets should be depreciated. This is a requirement both of accounting standards and company law. The relevant references are Statement of Standard Accounting Practice 12 'Accounting for depreciation' (specifically paragraph 15) and paragraph 18 of Schedule 4 to the Companies Act 1985. The legal requirement applies to investment properties but the 'true and fair override' is used when applying Statement of Standard Accounting Practice 19 'Accounting for investment properties'.

Problems that may be encountered involve disagreements over the value of assets and the appropriate amount of depreciation. In some instances, these matters are also uncertain and, if significant enough, a report modified for fundamental uncertainty may be appropriate.

5.5.2 Balance sheet and profit and loss account

If auditors express disagreement, SAS 600.8 requires (whenever practicable) a quantification of the effect on the financial statements. Many auditors only quantify the effect on the profit and loss account. Because depreciation has no tax effect the wording used refers to the overstatement (usually) of profit before and after tax. This practice is very common. It may be correct or incorrect depending on the materiality of the error in accumulated depreciation that affects the balance sheet.

There are three possible material circumstances:

- only the error in the charge to the profit and loss account is material
- only the error in accumulated depreciation in the balance sheet is material
- the error is material to both the profit and loss account and the balance sheet.

The illustrative reports may be tailored for each of these circumstances where necessary.

5.5.3 Capitalisation

Sometimes companies do not capitalise all the assets that they should, or include own-built assets at the wrong value. Charities often did not capitalise fixed assets, though following Statement of Recommended Practice 2 'Accounting by charities' (paragraph 51) they should now do so.

Report 522
D— e: Assets written off in year of acquisition

Qualified opinion arising from disagreement about accounting treatment

The company does not capitalise fixed assets unless the cost exceeds £ .... The effect of this policy is to understate the value of fixed assets shown in the balance sheet and to understate the profits in any year to the extent that the cost of fixed assets acquired in the year exceeds the depreciation that should have been charged in the accounts in respect of those assets. In addition, the profit and loss account should bear an appropriate element of the cost of assets acquired in earlier years that are still in use but have, instead, been fully expensed at the time of acquisition. In our opinion such assets should be capitalised and their costs depreciated over their expected useful economic lives as required by Statement of Standard Accounting Practice 12 'Accounting for depreciation' and paragraph 18 of Schedule 4 to the Companies Act 1985. It is not practicable for us to quantify the extent to which fixed assets, the [profit / loss] for the year and accumulated reserves are affected.

The financial statements do not include an explanation for this departure from an applicable accounting standard as required by paragraph 36A of Schedule 4 to the Companies Act 1985.

Except for the failure to capitalise and depreciate certain assets over their useful economic lives and except for the failure to include the disclosure required by paragraph 36A of Schedule 4 to the Companies Act 1985, in our opinion the financial statements give a true and fair view of the state of the company's affairs as at .... and of its [profit / loss] for the year then ended and have been properly prepared in accordance with the Companies Act 1985.

Report 523
D— e: Fixed asset capitalised at wrong amount (UITF Abstract 5 not followed)

Qualified opinion arising from disagreement about accounting treatment

As more fully explained in note ..... a property was transferred from current assets to fixed assets when a proposed sale did not proceed and the company then decided to hold the property for letting. The property is included in fixed assets at £ ..... the amount at which the proposed sale was to have realised. This treatment is not in accordance with Urgent Issues Task Force Abstract 5 'Transfers from current assets to fixed assets' (UITF Abstract 5) which requires such transfers to be at net realisable value. In our opinion, the transfer should have been accounted for in accordance with UITF Abstract 5 and, to the extent that the asset's net realisable value was less than its previous carrying value, the reduction in value at the date of transfer should have been charged in the profit and loss account, reflecting the loss to the company while the asset was held as a current asset. In the absence of a professional valuation as at the date of transfer it is not practicable to quantify the effects on the financial statements.

Except for the failure to account for the transfer of the property in accordance with UITF Abstract 5, in our opinion the financial statements give a true and fair view of the state of the company's affairs as at .... and of its [profit / loss] for the year then ended and have been properly prepared in accordance with the Companies Act 1985.

There are also likely to be problems in connection with the carrying value of the above investment property in the balance sheet.

5.5.4 Depreciation not charged

Many companies have decided not to depreciate buildings and have provided appropriate justification in their accounts. This practice was originally known to selected auditors as 'the brewery crumple', because brewers were the first industry to explore this route for licensed premises. The practice soon spread to any business that could demonstrate that enough was spent on maintaining property to keep its residual value at or above cost. A typical accounting policy is that disclosed in the March 1992 accounts of Argyll Group PLC:

> The group policy is to maintain its properties to a high standard through a continual programme of refurbishment and maintenance. In accordance with this practice, depreciation is not provided on freehold and long leasehold properties where, in the opinion of the directors, the residual values (in terms of original cost) are such that any depreciation charge would be immaterial.

Inevitably, the practice spread to some companies that had a less than perfect case to support the treatment. Inevitably, auditors had a hard time resisting the tide's flow. The ICAEW book *Financial Reporting 1992-93* reported that some 24 per cent of the companies in its survey did not depreciate some of their fixed assets.

Oddly enough, at the time this book was being written, there was the first sign of the tide turning. The March 1993 annual accounts of Argyll Group PLC saw a change in accounting policy and properties are now being depreciated over 40 years.[5] Other stores, such as Sainsburys and Tesco, seem to be following this lead. On 13 April 1994 the *Financial Times* reported that Tesco's profits had been hit by a £68.5 million depreciation charge following a decision to depreciate buildings and land premiums.[6] Press reports indicate that analysts are concerned that food retailers not depreciating stores could eventually be forced to make big write downs of property.

The following illustrative report uses a device that has been popular with some auditors, including the largest firms. In order to quantify the effect of the disagreement auditors have been assuming a particular useful economic life for the assets concerned. This is an informative approach but auditors may get drawn into remeasuring too much in the accounts if the approach is taken to its logical conclusion. For example, if a property is sold auditors might want to report their versions of the unamortised cost and hence the profit or loss on disposal. Published (pre SAS 600) examples also commonly suffered from wording difficulties, for example:

- the wording did not indicate clearly that the useful economic life was mentioned only for illustration

---

[5] Company law requires special reasons to justify a change in accounting policy. This is discussed further in the appropriate subsection of this chapter.

[6] The full story, as shown by notes 4 and 5 in Tesco's 26 February 1994 accounts, is more complex.

- the estimated residual value of the assets was often ignored
- the amounts disclosed were precise rather than rounded.

Report 524
D — e: Depreciation not charged

Qualified opinion arising from disagreement about accounting treatment

As explained in the accounting policies note on page ....., no depreciation is charged on freehold buildings. This is contrary to the requirements of Statement of Standard Accounting Practice 12 'Accounting for depreciation' and paragraph 18 of Schedule 4 to the Companies Act 1985. In our opinion, the cost less estimated residual value of each such asset should be charged to the profit and loss account on a systematic basis over its expected useful economic life. Had such a policy been adopted and if, for the sake of illustration only, the relevant assets had a useful economic life of 50 years and no residual value, the profit before and after tax would have been reduced by £ ..... (preceding year £ .....) and the accumulated reserves and fixed assets reduced by £ ..... (preceding year £ .....).

The financial statements do not include an explanation for this departure from an applicable accounting standard as required by paragraph 36A of Schedule 4 to the Companies Act 1985.

Except for the failure to depreciate freehold buildings and except for the failure to include the disclosure required by paragraph 36A of Schedule 4 to the Companies Act 1985, in our opinion the financial statements give a true and fair view of the state of the company's affairs as at .... and of its [profit / loss] for the year then ended and have been properly prepared in accordance with the Companies Act 1985.

The above report gives comparative amounts for the calculated figures. Readers would be confused if the movement in the accumulated depreciation was not exactly the same as the charge for the current year.

Instead of auditors giving an example to show the magnitude of the financial effect it is perhaps more realistic to expect them to report that it is not practicable to quantify the effect. This is done in the final example in this subsection which deals with depreciation at the wrong rate (over too short a period).

5.5.5 Depreciation at wrong rate

Report 525
D — e: Depreciation at wrong rate

Qualified opinion arising from disagreement about accounting treatment

As set out on note ..... , the company's depreciation policy writes off assets over periods shorter than their expected useful economic lives. This is not in accordance with Statement of Standard Accounting Practice 12 'Accounting for depreciation' or the requirements of paragraph 18 of Schedule 4 to the Companies Act 1985. In our opinion assets should be depreciated over their useful economic lives. It is not practicable for us to quantify the extent to which fixed assets, the [profit / loss] for the year and accumulated reserves are understated.

> The financial statements do not include an explanation for this departure from an applicable accounting standard as required by paragraph 36A of Schedule 4 to the Companies Act 1985.
>
> Except for the failure to depreciate assets over their useful economic lives and except for the failure to include the disclosure required by paragraph 36A of Schedule 4 to the Companies Act 1985, in our opinion the financial statements give a true and fair view of the state of the company's affairs as at .... and of its [profit / loss] for the year then ended and have been properly prepared in accordance with the Companies Act 1985.

Before leaving the subject of depreciation it is perhaps worth mentioning for the benefit of less experienced auditors that it is very difficult to issue a qualified opinion where the client is being overprudent in depreciating assets. A common accounting policy is to write off cars at 25% per annum on a straight line basis. Unless the vehicles are very high mileage indeed it is obvious that the residual value is being ignored. There are many practical reasons why auditors do not get too worried about this and similar matters of 'industry practice'. It is too late in this book to start a discussion about the *'directionality of materiality in accounting estimates.'* Instead, it is probably sufficient to argue that, given a reasonably large number of individual assets, the total annual depreciation charge is approximately correct. This is because any profit on disposal is treated as an adjustment to accumulated depreciation. Year on year, the overall depreciation charge approximates the theoretical one (i.e. the one that would have been calculated had the useful economic lives and residual values been known in advance). For example, a fleet of 20 cars, 5 replaced each year when fully depreciated, will have an annual depreciation charge of 25% of cost less 25% of the total projected profit on disposal (i.e. 5 out of 20 cars).

A discussion of the possible materiality arguments concerning depreciation of property is included in section 3.10 'Deciding on a modification' in chapter 3 'Modified Reports'. Although the figures used in the discussion are only for the purposes of the continuing example in that section, the arguments may be encountered in practice.

5.5.6 No permanent diminution

It is always difficult to tell the difference between a permanent diminution in the value of a fixed asset and a temporary fluctuation in value. Even an apparently simple case (such as a building having burnt to the ground) can be complex if the historical cost or valuation is not recent. For example, the value of a building may be irrelevant if the underlying land value has risen.

One view is that 'permanent' is a very long time indeed and so almost any change in value is temporary. This line of reasoning cannot be used once a decision has been taken to dispose of an asset nor is it therefore proof against the need to consider write downs if the company may no longer be a going concern.

The other view is that 'permanent' refers only to the foreseeable future. This view has increasingly being taken by auditors when considering property values in a recession.

The following published extract shows auditors treating the problem as a fundamental uncertainty. It would be a very brave firm of auditors' who went as far as disagreement.

Report 526
FU: Carrying value of property, Trace Computers PLC, 31 May 1993, Touche Ross & Co.

Fundamental uncertainty

> In forming our opinion we have considered the adequacy of disclosure in note 12 which explains the basis for carrying certain of the Group's freehold premises at a cost of £4.6 million compared to its current market value of £2.25 million. The eventual recovery in the value of the premises up to cost is uncertain. Should the property market relevant to these premises not recover as anticipated, provision may be required against its carrying value to recognise any permanent diminution in value. Our opinion is not qualified in this respect.

The relevant note to the accounts was:

> The Group's freehold premises at 224-232 St. John Street, London EC1, which are held for long-term occupation, are stated at cost of £4,606,721. The directors have been advised that the present market value of these premises is less than cost, at approximately £2.25 million, but believe the shortfall to represent only a temporary diminution in value. As a result, no adjustment has been made to the book value. The directors recognise that there is inevitably uncertainty surrounding the recovery in the value of the property as it involves a prediction of future events and trends over a prolonged period.

Note the intelligent use of rounding in the auditors' report. The magnitude of the possible shortfall against cost if the diminution turns out to be permanent is a pointer to the auditors' view on when an inherent uncertainty becomes a fundamental one. The 1993 accounts of Trace Computers PLC revealed a profit after taxation of £150,000 and shareholders' funds of £2 million.

5.5.7 Investment properties not at market value

Some companies have no in-house property expertise and have an investment property 'by accident' or simply because it seemed like a good place to invest surplus funds. In such circumstances the directors do not want to spend money on a professional valuation *'merely to keep their auditors happy'*.

Inevitably, as the purchase price information or valuation that there once was becomes older, auditors will consider the implications for their report. The following illustration is based on many reports that were published pre SAS 600.

Report 527

D — e: Investment properties not at market value

Qualified opinion arising from disagreement about accounting treatment

> As explained in note ..... the investment property has been included in the accounts at historical cost of £ ..... rather than at market value as required by Statement of Standard Accounting Practice 19 'Accounting for investment properties'. In the absence of a valuation, we are unable to quantify the effect, if any, on reserves and tangible fixed assets of this non-compliance.
>
> In our opinion the financial statements give a true and fair view of the company's [profit / loss] for the year to .... and except for the failure to include the investment property at market value of its state of affairs as at .... and have been properly prepared in accordance with the Companies Act 1985.

It is assumed that the departure from the SSAP is fully disclosed in the accounts. Note that there is normally no effect on the profit and loss account. Auditors looking for trouble may wish to consider whether, had the property been at an up-to-date valuation last year, there could have been any event giving rise to a profit and loss movement, for example a permanent diminution in value.

Auditors and clients may be affected by the fact that under SAS 600 the above report is a qualification. To avoid a qualification the directors might value the property and disclose in the accounts that (not having any expertise in property) they are unsure of the valuation. As the accounts now arguably comply with SSAP 19, the auditors have to decide whether the inherent uncertainty is fundamental. If it is not, they issue a standard report. If the uncertainty is fundamental they modify their report for a fundamental uncertainty, thus avoiding a qualified opinion. For smaller companies the attractiveness of this scheme is likely to be mitigated only by the directors' lack of understanding about the subtle differences between two types of modification and their greater concern for actually getting on with running their business.

5.6 Taxation

It is not common for taxation matters to affect the auditors' report. Taxation is relatively easy to compute and problems are therefore normally limited to disputes with the Inland Revenue or the estimation of deferred tax.

Most uncertainties over taxation will not be fundamental. If an uncertainty is fundamental it may be coupled with a going concern modification unless the company can withstand an adverse outcome and continue in business.

Report 528
FU: Taxation, Inland Revenue dispute

Fundamental uncertainty

> In forming our opinion, we have considered the adequacy of the disclosures made in the financial statements concerning the Inland Revenue investigation into the company's affairs. It is not possible to quantify the potential effects of the resolution of this uncertainty. Details of the circumstances relating to this fundamental uncertainty are described in note ..... . Our opinion is not qualified in this respect.

The above illustration is very stark and auditors may come under pressure from directors to include further wording. This might be a comment on the level of provisions made or on the strength of the directors' case.

Report 529
D— e: Deferred tax full provision, Courage Limited, 30 June 1992, Price Waterhouse (based on)

Qualified opinion arising from disagreement about accounting treatment

> As explained in Note 1(c), deferred tax has been provided in full for certain timing differences arising on capital allowances instead of being provided to the extent that it is probable that the liability will crystallise in the foreseeable future as required by Statement of Standard Accounting Practice No 15 *'Accounting for deferred tax'*. The effect of so doing has been to decrease the tax charge for the year by £16,271,000 (1991 £1,806,000) and retained earnings at 30 June 1992 by £45,117,000 (1991 £61,388,000)
>
> Except for the effects of accounting for deferred tax in the manner described in the preceding paragraph, *in our opinion the financial statements give a true and fair view of the state of the company's affairs as at .... and of its [profit / loss] for the year then ended and have been properly prepared in accordance with the Companies Act 1985.*

The words in *italics* have been introduced for the purposes of the illustration. The original report was issued before SAS 600. The report illustrates the importance of ensuring that the quantification of the effects 'adds up'. The effect on the current year's tax charge exactly accounts for the difference between the two balance sheet effects.

The vocabulary is derived from SSAP 15, which prefers 'tax' to 'taxation'.

5.7 Pension costs

SSAP 24 'Accounting for pension costs' came as a shock to many companies. It introduced very detailed disclosure requirements and an unfamiliar method of allocating costs to accounting years. The directors of many smaller companies did not see the need for it and would not change their methods from a cash basis. Even when the standard was acknowledged, some of its requirements produced unpalatable results. For example, the need to provide all of the cost of an ex gratia pension when it was awarded. Even if companies and their auditors went in for complex discounted cash flow calculations to mitigate the damage, the immediate 'cost' could be out of all proportion to the directors' understanding of the commitment.

Pension costs are very difficult to quantify and report if the auditors disagree with the client's accounting. Obviously, if there is no actuarial report available, quantification is not practicable. However, if a report is available the consequences can spread over many years and, if material, result in a long series of modified reports.

The two illustrations below also demonstrate how the wording of reports may be varied by changing the relative positions of the 'in our opinion' and quantification aspects in the first paragraph.

Report 530
D— e: Pension surplus credited in full to profit and loss account

Qualified opinion arising from disagreement about accounting treatment

As explained in note ..... , in accordance with actuarial advice, the company has not made any contributions to its employees' pension scheme during the year. The profit and loss account includes no pension costs for the year. This is not in accordance with Statement of Standard Accounting Practice 24 'Accounting for pension costs' (SSAP 24) which requires that such variations from the regular cost of pensions should be allocated over the expected remaining service lives of the current employees in the scheme. The effect of the company's accounting treatment is to report future cost reductions as part of its results for the year. In our opinion the profit and loss account should include a charge for pension costs of £ ..... together with attributable taxation of £ ..... and the net assets of the company should be reduced by £ ..... .

Except for the failure to account for pension costs in accordance with SSAP 24, in our opinion the financial statements give a true and fair view of the state of the company's affairs as at .... and of its [profit / loss] for the year then ended and have been properly prepared in accordance with the Companies Act 1985.

The above report includes extra wording to try to explain the complex effects of the failure to comply with SSAP 24. The vocabulary is derived from SSAP 24.

Report 531
D— e: SSAP 24 not complied with for ex gratia pensions

Qualified opinion arising from disagreement about accounting treatment

As explained in note ..... , during the year the company granted ex gratia pensions to two former senior employees. The monthly costs of such pensions have been charged to the profit and loss account. In our opinion, the cost of providing such pensions should have been accounted for in accordance with Statement of Standard Accounting Practice 24 'Accounting for pension costs' (SSAP 24) which requires the capital cost of such pensions to be charged in full in the period in which they are granted. The capital cost of the pensions concerned, as indicated by the costs of buying annuities to provide equivalent benefits, would have been in excess if the amounts charged to the profit and loss account by some £ ..... .

Except for the failure to account for ex gratia pensions in accordance with SSAP 24, in our opinion the financial statements give a true and fair view of the state of the company's affairs as at .... and of its [profit / loss] for the year then ended and have been properly prepared in accordance with the Companies Act 1985.

The report includes a positive opinion as to the auditors' preferred treatment. The capital cost of an ex gratia pension need not be the same as the cost of buying an equivalent annuity (if indeed a direct equivalent can be found) but the quantification is useful.

5.8 Goodwill

Over the years, accounting for goodwill has varied between capitalisation (with or without amortisation) and immediate write off. If auditors disagree with an accounting treatment they face the possibility of a modification appearing for many years as the effects unwind. They also have to face the problem posed by an accounting standard that allows two different treatments. The following illustration is based on a published report (Butler Advertising Ltd, 31 March 1991, Touche Ross [pre SAS 600]). Because of the complex quantification the auditors' view (that SSAP 22 should have been followed) has not been stated explicitly.

Report 532
D— e: Goodwill not in accordance with SSAP 22

Qualified opinion arising from disagreement about accounting treatment

As explained in note ..... the company has a policy of attributing a residual value to purchased goodwill and to the extent that the original value exceeds residual value goodwill is amortised over 10 years. This is not in accordance with Statement of Standard Accounting Practice 22 'Accounting for goodwill' (SSAP 22) which requires that the entire amount of purchased goodwill is either written off against reserves immediately or amortised over its useful economic life. SSAP 22 does not allow the recognition of a residual value. Had the company followed the requirements of SSAP 22 the goodwill in the balance sheet of £ ..... would either have been transferred to a goodwill reserve, or been amortised. If amortised over a ten year period £ ..... would have been charged against current year profit and loss and £ ..... would have been charged as a prior year adjustment and the balance of £ ..... would have been carried in the balance sheet for future amortisation.

Except for the failure to account for goodwill in accordance with SSAP 22, in our opinion the financial statements give a true and fair view of the state of the company's affairs as at .... and of its [profit / loss] for the year then ended and have been properly prepared in accordance with the Companies Act 1985.

5.9 Illegal distributions

Part VIII of the Companies Act 1985 contains provisions designed to restrict and control the payment of dividends (or the making of other distributions). The general rule in section 263 (1) is that a company shall not make a distribution except out of profits available for the purpose.

For these purposes a company's profits available for distribution are its accumulated, realised profits, so far as not previously utilised by distribution or capitalisation, less its accumulated, realised losses, so far as not previously written off in a reduction or reorganisation of capital duly made.[7]

Auditors may be faced with reporting on accounts showing a distribution that is prima facie illegal. Because of the way that distributions may be properly justified on the basis of accounts, the legality of a distribution (even one that is prima facie illegal) may be in doubt until the matter is before a court. As most such circumstances do not get resolved in court, legal advice may be taken to ascertain the likely view that would prevail.

The penalty for an illegal distribution is not severe. In essence, a member who knew it was illegal is liable to repay it.

If auditors form a view that a distribution is illegal the question remains as to whether, and if so how, they should modify their report. The Department of Trade and Industry inspectors of Bestwood criticised the auditors (BDO Binder Hamlyn) for not qualifying their opinion on accounts containing an unlawful distribution. They considered that *'the view expressed to us by Binders was that there is no specific requirement for the auditor to note in the audit report that a dividend had been paid unlawfully.'* The DTI inspectors found Binders' view 'disturbing'.

It is currently true that there is no requirement for auditors to report an illegal dividend. The APB has issued proposed SASs on illegal acts and consideration of law and regulations that provide guidance in this area. That guidance may be interpreted as resolving auditors' action into two categories (it is assumed that the illegal distribution is material):

1 if the accounts properly disclose the illegality and its consequences
2 if there is no such disclosure.

In the absence of appropriate disclosure (case (2)) the auditors may issue an except for opinion expressing disagreement with the lack of disclosure.

If the disclosure is adequate (case (1)) the auditors have to decide between:

- keeping silent
- including explanatory material outside the scope of SAS 600
- issuing a modification for fundamental uncertainty.

The last alternative would only be appropriate if the dividend was very significant and the possibility that repayment might come about was inherently uncertain.

---

[7] This is not intended to be anything other than a brief introduction to the legal position.

Following the DTI report the preferred option ought to be to include explanatory material. This is illustrated below.

Report 533
OTS: Illegal distribution

Basis of opinion

We conducted our audit in accordance with Auditing Standards issued by the Auditing Practices Board. An audit includes examination, on a test basis, of evidence relevant to the amounts and disclosures in the financial statements. It also includes an assessment of the significant estimates and judgements made by the directors in the preparation of the financial statements, and of whether the accounting policies are appropriate to the company's circumstances, consistently applied and adequately disclosed.

We planned and performed our audit so as to obtain all the information and explanations which we considered necessary in order to provide us with sufficient evidence to give reasonable assurance that the financial statements are free from material misstatement, whether caused by fraud or other irregularity or error. In forming our opinion we also evaluated the overall adequacy of the presentation of information in the financial statements.

Legality of dividend

Section 263 of the Companies Act 1985 states that a distribution shall not be made except out of profits available for that purpose. The dividend of £ ..... was paid at a time when the company had net realised losses and as a consequence it may have been paid illegally. If so, under section 277 of the Companies Act 1985, any member who knew or had reasonable grounds for believing that it is was illegal is liable to repay the amount they received to the company. Our opinion is not qualified in this respect.

5.10 Charities, completeness of income

Much of the content of the earlier section dealing with completeness of income for a small company may be relevant to a charity. An illustrative report is given below for a charity experiencing difficulty in applying proper control over voluntary donations until they are entered in the accounting records.

Some auditors have been able to issue standard reports on charities with donation income because of a combination of the degree of control over such things as collections and the probable immateriality of any uncertainty in relation to the accounts as a whole (carefully worded income recognition accounting policies also help here). Where, however, auditors consider that a real problem exists they are forced by SAS 600 to issue a qualified report. Some charities may notice the change from a 'subject to' modification in one year to an except for opinion following the adoption of SAS 600. For companies, this is now more likely to be coupled with wording about 'information and explanations' and 'accounting records' and so the new opinion could be interpreted as being much more critical of the charity.

There is no escape route for auditors. The choice is between a standard report and a scope limitation. There is no fundamental uncertainty about the level of income (in SAS 600 terms) because, to be treated as such, there must be an inherent uncertainty. Inherent uncertainty is defined, by SAS 600, as *'an uncertainty whose resolution is dependent upon uncertain future events outside the control of the reporting entity's directors at the date the financial statements are approved'.* The theoretical level of income will not be made certain by future events.

Where a scope limitation is reported, the charity may welcome appropriate wording, as recommended by paragraph 71 of SAS 600, making it clear that the scope limitation is outside the control of the auditors and the 'directors' of the charity.

In the following illustrative report it is assumed that the company is limited by guarantee and that the directors are not called anything else. Because there is no standard report for a guarantee company given elsewhere in this book, the report is presented in full.

Report 534
SL — e: Charity (guarantee company), completeness of income

AUDITORS' REPORT TO THE MEMBERS OF ....

We have audited the financial statements on pages ..... to ..... which have been prepared under the historical cost convention [as modified by the revaluation of certain fixed assets] and the accounting policies set out on page ..... .

Respective responsibilities of directors and auditors

As described on page ..... the company's directors are responsible for the preparation of financial statements. It is our responsibility to form an independent opinion, based on our audit, on those statements and to report our opinion to you.

Basis of opinion

We conducted our audit in accordance with Auditing Standards issued by the Auditing Practices Board except that the scope of our work was limited as explained below.

An audit includes examination, on a test basis, of evidence relevant to the amounts and disclosures in the financial statements. It also includes an assessment of the significant estimates and judgements made by the directors in the preparation of the financial statements, and of whether the accounting policies are appropriate to the company's circumstances, consistently applied and adequately disclosed.

We planned and performed our audit so as to obtain all the information and explanations which we considered necessary in order to provide us with sufficient evidence to give reasonable assurance that the financial statements are free from material misstatement, whether caused by fraud or other irregularity or error. However, the evidence available to us was limited because this charity derives [a substantial proportion / approximately a two thirds / OTHER DESCRIPTION] of its income from voluntary donations. These cannot be fully controlled until they are entered in the accounting records, and are not therefore susceptible to independent audit verification. This limitation, which is common to many other charities of similar size and organisation is outside of the control of the directors.

In forming our opinion we also evaluated the overall adequacy of the presentation of information in the financial statements.

Qualified opinion arising from limitation in audit scope

Except for any adjustments that might have been found to be necessary had we been able to obtain sufficient evidence concerning voluntary donations, in our opinion the financial statements give a true and fair view of the state of the company's affairs as at .... and of its [surplus / excess of income over expenditure] for the year then ended and have been properly prepared in accordance with the Companies Act 1985.

In respect alone of the limitation on our work relating to voluntary donations:

- we have not obtained all the information and explanations that we considered necessary for the purposes of our audit; and

- we were unable to determine whether proper accounting records had been kept.

The wording of the description of the scope limitation in the basis of opinion section derives from the Auditing Guideline 301 'Charities'. The Guideline was issued well before SAS 600 and is due for updating. The wording is not without difficulties. The original wording was not quantified, whereas the relevant examples in appendix 2 to SAS 600 include some quantification and some mention of the effect on the accounts. To go some way towards meeting this need, but without losing wording that may be familiar to users, the suggested wording in square brackets commences with the Guideline's *'a substantial proportion'* but continues with alternative wording that is more quantified.

As a consequence, the word order has been changed to prevent wording about similar charities referring incorrectly to the proportion of donations that is particular to the charity concerned. This change has also facilitated the creation of three sentences instead of one and the opportunity has been taken to make an explicit statement that the limitation is outside of the control of the directors.

A final difficulty with the wording of the Guideline is that it refers to lack of control over donations *'until they are entered in the accounting records'*. This makes the opinion about accounting records look out of place. Accounting records are discussed fully earlier in this book. Auditors unhappy with the illustrative wording may wish to start from another point and use words that do not draw attention to the possible difficulty.

5.11 Reporting verbally

Over the years, auditors have delighted in attending annual general meetings to exercise their rights and do other things. The Auditing Committee of the ICAEW has seen fit to attempt to curb the more exuberant verbal expressions of opinion by the issue of FRAG 1/94.[8] Auditors are not required to read out their report but that has not stopped some doing so. One of the contributors to this book suggested that a former managing partner of a firm that merged with one of the Big Six should be contacted to discover the exact wording of his 'well spirited rendition' of the auditors' report invariably delivered to the directors in their box at Ascot.

FRAG 1/94 rightly warns that reading a SAS 600 auditors' report in full is *'a lengthy process which may not be appreciated'.*

Auditors who choose to read out only highlights of the report are solemnly advised to ensure that what is read out cannot be construed as the full report, and modifications (if any) are made clear. FRAG 1/94 (which was not issued on 1 April 1994) goes on to give an example of suitable wording for a group:

> Ladies and gentlemen
>
> [The firm's] report on the annual financial statements is set out on page x of the annual report and accounts. This includes confirmation that we have performed our audit in accordance with Auditing Standards and that in our opinion the financial statements give a true and fair view of the state of affairs of the company and the group as at [date] and of the profit of the group for the year then ended and have been properly prepared in accordance with the Companies Act 1985.

And where appropriate:

> I would also draw your attention to page y which sets out [the firm's] report on the directors' statement of compliance with the Cadbury Committee's Code of Best Practice. This includes confirmation that we have reviewed the statement insofar as it relates to the paragraphs of the Code which the London Stock Exchange has specified for our review, and that it appropriately reflects the company's compliance with the specified paragraphs of the Code.

FRAG 1/94 is open to criticism because it pays no attention to the differences of house style (or accent) that auditors may adopt and gives no guidance on reporting in Welsh.

---

[8] FRAG 1/94 does not include some vital information: namely, what the final FRAG in 93 was. Auditors are now driven to distraction in trying to ensure that they have not missed some other vital piece of guidance merely because they could not discover that their file of FRAGs was incomplete. At least the 'TR' series of pronouncements could be audited for completeness. Perhaps this is the price that has to be paid for progress.

6 TABLE OF REPORTS

6.1 Introduction

This table lists the example reports in the book. It has been compiled from the headings for the individual reports. Some short examples and illustrations of errors have not been listed as they do not make sense out of context.

The reports are numbered in a sequence within each chapter. The meanings of the abbreviations use are given below. Scope limitation modifications are often accompanies by modifications for information and explanations and uncertainty over accounting records; these linked modifications are normally not shown in the headings of reports.

Reports are listed first in numerical order (subsection 6.2), then in alphabetical order of the first modification in each report (subsection 6.3).

1 Main abbreviations

STD standard report (mainly found in chapter 2 'The Standard Report')
SL scope limitation
D disagreement
FU fundamental uncertainty
— e except for opinion
— a adverse opinion
— d disclaimer of opinion.

2 Abbreviations for statutory requirements and other matters

I&E information and explanations
AR accounting records
BR branch returns
AARR agreement with accounting records and returns
DR directors' report not consistent with accounts
Sch 6 omission of disclosures required by Schedule 6
RofD responsibilities of directors
OTS outside the scope of SAS 600.

6.2 Reports in numerical order

6.3 Reports in modification order

INDEX

This index is arranged alphabetically letter-by-letter. As a consequence, references to sections of the Companies Act 1985 and similar numerical entries are not in numerical order, for example section 43 is listed below section 389.

Main references are in **Bold.** Although the index has entries for Companies Act sections and SASs by number, it is normally better to locate relevant material through its subject.

Abbreviations are cross-referenced to the words they stand for and the index may, therefore, be used as a key to abbreviations. Abbreviations used in the headings of reports are explained in the introduction to the Table of Reports on page 359. Where relevant, the Table of Reports shows the companies and auditors involved and that information is not, therefore, duplicated in this index.
